The Handbook of Artificial Intelligence

The Handbook of Artificial Intelligence

Volume II

Edited by

Avron Barr

and

Edward A. Feigenbaum

Department of Computer Science
Stanford University

ADDISON-WESLEY PUBLISHING COMPANY, INC.

Reading, Massachusetts   Menlo Park, California   New York
Don Mills, Ontario   Wokingham, England   Amsterdam   Bonn
Sydney   Singapore   Tokyo   Madrid   San Juan
Santiago   San Juan

Library of Congress Cataloging in Publication Data:

The handbook of artificial intelligence.

    Bibliography: p. 381
    Includes index.
    1. Artificial intelligence. I. Barr, Avron, 1949–
    II. Feigenbaum, Edward A.
Q335.H36   001.53′5   80–28621
ISBN 0-201-16889-8
ISBN 0-201-11812-2
ISBN 0-201-16886-3 (pbk.)
ISBN 0-201-11813-0 (pbk.)

Printed in the United States of America

BCDEFGHIJ-DO-89
Second Printing, September 1989

To Herbert A. Simon, scholar and teacher,
In honor of his sixty-fifth birthday and
In recognition of his seminal contributions
to the scientific study of thinking and
to the field of Artificial Intelligence

CONTENTS OF VOLUME II

LIST OF CONTRIBUTORS

Non-Stanford affiliations indicated if known.

Chapter Editors

Janice Aikins (Hewlett-Packard)
James S. Bennett
Victor Ciesielski (Rutgers U)
William J. Clancey
Paul R. Cohen
James E. Davidson
Thomas G. Dietterich

Bob Elschlager (Tymshare)
Lawrence Fagan
Anne v.d.L. Gardner
Takeo Kanade (CMU)
Jorge Phillips (Kestrel)
Steve Tappel
Stephen Westfold (Kestrel)

Contributors

Robert Anderson (Rand)
Douglas Appelt (SRI)
David Arnold
Michael Ballantyne (U Texas)
David Barstow (Schlumberger)
Peter Biesel (Rutgers U)
Lee Blaine (Lockheed)
W. W. Bledsoe (U Texas)
David A. Bourne (CMU)
Rodney Brooks (MIT)
Bruce G. Buchanan
Richard Chestek
Kenneth Clarkson
Nancy H. Cornelius (CMU)
James L. Crowley (CMU)
Randall Davis (MIT)
Gerard Dechen
Johan de Kleer (Xerox)
Jon Doyle (CMU)
R. Geoff Dromey (U Wollongong)
Richard Duda (Fairchild)
Robert S. Engelmore (Teknowledge)
Ramez El-Masri (Honeywell)
Susan Epstein (Rutgers U)
Robert E. Filman (Hewlett-Packard)
Fritz Fisher (Ramtek)

Christian Freksa (Max Plank, Munich)
Peter Friedland
Hiromichi Fujisawa (CMU)
Richard P. Gabriel
Michael R. Genesereth
Neil Goldman (ISI)
Ira Goldstein (Hewlett-Packard)
George Heidorn (IBM)
Martin Herman (CMU)
Annette Herskovits
Douglas Hofstadter (Indiana U)
Elaine Kant (CMU)
Fuminobu Komura (CMU)
William Laaser (Xerox)
Douglas B. Lenat
William J. Long (MIT)
Robert London
Bruce D. Lucas (CMU)
Pamela McCorduck
Mark L. Miller (Computer Thought)
Robert C. Moore (SRI)
Richard Pattis
Stanley J. Rosenschein (SRI)
Neil C. Rowe
Gregory R. Ruth (MIT)
Daniel Sagalowicz (SRI)

Contributors (continued)

Behrokh Samadi (UCLA)
William Scherlis (CMU)
Steven A. Shafer (CMU)
Andrew Silverman
David R. Smith (CMU)
Donald Smith (Rutgers U)
Phillip Smith (U Waterloo)
Reid G. Smith (Schlumberger)
William R. Swartout (ISI)

Steven L. Tanimoto (U Washington)
Charles E. Thorpe (CMU)
William van Melle (Xerox)
Richard J. Waldinger (SRI)
Richard C. Waters (MIT)
Sholom Weiss (Rutgers U)
David Wilkins (SRI)
Terry Winograd

Reviewers

Harold Abelson (MIT)
Saul Amarel (Rutgers U)
Robert Balzer (ISI)
Harry Barrow (Fairchild)
Thomas Binford
Daniel Bobrow (Xerox)
John Seely Brown (Xerox)
Richard Burton (Xerox)
Lewis Creary
Andrea diSessa (MIT)
Daniel Dolata (UC Santa Cruz)
Lee Erman (ISI)
Adele Goldberg (Xerox)
Cordell Green (Kestrel)
Norman Haas (Symantec)
Kenneth Kahn (MIT)
Jonathan J. King (Hewlett-Packard)
Casimir Kulikowski (Rutgers U)
John Kunz
Brian P. McCune (AI&DS)
Jock Mackinlay

Ryszard S. Michalski (U Illinois)
Donald Michie (U Edinburgh)
Thomas M. Mitchell (Rutgers U)
D. Jack Mostow (ISI)
Nils Nilsson (SRI)
Glen Ouchi (UC Santa Cruz)
Ira Pohl (UC Santa Cruz)
Arthur L. Samuel
David Shur
Herbert A. Simon (CMU)
David E. Smith
Dennis H. Smith (Lederle)
Mark Stefik (Xerox)
Albert L. Stevens (BBN)
Allan Terry
Perry W. Thorndyke (Perceptronics)
Paul E. Utgoff (Rutgers U)
Donald Walker (SRI)
Harald Wertz (U Paris)
Keith Wescourt (Rand)

Production

Max Diaz
David Eppstein
Lester Ernest
Marion Hazen
Janet Feigenbaum
David Fuchs
José L. González
Dianne G. Kanerva
Jonni M. Kanerva

Dikran Karagueuzian
Arthur M. Keller
Barbara R. Laddaga
Roy Nordblom
Thomas C. Rindfleisch
Ellen Smith
Helen Tognetti
Christopher Tucci

PREFACE

THE PROJECT to write the *Handbook of Artificial Intelligence* was born in the mid-1970s, at a low ebb in the fortunes of the field. AI, in our view, had made remarkable contributions to one of the grandest of scientific problems—the nature of intelligence, in humans and in artifacts. Yet it had failed to communicate its concepts, its working methods, its techniques, and its successes to the broad scientific and engineering communities. The work remaining to be done was almost limitless, but the number of practitioners was few. If AI were to succeed, it would have to communicate more clearly and widely to others in science and engineering. So we thought, and thus were we motivated to assemble and edit these volumes.

In the last few years, we have seen an astonishing change in the perception and recognition of AI as a science and as a technology. Many large industrial firms have committed millions of dollars to the establishment of AI laboratories. The Japanese have even committed a national project, the so-called Fifth Generation, to the engineering of "knowledge information processing machines," that is, AI-oriented hardware and software. Newspaper, magazine, and broadcast features on AI are common. A lively new professional society, the American Association for Artificial Intelligence, has been formed. And university graduate-school enrollments in AI are booming. Indeed, Volume I of the *Handbook* was the main selection, in August 1981, of one of the major book clubs; it is now undergoing its second printing and is being translated into Japanese.

The crisis we face now is a crisis of success, and many wonder if the substance of the field can support the high hopes. We believe that it can, and we offer the material of the three massive volumes of the *Handbook* as testimony to the strength and intellectual vigor of the enterprise.

The five chapters in this volume cover three subfields of AI. Chapter VI, on *AI programming languages*, describes the kinds of programming-language features and environments developed by AI researchers. These languages are, like all programming languages, not only software tools with which the many different kinds of AI programs are constructed, but also "tools of thought" in which new ideas and perspectives on the understanding of cognition are first explored. Of note here is the extended discussion of LISP—by far the most important tool of either kind yet invented in AI.

Chapters VII through IX are about *expert systems,* in science, medicine, and education. These systems, which vary widely in structure and behavior, all focus on one important methodology, called the *transfer of expertise.* Early in AI's history, researchers agreed that high performance on difficult problems would require large amounts of *real-world knowledge,* the knowledge that a human expert in a particular domain has extracted from his (or her) experience with the problems he solves. The idea of expert-systems research was to find ways of transferring the necessary kinds and quantities of knowledge from human experts to AI systems. This technology has advanced to the point where these systems can perform at the level of human experts and may be available commercially in the next few years.

Finally, Chapter X reviews the area of AI research called *automatic programming*. This research has focused on systems that can produce a program from some "natural" description of what it is to do or that attend to some other important aspect of programming, like verifying that a program does what it was intended to do. For example, some automatic-programming systems produce simple programs from examples of input/output pairs or from English *specifications* of the program's intended behavior. But there is a much deeper purpose to automatic-programming research than just easing the burden of the programmer. To achieve their pragmatic goals, these systems must *understand* programs just as other AI systems understand language or chess or medical diagnosis. They must reason about programs and about themselves as programs, and, as we discuss in Chapter X, this is a central and characteristic feature of many AI systems.

Acknowledgments

The chapter on AI programming languages was first drafted by Steve Tappel and Stephen Westfold. Johann de Kleer and Jon Doyle contributed the excellent article on dependencies and assumptions. A thorough review and additional material were supplied by Christian Freksa. Other reviewers included Robert Balzer, Cordell Green, Brian McCune, and Harald Wertz.

The chapter on scientific-applications research was edited by James Bennett, Bruce Buchanan, Paul Cohen, and Fritz Fisher. Original material and comments were contributed by, among others, James Davidson, Randall Davis, Daniel Dolata, Richard Duda, Robert Engelmore, Peter Friedland, Michael Genesereth, Jonathan King, Glen Ouchi, and Daniel Sagalowicz.

Chapter VIII, on research in medical applications of AI, was edited by Victor Ciesielski and his colleagues at Rutgers University. James Bennett and Paul Cohen continued work on the material. Others who contributed to or reviewed this material include Saul Amarel, Peter Biesel, Bruce Buchanan, Randall Davis, Casimir Kulikowksi, Donald Smith, William Swartout, and Sholom Weiss.

The educational-applications chapter was compiled by Avron Barr and William Clancey, and, once again, James Bennett and Paul Cohen continued the editing process. Contributors and reviewers included Harold Abelson, Lee Blaine, John Seely Brown, Richard Burton, Andrea diSessa, Adele Goldberg, Ira Goldstein, Kenneth Kahn, Mark Miller, Neil Rowe, Albert Stevens, and Keith Wescourt.

Finally, the automatic-programming chapter was edited by Bob Elschla-
ger and Jorge Phillips, working from original material supplied by David
Barstow, Cordell Green, Neil Goldman, George Heidorn, Elaine Kant, Zohar
Manna, Brian McCune, Gregory Ruth, Richard Waldinger, and Richard Waters.

The design and production of the volume were the responsibility of Dianne
Kanerva, our professional editor, and José González. The book was typeset
with TEX, Donald Knuth's system for mathematical typesetting, by David
Eppstein, Janet Feigenbaum, José González, Jonni Kanerva, Dikran Karagueuzian, and Barbara Laddaga. Our publisher William Kaufmann and his
staff have been generous with their patience, help, and willingness to experiment.

The Advanced Research Projects Agency of the Department of Defense
and the Biotechnology Resources Program of the National Institutes of Health
supported the *Handbook* project as part of their longstanding and continuing
efforts to develop and disseminate the science and technology of AI. Earlier
versions of material in these volumes were distributed as technical reports of
the Department of Computer Science at Stanford University. The electronic
text-preparation facilities available to Stanford computer scientists on the
SAIL, SCORE, and SUMEX computers were used throughout the writing and
production of the *Handbook*.

Chapter VI

Programming Languages
for AI Research

CHAPTER VI: PROGRAMMING LANGUAGES FOR AI RESEARCH

A. OVERVIEW

ARTIFICIAL INTELLIGENCE is a branch of computer science—the study of the relation between computation and cognition. Research in AI involves writing programs that attempt to achieve some kind of intelligent behavior. Besides the computers themselves, the most important tools in AI are the programming languages in which these programs are conceived and implemented.

A programming language provides a means of specifying the objects and procedures needed to solve certain classes of problems. Languages such as FORTRAN and COBOL were developed to make this specification easier by supplying higher level algebraic and business primitives, respectively (and also to establish vocabularies that could be used on a variety of machines). Contemporaneously with the development of these languages, researchers in AI were developing their own programming languages with features designed to handle AI problems.

Once a programming language has been designed, the implementation of that language is itself a serious and time-consuming programming task. There must at least be a translator from the high-level language to the particular machine's language (a *compiler* or *interpreter*) as well as a *run-time environment* that supports the new objects and procedures allowed in the language. For example, the SIN function supplied in languages like FORTRAN makes it convenient to do trigonometric calculations and requires, since SIN is not a primitive function on most computers, a procedure in the run-time environment that calculates the value of the function on the arguments supplied while the program is running. Most AI programming languages, in addition to supporting many quite novel high-level features, offer splendid environments for writing, debugging, and modifying programs.

AI programming languages have had a central role in the history of Artificial Intelligence, serving two important functions. First, they allow convenient implementation and modification of programs that demonstrate and test AI ideas. Second, they provide vehicles of thought: As with other high-level languages, they allow the user to concentrate on higher level concepts. Frequently, new ideas in AI are accompanied by a new language in which it is natural to apply these ideas.

Symbol Manipulation and List Processing

The first and most fundamental idea in AI programming languages was the use of the computer to manipulate arbitrary symbols—symbols that could stand for anything, not just numbers. This idea, and the *list-processing*

3

techniques that followed from it, were first introduced in the IPL language, one of the earliest programming languages of any kind.

IPL was created by Newell, Shaw, and Simon (1957) for their early AI work on problem-solving methods. Its design was guided by ideas from psychology, especially the intuitive notion of *association*. The primary elements of the language were symbols, as opposed to numbers. To form associations of these symbols, list processing was introduced, which allowed programs conveniently to build data structures of unpredictable shape and size: When parsing a sentence, choosing a chess move, or planning robot actions, one cannot know ahead of time the form of the data structures that will represent the meaning of the sentence, the play of the game, or the plan of action, respectively. The unconstrained form of data structures is an important characteristic of AI programs and is discussed further in Article VI.C1.

The problem of *unpredictable shape* of data structures was solved in IPL by the use of primitive data elements (now commonly called *cells*) consisting of two fields, each of which could hold either a symbol or a *pointer* to another cell. This simple arrangement, called a *list structure*, allows arbitrarily branched binary trees to be constructed. List structure is an extremely *general* data structure: For instance, an array, normally implemented as a sequence of words in memory, can be thought of as a list of cells whose left halves each contain a symbol and whose right halves each contain a pointer to the next memory location. The problem of *unpredictable size* was handled by having a *free list* of cells that are to be allocated to the various data structures as required.

As AI programming languages evolved, these simple list-structure ideas were expanded to include utilities that allowed truly convenient application. For instance, a programmer should not have to attend to the fact that, as a program runs, cells in temporary list structures have to be returned to the free list or else the program runs out of memory space. Eventually, these chores would be attended to automatically by the operating environments of AI programming languages. This is the sense in which a programming language can free the programmer from attending to detail, allowing him (or her) to think at a higher level, that is, in terms of list structures instead of memory addresses or even arrays. (See Article VI.B for a complete discussion of list processing.)

Another feature introduced in IPL is the *generator*, a procedure for computing a series of values. It produces one value each time it is called and is then suspended, so that it starts from where it left off the next time it is called (see Article VI.C3). This important idea was to turn up later in CONNIVER and similar languages.

Many of the first AI programs were written in IPL. These include the Newell-Shaw-Simon Chess Program (Article II.C5c, in Vol. I), the Logic Theorist (Article II.D1), the General Problem Solver (Article II.D2), SAD–SAM

(Article IV.F1), EPAM (Article XI.D, in Vol. III), Feldman's two-choice decision model, and Tonge's Assembly Line Balancing Program; many of these are described in the *Computers and Thought* collection (Feigenbaum and Feldman, 1963). Some later programs written in IPL are Quillian's memory model (Article XI.E1, in Vol. III) and REF–ARF (Fikes, 1970).

LISP

In the very early years of AI research, the idea of list processing was incorporated, along with some other novel ideas about programming, into the language that has become the mainstay of AI programming. Since its invention in 1958 by John McCarthy, LISP has been the primary AI programming language—used by the vast majority of AI researchers in all subfields. The reasons for this are in part historical: LISP was established early, several large systems have been developed to support programming in the language, and all students in AI laboratories learn LISP, so that it has become a shared language. However, the language continues to be the natural vehicle for AI research because there are features of LISP that are critically important in AI programming. As John McCarthy (1978) himself put it in an excellent article on the history of LISP:

> LISP is now the second oldest programming language in present widespread use (after FORTRAN). . . . Its core occupies some kind of local optimum in the space of programming languages given that static friction discourages purely notational changes. Recursive use of conditional expressions, representation of symbolic information externally by lists and internally by list structure, and representation of program in the same way will probably have a very long life. (p. 221)

In truth, computer science has explored the "space of programming languages" with only a few dozen experiments—an understanding of what it means to be a "local optimum" must await major advances in the study of computation. But LISP has survived and flourished where many competing programming languages have been all but forgotten. The following treatment of LISP's distinguishing features is meant to illustrate its nature and importance. A full discussion of the language, along with sample programs, is to be found in Article VI.B and in the several references given there.

Applicative style. Besides its use of list structures as its primitive (and only) data type, LISP probably differs most from other programming languages in its style of describing computations. Instead of being described as sequences of steps, LISP programs consist of functions defined in a rather mathematical format. Each function call is represented as a list, the value of whose first element is the name of the function and the values of whose other elements are the arguments. For instance, consider the LISP definition of the function FACTORIAL(N)

```
FACTORIAL (N):
    (COND ( (EQUAL N 1)                    1                     )
          (  TRUE    (TIMES N (FACTORIAL (DIFFERENCE N 1))) ) ) ,
```

where the function EQUAL takes two arguments and returns TRUE if they are equal, the function COND takes pairs of expressions as its arguments and evaluates the left expression in each pair in sequence until one left half evaluates to TRUE, and then COND returns the value of the right half of that pair. The LISP definition of the function FACTORIAL looks very much like its recursive mathematical definition:

$$N! = \begin{cases} 1, & \text{if } N = 1 \\ N(N-1)!, & \text{if } N > 1. \end{cases}$$

Thus, the basic LISP procedure specification involves, not a sequence of program steps, but a function definition in terms of applications of functions to arguments (especially recursive applications of the same function to a "depleted" argument). This *applicative style* of programming, pioneered in LISP (and also used in APL), has been suggested by a number of people (e.g., Backus, 1978) to be a more appropriate style than the von Neumann-machine-oriented sequential languages that currently dominate (in which a program consists of a sequence of instructions, much like machine-language programs, which are a collection of instructions in sequential memory locations). This orientation, and the use of embedded parentheses to indicate list structure, gives LISP programs a distinctly different appearance from those in other languages. In fact, people who know other programming languages frequently have difficulty learning LISP, while many people with a mathematical background find LISP an easy first language to learn.

The design of LISP and of ALGOL overlapped in time, with McCarthy involved with both. McCarthy was influential in the decision to include both conditional expressions and recursion in ALGOL–60, having already decided to include them in LISP. However, in LISP these two features, conditionals and recursion, form the core of the programming style in procedure definitions, much as variable assignment and loops do in ALGOL.

Programs as data. One characteristic of LISP that is unique among high-level programming languages and that seems particularly important in AI work is the representation of the programs themselves in the same data structure as all the other data, namely, list structure. This simple device has proved central to AI programs whose purpose is often to manipulate other programs, sometimes themselves. For instance, a program that is to *explain* its line of reasoning must examine its operation in reaching a conclusion— it must determine what functions were called and with what values (see, e.g., Article IX.C6). Programs that *learn* to do some task, for another example, often involve procedures that create and modify new procedures to accomplish the task (see Chap. X, in this volume, and Chap. XIV, in Vol. III).

The idea is simply that in most programming languages the executing program does not have access to the actual code, while any procedure in LISP can manipulate another procedure as easily as it can other data. For example, since the first element of a function call is the name of the function to be called, a general-purpose procedure that returns the value of the first element of a list will, when applied to a function call like (TIMES X Y), return the name of the function to be called, TIMES. Imagine trying to write a FORTRAN program that analyzes another program written in the usual FORTRAN syntax.

Another ramification of the program-as-data idea is that LISP programming environments tend to be extremely interactive: Since programs can be manipulated easily by other LISP programs, utilities such as program editors and debugging facilities can be written in LISP. Thus, they can be easily tailored by each programmer for a specific application or even used by a program to edit or monitor another program (see Article VI.C5).

Associations. The idea of associations of symbols, mentioned as a central motivation of IPL, was implemented in LISP in a simple and elegant mechanism called *property lists*. Symbols in LISP are called *atoms*, and every atom can have several properties associated with it—more precisely, the user can define properties and associate them with each atom. For instance, there might be associated, with each atom that represents a person, a property called SEX with the symbols for MALE and FEMALE as values. And there might be other properties of each person called MOTHER and FATHER whose values are the symbols for other people. Property lists are thus a very general way of *associating* symbols (see related work on *knowledge representation* in Chap. III, in Vol. I). Once again, the job of a LISP programming, run-time environment is to make this simple but powerful tool of property lists convenient to use (see Article VI.C2).

LISP as a target language. Finally, McCarthy (1978) points out another feature of LISP that, although in part an accidental side effect of its first implementation, proved to be important. It is that programs are represented in a simple syntax, namely, as lists:

> One can even conjecture that LISP owes its survival specifically to the fact that its programs are lists, which everyone, including me, has regarded as a disadvantage. Proposed replacements for LISP, e.g., POP-2 (Burstall, Collins, and Popplestone, 1968, 1971), abandoned this feature in favor of an ALGOL-like syntax leaving no target language for higher level systems. (p. 221)

In other words, since the LISP language syntax is so simple, LISP programs that produce other programs as their output do not have to worry about expressing their results in a complex format. Many of the systems described in this chapter and throughout the *Handbook* are indeed programs of this sort.

LISP today. Current LISP programming environments are themselves very large LISP programs. MACLISP from M.I.T. and INTERLISP from BBN and Xerox are the most highly developed systems, although there are several others. All of these systems offer support for creating and modifying procedures, for managing the hundreds of individual procedures that make up a LISP program, and for debugging those systems interactively. LISP lends itself to incremental program-writing. Functions can be defined incrementally, without declarations; data structures and variable names (atoms) can be created dynamically. Using the interpreted form of functions, it is simple to make *try-and-see* modifications to functions. The implementors of the major LISP environments have tended to stay in close contact with the users (since the LISP systems are LISP programs, the implementors are users), with the result that the LISP systems have tended to evolve relatively rapidly.

The system that has gone farthest in including user facilities is INTERLISP (Teitelman et al., 1978), which evolved from a series of LISP systems at BBN, notably 940 LISP in 1967 and BBN LISP in 1970. In addition to highly developed versions of the facilities described above, INTERLISP has the following features:

1. *A uniform error-handling system*, which allows some kinds of automatic error correction, such as spelling correction, entry to a special, flexible debugging facility, and handling of particular error conditions by user functions;

2. *CLISP*, which is an alternative, extensible, expression syntax;

3. *Programmer's Assistant*, which keeps track of a user's commands and so allows selected commands to be undone, retried, or changed and retried;

4. *Masterscope*, which is a cross-referencing facility to create a model of a user's program that can be used to help manage a large system;

5. *File Package*, which offers assistance such as storing functions that have been altered during a debugging session on a permanent file.

MACLISP has been under continuous development at M.I.T. since about 1966. It was developed in parallel with INTERLISP, and frequently a feature in one that was found to be useful was implemented in the other. There has, however, been more emphasis on efficiency in the use of time and space in MACLISP. Some of the main forces pushing in this direction were the increasing requirements of MACSYMA (Article VII.D1) and, to a somewhat lesser extent, of higher level AI programming languages like MICRO–PLANNER and CONNIVER, which were implemented in MACLISP. In contrast to INTERLISP, where most of the user facilities reside in the system, user facilities in MACLISP are in separate programs and are loaded automatically when required. The code produced by the MACLISP compiler is very efficient. Particular effort was directed at producing efficient compiled arithmetic, and by 1974 this objective had been accomplished to such an extent that the efficiency of compiled arithmetic in MACLISP was comparable to that of FORTRAN.

Several personal computers designed specifically for LISP programming are now available. These "LISP machines" offer complete, powerful computation facilities, very good graphics interfaces, interfaces to networks for sharing resources between personal work-stations, and all the features of the advanced LISP programming environments.

PLANNER and CONNIVER

We have said that a high-level programming language supplies some useful data and control concepts and makes it easier to use these constructs. For instance, list structure is a high-level data type, and LISP offers primitives for manipulating lists and run-time facilities to take care of bookkeeping and collecting unused cells, thus freeing the programmer from concern about these details and making it easier for him to think in terms of the list-structure concepts.

Representing knowledge. Carl Hewitt (1971) developed the PLANNER language around an idea about knowledge and reasoning in problem solving. In PLANNER, the programmer expresses his program in terms of a collection of statements, called *theorems*, about how to achieve goals given certain preconditions and about what to do should certain situations arise in the process. PLANNER encourages the encoding of *procedural knowledge*— knowledge about how to do things—and offers utilities for using that kind of knowledge in a particular style of problem solving (see Article III.C2, in Vol. I, on procedural knowledge representation). For example, the PLANNER theorem

```
(CONSE (MORTAL ?X) (GOAL (HUMAN +X)))
```

states that one way to show that someone (?X) is mortal is to show that they are human. The pattern (MORTAL ?X) is stored in a database. Later, in solving a problem, should some goal come up that matches the pattern, for example, (MORTAL (MOTHER HARRY)), the system knows that this *consequent theorem* might be useful; that is, if it can prove that Harry's mother must be human, it can conclude that she is mortal. This automatic retrieval of relevant facts is called *pattern-directed invocation* of procedures and is commonly used in *expert-systems* research in AI (see Chaps. VII, VIII, and IX; also, Waterman and Hayes-Roth, 1978). Article VI.C4 discusses the pattern-matching facilities of AI programming languages.

Control of reasoning. PLANNER offers facilities for *automatic backtracking:* The PLANNER run-time environment takes a goal to be achieved and a collection of theorems like the one above and attempts to find a theorem to achieve the goal. If the first theorem that matches the goal must in turn be proved (e.g., proving that mothers are human, so that one can conclude that Harry's mother is mortal), the system attempts to prove this goal in the same way, that is, by matching it against the knowledge base of theorems. This process continues, recursively, until either it succeeds in finding a fact that proves some goal or the line of attack fails. In this case, the system *automatically backtracks* to the most recent point of deciding between several alternative theorems for proving a goal and tries another theorem.

Only a portion of PLANNER was actually implemented, as MICRO–PLANNER (Sussman, Winograd, and Charniak, 1971). It included pattern-directed invocation of procedures and automatic backtracking. There are two types of procedures: *consequent theorems* and *antecedent theorems*. A consequent theorem is called when its pattern matches a subgoal to be solved; an antecedent theorem is called when its pattern matches an assertion added to the database (there is another kind of antecedent theorem for assertions deleted from the database). An important program written in MICRO–PLANNER is Winograd's SHRDLU (see Article IV.F4, in Vol. I).

CONNIVER was developed in reaction to the rigidity of the conception of backtracking in MICRO–PLANNER (Sussman and McDermott, 1972). The CONNIVER program retained many of the ideas of PLANNER, but at a lower level, so that fewer of the mechanisms were imposed on the user. In particular, Sussman and McDermott objected to the use of automatic backtracking. In MICRO–PLANNER, most of the information gained from following a wrong choice was lost upon failure. As a result, programs tended to get bogged down in blind backtracking.

Contexts. CONNIVER introduced the idea of a *tree of contexts* in the database. This tree represented simultaneously the different situations for different choices of actions. A powerful pattern matcher allowed flexible associative access to the database. A version of the *spaghetti stack* (see Article VI.C3) was also implemented (rather inefficiently, because it used lists rather than a stack). Together, the spaghetti stack and context tree allowed a problem solver, for example, to suspend a process that was working on one subproblem, continue work on another subproblem that seemed more promising, and then, at some later point, resume the process working on the original subproblem if necessary. Sussman's HACKER system (Article XV.C, in Vol. III) was written in CONNIVER. Continued research on the role of contexts in reasoning is described in Article VI.D.

The important point about PLANNER and CONNIVER, which are as much knowledge-representation languages as programming languages, is that they made some high-level *control* constructs (as well as data structures) convenient to use. These languages were very influential in the history of AI (see Article III.A, in Vol. I), but neither is used anymore. They can be viewed as empirical studies of the space of programming languages—studies on how to specify reasoning and problem-solving activities.

Other Languages Covered

The articles in Section VI.C attempt to analyze the issues explored in programming-language research in AI by comparing seven major languages: LISP, PLANNER, CONNIVER, QLISP, POP-2, SAIL, and FUZZY. By way of preparation for this study, the last four will be introduced here briefly.

SAIL. Developed in 1969 at the Stanford Artificial Intelligence Laboratory, the SAIL language is based on ALGOL-60 with extended string, macro, and input/output capabilities (Feldman et al., 1972). It thus has the typical block structure and is compiler based, like the majority of modern programming languages. But incorporated into SAIL from the beginning was an associative retrieval formalism called LEAP (Feldman and Rovner, 1969), which allowed rapid lookup of multiply indexed facts in a small database. SAIL was designed especially for those AI systems, such as vision and speech-understanding systems, that required fast arithmetic as well as some of the symbol-manipulation facilities available in LISP. The language was extended in 1973 to include listlike data structures, records, coroutining, and a powerful interactive debugging environment (Reiser, 1975, 1976).

QLISP. The problem-solving language QA1 was developed by Cordell Green at SRI International in the mid-1960s as an attempt to formalize the ideas in Bertram Raphael's SIR program (see Article IV.F1, in Vol. I). This effort was followed immediately by QA2, which applied the ideas of *resolution theorem proving* as the inference-making mechanism. QA2 introduced the now standard method for extracting answers from the process of proving theorems with existentially quantified variables—that is, binding values to the variables that satisfy the theorem (see Chap. XII, in Vol. III). QA3 was an improved implementation of QA2, in which Green explored how to tackle various types of problems with a resolution theorem prover, including program synthesis, verification, and problem solving (Green, 1969). QA3 was also used in STRIPS (Article II.D5, in Vol. I).

QA4 was developed by Rulifson and others (1971) at SRI around the time that MICRO-PLANNER was implemented at M.I.T. QA4 was intended to overcome certain problems with QA3—specifically the difficulties in guiding the search to *relevant* facts and theorems in trying to derive a proof. It was necessary somehow to specify procedural and domain-specific knowledge about what facts to use and when to use them, in a way that a theorem prover—the underlying inference engine—could use. Theorems or procedures had to be indexed by their purposes, an idea that led to the implementation of *pattern-directed invocation* similar to that of PLANNER. QA4 was the first language to develop the idea of representing assertions *uniquely*, in the way that simple symbols are represented uniquely, so that properties can be associated with assertions. QA4 adopted a context mechanism like that of CONNIVER and also had a general control structure.

To make the language more widely available and to take advantage of the new facilities in INTERLISP, a cleaner implementation of QA4 was embedded in INTERLISP and called QLISP. When the spaghetti stack was implemented in INTERLISP, QLISP was modified to take advantage of it. Unlike MICRO–PLANNER and CONNIVER, which are interpreted languages on top of LISP, QLISP is basically a subroutine package for INTERLISP, making it much easier to mix QLISP with INTERLISP in programming. (This extended-language design has been found advantageous in current representation-language research as well.)

Some special features of QLISP are its extra data types, such as sets, tuples, and bags, together with procedures for handling them, and QLISP's ability to use them in pattern matching. Pattern matching plays a major role in QLISP, being used for such things as constructing data. QLISP also makes the distinction, blurred in PLANNER, between (a) finding the truth of an assertion by a simple lookup in the database and (b) finding it by deduction using *consequent theorems*, as described above. QLISP also introduced the notion of a *team* of procedures that the programmer could specify as worth considering anywhere that a pattern-directed procedure invocation might occur. (A team consisting of a single procedure corresponds to the traditional subroutine call. At the other extreme, a team consisting of all the goal-achieving procedures in the system corresponds to the nondeterministic style of PLANNER.) The NOAH systems (Article XV.D1, in Vol. III) and the DEDALUS systems (Article X.D5) were written in QLISP.

POP–2. AI researchers at the University of Edinburgh developed the POP–2 language because good implementations of LISP were not available on the machines they were using and because they disagreed about the usefulness of some of the features of LISP and thought that others could be improved (Popplestone, 1967). POP–2 is still the most common AI language in Great Britain, but it has not found broad use elsewhere. It has many of the properties of LISP but an ALGOL-like syntax. Like LISP, it is interactive and allows general manipulation of functions, but it has several novel features, including partially applied functions, dynamic lists (generators), and explicit stack manipulation, allowing multiple-valued procedures. POP–2 was intended for efficient implementation on the medium-sized machines available to the designers of the language.

POPLER is a language based on PLANNER and embedded in POP–2 (Davies et al., 1973). It has an implementation of the spaghetti stack and makes the same distinction as QLISP between testing the database and calling consequent procedures. POPLER further distinguishes between those procedures that deduce the value of an assertion in a world model from those that achieve the assertion as a goal, producing a new world model from the old model.

FUZZY. The most recently developed language included in this study illustrates current work in AI programming languages. The design of the FUZZY language (Le Faivre, 1977) was motivated by the theory of fuzzy sets (Zadeh, 1965; Gupta, Saridis, and Gaines, 1977), a generalization of Boolean set theory that allows for "graded" set membership (rather than all-or-none). For many natural-language concepts, for instance, there is no sharp boundary between situations for which the concept applies and situations for which it does not. Consider, for example, the concept *young*. We may say that people under 10 years of age are young and those above 60 years are not young. However, there is no particular day at which a person's age switches from "young" to "not young"; rather, this is a gradual transition. In fuzzy set theory, the concept of young in this context is expressed by a "membership function" representing the degree to which a person of a particular age can be considered to be young.

Many AI systems deal explicitly with fuzzy information (see, e.g., the *certainty factor* in MYCIN, Article VIII.B1), and FUZZY is designed to facilitate certain types of reasoning with fuzzy sets. It has been used for various AI projects, including the AIMDS/BELIEVER system at Rutgers University (Schmidt and Sridharan, 1977) and HAM–RPM, a knowledge-based conversationalist at the University of Hamburg (Wahlster, 1977).

Logic Programming

Two languages based on first-order predicate calculus are PROLOG and FOL. PROLOG programs consist of "axioms" in first-order logic together with a theorem to be proved. The axioms are restricted to implications with the left- and right-hand sides in *horn-clause* form. If the theorem contains existentially quantified variables, the system will return instantiations of these that make the theorem true (if such exist) using methods developed from those of QA3. The style of programming is similar to that demonstrated in QA3 and, to a lesser extent, PLANNER. Automatic backtracking is used, but the programmer may add annotation to control the order in which clauses and axioms are considered. A compiler has been implemented for PROLOG that allows programs in a variety of domains to be executed in about the same time as corresponding compiled LISP programs. (See Clocksin and Mellish, 1981; Warren, Pereira, and Pereira, 1977.)

Another direction of logic—the uses of meta-theory—has been explored in FOL (Weyrauch, 1979). This program is primarily a proof checker that accepts logic statements and proof-step commands that can be carried out and tested for correctness. However, it provides a powerful theory-manipulating structure that allows the building of arbitrary meta-theory. Thus, for example, a theorem may be proved not only within a theory but also with the help of the meta-theory. Proving a theorem by going through the meta-theory corresponds closely to executing a procedure to produce the theorem.

Modern AI Programming Environments

Current programming in AI research laboratories is done predominantly on Digital Equipment Corporation's PDP–10s and PDP–20s in LISP, principally MACLISP or INTERLISP. Other LISP dialects, for the DEC VAX machine and for several other machines, are in relatively sparse use, as are some other general-purpose languages like SAIL, POP–2 (used mostly in Great Britain), and PROLOG (used mostly in Europe). Work on languages as specialized as PLANNER comes under the heading of knowledge representation these days and is reported in Chapter III (in Vol. I). The recently introduced LISP machines promise to alter AI programming environments radically.

References

The review article by Rieger, Rosenberg, and Samet (1979) gives examples of procedures in several languages. More complete introductions to AI programming include Charniak, Riesbeck, and McDermott (1979), Schank and Riesbeck (1981), and Winston and Horn (1981).

B. LISP

THE BEGINNINGS of LISP date from the first days of computing machinery: John McCarthy, who invented the language in 1958, states that he was motivated by a desire to implement a practical list-processing language for AI work on the IBM 704 computer. As his ideas about the language developed, McCarthy came to see LISP as an elegant mathematical tool as well. His first paper on LISP, in 1960, described it both as a practical programming language and as an idealized model of computation suitable for use in recursive-function theory.

McCarthy (1978) cites the following as the key ideas about computation that are embodied in LISP:

1. Computing with symbolic expressions rather than numbers; that is, bit patterns in a computer's memory and registers can stand for arbitrary symbols, not just those of arithmetic.

2. List processing, that is, representing data as linked-list structures in the machine and as multilevel lists on paper.

3. Control structure based on the composition of functions to form more complex functions.

4. Recursion as a way to describe processes and problems.

5. Representation of LISP programs internally as linked lists and externally as multilevel lists, that is, in the same form as all data are represented.

6. The function EVAL, written in LISP itself, serves as an interpreter for LISP and as a formal definition of the language.

This article concentrates on describing LISP as a practical programming language. After a sketch of the basic design of the language, enough of the most important language constructs are defined to allow readers to understand small LISP programs and some sample programs are provided. After the definitions, some general implications of the structure of LISP for the way it is used in AI are discussed, and some of its drawbacks are mentioned. A more complete introduction to the language can be found in several books mentioned at the end of this article.

Description of LISP

Data structure. In basic LISP there is only one data type, namely, *list structure*. In most LISP programming situations, a datum takes the specific

15

form of a *list* or an *atom*. Atoms have identifiers such as I-AM-AN-ATOM, 3, XYZ, or NIL. They have no component parts—hence, the name—but various properties or attributes can be attached to individual atoms. The most important attribute an atom can have, besides its name, is a *value*—in the same sense that variables have values. Certain atoms have standard values: The atom NIL has the value NIL, T has the value T, and any numerical atom, such as 12, 1.732, or -1.066E3, has the corresponding integer or floating-point number as its value. (Note that the atoms are not "typed"—any atom, besides these constants, can have any value bound to it.)

A list is defined recursively as a sequence of zero or more elements enclosed in parentheses,

$$(\text{element}_1 \ldots \text{element}_n),$$

where each element is either an atom or a list. (The definition is *recursive* because it mentions the thing being defined in the body of the definition.) The *null* or *empty* list is written as ( ) or NIL. NIL, you will remember, is also an atom. In fact, NIL has the distinction of being the only LISP datum that is both an atom and a list. Some other examples of LISP lists are:

> (SPOT RAN HOME)
>
> (SPOT RAN (TO JANE))
>
> (SPOT RAN (TO (JANE AND DICK))) .

The inherently recursive structure of lists is very flexible and turns out to be a convenient representation for many kinds of information:

(2 3 5 7 11 13 17 19)	A set of numbers.
((- B) + (SQRT ((B * B) - (4 * A * C))))	An algebraic expression.
(I (saw ((that (gasoline can)) explode)))	A parsed sentence.
(GREEN GRASS)	An assertion.
(AND (ON A B) (ON A C) (NOT (TOUCH B C)))	A conjunctive clause.

The internal representation of LISP lists is built from primitives called *CONS cells*. Each CONS cell is an address that contains a pair of pointers, and each pointer can point either to an atom or to another CONS cell. In a typical LISP implementation, the CONS cells are computer words with pointers in their right and left halves, like the cell z diagrammed below:

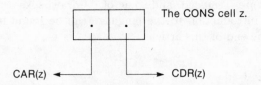

The CONS cell z.

CAR(z) ◄——— ———► CDR(z)

The left-half pointer points to the CAR of the cell z; the right half, to the CDR (pronounced cood-er; the names originated in the architecture of the

IBM 704). The list (A B C) is represented by three CONS cells whose left halves point to the atoms A, B, and C, and whose right halves are used to link the cells together:

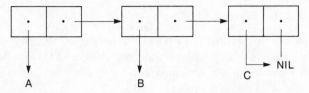

In mathematics, *sets* are taken as the fundamental objects, and other concepts, such as ordered pairs, sequences, tuples, and relations, are defined in terms of sets. LISP data may be regarded as an alternative formalism in which the ordered pair, represented by the CONS cell, is fundamental. Sequences and sets are then represented by LISP lists, an n-tuple by a list of length n, and a relation by a list of tuples.

The list structure of LISP can be used to model essentially any data structure. For example, a two-dimensional array may be represented as a list of rows, and each row in turn as a list of elements. Of course, for many purposes, this implementation of arrays would be relatively clumsy or inefficient, but the point is not so much to model standard data structures with lists as to model the complicated and often unpredictable data structures that arise in many symbol-manipulation tasks (see below).

Control structure. LISP's control structure is primarily *applicative*—the flow of control is guided by the application of functions to arguments, where the arguments in turn may be applications of functions. This contrasts with the sequential control structure of most programming languages, in which separate statements are executed one after another. Compare, for example, the ALGOL-like and LISP-like versions of a program to compute the two square roots of a nonnegative number:

```
ALGOL-like:    procedure ROOTS (value X: real; R1, R2: real);
               begin
               R1 ← SQRT (X);
               R2 ← -R1
               end

LISP-like:     ROOTS (X): (BOTHSIGNS (SQRT X))
                  where BOTHSIGNS (Y): (LIST Y (MINUS Y)) .
```

The LISP function ROOTS applies the duplicating function BOTHSIGNS to the result of the function SQRT. In LISP, statements are not differentiated from expressions, nor are procedures differentiated from functions. Each function, whether it is a language primitive or defined by the user, returns a single value in the form of a pointer to a list structure.

Syntax. LISP syntax reflects its uniform control structure. A LISP expression is defined recursively either as an atom, which when evaluated returns its *value*, or as a list of the form

$$(F\ e_1 e_2 \ldots e_n).$$

When evaluated, this expression first evaluates (again recursively) the arguments e_1 through e_n, which may be atoms or lists, and then calls (evaluates) the function F with those values as arguments. For example, the expression (TIMES 3 (PLUS 4 1)) would evaluate to 15.

Dynamic scoping. The scoping rule of LISP is also closely linked to its applicative control structure. Purely dynamic scoping is used: During the evaluation of a function F, a nonlocal variable x will have the value bound to it most recently in the calling hierarchy. In other words, if x was assigned a value by the function that called F, say, G, that will be its value when F is evaluated; otherwise, the value for x would be the one bound to it by the function that called G; and so on. Scoping in LISP, then, depends only on the calling order of functions (dynamic scoping) and in no way depends on when or where they were declared in the program text (static scoping).

Recursion. Dynamic scoping allows the free use of recursive functions—functions that can call themselves. Recursive functions are most easily understood as operations that are defined in terms of themselves. For example, the factorial function, $N!$, on the positive integers is defined as 1 when $N = 1$ and otherwise as $N(N - 1)!$. Thus, the control structure of LISP, like the data structure, is uniform and based on a recursive definition. In the sample LISP programs presented later in this article, we illustrate recursion with a LISP version of the factorial function and other LISP programs.

Storage allocation and garbage collection. LISP relies completely on dynamic allocation of space for data storage. During execution of a program, each evaluation of the CONS function causes one CONS cell to be allocated to the list structure being manipulated. Gradually, the program's available space (e.g., the *free list* of CONS cells) is used up. Fortunately, after the program has used a CONS cell, it often forgets all about it—that is, it retains no direct or indirect pointer to it and will never access it again—so these old CONS cells can be recycled. When the available storage gets low, LISP systems suspend the user program and call the *garbage collector*, which locates all the forgotten cells and makes them available again to the user program.

Comparing this scheme to static allocation, in which each variable or array has a fixed amount of storage reserved for it before the program is executed, it is clear that static allocation requires less overhead. But for LISP, in which list structures grow unpredictably, static allocation would be hopelessly restrictive. The time spent in garbage collection is part of the price paid for the flexibility of LISP's data structure.

LISP's Primitive Functions

There are only a few basic LISP functions in terms of which other LISP functions can be defined. (Most LISP programming environments offer a very large set of utility functions for the convenience of the programmer. They include systems functions for writing files, etc., and other functions written in terms of these few primitives.) With the exception of the function CONS, which causes a CONS cell to be made, none of these basic functions has any side effects, so they can be described by the value they return.

Most LISP functions evaluate their arguments before computing anything from them. (Here, only the function QUOTE does not.) Beginner's problems with LISP frequently stem from not making the distinction between an expression and the value of that expression. For instance, if the value of the atom A is ALDO, then the value of the expression A is ALDO, but the value of the expression (QUOTE A) is A. The value of an unbound atom is undefined in LISP and will cause an error in all implementations.

In Table B–1, let the atom X have as its value (TIMES 3 (PLUS 4 1)), which is a list. The symbols e, e_1, p_1, etc., stand for any expressions given as arguments to the functions, and e, e_1, p_1, etc., stand for the values of those expressions. The seven functions have the power to compute anything that can be computed—they have the computing power of a Turing machine. However, they do not allow one to write programs in the style common to most programming languages, that is, as a sequence of statements that operate by causing side effects. The prime example of this kind of statement is *assignment*, performed by the SET function in LISP:

Expression	Value	Comment
(SET e_1 e_2)	e_2	Like all LISP functions, SET
(SET 'Y (EVAL X))	15	returns a value, but its real
(SET 'Y X)	(TIMES 3 (PLUS 4 1))	purpose is its side effect.
(SETQ Y X)	(TIMES 3 (PLUS 4 1))	The more commonly used
		form, SETQ, automatically
		quotes its first argument.

Another construct imported to LISP from other programming languages is the sequential-statement program format. In LISP, this is accomplished with the PROG function. (It is really stretching terminology to call PROG a function, since it is basically a BEGIN–END block with local variables. However, PROG does have the standard LISP-function syntax and does always return a value.) Here is what a PROG block looks like:

$$(\text{PROG} (\text{atom}_1 \ldots \text{atom}_M) \, e_1 e_2 \ldots e_n).$$

TABLE B–1

LISP Primitive Functions

Expression	Value	Comments
e X	e (TIMES 3 (PLUS 4 1))	An expression is an atom or a list of the form $(F\ e_1 \ldots e_n)$.
(QUOTE e) (QUOTE X)	e X	QUOTE is essential to manipulate an expression itself, rather than its value. We abbreviate (QUOTE e) as 'e.
(CAR e) (CAR X)	first element of e TIMES	Not defined if e is not a list.
(CDR e) (CDR X) (CADDR X)	the rest of e (3 (PLUS 4 1)) (PLUS 4 1)	Not defined if e is not a list. (CAR (CDR e)) is abbreviated (CADR e), (CDR (CDR (CAR e))) is abbreviated (CDDAR e), etc.
(CONS e_1 e_2) (CONS 'F X) (CONS '(A B) '(A B)) (CONS NIL NIL)	prefix e_1 onto e_2 (F (TIMES 3 (PLUS 4 1))) ((A B) A B) (NIL)	Has side effect of setting up a CONS cell. (CAR (CONS e_1 e_2)) is e_1, (CDR (CONS e_1 e_2)) is e_2.
(EQUAL e_1 e_2) (EQUAL '(B) (CONS 'B NIL)) (EQUAL X 15) (EQUAL (EVAL X) 15)	T if $e_1 = e_2$ T NIL T	Note how NIL is used to mean "False." (EQUAL e 'e)) = NIL, usually, but (EQUAL NIL 'NIL) = T.
(ATOM e) (ATOM (CAR X)) (ATOM (CADDR X))	T if e is an atom T NIL	(ATOM NIL) = T.
(COND $(p_1\ e_1) \ldots (p_n\ e_n)$) (COND (NIL 'A) (T 'B))	If $e_1 = $ T then p_1 else if $e_n = $ T then p_n. B	This is the basic branching function of LISP.
(EVAL e) (EVAL X)	value of e 15	EVAL is the opposite of QUOTE; (EVAL 'e) = value(e).

PROG does not evaluate its first argument, which has to be a list (possibly empty) of atoms. Each of these atoms is a local variable inside the PROG block. The subsequent expressions e_1, e_2, etc., are evaluated in that order. The special function (RETURN e_0) causes termination of the PROG, returning the value of e_0.

A few of the more commonly used nonprimitive functions are defined here in terms of LISP primitives:

(NULL e) or (NOT e) $\leftrightarrow$ (COND (e NIL) (T T))

(OR $e_1 \ldots e_n$) $\leftrightarrow$ (COND (e_1 T) $\ldots$ (e_n T) (T NIL))

(AND $e_1 \ldots e_n$) $\leftrightarrow$ (COND ((NOT e_1) NIL) $\ldots$ ((NOT e_n) NIL) (T T))

(LIST $e_1 \ldots e_n$) $\leftrightarrow$ (CONS e_1 (CONS $\ldots$ (CONS e_n NIL) $\ldots$)).

Thus, (NULL e) returns T only if e evaluates to NIL, and (OR $e_1 \ldots e_n$) returns T if and only if e evaluates to TRUE.

User-defined functions in LISP are written in a notation derived from the lambda-calculus of Church (1941). The LAMBDA function in LISP corresponds loosely to a procedure declaration in an ALGOL-like language, in the same way that PROG corresponds to a BEGIN–END block. The expression

$$\text{(LAMBDA (atom}_1 \ldots \text{atom}_m) \, e)$$

evaluates to a function of m parameters, where e is the LISP form of an expression to be evaluated. When a function is called, giving m expressions as actual parameters, *all* actual parameters are evaluated and their values are bound to the formal parameter atoms. Thus, if the user defines the function EXCHANGE as:

EXCHANGE: (LAMBDA (Y) (LIST (CADR Y) (CAR Y))),

the value of (EXCHANGE '(A B)) would be (B A). We have now introduced enough of LISP to go through some sample programs.

Examples of LISP Programming

FACTORIAL—A simple recursive program. This example was chosen for the sole purpose of showing how recursion works in LISP. Even so, it is not unrealistically simple.

FACTORIAL: (LAMBDA (N) (COND ((EQUAL N 1) 1)
                          (T (TIMES N (FACTORIAL (SUB1 N))))))

The evaluation of an expression like (FACTORIAL 3) proceeds as follows: First, N is bound to 3 and then the (COND...) expression is evaluated. COND takes a list of pairs of expressions as its arguments—the first pair is composed of the expressions (EQUAL N 1) and 1. If the left half of the pair evaluates to TRUE, the value of the right half is returned as the value of the COND. Otherwise, the next pair is processed.

In this case, since (EQUAL N 1) evaluates to NIL, that is, "false," the next pair, composed of T and (TIMES N (FACTORIAL (SUB1 N))) must be evaluated. Since T always evaluates to TRUE—it is a special symbol—the value of the COND expression is the value of (TIMES 3 (FACTORIAL 2)), so FACTORIAL must be called again with an argument of 2. These recursive calls in the evaluation of (FACTORIAL 3) can be summarized as follows:

value of (FACTORIAL 3) $= 3 \times$ value of (FACTORIAL 2)

value of (FACTORIAL 2) $= 2 \times$ value of (FACTORIAL 1)

value of (FACTORIAL 1) $= 1$.

The third call of FACTORIAL in this evaluation binds N to 1 and, since the case of $N = 1$ is treated specially in the definition of the function, it can return a numeric value, namely, 1, without recursion. Most recursive-function definitions are of this form: a general case involving a recursive call with a "diminished" argument and a special case for some known value of the argument.

The various calls to FACTORIAL are "stacked" like any other procedure calls, so that after (FACTORIAL 1) is evaluated—"returns" a value—the evaluation of (FACTORIAL 2) continues; and so on.

Recursion is a programming method of great power in tasks that have an inherently recursive structure, which is the case in much of AI problem solving. If the programmer can think of a way to reduce the general problem to simpler problems of the same form, which finally reduce to one or two special cases, he need not state the step-by-step solution to the general case. In our FACTORIAL example, this reduction was accomplished in the very definition of the FACTORIAL function, $N! = N(N-1)!$, which was itself recursive. If we had been given an alternate definition of FACTORIAL, like

$$N! = N(N-1)(N-2) \cdots 1,$$

we might have written a more standard program, perhaps using a loop, to evaluate the function. The power of thinking recursively in AI is illustrated in the next example.

"Tower of Hanoi"—Recursive problem solving. In the "Tower of Hanoi" puzzle, a tower formed by disks stacked on a peg must be transferred to another peg, say, from peg A to peg B in Figure B–1, moving only one disk at a time and never placing a larger disk on top of a smaller. (Peg C may be used for temporary storage.)

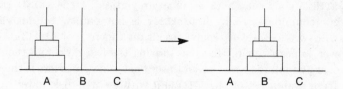

Figure B–1.   The "Tower of Hanoi" puzzle.

In looking for a recursive solution to the problem, one would notice that to move a tower of just two disks, one would move the smaller disk from peg A to peg C, then move the big disk from peg A to peg B, and finally move the little disk back on top on peg B. Now the general problem of moving a tower of N disks can be reduced to three steps, as shown in Figure B–2: Transfer the subtower of disks 1 through $N-1$ from peg A to peg C, move the biggest disk, N, from peg A to peg B, and then transfer the subtower back from peg C to peg B.

Of course, in the special case of only one disk ($N = 1$), the solution is trivial—just move the disk from peg A to peg B. Now we can directly write a recursive program to find the general solution.

```
MOVETOWER:
  (LAMBDA (DiskList PegA PegB PegC)
    (IF DiskList THEN
      (PROG ()
        (MOVETOWER (CDR DiskList) PegA PegC PegB)
        (PRINT (LIST 'Move (CAR DiskList) 'from PegA 'to PegB))
        (MOVETOWER (CDR DiskList) PegC PegB PegA)))) .
```

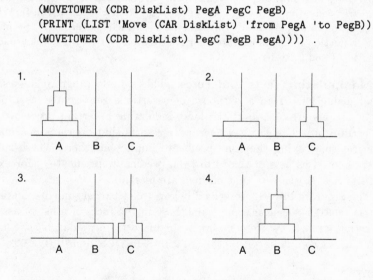

Figure B–2.   Solution of the "Tower of Hanoi" puzzle.

The IF...THEN construct here is an abbreviation of the COND statement that is very commonly used. If DiskList is not empty, the MOVETOWER function will first execute a recursive call on the rest of DiskList to move the subtower to peg C, print that it is moving the last disk, and then execute another recursive call to move the subtower back to peg B. Here is the printout resulting from evaluation of MOVETOWER with a three-disk tower:

```
(MOVETOWER '(Disk1 Disk2 Disk3) 'A 'B 'C):
                    (Move Disk1 from A to B)
                    (Move Disk2 from A to C)
                    (Move Disk1 from B to C)
                    (Move Disk3 from A to B)
                    (Move Disk1 from C to A)
                    (Move Disk2 from C to B)
                    (Move Disk1 from A to B)
                    NIL .
```

Observe the following points:

1. NIL is returned as the value of the PROG.

2. Each instance of the function MOVETOWER calls two other instances. The reader is invited to draw the tree of recursive calls to MOVETOWER and calculate how many moves it takes for N disks. By the way, it is not hard to see that this solution is optimal.

3. One may regard the tree of calls to MOVETOWER as a problem-reduction tree consisting entirely of AND nodes (see Article II.B2, in Vol. I). When the subproblems are of the same form as their *parent* nodes, problem-reduction methods lead to recursive solutions—a very general situation in AI and a strong point of LISP.

Manipulating facts and rules. This sample program makes simple logical deductions from a database of assertions represented as LISP lists. The assertions are of two kinds: facts indicating a certain predicate is true of a certain object (e.g., (MAN Socrates) asserts that Socrates is a man) and a general rule saying that one predicate implies another. These rules will be represented as lists of the form (ALL predicate$_1$ predicate$_2$); for example, (ALL MAN MORTAL) asserts that all men are mortal.

The program PROVE, described below, takes two arguments, a statement such as (MORTAL Socrates) and a database in the form of a list of assertions, and returns T if the statement can be deduced from its database, NIL if not. PROVE uses two auxiliary functions, FINDASSERTION and PROVESIT.

```
PROVE:
        (LAMBDA (Statement DataBase) (FINDASSERTION DataBase))
```

```
FINDASSERTION:
        (LAMBDA (RestOfDataBase)
            (COND ((NULL RestOfDataBase) NIL)
                  ((OR (PROVESIT (CAR RestOfDataBase)))
                      (FINDASSERTION (CDR RestOfDataBase)))))
PROVESIT:
        (LAMBDA (Assertion)
            (OR (EQUAL Statement Assertion)
                (AND (EQUAL (CAR Assertion) 'ALL)
                     (EQUAL (CADDR Assertion) (CAR Statement))
                     (PROVE (CONS (CADR Assertion) (CDR Statement))
                            DataBase))))
```

We would describe this system of three functions in English by saying that a statement can be proved from a database if the first assertion in the database proves it, or it can be proved from the rest of the database. (The LISP function OR returns the value of the first clause that does not evaluate to NIL.) An assertion in the database *proves* a statement of the form (predicate object) if it is either identical with the statement or of the form (ALL predicate$_2$ predicate) and the new statement (predicate$_2$ object) can be proved from the database.

Evaluation of the form (PROVE '(MORTAL Socrates) '((MAN Socrates) (ALL MAN MORTAL))) builds up the following tree of function calls before returning T:

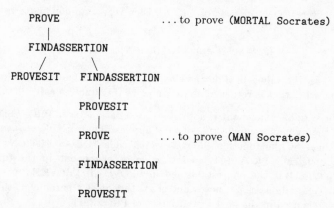

Observe the following points:

1. Clarity is enhanced by splitting the prover, which *could* be written as a single function, into three smaller functions that each perform an identifiable subtask.

2. The three functions are purely applicative—no assignments or PROG statements. LISP programs tend to be most elegant when written in this style, but for MOVETOWER it would have been clumsy.

3. Though they do not directly call themselves, the functions PROVE and PROVESIT are still considered recursive, since the system of three functions is mutually recursive—from each function, there is a chain of calls leading back to itself:

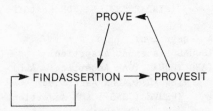

4. FINDASSERTION illustrates a very common scheme for recursion "down a list," meaning that the diminished argument of the recursive call is the *rest* of the original list argument after processing its CAR. This general form can be expressed symbolically as the pattern:

```
F: (LAMBDA (X) (COND ((NULL (X) NIL)
                      (T (G (H (CAR X)) (F (CDR X)))))))),
```

where F, G, and H are arbitrary functions. In FINDASSERTION, G = OR and H = PROVESIT, making

$$(\text{FINDASSERTION } '(e_1 \ldots e_n))$$
$$= (\text{OR } (\text{PROVESIT } e_1) \ldots (\text{PROVESIT } e_n)).$$

If G were CONS instead of OR, another very common pattern would result:

$$(F \ '(e_1 \ldots e_n)) = ((H \ e_1) \ldots (H \ e_n)),$$

that is, the values of H on the elements e_1 to e_n would be CONSed into a new list that is returned as the value of the function call.

5. The variable **statement** is not defined as a parameter to PROVESIT, and so the dynamic scoping rule of LISP applies. The variable **statement** is defined by the function PROVE, which calls FINDASSERTION, which in turn calls PROVESIT, so the value of **statement** in the function PROVESIT is the one established in PROVE. If PROVESIT now calls PROVE and passes it a new value of **statement** as a parameter, this new value is used in the next instantiation of PROVESIT.

Some Important Features of LISP

As described above, data and programs in LISP are highly recursive and are represented as nested lists. There are even closer connections between them.

Programs mirror data. In LISP, functions may be written so as to mirror the structure of the data they operate upon. As an example, the function SUBSTITUTE takes any list Object and generates a copy of it in which every occurrence of a given atom Old is replaced by another list or atom New.

```
SUBSTITUTE:
    (LAMBDA (Object Old New)
        (COND ((ATOM Object) (COND ((EQUAL Object Old) New) (T Object)))
              (T (CONS (SUBSTITUTE (CAR Object) Old New)
                       (SUBSTITUTE (CDR Object) Old New)))))
```

Suppose we evaluate (SUBSTITUTE '(PLUS (TIMES A X) X) 'X (PLUS 2 3)), replacing all occurrences of X with (PLUS 2 3). SUBSTITUTE is called a total of 13 times. If we draw out the internal representation of (PLUS (TIMES A X) B) in terms of CONS cells and pointers, we find that it contains six CONS cells and seven atoms. In evaluating this structure, SUBSTITUTE is called exactly once for each of these pieces, and the tree structure of instances of SUBSTITUTE is, in general, isomorphic to the internal structure of its argument. There are two cases: Either Object is an atom, and the appropriate value is returned without recursion, or Object is a list, in which case SUBSTITUTE is applied recursively to the CAR and CDR of Object and the results CONSed together. Note that should Old not occur in Object, the body of SUBSTITUTE simplifies to:

```
(IF (ATOM Object)
    THEN Object
    ELSE (CONS (CAR Object) (CDR Object))) .
```

This parallelism of control structure to data structure is an enormous help in dealing with complex nested data. It is very characteristic of programming in LISP that, in writing functions, one need only concern oneself with the *recursive definition* of the data and not with all possible cases, much as a language is adequately and conveniently described by its grammar for many purposes.

Programs are data. The internal representation of a LISP program (assuming it has not been compiled) is the same as that of any other multi-level list, that is, CONS cells and atoms. LISP is unique among programming languages in storing its programs as *structured* data. (Of course, many languages store programs unstructured, as bit strings or sequences of tokens.) This property is very important, for several reasons.

First, it is particularly easy to write LISP programs that generate LISP expressions and programs, as in *automatic-programming* research (Chap. X). Second, functions can be passed as parameters to other functions (just as any list structure can). For instance, suppose we had a function to do minimax game-tree search as in chess-playing programs (see Article II.C5a, in Vol. I). We could pass as a parameter to the search routine its *evaluation function*—the code that evaluates the positions to determine which are "best" to pursue. Changing this parameter, under the control of some strategy, would cause different moves to be chosen, depending possibly on global strategy, known traits of the opponent, or other considerations. Third, there is procedural representation of knowledge: LISP procedures for deducing facts can be stored in a database as if they *were* facts.

Last, and most important, is the manner in which LISP can be a foundation for more advanced languages. The method is to write an interpreter, in LISP, for a new LISP-like language. Syntactic constructs of the new language are represented as multilevel lists just as in LISP itself, making the interpretation relatively easy to do. The special AI languages MICRO–PLANNER, CONNIVER, and QLISP were all implemented in this way.

LISP is interpretive. Originally LISP was to be a compiler-based language. While design of the first compiler was under way, it was recognized that the LISP function EVAL was in essence a LISP interpreter. Before, EVAL had been of only theoretical interest and existed only on paper. It was soon hand-coded, and long before a compiler had been implemented, a LISP interpreter became available.

Interpretive execution (or evaluation) has strong advantages during program *development*, chiefly in that it permits interactive programming. Once a program is fully operational, it is usually compiled for greater speed. Another important consequence of interpretation is greater flexibility of the language itself. An interpreter is much more accessible to change than a compiler, especially LISP interpreters, which tend to be written almost entirely in LISP itself.

LISP is interactive. Any interactive language system must be interpreter based rather than compiler based. Interpretation for LISP is far easier than for most languages, because of its uniform syntax. Other features like dynamic allocation and the absence of type declarations also suit it to interactive use. Essentially all existing LISP systems are interactive.

Since LISP encourages the composition of large programs out of many small functions, large programs can be developed incrementally by writing and debugging the component functions one at a time. There are a few large LISP systems that provide not only the direct language support but also an entire "environment" for interactive LISP programming, including editors, debugging and tracing facilities, and alternative syntactic forms more convenient than the pure list notation. These LISP systems also extend the basic language with additional special-purpose functions and sometimes new data types (see Sec. VI.C).

Disadvantages of LISP

Ugly syntax. A common complaint about the list-structure format of LISP programs is that it makes them difficult to read. The only syntactic items are separators, such as spaces and parentheses, which provide most of the structure. This way of representing structure is convenient for the machine to read, but inconvenient for humans. In practice, facilities are provided for printing out programs so that the structure is also indicated with indention. No attempted alternative formats have caught on (with, perhaps, the exception of the CLISP dialect provided in the INTERLISP system). The utility of LISP's structured representation of code outweighs the nuisance of its external form.

One data type. Not having distinct data types is harmful when it prevents type-checking at run time, where bugs can often be detected early. However, many LISP systems do support additional data types, such as strings, arrays, and records (see also QLISP in Article VI.C2).

Inefficiency. Any language is relatively slow when executed interpretively. Speed is traded for convenience and extensibility. Some LISP compilers, however, produce fairly efficient code: Because of its use in the MACSYMA system, MACLISP produces very efficient code for numeric calculations.

Lack of a language standard. Unlike FORTRAN and other well-known languages, there has never been an attempt to agree on a standardized LISP. The absence of a language standard and the proliferation of incompatible versions make LISP badly suited to be a production language, and in AI research work there are severe difficulties in transporting LISP programs to machines running a different LISP.

Conclusion

It has always been the case that almost all LISP use has been in the AI community and that almost all AI research employs LISP or a language built on LISP. Although it is really a general-purpose, list-processing language, LISP has not found a niche outside of the AI community. But among AI researchers, the various shortcomings of the language have never outweighed their feeling for its power and elegance as a tool for programming and for thought.

References

Introductory texts on LISP include the books by Weissman (1967), Friedman (1974), and Siklossy (1976), and the second half of Winston's (1977) text on Artificial Intelligence. Allen (1978) gives a complete introduction to the theory and practice of LISP programming. Pratt (1979) is an excellent, short introduction. McCarthy (1978) is a fascinating historical study of the theoretical origins of the language.

The practical side of AI programming is covered more thoroughly in the books by Winston and Horn (1981); Charniak, Riesbeck, and McDermott (1979); and Schank and Riesbeck (1981).

C. AI PROGRAMMING–LANGUAGE FEATURES

C1. Overview

THE PURPOSE of this section on AI programming-language features is two-fold: to present some powerful programming techniques and to show how they are implemented in some major AI languages. We describe the special data representations, control structures, pattern-matching capabilities, and programming environments that have been developed for AI programming— each representing a data point in AI researchers' exploration of the "space of programming languages." We attempt to explain why these peculiar features developed by discussing some of the applications they have found in AI languages.

In these articles, we focus on more advanced features, built on the basic features of LISP: symbol manipulation, list processing, and recursion. These are attempts to supply primitives in the languages for some higher level conception of data or control. We look at seven AI languages: basic LISP, PLANNER, CONNIVER, QLISP, SAIL, POP-2, and FUZZY. While the approach we take is largely comparative, the comparisons are intended to bring out significant trade-offs and alternatives rather than suggest a best language for a particular purpose. In fact, except for LISP, none of these languages is in widespread use (see Article VI.A).

No previous knowledge of the languages is assumed here. Nor is any attempt made to help the reader learn how to program in them. Experience in programming and familiarity with basic concepts of computer science (data types, variables, procedures, etc.) will be very helpful, but not essential, in understanding the discussion.

AI Programming

From the start, it must be admitted that the class of "AI programs" is not clearly defined. As discussed in Article VI.A, some general features of AI problems, such as recursive processing and the unpredictable form of data, dictate some of the structure of the programs. But the variety of the language features developed to handle even these basic issues shows that the practice of AI programming is still more of an art form than a technology.

Data structure. Some feeling for the difficulties of designing data structures for an AI program may be gained from Chapter III (in Vol. I) on knowledge representation. The simple representation known as a *semantic* *network*—a collection of nodes, representing objects and properties, linked together by a network of labeled links—will serve to illustrate these problems (see Article III.C3, in Vol. I). As a first cut, a semantic net can be implemented as a set of *records*, one per node of the net, each having a field for each kind of link that can emanate from the node. However, a host of difficult issues soon arises:

1. What happens if there are many kinds of links (although any node has only a few)? In this case, records would be impractical and a *property list*, that is, a list of name-value pairs for each property a given node has, would be more appropriate.

2. Suppose we need to find all nodes having a certain kind of link—do we need some kind of index?

3. How is inconsistency in the net to be detected as new facts are added? For example, if "Terry ISA man" is already encoded, what happens when "Terry ISA woman" is asserted?

These sorts of issues demonstrate the trade-offs between alternative data structures. Each programming language offers primitives for certain types of data structures, including a wide range of data types (each with appropriate operations and semantics) and facilities for dealing with large databases. But to the extent that an AI language attempts to offer standard data facilities, it will have to embody choices on difficult issues like those listed above, and it is not to be expected that the choices will be optimal for all applications.

Control structure. AI programs are generally quite large and, like most large systems, are made up of many modules each carrying out a certain kind of subtask. These subtasks must be intelligently sequenced to perform the whole task properly. How the task can be divided up and how the sequencing can be accomplished are highly dependent on the control-structure facilities offered by the programming language.

In most programming languages, modules must obey a strict *calling hierarchy:* At any point in the execution, the options are very limited as to what to do next—that is, only a few alternatives can be indicated by conditional statements (IF–THEN statements, CASE statements, loop-exit tests, etc.). This primitive control structure is inappropriate in many situations in which the programmer wishes to specify the alternatives less rigidly, leaving the decision to the program.

In the HEARSAY–II speech-understanding system (Article V.C1, in Vol. I), for example, several modules monitor a global database, called the *blackboard*, for situations in which they can act. The action of one module (e.g., phonetic analysis, syntactic analysis) modifies the blackboard and may trigger activity in other modules. The actual flow of control in the system is radically different on each new utterance it analyzes, with some analyses depending much more on syntactic constraints and some being driven more by the data. In HEARSAY–II, each activation of a given module is independent of its last activation. In other control structures, it is possible for modules to have an internal state that survives from activation to activation.

Pattern matching. Both the data structures and the control mechanisms of AI programs are less rigidly specified and more complex than those of more general languages. Furthermore, there is a greater complexity in their interaction. On the one hand, the control structure becomes increasingly "data driven"—procedures are *invoked* by the situation rather than being called in a planned sequence. On the other hand, more powerful operations for accessing the data structures are introduced. A striking fact about AI programming languages is the extensive use of *pattern matching* to mediate both directions of interaction, and so pattern matching is taken up here as a separate type of language feature.

In HEARSAY–II, for example, the program modules can be described as looking for certain *patterns* in the global blackboard. The use of pattern-matching in controlling the execution is called *pattern-directed invocation* of procedures and was introduced in the PLANNER language. In the other direction, consider the problem of finding an object with certain properties in a semantic-network database. Since the object being sought can be described in terms of a small network fragment, the retrieval process is really just matching the fragment to the same pattern in the database—a *subgraph-isomorphism* problem. Unfortunately, the best known algorithms for subgraph isomorphism require exponential time, so it is not practical as a pattern-matching method. Different AI programming languages have offered various compromise retrieval schemes.

Programming environment. AI programs are among the largest and most complex computer systems ever developed and present formidable design and implementation problems. This brings up the fourth aspect on which we compare AI programming languages, namely, their programming-support facilities. Because they are usually developed as research projects, AI programs tend to undergo drastic revisions. And since they are quite large, programmers have difficulty keeping track of things. However, this is a human limitation that the machine can help overcome. AI researchers, in their capacity as language designers and programmers, have pioneered an interactive mode of programming in environments with extensive support: editors, trace and debugging packages, and other aids for the construction of large, complex systems.

Languages Covered

High-level computer languages tend to fall into two broad classes. The programs that are written in the ALGOL-like, or block-structured, languages are recognizable by the many block-delimiting BEGIN and END statements. These languages usually allocate space for variables, arrays, and other data before the program is executed (at *compile time*), so that during execution the space available for its data is fixed. The nested structure of the blocks defines the *scope* of the program variables, that is, the region of the program in which they are accessible, and similarly defines which procedures can call which other procedures. Only one of the seven AI programming languages discussed in this chapter, SAIL, is of the block-structured type.

The LISP-like languages are characterized by *dynamic allocation* and *dynamic scoping*. Dynamic allocation means that the space to be used by a data object is not fixed ahead of time but is allowed to grow and shrink as needed—an essential attribute for list processing. Dynamic scoping means that any procedure can call any other, and variable values are passed down the control chain rather than being determined by the static block structure. That is, once a variable is declared or otherwise allocated during the execution of, say, procedure A, it can be accessed from within any procedure B that A calls, or any procedure C that B calls, and so forth, regardless of where A, B, and C appear in the actual program text. LISP-like languages are often interpreted—the run-time environment is available during the program-writing process so that procedures can be easily tested—which encourages an interactive style of programming. PLANNER, CONNIVER, and QLISP are all LISP-like, being built upon LISP itself. (To avoid confusion of LISP dialects, we speak here of "basic LISP," which corresponds roughly to the LISP 1.5 defined by McCarthy et al., 1962.)

The POP–2 language shares characteristics of both ALGOL-like and LISP-like languages. It was developed at Edinburgh University as an attempt to implement LISP-like ideas in an ALGOL-like syntax. The newest language covered, FUZZY, brings together many of the constructs of previous languages in a LISP-embedded form much like that of QLISP.

References

A thorough introduction to some AI programming-language features in the context of detailed examples of AI programming techniques can be found in the book *Artificial Intelligence Programming* by Charniak, Riesbeck, and McDermott (1979).

C2.   Data Structures

THE GENERAL GOALS of a data representation are (a) to mirror, in a natural and convenient way, certain features of the entities in which the programmer views the problem at hand and (b) to be efficient in storage space and in the time required to operate on the data. These goals often come into conflict. In AI programs, data structures tend to become large and complex. But complex data structures are inefficient, so there is a tendency to sacrifice some naturalness and convenience in order to make do with simpler data structures. The data-structure offerings of various languages may be viewed as compromises toward some kind of optimum. In the context of AI programming languages, we will discuss three data-structure issues: data types, problems of storage and retrieval in large databases, and division of the database into contexts.

Data Types

Every computer-programming language offers a selection of data types: integers, reals, arrays, strings, records, and so on. AI programming languages always include some "list" data type or types because of the fundamental importance of list processing in AI programs. Lists and list processing are discussed in the LISP article (Article VI.B). Here, our main concern will be with the new data types introduced in AI languages, including:

1. *Set*—a collection; unlike a list in that it is not ordered and each symbol can appear only once.

2. *Bag*—like a set, but with repeated elements.

3. *Tuple*—basically a list of fixed length; for example, an ordered pair is a 2-tuple.

4. *Record*—like a tuple with *named* components, so the progammer need not keep track of their actual position.

5. *Function*—a procedure treated as data (see Article VI.A).

Some languages also allow users to define their own data types.

Database Storage and Retrieval

As AI systems involve the application of ever more knowledge to the problems they address, there is a growing concern with questions of how to organize and access large knowledge bases. The term *knowledge base* indicates that these AI databases are not merely big files of uniform content but are collections of facts, inferences, and procedures that correspond to the kinds of things people *know* (see Article III.A, in Vol. I). The ideal, from the programmer's point of view, would be a system that can retrieve data according to any specification that might be constructed by the program. However, the less that is known at the time the knowledge is encoded and stored about how it is going to be eventually used, the harder it is later to retrieve appropriate facts—computational limits on retrieval are real constraints in AI programming. Ideally, again, the programmer would like the language system to perform certain updating and bookkeeping tasks, even to the extent of automatically detecting inconsistencies in the knowledge base.

The languages covered here all have a set of database features that are of considerable utility and are reasonably efficient for some kinds of retrieval. A programmer designing, say, a semantic-network knowledge base (which none of the languages offers), would have to construct the semantic-net primitives from whatever database primitives the AI programming language does provide.

The selection of a good set of database primitives is crucial. There is still much debate on the relative utility of alternative schemes. One common scheme uses multiple indices: Incoming data are indexed by several of their attributes. Data about books, for instance, might be indexed by author, title, and subject, and the retrieval process would then be simple and fast: An attribute and its value are specified (e.g., AUTHOR–VONNEGUT), and the system looks in the appropriate index, finds the entry (if any) for that value, and retrieves all items listed for that entry. McDermott (1975) argues that multiple indexing can be implemented efficiently even when the database is split into contexts (see below).

A more advanced scheme, introduced by Carl Hewitt in the PLANNER language, retrieves data according to a *pattern*, a sort of structural sketch of an item with some pieces left undefined. The system retrieves all items that fit the general pattern. Implementation must be done carefully, however. The simpleminded approach of scanning the entire database and testing each item against the pattern—the British Museum algorithm—is out of the question for large databases.

Contexts

Beyond pattern-directed retrieval, one can speak of semantically directed retrieval in which items are somehow located by their meaning, rather than by their explicit structure. One can also raise legitimate objections to the whole idea that databases should consist of a set of separate items. We will leave these issues aside—no AI programming language has attained such a level of sophistication. There is, however, one quite standard technique that starts to move away from the crude notion of a set of items. This is the division of a database into *contexts*.

The basic idea of this technique is to replace the global database with a tree of distinct databases called contexts (see Fig. C2–1). The contexts are arranged in a tree because each represents a distinct *state* of the world (or set of assumptions about its state): As the world changes, a context naturally gives rise to "descendant" contexts, which differ slightly from each other and from their common parent. Conceptually, each context is a full database in its own right. In reality, most of the information in a given context will be the same as in the (parent) context just above it, so that, to save space, only the differences are actually stored. The root of the tree, of course, must actually be a full database.

Contexts have been found especially useful in hypothetical reasoning systems. In robot planning, for example, the robot can simulate alternative sequences of actions, creating contexts to represent the different states of the world that result. If the consequences of an action are undesirable, the robot planner can delete the context and try something else. (See Article VI.D for further discussion.)

A process at any given time uses one specific context as its database—the current context. Referring to Figure C2–1, assume that the current context is A and that no other contexts exist yet. The following context-manipulation primitives may offer a clearer idea of what context mechanisms look like.

1. PUSH. This creates a new context as a descendant of the current context and enters it. Initially the contents of the new context are identical to its parent. If we PUSH from context A, context B is created and becomes

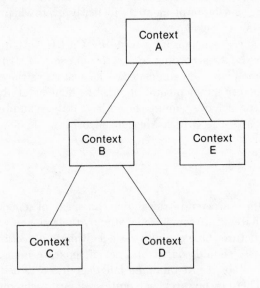

Figure C2–1. A tree of contexts.

the current context. And if we PUSH again, C is created and becomes the current context.

2. SPROUT ⟨cxt⟩. This is like PUSH, except that the new context is a descendant of the designated ⟨cxt⟩ and is not automatically entered. SPROUT A creates E, and SPROUT B creates D. We are still in C.

3. POP. This is the inverse of PUSH. It moves up the context tree to the parent of the current context. POP may be destructive; that is, the current context may be deleted. POP puts us back in B.

4. SWITCH ⟨cxt⟩. This leaves the current context and enters the designated context ⟨cxt⟩. SWITCH E makes E be the current context, that is, puts us in E.

5. DELETE ⟨cxt⟩. This deletes the context ⟨cxt⟩ and all its descendants. DELETE B deletes B, C, and D.

LISP

In looking now at the data-structure features of the individual languages, we see that basic LISP has little in the way of sophisticated data facilities, but it provides a flexible base on which they may be built. As described in Article VI.B, the original LISP had only one data type, namely, list structure built from *CONS cells* and *atoms*. This makes for a simple and elegant language, but at considerable cost in efficiency and readability. A list-structure representation of arrays, for instance, is highly inefficient, and the access of its elements by a chain of *CAR* and *CDR* list-selector functions is somewhat opaque to the reader of a program. To supplement lists, later versions of LISP have tended to add more data types. Integer, real, string, array, and record types are more or less standard. Many versions also allow the user to define new data types. Finally, LISP was the first computer-programming language to represent procedures as data in a practical way (see Article VI.A).

LISP provides a database facility of a crude sort through the *property list*. Every atom has attached to it a list of property-value pairs; for instance, the property list of atom K2 might include the property RANGE paired with the value HIMALAYAS. The main deficiency of property lists as a database mechanism is that they are indexed only one way; given atom K2, we can retrieve all its property-value pairs (or its value for any given property), but we cannot efficiently retrieve all atoms having the RANGE property HIMALAYAS.

Pattern-matching data-retrieval and context mechanisms are not provided in basic LISP, though, as we shall see, they are relatively easy to include in languages built on top of LISP. The recursive structure of LISP is especially well suited to implementing pattern matchers.

PLANNER

PLANNER was the first language to implement a general-format associative database. The particulars of PLANNER's database stem from its theorem-proving semantics, in which having a theorem that can prove a fact is equivalent to having the fact explicitly stored. The global associative database can store two semantically different classes of data items. The first class is *assertions*, which are LISP lists. Their elements may be of any MACLISP type (because PLANNER is implemented in MACLISP). All assertions in the database are assumed to be true for purposes of PLANNER's automatic-deduction control structure. But beyond that, assertions are treated merely as lists with no inherent semantics. Thus, either (RED MARS) or (MARS RED), or even (MARS IS RED), could have the same meaning, if the PLANNER program is written so as to manipulate them appropriately. Some examples of assertions are the following:

```
(COLOR GRASS GREEN)
(HOT SOUP)
(LOCATION PUMP-BASE (10 4 50)).
```

The second class of data items is procedural data in the form of *theorems*, which typically state when they can be invoked and what their effects will be. (PLANNER theorems are explained further in Articles VI.C3 and VI.C4.) Assertions are explicitly added to the database by an ASSERT operation and deleted by ERASE. They may also be added implicitly: Whenever an assertion is added to or deleted from the database, it may trigger certain PLANNER theorems to perform updating operations or consistency checks. More will be said about these "antecedent theorems," or *demons*, in Article VI.C3. Theorems can also be added and deleted in the database, but this is seldom actually done by a PLANNER program.

CONNIVER

It is sometimes helpful to view CONNIVER as a restructured and extended PLANNER (both are built on MACLISP). All the PLANNER data types are carried over to CONNIVER, with three important additions:

1. possibility lists,

2. tags, and

3. context tags.

Possibility lists and tags are discussed in Article VI.C3. *Possibility lists* are used during fetch operations on the database, and *tags* are used for jumping from one process to another in CONNIVER's generalized control structure. *Context tags* designate contexts, which we discuss shortly.

The database facilities of CONNIVER are virtually identical to those of PLANNER. Again, the database contains assertions and theorems (called *methods* in CONNIVER) that are all assumed to be true and that are accessed by pattern matching. The only important difference between the PLANNER and CONNIVER databases is that CONNIVER's database is organized into contexts.

The global variable CONTEXT holds the context tag of the current context. By storing tags for other contexts and then reassigning CONTEXT to one of them, the program switches its context. Context tags are generated by standard functions like the following:

(PUSH–CONTEXT ⟨context tag⟩) sets up a new context as a direct descendant of ⟨context tag⟩ and returns a context tag representing it.

(POP–CONTEXT ⟨context tag⟩) returns a context tag representing the direct ancestor of ⟨context tag⟩.

CONNIVER has the most fully developed context mechanism of the languages discussed here. Some context mechanisms were implicitly present in PLANNER but were tied to the backtracking control structure and were inaccessible to the programmer. CONNIVER made them explicit and also permitted general switching from any node on the context tree to any other, which is more general than the strict hierarchical movement done during PLANNER deductions. In terms of *search methods* described in Chapter II (in Vol. I), CONNIVER programs can execute a breadth-first or best-first search (or any other kind), whereas PLANNER programs are constrained to a depth-first search.

QLISP

QLISP has a wide range of data types. All the data types of INTERLISP are available in QLISP: integers, reals, strings, lists, pointers, arrays of any of the previous types, and records with fields of any of the previous types. And the user can define new data types.

The unique data types that QLISP provides are TUPLE, VECTOR, BAG, and CLASS. The names are a bit confusing. VECTORs correspond to what we called tuples in the introduction to this chapter—lists of fixed length. QLISP TUPLEs are just like VECTORs except that their first component is a function. A CLASS is a set, that is, an unordered collection of distinct elements. A BAG is like a set except that it may contain more than one copy of an element. For two QLISP objects to be equal, they must be of the same data type and

have the same components. In the case of CLASS and BAG, the order of the
components does not matter. Here are some examples:

(TUPLE F A)	$\neq$ (VECTOR F A)
(VECTOR A B C)	$\neq$ (VECTOR B A C)
(CLASS B C A)	$=$ (CLASS A B C A)
(BAG A A B C)	$=$ (BAG C A B A) $\neq$ (BAG A B C)
(BAG C A)	$\neq$ (CLASS C A)
(BAG B (CLASS C A B C) A A)	$=$ (BAG B A (CLASS C A B) A)

Every datum stored in the database is first transformed to a canonical
form, such that any two data that are theoretically the same, for example,
(BAG B A A C) and (BAG C A B A), will map onto the same canonical representation, in this case, (BAG A A B C). Pattern matching is greatly simplified
by this. In theorem proving, for example, a BAG is the natural representation
for the operands of functions such as PLUS, where repetition is important but
order is not. QLISP easily can prove that (PLUS (BAG A B C D)) is equal to
(PLUS (BAG C D B A)) by canonicalizing the BAGs, since the two expressions
then become identical.

Canonical representation also allows QLISP to make use of two unique
database methods. First, the entire database is stored as a discrimination
net (see Article XI.D, in Vol. III). Only the canonical forms are put in the
net, making it feasible to search the database in a uniform top-down manner.
Retrieval in general, and especially pattern matching, is thereby simplified.
QLISP, unfortunately, stores every subexpression of an item as a separate item
in the discrimination net and suffers from excessive use of space.

Second, since every object is uniquely represented, a property list just
like that attached to atoms in LISP can be attached to *every* object in the
database. In LISP, only atoms are uniquely represented and only atoms can
have a property list. Here is a QLISP property statement:

(QPUT (TUPLE PHONE-NUMBER-OF MIKE) LENGTH 7) .

This sample statement adds a TUPLE representing Mike's telephone number to
the database, if it is not already there, and says that the LENGTH property of
the number has the value 7. Object properties provide an elegant solution to
the problem, from which PLANNER and CONNIVER suffer, of being unable
to distinguish the mere *presence* of a statement in the database from its *truth*.
In QLISP, truth or falsity is indicated by setting the MODELVALUE property
of a statement to be T or NIL. Thus, to claim it is *true* that grass is green,
one executes

(QPUT (VECTOR COLOR GRASS GREEN) MODELVALUE T) .

For automatic inference and updating of the database, IF–ADDED and
IF–REMOVED demons similar to those of PLANNER and CONNIVER are available in QLISP. Context mechanisms for QLISP were inherited from QA4,

an ancestor of QLISP, where they were developed independently of those of CONNIVER.

SAIL

SAIL has three categories of data types. First, there are the types inherited from ALGOL—integers, reals, Booleans, strings, and arrays. Second, the user can define record types, in which the components of a record are specifiable as any of the above types or as some record type. Records are especially important in AI applications in SAIL because they can serve as building blocks for list structures. The CONS cell of LISP is essentially a record with two components (CAR and CDR), whereas SAIL records can have any number of components. More general list structures can be built. However, the LISP approach has the advantage that standard functions are available for searching lists, deleting from lists, appending lists, and so forth; in SAIL, these must be defined by the user. The third data category is the most interesting, namely, the *items* of SAIL's associative-database mechanism.

Items were the major feature of the earlier LEAP language, which was incorporated into SAIL (Feldman et al., 1972). The motivation for LEAP was to implement an efficient software scheme for associative processing, or the accessing of data by partial specification of its content rather than by the address of the storage location it happens to reside in. An item is either a primitive identifier (atom) or a triple of items. Triples are formed by the association of three items:

$$\text{Attribute} \otimes \text{Object} \equiv \text{Value}.$$

Here are examples of associative triples:

```
COLOR     ⊗ MARS ≡ RED
CLASS     ⊗ RED  ≡ COLOR
SATELLITE ⊗ MARS ≡ PHOBOS
SATELLITE ⊗ MARS ≡ DEIMOS .
```

Notice that items are not restricted to any one position in associations, nor does the value have to be unique. In fact, the labels "Attribute," "Object," and "Value" are mere conveniences with no special significance. Associations can themselves be items:

```
DISCOVERER ⊗ [COLOR ⊗ MARS ≡ RED] ≡ ANONYMOUS .
```

Associations are created and removed from the global database by the statements:

$$\begin{array}{llll} \text{MAKE} & \langle \text{item}_1 \rangle \otimes \langle \text{item}_2 \rangle \equiv \langle \text{item}_3 \rangle \\ \text{ERASE} & \langle \text{item}_1 \rangle \otimes \langle \text{item}_2 \rangle \equiv \langle \text{item}_3 \rangle \end{array}$$

Associations in the SAIL database are triply indexed and can be retrieved quite efficiently. (Retrieval statements are explained in Article VI.C4.) There are no facilities for automatic updating or consistency checking for the SAIL database.

POP-2

POP-2 has a quite rich collection of data types. Many of them are standard special cases of more general types, as indicated below. For example, the POP-2 data type STRIP is a sequence of elements of any type, and the data type STRING is a STRIP of CHARACTERs. Specializations of the RECORD data type include POINTER, ATOM, and ORDERED PAIR (like the LISP CONS cell). And the POP-2 ARRAY data type is a specialization of the FUNCTION data type (conceptually an array, as a function from the index to the element). Data types are classified as simple and composite. Integers, Booleans, reals, pointers, and atoms are simple; the rest are composite. User-defined data types are allowed.

POP-2 has the helpful property (for clarity and ease of programming) of treating all data types in a uniform way. Data of any type can be—

1. used as the actual parameters of functions,

2. returned as the results of functions,

3. assigned to variables of their type, or

4. tested for equality.

Components of composite data types are always accessed by four kinds of functions, illustrated below for the type LIST. In the case of user-defined types, the user must supply the four kinds of functions. Note that the destructor function shown here produces two outputs. In general, POP-2 functions can produce multiple outputs. Also note that the selector and the updater have the same name.

Kind of function	For lists
constructor	cons(x, (y z)) = (x y z)
destructor	dest((x y z)) = x, (y z)
selector	hd((x y z)) = x, tl((x y z)) = (y z)
updater	hd(MY-LIST) ← x, tl(MY-LIST) ← (y x)
	Now MY-LIST = (x y x) .

Associative database and context facilities are not part of the basic POP-2 language, but some facilities are available in POP-2 libraries.

FUZZY

Much like PLANNER, the programming language FUZZY maintains a database of assertions. However, FUZZY assertions include a *Z-value* indicating the degree of certainty, for example, ((CHANCE OF RAIN) . 0.30). FUZZY maintains an associative network of assertions quite similar to that of PLANNER and CONNIVER. Any arbitrary LISP list structure may be entered into this net. In addition, an assertion may have a *Z*-value associated with it, if desired. The *Z*-value of the assertions can be used to control success and failure of retrieval or subsequent actions.

FUZZY has a context mechanism that activates and deactivates associative nets of assertions. It is also possible to save the state of the entire system in order to allow for later restoration. Functions are available to compute differences between states and to add differences to a state. State changes can be set, if desired, so that they cannot be undone by a subsequent restoration. This feature is useful to control backtracking. Several FUZZY primitives exist in backtrackable and in finalizing versions to give the programmer easy control over the global control mechanisms.

Summary

Data types. The languages vary considerably in the number and kinds of data types they offer. Basic LISP is at one extreme: It began with exactly one data type, with a few supplementary ones added later. Advantages of a sparse set of data types accrue mostly to the writers of LISP compilers and interpreters, whose job is simplified because there are fewer operations and less need for type conversion. Also, the relatively small compilers and interpreters that are produced help conserve available core space. From the *user's* point of view, however, there is little to recommend such a small set of data types, except that it (almost) removes the need for type declarations.

Later versions of LISP, such as INTERLISP and MACLISP, and to an even greater extent the languages QLISP and POP–2, have provided rich sets of data types and the access functions that go with them. Programming is easier because the data structures can more closely mirror the programmer's ideas, and type checking becomes available. Efficiency is improved because the standard data types can be implemented closer to the machine level than equivalent structures built of more primitive units. For example, a SAIL or POP–2 record uses fixed-offset fields and avoids the overhead of the pointers needed in an equivalent LISP list structure.

A related issue is whether to allow user-defined data types. The advantages are similar to those of having many data types, but when user-defined data types have been allowed, as in POP–2, they have not found great utility. Probably the main reason is simply the extra effort required from the user (who has to define all the primitive operations on each new data type). User-definable data types also result in "unique" programs that other people may have difficulty understanding.

Large database facilities. Database facilities were present in a crude form in the LISP property-list feature. The next level of complexity is represented by the multiple-index scheme of SAIL associations. Next above the use of fixed-form associations is the structural pattern-match as a general retrieval mechanism, found in PLANNER, CONNIVER, QLISP, and FUZZY. Appropriate retrieval is somewhat hampered in PLANNER and CONNIVER, however, because they cannot attach properties to assertions as QLISP can. PLANNER also keeps the possibilities lists hidden from the programmer, who always has to operate at the goal level even though it may be inefficient to do so.

Context mechanisms. Context mechanisms may also be arranged in a loose ordering of complexity, starting with the scoping rules that virtually all languages have. These provide a new context whenever a new function or block is entered and restoration of the previous context upon exit. This basic level of context manipulation is extremely useful in programming practice. Next comes the ability of a program to PUSH and POP contexts on demand, whenever they are needed, rather than in rigid correspondence to the structure of the program. In both these forms, the contexts existing at any given time are simply those in the direct line from the global context down to the current context. CONNIVER is more advanced and allows a whole tree of contexts to exist, with freedom for the program to SPROUT new contexts below any existing context and to jump around arbitrarily between contexts.

To sum up very briefly, LISP introduced a simple and flexible data type and a way to represent functions as data. PLANNER introduced the general associative database, and CONNIVER improved it by the addition of contexts. QLISP and FUZZY increased the power of the database by defining special data types and putting everything into a discrimination net. SAIL went in another direction, developing an efficient multiple-index scheme. Finally, POP-2 showed how a wide range of data types can all be treated in a clear and uniform way.

C3. Control Structures

THE MOST IMPORTANT of the AI control structures we discuss in this article is *coroutining*. The central idea here is to relax the strict control hierarchy found in most languages (including LISP), in which every procedure runs for a while, then returns control to the procedure that called it, and vanishes. Coroutines are procedures that can pass control to *any* other coroutine and, furthermore, can suspend themselves and continue later. To make these concepts more precise, we need some new terminology.

First of all, it is loose terminology to talk about procedures or coroutines suspending or vanishing; a procedure is a piece of code. To draw the distinction, an instantiation of a procedure, a copy of the code that is actually running, will be called a *process*. For a process to *suspend*, its current *state* must be saved—that is, the current values of its variables and the point at which to resume execution. There is initially only one process, and it can *create* new processes. Once created, a process can be in one of three states: running, suspended, or terminated. If control is transferred to the process when it is created, it is running; otherwise, it is suspended. A running process can *resume* or *activate* some other process, that is, pass control to the other process, causing itself to suspend. While a process is suspended, its state is preserved but nothing happens. A running process can also *terminate* as it passes control to another process.

Bobrow and Wegbreit (1973) provide a formal, clear model for general coroutining in terms of *stack frames*, a construct that has the advantage of being efficiently implementable in current machine architectures. Their model unified the various types of procedural interconnections seen in previous AI languages (e.g., recursion, coroutines, generators, FUNARGs, FUNVALs). Each process is represented by one stack frame, which contains the process state and links indicating where control was passed from and where the values of free variables are to be obtained.

The *generator* is a common specialization of the coroutine. Generators are used when a potentially large set of results may be produced by a function (e.g., one that looks for *matches* in a database) but only a few of these are needed at a time. A generator is a coroutine that runs until it produces one item and then suspends itself. When a process needs another piece of information, it resumes the generator. A generator always returns control to the routine that activated it. This continues until there are no more items to produce, and the generator terminates.

In a coroutining regime, only one process is running at any given time. There can be a considerable amount of communication and cooperation between processes, but it is rather awkward, since process A must suspend itself in order to pass information to process B. In a *multiprocessing* regime,

45

many processes can run at once and freely pass messages back and forth. SAIL is the only language covered here that allows for multiprocessing, and its facilities are primitive. With the declining cost of computation, however, there is increasing interest in models for parallel communicating processes (see Hewitt, 1977; Kornfeld, 1979; Kornfeld and Hewitt, 1981; Smith and Davis, 1981).

Coroutining and multiprocessing only provide more flexibility in the flow of control, without alleviating the problem of determining *where* control is to flow. The most common programming-language facility for directing the flow of control is the conditional statement (e.g., an IF or CASE statement), which chooses one of a few predetermined directions. Some AI programming languages introduce the much more powerful method of *pattern-directed invocation*, described in Article VI.C4.

Another important control concept is the *demon*. Implementations differ, but, in concept, a demon is a kind of suspended process that "waits" for a certain kind of event to occur (e.g., a certain kind of update operation on a database). When such an event occurs, the demon is activated automatically, performs its job, and either terminates or suspends in wait for the next event. Typically, demons are used to make inferences as new information comes in, to perform bookkeeping tasks of some kind, or to recognize important occurrences.

LISP

Basic LISP lacks any coroutining or multiprocessing facilities. The LISP control structure is suited to AI programming mainly by its emphasis on recursion (see Article VI.B). Recursion allied with LISP's dynamic scoping rule allows functions to be used by other functions in a context-free manner: A function's behavior depends only on its arguments and the values that its free variables have when it is called; the context in which the function was originally defined is not significant. Furthermore, any function is allowed to call any other function. This freedom makes it easier in many cases to put together separate modules to form an AI system.

The FUNARG mechanism of LISP permits functions to be used in a context-dependent or history-dependent way when desired. A FUNARG is a call to a LISP function together with an environment, or *context* (see Article VI.C2), for the variables used by the function. For example, FUNARGs can be used to implement generators: Suppose we tried to write a generator as an ordinary LISP function. We would define a function that generates just one item each time it is called and changes the state of the generation process by updating a free variable. Here is such a generator for squares of numbers:

```
NextSquare:   (LAMBDA NIL
              (PROG NIL
              (SETQ N (ADD1 N))
              (RETURN (TIMES N N))))
```

NEXTSQUARE uses the free variable N to hold the state of the generation. If initially N = 3 and we call NEXTSQUARE repeatedly, we will get the sequence 16, 25, 36, ...

However, NEXTSQUARE is not really a generator. It is not an independent process, because if any function happens to use a variable called N locally and calls NEXTSQUARE, then NEXTSQUARE will use the local value of N and the sequence will be disrupted. A true generator results when we construct a FUNARG, say, GENSQUARE, which consists of the function NEXTSQUARE and a pointer to an environment (in which N has some initial value, say, 3). If we repeatedly evaluate (GENSQUARE), we get 16, 25, 36, ... as before, only GENSQUARE always uses that N which is in its specified environment and so is unaffected by local versions of N. In general, FUNARGs act much like coroutines; they "activate" when their function is called and "suspend" when it exits. Unlike general coroutines, FUNARGs always return control to the function that called them.

PLANNER

While CONNIVER has a control structure very much like that of LISP, with the addition of full coroutining facilities, PLANNER extends the LISP control structure in a completely different direction. PLANNER is somewhat like a backtracking version of LISP—functions call each other recursively as in LISP, but when a function fails (returns NIL), it is *automatically called again* using the next possible value of the argument. This continues until either the function succeeds or all arguments have failed.

The control structure of PLANNER is very interesting. The important point to keep in mind is that PLANNER is *always* goal directed. Functions are invoked because they might possibly cause a goal to be satisfied, *not* because some other function called them. PLANNER functions simply do not call each other; they just state a goal and the system chooses functions to apply toward that goal.

A rather strong analogy may be drawn to the control structure of GPS (Article II.D2, in Vol. I). Both systems completely separate domain-dependent information from the control structure and employ a uniform depth-first search to solve problems. In both systems, the problem is represented by a goal to be reached or established. The starting point is different, however; GPS is given a single initial object (which may be thought of as the initial state of the world) that it then tries to transform into the goal object. PLANNER is given a whole database of facts and tries to prove that the goal follows from them.

Thus, although GPS's paradigm is actions on the world and PLANNER's is theorem proving, the actual methods they use are quite similar:

1. Each first will check to see if the goal is equal to the initial state (or some fact in the database). If not, GPS looks for an *operator* that will

reduce the difference between the goal state and the initial state, and PLANNER looks for a *theorem* that can prove the goal from the database.

2. Each then sets up *subgoals*. For GPS, the subgoals are (a) to transform the initial state into a state to which the chosen operator can be applied and (b) to transform the result of the operator into the goal. The whole GPS method is applied recursively to these two subgoals. PLANNER theorems can set up any number of subgoals, namely, whatever facts must be established before the theorem will imply the goal. Again, the whole PLANNER method is applied recursively to each subgoal.

3. If at any point a subgoal fails, both GPS and PLANNER will backtrack and try to apply a different operator or theorem.

4. The net result is a depth-first search of an AND/OR tree (OR nodes wherever there is a choice of operators or theorems, AND nodes for the subgoals induced by each operator or theorem).

In addition to the goal-directed or *consequent theorems*, PLANNER programs can have *antecedent theorems*, which are a type of demon that triggers when facts are added to the database or deleted from it. (GPS has nothing analogous.) Demons can modify the database in arbitrary ways, generally filling out implications of a new fact or doing some kind of bookkeeping. Deductions that would have to be made anew each time a goal called for them can be done just once by an antecedent theorem, as in the following example.

Suppose a common goal is to establish that so-and-so is mortal. A consequent theorem for this would read

```
(CONSE (MORTAL ?X) (GOAL (HUMAN +X))) .
```

In other words, this theorem will establish that something is mortal if the subgoal of proving that it is human is satisfied. Alternately, write the antecedent theorem

```
(ANTE (HUMAN ?X) (ASSERT (MORTAL +X))) ,
```

which watches for any assertions of the form (HUMAN ...) to be added to the database and then causes (MORTAL ...) also to be added.

Here is a more extensive example of PLANNER in action. Suppose we have a consequent theorem giving one set of conditions under which an object can be deduced to be broken,

```
(CONSE (BROKEN ?X)
       (GOAL (FRAGILE +X))
       (GOAL (HEAVY ?Y))
       (GOAL (ON +Y +X))) ,
```

and a database containing the following assertions, among others,

```
(HEAVY Jumbo)
(FRAGILE Violin)
(ON Jumbo Teacup)
(FRAGILE Teacup) .
```

Now let's see what happens when the following PLANNER program is executed:

```
(GOAL (BROKEN ?V)) .
```

It will first scan the database looking for broken things and then use consequent theorems to deduce that other things are also broken. The backtracking search produces the tree shown in Figure C3–1.

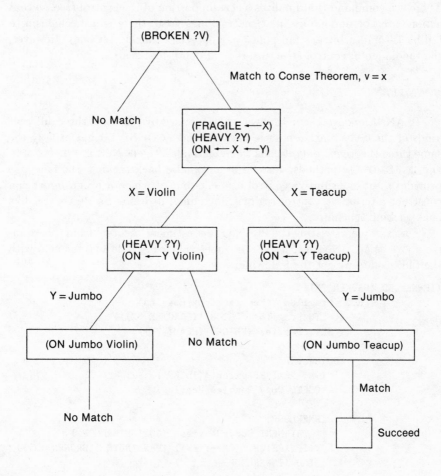

Figure C3–1. A PLANNER execution tree.

PLANNER does pure *depth-first search* (see Chap. II, in Vol. I). In the tree shown in Figure C3–1, search proceeds top to bottom and left to right. Initially, the goal is to match or prove (BROKEN ?V). This fails to match any assertion in the database, but it does match the consequent theorem that is illustrated. That theorem sets up three subgoals (FRAGILE, HEAVY, and ON). These are processed in the same way, first matching (FRAGILE ←X) against the database entry (FRAGILE Violin) and, when that choice eventually fails, *backtracking* to match that clause against the other database fact, (FRAGILE Teacup). When all three clauses eventually get matched, control returns to the original goal and the pattern ?V is bound to the value of X, namely, Teacup. The goal (BROKEN ?V) has been satisfied by the deduced fact (BROKEN Teacup).

PLANNER control structure is actually not quite so rigid as pictured here. There is a command that finalizes a certain portion of the control tree, so that actions are not undone during backtracking. Also, there is a mechanism to fall back to an arbitrary fail point (as opposed to the closest one). However, the fundamental control structure is rigid depth-first search.

CONNIVER

PLANNER control structure was characterized by the use of three different kinds of theorems and automatic backtracking. CONNIVER has exactly the same three theorems, only it calls them methods—the IF–NEEDED, IF–ADDED, and IF–REMOVED methods. Instead of automatic backtracking, the language provides a set of primitive control elements out of which a programmer can construct alternative control regimes, including, if desired, a PLANNER-like backtracking scheme.

For example, rewriting the PLANNER consequent theorem from the example above as a CONNIVER IF–NEEDED method (see Article VI.B for help with the LISP code), we get the following:

```
(IF-NEEDED (BROKEN ?X)
          (PROG (Fragiles Y Heavies Copy-Heavies)
              (CSETQ Fragiles (FETCH '(FRAGILE ?X)))
              (CSETQ Heavies (FETCH '(HEAVY ?Y)))

           OUTERLOOP:
             (TRY-NEXT Fragiles '(ADIEU))
             (CSETQ Copy-Heavies Heavies)

           INNERLOOP:
             (TRY-NEXT Copy-Heavies '(GO 'OUTERLOOP))
             (IF (FETCH '(ON ←Y ←X)) THEN (NOTE '(BROKEN ←X)))
             (GO 'INNERLOOP)          )) .
```

A problem with the PLANNER-language solution was its repetition of the search for heavy objects each time a new fragile object was being tested.

This was forced, because the automatic backtracking mechanism assumes that later choices are dependent on earlier ones, even when, as in this case, they are independent. In CONNIVER, the list of heavy objects can be fetched once and used again. Accordingly, the first section of the program finds all fragile objects and all heavy objects.

In the second section of the CONNIVER program, the generator statement (TRY-NEXT Fragiles '(ADIEU)) grabs the next fragile object in the list and binds X to it. The (ADIEU) is executed when there are no more fragile objects; it causes the method to terminate.

In the third section, the inner loop scans through all heavy objects in the same fashion, and each pair of a fragile X and a heavy Y is tested to see whether Y is ON X, and if so, the method NOTEs this and moves on. Noting an item involves adding it to a "possibilities list." That possibilities list becomes the result of the IF-NEEDED method, after (ADIEU) is executed. Thus, the effect of the method is to return a list of all deducible instances of (BROKEN ?V), which will be just ((BROKEN Teacup)), assuming the same database as in the PLANNER version of the example.

Unlike PLANNER, CONNIVER's possibilities lists are a separate data type and may be manipulated by a user program. In many respects, CONNIVER is like a PLANNER program in which implicit control and data structures are made explicit and put under the control of the programmer. Greater flexibility results, at the cost of longer and less organized programs.

CONNIVER allows general coroutining. As one application, a program can be written to do breadth-first or best-first search; PLANNER, you will recall, always does depth-first search (see Chap. II, in Vol. I). Another use of coroutining is the implementation of generators. The broken-object finder above can be turned into a generator simply by adding (AU-REVOIR) after (NOTE '(BROKEN +X)). AU-REVOIR is the CONNIVER function that suspends the current process and resumes whichever process called it. Now each time the method is called, it finds one broken item, produces it, and then suspends. The advantage of this technique is that the calling process can ask for broken items only as it needs them, and the generator may not have to find them all.

QLISP

The GOAL statement in QLISP works like the one in PLANNER, first searching the database to try to match the pattern there and then invoking consequent theorems (IF-NEEDED methods) to try to derive it. Automatic backtracking takes place whenever one of the theorems fails. The main difference is that in QLISP the consequent theorems to be tried must be listed explicitly in the GOAL statement itself. For instance:

```
(GOAL (MORTAL Socrates) APPLY Grim Reapers).
```

`Grim Reapers` would be the class of theorems, which might include theorems similar to the PLANNER consequent theorem we saw before to establish Socrates' mortality: `(CONSE (MORTAL ?X) (GOAL (HUMAN ←X)))`. It is called an *APPLY team*. (In PLANNER, the APPLY team for every goal is the set of all known theorems.) Database operations may also have APPLY teams, which take the place of the IF–ADDED and IF–ERASED demons of PLANNER and CONNIVER.

SAIL

The most interesting feature of SAIL's control structure is its multi-processing capability, something none of the other languages covered here has. The designers of SAIL wanted to allow parallel exploration and coopera-tion by problem-solving processes (Feldman et al., 1972). There was also the need, imposed by address-space limitations, to split large hand-eye systems in robotics into multiple communicating processes.

Multiprocessing is implemented within the ALGOL-like block structure of SAIL. Any process (an invocation of a SAIL procedure) can SPROUT another process. The standard ALGOL scope rules are followed just as if the new process were started by a procedure call; thus, related processes are automati-cally able to share a common database. The JOIN primitive suspends a process until other processes (named in the JOIN statement) have terminated, at which point the first process resumes execution. JOIN is used as a synchronization primitive, as shown in the following example:

```
SPROUT(P1, GRAB(HAND1, HAMMER));
SPROUT(P2, GRAB(HAND2, NAIL));
...
JOIN(P1, P2);
POUND(HAMMER, NAIL);
...
```

The variables P_1 and P_2 hold the (unique) names assigned to the new processes. The names are used to identify processes in later commands.

Interprocess communication is handled by a "mail" system implemented as a message-queuing system. The mail is delivered (whenever possible) by the process scheduler. Processes can simply check for messages as they go along or they can place themselves in a queue while waiting for an appropriate message. Using the first method, the robot's grab-hammer process could inform the grab-nail process about the movements of the arm and hammer, so the grab-nail process could avoid a collision with the other arm.

Demons can be implemented by means of the second message-passing scheme. To set up a demon, a process is created that immediately places itself in a queue waiting for a certain kind of message that is sent out whenever a database update is done. Demons that are waiting for such a message will be activated, simulating a direct activation of demons by the database update.

Coroutining is a special case of multiprocessing, in which only one process is active at any time. The coroutining primitives CREATE, TERMINATE, ACTIVATE, and SUSPEND can all be implemented using SAIL's message-passing mechanism.

POP–2

The POP–2 control structure is much like that of LISP. The basic language is very simple, partly in the interests of fast compilation, and contains none of the specialized AI control structures found in PLANNER, CONNIVER, and QLISP. Some of these features, including coroutines and multiprocessing primitives, are available in POP–2 libraries. The POPLER library (Davies et al., 1973) implemented the spaghetti stack, backtracking, database demons, and pattern matching in the manner of PLANNER.

The basic POP–2 language does provide for the use of generators to construct *dynamic lists*. The programmer defines a function of no arguments, say, F, and applies the POP–2 function FNTOLIST to F. The result is the list LF of values that F produces on successive calls. Of course, F has to read and change a free variable, representing the state of the generation, or else every element of LF would be the same. Now comes the interesting part. The program can operate on LF just as on ordinary (static) lists. But, in fact, LF is not all there; it starts empty and new elements are added onto the back of it only as needed. This means that LF can be conceptually very large or even infinite, and it does not matter so long as only the initial part of it is used.

Dynamic lists allow the programmer to abstract away from the details of how a list is produced, whether it is computed once and for all or is extended when needed. Similarly, the *memo function* allows abstraction from the details of how a function is computed. Memo functions are provided by one of the POP–2 libraries. The name comes from the notion that a function, if it is called several times with the same argument, would do better to "make a memo of it" (the answer) and store it in a lookup table.

FUZZY

FUZZY procedures have a more general global-control mechanism than PLANNER theorems have. The procedure demons are given control not only upon failure of an expression (as in MICRO–PLANNER) but also after successful termination of a top-level expression. This makes it possible to evaluate globally the results returned by the expressions of a procedure. With each procedure a variable is associated that maintains an "accumulated Z-value" for the demon's calculations. The procedure demon is called a last time when the procedure is exited in order to make any necessary final computations (e.g., concluding statistics).

There are several levels at which information is accessed in a knowledge base:

1. Explicitly available information is requested.

2. An explicit procedure is invoked to retrieve the desired information.

3. A goal is specified and the system is left to decide how to achieve it.

All three methods are possible in FUZZY:

1. The FETCH statement retrieves assertions that are explicitly stored in the associative net by pattern matching.

2. FUZZY procedures can be called by name.

3. If FUZZY procedures have been stored in the associative net, they can be invoked by pattern matching through the DEDUCE statement. This relieves the programmer of keeping track of which particular procedures may be used to achieve a certain task and allows the easy addition of new procedures to the associative net that can be utilized automatically by existing programs without change.

4. The GOAL statement combines the FETCH and DEDUCE statements. It first checks whether the desired information is explicitly available in the net of assertions. If it fails, it then attempts to deduce the goal by invoking DEDUCE procedures that match the specified pattern.

In addition, FUZZY supports ASSERT and ERASE procedures, which are invoked automatically when assertions of corresponding patterns are added and removed, respectively, from the associative net.

The following program illustrates how FUZZY may deal with both vague and incomplete information. The vagueness is expressed here by Z-values associated with assertions. Incomplete information in this example is manifested by the absence of useful assertions. This "missing information" does not force the procedure into failure, but rather lowers the confidence in the result obtained by the procedure:

```
=== NET ===
((CHANCE OF RAIN) . 0.8)
((DRYNESS DESIRED) . 0.7)
((BLUE SKY) . 0.4)

=== DEDUCE ===
(PROC NAME: UMBRELLA DEMON: CONFIDENCE (RAIN PROTECTION)
     (BIND ?SK (FETCH ((*OR CLEAR BLUE) SKY)))
     (BIND ?BU (FETCH (BURDENSOME UMBRELLA)))
     (BIND ?DD (FETCH (? DESIRED)))
     (IF (ZAND THRESH: 0.9 (ZNOT !SK) !DD !BU)
   THEN: (SUCCEED @"STAY HOME!")
   ELSE: T)
     (BIND ?CR (FETCH (CHANCE ??)))
```

```
(IF (MINUSP (DIFFERENCE (PLUS (ZVAL !CR) (ZVAL !DD))
                        (PLUS (ZVAL !SK) (ZVAL !BU))))
   THEN: (SUCCEED @"DON'T TAKE UMBRELLA" ZACCUM)
   ELSE: (SUCCEED @"TAKE UMBRELLA" ZACCUM)))


===========
(DEFPROP CONFIDENCE
 (LAMBDA (RESULT THRESHOLD C-LEVEL)
  (COND [(EQ RESULT FAIL) (COND [(*GREAT C-LEVEL 0.25)
                                 (DIFFERENCE C-LEVEL 0.25)]
                                [T (FAIL)])]
        [(EQ RESULT DONE) C-LEVEL]
        [(*LESS (ZVAL RESULT) THRESHOLD) (FAIL)]
        [T C-LEVEL]))
 EXPR)
        (;   RESULT    = result of last top-level expression
             THRESHOLD = criterion for forcing procedure to fail
             C-LEVEL   = current confidence level)
```

The program listing includes the associative net, containing some declarative knowledge about a potential umbrella carrier and his situation. Next is the procedural associative net containing a DEDUCE procedure to give advice whether or not to carry an umbrella in a given situation. Finally, there is a LISP procedure that is used by the DEDUCE procedure UMBRELLA as a procedure demon. The procedure UMBRELLA uses assertions and their modifiers to calculate the projected payoff for carrying an umbrella. The demon CONFIDENCE watches this calculation and determines a confidence measure for the result obtained by UMBRELLA. This is done as follows. UMBRELLA looks for four types of assertions in the associative net:

1. information about the blueness or the clearness of the sky,
2. information about the burden of carrying an umbrella,
3. information about a desired goal that can be satisfied with an umbrella, and
4. information about the chance that an event would occur that would make an umbrella desirable.

The most reliable advice can be given by UMBRELLA if all four pieces of information can be found. If a piece of information cannot be found (i.e., if the corresponding FETCH returns FAIL), the demon reduces the confidence level ZACCUM, which is returned as the Z-value of UMBRELLA. Observe that the Z-value can be used in a single program to do different kinds of qualifications.

Summary

In the chronological sequence PLANNER, CONNIVER, QLISP, we observe an increase in the variety of control structures and in the programmer's access to them. This development seems to address two major needs: to concisely express powerful control techniques and to make complicated programs as efficient as possible. PLANNER took a giant step in the direction of increased power by shifting the entire domain of discourse in which programs are written from the imperative level (do this, then do that, etc.) to the level of goals. The programmer formulates problems in terms of goals that are to be established, writing "theorems" that reduce a goal to subgoals, and sets the automatic-deduction mechanism going. This approach suffers from the inefficiency of its central method, automatic backtracking, and the inability of the user to remedy this by expressing himself at the imperative level on occasion. Automatic backtracking in PLANNER is convenient if the user has absolutely no good idea of how to guide the program.

CONNIVER was developed largely in response to these problems. Sussman and McDermott (1972) argue the following points against PLANNER and for CONNIVER:

1. Programs that use automatic backtracking often result in the worst algorithms for solving a problem.

2. The most common use of backtracking can almost always be replaced by a purely recursive structure that is not only more efficient but also clearer, both syntactically and semantically.

3. Superficial analysis of problems and poor programming practice are encouraged by the ubiquity of automatic backtracking and by the illusion of power that a function like GOAL gives the user merely by brute-force use of invisible failure-driven loops.

4. The attempt to fix these defects by the introduction of failure messages is unnatural and ineffective.

CONNIVER retreats to the imperative style of programming with some automatic-deduction primitives kept on, namely, the three kinds of theorems or methods. In addition, it gives the user the flexibility implied by coroutines, which permit techniques like breadth-first or depth-first search to be expressed conveniently.

QLISP reintroduces automatic backtracking, but as optional and under restrictions (that the consequent theorems to try must be named as a *team*). Over all, it includes practically every control structure found in PLANNER or CONNIVER.

All three of these LISP-based languages rely heavily on pattern matching to guide the flow of control. The basic technique is pattern-directed invocation, in which the function to execute next is chosen by its match to a pattern in the database. A problem here is that, in current schemes, there is little information passed between the alternative functions that match in a given situation. It seems plausible that cooperation and sharing of information between the different functions attempting a goal might be better. This is part of the idea behind SAIL's message-passing, multiprocessing primitives (see also Article V.C1, in Vol. I).

Davis (1976) discusses and compares several control schemes in the context of his own program, TEIRESIAS, which uses strategy *rules* to decide how to sequence the application of other rules (Article VII.B). One major dimension along which control schemes vary is the degree of data-drivenness. In the usual calling-hierarchy scheme, conditional statements (and loop tests) interrogate a single data value and select from a few predetermined paths depending on the value. In the most complex control scheme, the decision about what to do next would be "reasoned about" with the full power of the problem solver, considering all of the data available. The control activities offered in AI programming languages explore the possibilities between these extremes.

References

The book *Pattern-Directed Inference Systems* by Waterman and Hayes-Roth (1978) is a good place to begin.

C4. Pattern Matching

PATTERN–MATCHING FACILITIES are supplied in AI programming languages for two major tasks: finding entries in a database and choosing which procedure to execute next. Pattern matching can be viewed as a form of *content addressing:* In most computer languages, a datum has to be accessed by its name, for example, the name of a variable. The general idea of content addressing is to eliminate this need for arbitrary names of things and to access an item of data by specifying its form (or meaning) instead. A pattern, such as ((FATHER-OF ?X) ?Y), is used as a kind of sketch of the datum being sought in the database and "matches" against stored items like ((FATHER-OF MARY) (FLIES KITES)). Thus, the name or address of the stored information need not be remembered. This is known as *pattern-directed retrieval*, or retrieval by pattern match.

Similarly, patterns can be used to make less rigid control regimes possible by eliminating the need to call specific procedures by name. In *pattern-directed invocation*, described in Article VI.C3, the tests-and-branches form of program control is replaced by associating each procedure with a pattern and then, at decision points, matching them all against the current situation or goal to determine which to execute next.

These techniques can relieve the AI programmer of a great burden: Modularization of programs is much easier to accomplish because the programmer does not have to specify which calls what, or what access path is taken to get to an item in the database. Of course, a price must be paid—the overhead of running the pattern matcher.

Typically, a pattern is a structure with variables embedded in it, and it matches another structure if it could be made identical to that structure by replacing its variables with some values. Occurrences of the same variable must be replaced by the same value. For example, (A ?X C ←X) will match (A B C B) but not (A B C D), because once the variable ?X has been *bound* to B in the match, it cannot then be bound to D. The power (and overhead) of a pattern-matching facility is partly related to the types of *pattern variables* that can be handled. Here are some common pattern-variable types, expressed in terms of matching patterns in lists:

1. An "open" variable (?X) matches to any element of a list, and binds X to that element.

2. A "closed" variable (←X) must have already been bound, as in the example above, and matches only the value already bound to X.

3. A "restricted" variable may have arbitrary restrictions placed on it. These restrictions are *procedurally attached* to the variable in some way,

for example, as a predicate (Boolean function) that must be TRUE in order for the variable to match.

4. Segment variables match to a sublist of any length, rather than to an element. Open and closed segment variables are denoted ??X and ←←X, respectively.

To avoid confusion, the different kinds of pattern variables will always be written ?X, ←X, and so on, ignoring the varying notations of the different AI programming languages.

Some examples may clarify these ideas. Suppose we want to match the form

$$(A \ B \ (C \ A) \ B)$$

against the following patterns:

Pattern	Match	Bindings
?X	yes	X = (A B (C A) B)
(?X ←X (C A) B)	no	
(?X B (C ←X) B)	yes	X = A
(?X ?Y (C A) B)	yes	X = A, Y = B
(?X ?X (C A) B)	illegal pattern	
(A B ?Z B)	yes	Z = (C A)
(??X)	yes	X = (A B (C A) B)
(??X (←←X) B)	no	
(??X (←←Y) B)	yes	X = (A B), Y = (C A)
(A ??Z)	yes	Z = (B (C A) B)
(B ??Z)	no	

Typically, patterns are matched against forms that contain no variables. Some systems, notably QLISP, allow for patterns to be matched against patterns.

LISP

As was the case in control-structure facilities, basic LISP has no pattern-matching constructs. But, again, LISP does lend itself to implementing such mechanisms, and it is appropriate to say a little about this.

Patterns typically take the form of nested structures, standing for a mathematical formula, an assertion, or some kind of structured object, for instance. These can all be *uniformly* represented in list structure in LISP, as described in Article VI.B. Uniformity is a big advantage in that it allows the *same* pattern-matching algorithm to be used for these different kinds of objects. Pattern matching on nested structures is inherently a recursive process, since the same matching engine is applied to each nested level; thus, the central role of recursion in LISP is also helpful.

PLANNER

The big innovation in PLANNER was simply its more extensive *use* of pattern matching compared to previous programming languages. Access to the PLANNER database is exclusively by pattern-directed retrieval. Thus, the goal pattern

(?X SOCRATES)

will match to a database assertion

(MORTAL SOCRATES)

and X will be bound to MORTAL.

As another application of pattern matching, PLANNER functions (i.e., theorems) are always called through pattern-directed invocation. Consequent theorems have an attached pattern that is matched to the current goal and, if the match succeeds, the theorem is invoked. For example,

(CONSE (MORTAL ?Y) (GOAL (HUMAN ←Y))) .

With this consequent theorem, the goal (?X SOCRATES), meaning roughly *Tell me something about Socrates*, will match to the theorem's pattern (MORTAL ?Y), meaning *I can tell you when things are mortal*, with the upshot that the theorem establishes a subgoal (HUMAN SOCRATES). If it succeeds in proving this goal, it returns (MORTAL SOCRATES).

Similarly, antecedent and erasing theorems (Article VI.C3) have attached patterns, but these are matched against assertions that are being added to or deleted from the database, rather than against goals. The same pattern-matching method is used in all cases.

There is nothing particularly interesting about the implementation of PLANNER's pattern matcher. The implementors of MICRO–PLANNER deliberately chose the simplest scheme that would be adequate for their needs. The matching is only one level deep—(?X (?Y Plato)) is not a valid PLANNER pattern. (Full PLANNER, as opposed to the actually implemented sublanguage MICRO–PLANNER, specified general tree matching, which is the same as multilevel list matching.) For an extensive example of how PLANNER's pattern-matching facility is used, see Article IV.F4 (in Vol. I) on SHRDLU.

CONNIVER

CONNIVER uses pattern matching for the same purposes PLANNER does, but it allows functions to be invoked directly (imperatively) as well as through pattern-directed invocation. The pattern matcher is more powerful than that of PLANNER. For one thing, it handles multilevel patterns like (?X (?Y Plato)), which matches (MORTAL (TEACHER-OF Plato)). There is no restriction on the level of nesting. Second, while PLANNER and CONNIVER patterns are LISP list structures, CONNIVER, in fact, allows patterns to take the more general form of *s-expressions* (see Article VI.B). For example, the pattern (PLUS 0 . ?X) will match to (PLUS 0 1 2 3 4), binding X to the list tail, (1 2 3 4).

CONNIVER's pattern matcher can be applied independently to analyze the structure of data using the MATCH statement. For example, the function call

(MATCH ((FATHER-OF ?WHO) . ?WHAT) ((FATHER-OF FRED) WHISTLES DIXIE)),

which contains the pattern and the data to which it is to be matched, binds ?WHO to FRED and ?WHAT to (WHISTLES DIXIE).

So far, all the patterns we have shown contain just two kinds of objects: variables that must match something and constants like FATHER-OF and PLUS. CONNIVER adds flexibility by allowing variables that are assigned some constant value before the match is done; the effect is as if the variable were replaced by its value before the match begins.

QLISP

QLISP has by far the most powerful pattern-matching facility of the languages covered here. There are three contributing factors:

1. The special QLISP data types, BAG, CLASS, TUPLE, and VECTOR, used in patterns and data;
2. Segment variables;
3. A powerful *unification* algorithm.

Recall, from one of the examples of CONNIVER's pattern matching, that the pattern (PLUS 0 . ?X) will match to the form (PLUS 0 1 2 3 4), binding X to the list tail (1 2 3 4). Unfortunately, no such pattern will also match to (PLUS 1 0 2 3 4) or (PLUS 4 3 2 1 0), even though that might be convenient. LISP list structure forces a spurious ordering of the arguments. In QLISP, one can rewrite the pattern as

(PLUS (BAG 0 ??X)),

where ??X is a *segment variable*. A segment variable matches to any number of items, rather than a single one. Furthermore, the order of the items following BAG is irrelevant (see Article VI.C2). Hence, this pattern will match to any of the following objects:

(PLUS (BAG 0 1 2 3 4))	X = (BAG 1 2 3 4)
(PLUS (BAG 1 0 2 3 4))	X = (BAG 1 2 3 4)
(PLUS (BAG 4 3 2 1 0))	X = (BAG 4 3 2 1)
(PLUS (BAG 0))	X = (BAG) .

The so-called QLAMBDA functions in QLISP have a pattern instead of an argument list, much like consequent theorems in PLANNER. The QLISP programmer can exploit the power of QLISP pattern matching to express computations very concisely, as in these examples:

```
PlusZero:   (QLAMBDA (PLUS (BAG 0 ??X)) (PLUS (BAG $$X)))
PlusMinus:  (QLAMBDA (PLUS (BAG ??X ?Y (MINUS ?Y))) (PLUS (BAG $$X)))
BothSets:   (QLAMBDA
               (TUPLE (CLASS ?X ??OTHERS) (CLASS ?X ??YETOTHERS)) $$X).
```

PLUSZERO, if its pattern matches, has found a zero in the list of numbers to be added and will return the PLUS without the zero. PLUSMINUS finds an expression and its negative in the arguments and cancels them. BOTHSETS finds an element common to two sets (called classes in QLISP) and returns that element.

PLANNER and CONNIVER use pattern matching only in the contexts of pattern-directed retrieval and pattern-directed invocation. The QLISP programmer can call the pattern matcher directly, as well as use it implicitly in retrieval and invocation.

In most pattern-matching applications, only the pattern contains variables; it is matched to a constant object. QLISP's unification algorithm generalizes this to a "merge," or *unification*, of two patterns, both containing variables. The patterns unify if there is some substitution of values for variables such that the patterns become identical. For example, the pattern (A ?X) unifies with (?Y B) under the binding X = B, Y = A. QLISP uses a unification algorithm extended to handle its special data types and segment variables. Most commonly, one of the patterns contains no variables and unification reduces it to a standard match, but in some tasks, notably *theorem proving* (Chap. XII, in Vol. III), it is necessary to match against objects, like mathematical formulas, which themselves contain variables. (See Kahn, 1981, for a more complete discussion of unification.)

SAIL

In SAIL, pattern matching is used only in database retrieval. The major language construct for retrieval in SAIL is the FOREACH statement. Patterns are composed from four types of expressions:

1. Associative triples such as $X \otimes Y \equiv$ GREEN and MOTHER $\otimes$ ADRIAN $\equiv$ Z;

2. Restricted variables, using any Boolean function as the predicate;

3. Expressions of the form $X \in A$, where A is a set;

4. Matching procedures, which are essentially generators.

These interact in a manner best shown by example:

```
FOREACH X, Y SUCH THAT X IN AnimalSet AND Gregarious(X) AND
                Desert(Y) AND Range ⊗ X ≡ Y DO PRINT(X);
```

The conjunctive conditions in the FOREACH statement are processed left to right. In this example, a set-membership pattern is leftmost, so the system chooses some X in the set AnimalSet. Then X is tested to determine whether it satisfies the predicate GREGARIOUS (just a Boolean function). If GREGARIOUS returns FALSE, another X in AnimalSet is chosen, but if it returns TRUE, the process continues: The matching procedure DESERT generates a Y and the database is checked to determine whether Range ⊗ X ≡ Y. (If not, another DESERT is generated by the matching procedure.) X-Y pairs that meet all the conditions are passed on to the action part of the FOREACH statement (following the DO), which in this case consists merely of printing X. The net effect of this FOREACH, then, is to print out all gregarious animals that live in a desert.

In general, a FOREACH statement can include any number of variables and can have any number of conjoined conditions. The ordering of the conditions is critical for efficiency; for instance, if we had put the triple Range ⊗ X ≡ Y first in our example, the FOREACH statement would first find all appropriate triples in the associative database and then try each X-Y pair on the other conditions. (A matching procedure, when its variable is already bound, behaves like a Boolean function.) If the database includes a large amount of information concerning the ranges of animals, this would be highly inefficient. (Note that consequent theorems in PLANNER have a similar property, namely, that the order in which subgoals are listed can drastically affect the number of alternatives examined.)

POP-2

The basic POP-2 programming language does not have pattern matching. As with POP-2's control-structure features (Article VI.C3), the pattern-matching facilities are provided by various library packages that implement facilities similar to those in PLANNER, CONNIVER, and SAIL.

FUZZY

As in PLANNER and CONNIVER, a FUZZY variable is assigned a value through pattern matching. For example,

```
(MATCH (?X ??Y) ((A B) C D))
```

binds the FUZZY variable !X to (A B) and !Y to (C D). A greater selection of functions than in PLANNER and CONNIVER is available for restricting the structure of the pattern or the set of items that can match successfully; for example,

```
(*R ?OBJECT (FETCH (RED !OBJECT)))
```

will only match an object that is known to be red.

Summary

Once again, in the chronological sequence PLANNER, CONNIVER, QLISP, we see a general increase in sophistication of pattern matching and the range of its applications. PLANNER patterns are used implicitly to fetch assertions from the database and to choose a function (theorem) to invoke, but they are limited in their structure and cannot be used explicitly to analyze the structure of data items. QLISP patterns are, by comparison, very general, and much of the language's power depends on them. They serve as a major method for analyzing data, not just in the sense of extracting parts, but of performing quite complicated tests and searches as well.

Not surprisingly, pattern matching is expensive. In almost any particular case, the pattern-match algorithm will be more general than is really required, implying that replacing it with ad hoc code would yield a speedup. When the pattern contains segment variables (as in QLISP), the slowdown is especially severe. In this connection, it is interesting to note that QLISP is termed by its designers (Sacerdoti et al., 1976) a "language for the interactive *development* of complex systems" with the explicit intention that once a QLISP program works, the user can convert it to pure INTERLISP. This can even be accomplished in stages in the QLISP environment, because QLISP and INTERLISP can be freely mixed.

Some pattern-matching capabilities are not offered in any AI programming language. For one thing, all current languages do exact structural matches. A very desirable feature would be "best match" capability: Instead of matching exactly or failing, the matcher would do the best it could and return information on the points it could not find a match on (see Bobrow and Winograd, 1977, for speculations along this line).

C5.   Programming Environment

THE PURPOSE of a programming environment is to help the programmer in all phases of program development, from initial writing of the code through modification, debugging, assembling of modules, and documentation—not necessarily in that order. The principal limitation is feasibility. As will become apparent, designing and implementing the programming environment can easily be as much work as implementing the language itself.

Some AI programming languages have given rise to outstanding environmental facilities. In part, this is due to the character of AI researchers themselves, who include some of the world's consummate "hackers." Furthermore, the language implementors are in close contact with the language users—they are often the same people. It is also true that the programs these researchers have developed are particularly complex and difficult to manage.

AI programs tend to have certain characteristics that greatly influence the practice of programming. Most obviously, they are big. As with other large programs, designers and programmers usually try to break the system down into several discrete "modules" that can be written and tested separately. It often happens in AI programs that the modules will be heavily interdependent, no matter how the breakdown of the task is done; the programmer then has no choice but to write each module with the necessary flexibility for interactions. Finally, since the development of an AI program is usually a research effort, the program tends to be always in a state of flux, subject to frequent modification and occasional major restructuring. In other words, in the course of his (or her) research, an AI programmer may produce dozens or even hundreds of variations of his system, looking for the effects of changes in both design and implementation.

One programming style frequently used in AI projects emphasizes incremental development, module by module. Each new module is added to what already exists, and the expanded configuration is tested to see how it behaves with the new module added. During incremental development, not-yet-written modules may be simulated by a person interacting with the program. In other cases, the system will run with only some of its modules (see, e.g., Article V.C1, in Vol. I).

Another programming style, "structured growth," is described in Sandewall (1978):

> An initial program with a pure and simple structure is written, tested, and then allowed to grow by increasing the ambition of its modules. The process continues recursively as each module is rewritten. The principle applies ...to the flexibility of the data handled by the program, the sophistication

of deduction, the number and versatility of the services provided by the system, etc. (p. 60)

Sandewall notes that the classical *structured-programming* method of stepwise refinement is not often used in Artificial Intelligence.

To sum up briefly, AI programmers must impose some workable organization upon a large set of interacting modules, one that is flexible enough to allow constant modification, correction, and growth of the system. The support provided by a good programming environment is essential.

In looking further at the question of why AI languages tend to have highly developed environments, it is also significant that the programming-support system of a language often resembles an AI system in its own right. It may rely on a large database describing the program and consist of several modules (editor, debugger, etc.) that interact strongly. Consider, then, the advantages of developing environment facilities in an AI language, presumably the one being supported.

Although one's wish list of programming-support features might be endless, the following list includes the most important ones:

1. An *interactive language*, that is, one in which statements can be typed in as commands and are executed immediately. Compiler-based languages are generally not interactive.

2. A good *editor*, if possible, one that can deal with a program according to its structure as a program (not just as text composed of characters).

3. *Interactive debugging facilities*, that is, breaks, backtraces, and facilities for examining and changing program variables.

4. *Input/output routines*. The most common input/output actions should be specially supported by standard system input/output functions, so that the programmer is not burdened with such details.

In the following discussion of the environments of individual languages, keep these basic features in mind—not all of these languages have all the basic features, and some go well beyond them.

LISP

Basic LISP lends itself quite well to various environment facilities. All dialects of basic LISP have some environment features:

1. LISP is an interpreted language. This means that LISP is used naturally in an interactive mode, which is itself a very important environment feature. And since the support programs are also written in LISP, they will be interactive. Interpreted languages are also easier to debug, since it is the source program that is actually executed, rather than the relatively opaque object program that results from compiling the source code.

2. The simple syntax of LISP programs and the standard representation of programs in list structures have been pointed to as important features of LISP for AI programs that involve the creation, inspection, and manipulation of other programs. These features can be exploited by editing and debugging routines, which, of course, must themselves manipulate procedures.

3. The flexibility of function calling in LISP makes it easy for environment programs to call each other. For example, the debugger could call the editor to insert or remove breakpoint statements.

4. LISP has an elementary database facility—property lists and association lists—that is useful for storing information about user programs.

Almost any LISP system includes some debugging facilities and a scheme for printing LISP programs with indentions for easier reading. (Because of the rather difficult-to-read form of LISP functions in the usual embedded list format with parentheses, a "pretty printing" facility is an important programming aid.) The major LISP dialects, MACLISP and INTERLISP, are certainly among the most highly developed programming environments ever created.

INTERLISP

Although there are important differences in philosophy and performance between MACLISP and INTERLISP, in practice, the two languages offer very similar programming environments. For one thing, as was the case with the development of the languages themselves, features that prove useful in one system are copied over to the other. We discuss the major support facilities of INTERLISP here; some of the differences between these two major dialects were mentioned in Article VI.B.

The name INTERLISP stands for "Interactive LISP" and refers to a LISP programming system that has been developing steadily for over 10 years, both in language features and in programming-support facilities (see Masinter, 1981). The major environment features are mentioned here. INTERLISP is a "residential" system: The facilities reside in core and can be called without the user leaving LISP. Another important general point is that the facilities are well integrated with each other (although, on occasion, this integration can lead to unpredictable interactions and consequent difficulties; Sandewall, 1978, p. 51).

The INTERLISP editor operates directly on the list structure of programs and data. It is itself a LISP function, or, more precisely, an assemblage of functions. Thus, the user can define composite editor commands as macros or even define editing macros that call arbitrary LISP programs. Conversely, INTERLISP programs themselves can call the editor and give it commands.

INTERLISP's debugging package offers the standard facilities for breaking and tracing functions. Upon an error break, a new read-evaluate-print loop is entered, in which the user can ask for a backtrace or evaluate any LISP statement (including statements to examine or change variables). An extensive input/output file package is provided that assists in the difficult task of keeping track of the many functions and modules in a typical LISP program. In particular, the file package keeps track of which functions are being used, possibly read in from several of the programmer's disk files, and automatically updates the file copy of the code when the programmer edits a function in core.

The "Programmer's Assistant" monitors and records all user inputs and retains a history of the computation. For instance, the user can ask the Assistant to *repeat* a command or *undo* the effect of one. The intended impression is that of an attentive assistant who carefully watches what the programmer is doing and can take over some of the repetitious tasks when asked. The DWIM (Do What I Mean) facility attempts to figure out what the programmer really meant to say when he typed in an uninterpretable command; for instance, DWIM corrects spelling errors.

CLISP (Conversational LISP) is a set of convenient surface syntax constructs that are translated into ordinary LISP. It includes various abbreviations, a record package, a pattern-match compiler, algebraic notation, and other things. (CLISP is actually implemented through the error-catching mechanism of INTERLISP: Any input that cannot be recognized as LISP is analyzed to see if it is valid CLISP before the system indicates that an error has been made.)

PLANNER and CONNIVER

PLANNER and CONNIVER are interpreters written in MACLISP and have access to some of the MACLISP programming-support facilities. Neither system has been fully implemented or used extensively, so relatively little work has gone into additional support facilities.

One novel programming-support mechanism implemented in PLANNER concerns the style of tracing a program's execution. Tracing involves going back through the steps of a computation (function calls in LISP), usually from some error break. PLANNER offers a trace-as-you-go facility: By saying (THTRACE ⟨object⟩), the programmer can request a trace of a particular function, a goal, all goals, or various other "objects"; then, as his program runs, the system prints out information every time his object is activated. Considering that PLANNER's control structure results in an extensive tree of goals and actions, it does make sense to trace the whole tree as it develops, rather than backtrack from one particular node—which would reveal only one branch of the tree.

QLISP

QLISP is embedded in INTERLISP, and care was taken to preserve the extensive INTERLISP environment while extending the language with QLISP constructs. QLISP, like the INTERLISP package CLISP, is implemented by means of the error-catching mechanism: When the interpreter comes to a QLISP construct, it translates it into INTERLISP and executes that. It also stores the translated version, so that retranslation is not needed. In programs, LISP and QLISP can be freely mixed. QLISP is thus a surface extension of INTERLISP, whereas PLANNER and CONNIVER were distinct language systems built on top of MACLISP. Implementation of QLISP constructs through the error mechanism implies, by the way, that execution of pure LISP constructs is not slowed down at all by the presence of QLISP.

Some difficulties arose in trying to treat QLISP contructs as if they were on a par with INTERLISP constructs. For instance, because they are translated into INTERLISP before being executed, QLISP functions would not show up on a trace or backtrace. A special QTRACE facility had to be added to get around this problem. And some "unfortunate interactions" resulted from the clever adaptation of some of the INTERLISP support facilities to implement certain QLISP language features. For instance, the CLISP pattern-matching feature becomes unusable because QLISP uses it for its own pattern matching. The QLISP manual (Wilber, 1976) contains many warnings about how to avoid running into these painful effects. For the most part, though, INTERLISP environment features carry over directly to QLISP.

QLISP also offers a standard function, NEWSTATEMENT, that allows the user to define surface syntax and an execution routine for some new statement. This extensibility feature is employed typically to "provide alternative control structures for invoking the standard QLISP statements, or to provide special syntax for user-defined QLAMBDA functions" (Sacerdoti et al., 1976, p. 13).

SAIL

SAIL was designed with both real-time robotics applications and the PDP–10 computer in mind. For this reason, SAIL emphasizes convenient access to the operating system from within user programs. The language itself has many standard functions compiled as monitor calls to the operating system. The run-time environment includes especially convenient input/output facilities, such as interrupt handling. Provision is also made for linking SAIL programs to hand-coded assembly-language algorithms (for efficiency).

Since SAIL is a compiler-based language and is not interactive, the experience of writing and debugging SAIL programs is considerably different from the other AI programming languages we have discussed. Programs are written separately, with whatever text editor is convenient, and then compiled into machine code. Unlike the other languages in which each (small) function is written separately, SAIL programs are block structured and usually will have many procedures nested inside the main program. Testing of individual procedures (functions) is more difficult than in LISP because they usually cannot be run in isolation. Some of these drawbacks have been overcome by the interactive debugging system, BAIL, which has been added to the SAIL programming environment (Reiser, 1976).

POP–2

POP–2, although again not an interpreted language, has an *incremental compiler* that allows an interactive style of programming similar to that of LISP. The programmer can type in any statement and have it executed immediately, or he can define functions and edit them. POP-2 functions tend to be even smaller than LISP functions.

POP–2, as mentioned before, relies on library packages for its extended data, control, and pattern-matching features. This allows the core language to remain quite small. The packages, however, cannot be integrated as tightly as the features in INTERLISP, which in turn is a very large running program.

The POP–2 editor (which, incidentally, is neither especially powerful nor oriented to POP–2 syntax) does reside in core permanently. Some of the available packages include facilities for tracing and debugging, timing of individual functions, automatic documentation of the various packages, and special routines for debugging stack errors (the POP–2 stack, remember, is explicitly manipulable by the program).

Summary

The programming environment is the least AI-specific of the four aspects of AI programming languages discussed. At the same time, it is an area that AI languages have pioneered. The key word is *interaction*. In the environments we have examined, we can distinguish several different kinds of features that facilitate interactive programming. The most important, of course, is for the programming language itself to be interactive. In an interactive language, programs are built up of small modules (procedures, functions) that are each tested immediately after they are typed in, rather than after the entire program is completed and run through a compiler. This kind of interaction facilitates bug detection and correction.

The Programmer's Assistant feature of INTERLISP exemplifies another kind of interaction—at the meta-level, in a sense. User commands to the Assistant refer not to LISP objects but to the user's manipulations of LISP objects. For example, the Assistant may be told to repeat an action or show the recent history of user commands.

For smooth interaction it is important that the various components of an environment be well integrated with each other. INTERLISP is the only one of the languages covered that (by and large) accomplishes this integration. Almost any component can be called from within almost any other. In the other languages, components generally can be called only from the top level. INTERLISP also provides a concept of structural editing that many programmers find to be an extremely useful tool—the editor commands are specially designed for manipulating list structures.

The next general advance in AI programming environments will be facilitated by the special-purpose LISP machines now becoming available commercially. In these single-user work stations, the programmer has a powerful computational tool that is designed for LISP programming and that can be a highly integrated system—from the disk to the graphics display.

D. DEPENDENCIES AND ASSUMPTIONS

THIS ARTICLE outlines a technique for recording the inferential steps taken by a reasoning program, using *dependency records* to link conclusions with the reasons behind them. One important requirement on the design of intelligent programs is that they be responsibly humble about their conclusions and actions; that is, they should be able to explain their conclusions and actions in terms of the information supplied by their informants. This ability to defer responsibility for conclusions to their sources is crucial in the transfer of expertise from an expert to a program, for the expert must be able to assign credit or blame for unexpected conclusions and actions to forgotten, missing, or erroneous knowledge-base elements or procedures (see Article VII.B). Similarly, such restraint is crucial in any *learning* done by the program, for the program must be able to analyze the reasons for its own successes and failures (see Chap. XIV, in Vol. III).

These considerations alone are enough to suggest that intelligent programs should record information about their inferences, so that they can refer to these records during *credit* or *blame assignment*. In fact, several other considerations also suggest keeping these dependency records, namely, the control of program actions, the adoption and abandonment of assumptions, and the recovery of improperly abandoned conclusions.

Recorded dependencies aid in controlling the actions of a program, since credit assignment is important in *search* as well as in transfer of expertise and learning. One standard search technique that can be augmented in this manner is *chronological backtracking*, in which a space of hypothetical situations is being searched. An error or inconsistency encountered in one of these situations signals for backtracking—all actions and assumptions after the most recent choice point are retracted and the next alternative at that point is examined (see Chap. II, in Vol. I, and the discussion of PLANNER in Article VI.C3).

In situations in which the temporal order of previous choices is not of primary importance, however, chronological backtracking is needlessly inefficient. Instead, by examining a trace of the actions and assumptions at each successive situation, the source of the problem may be identified and the next alternative chosen in this light, avoiding searches through numerous irrelevant combinations of assumptions and actions. For example, in a chess-playing program that examines several alternative moves a few ply ahead, a threat discovered while considering one move could be an important constraint in deciding which alternative moves to explore (see Article II.C5c, in Vol. I).

In addition to their credit-assignment applications, recorded dependencies can also be used to maintain the set of currently active database elements.

72

There have been three other techniques used for this purpose, each of which has its problems:

1. *Manual changes* to the database, whenever a new assumption is made or action is taken, are the most straightforward way of keeping track of the current state of things. However, the job of keeping track of all the ramifications of the updates—new conclusions that can be drawn, old conclusions that are no longer valid, and so forth—gets to be a major problem in any reasonably sized knowledge base.

2. *Context* mechanisms, as supplied in several of the AI programming languages described in Article VI.C2, shared the problems of chronological backtracking (in which they played an important role). In particular, the context mechanisms of these languages needlessly discarded information discovered in an abandoned search.

3. *Change-triggered procedures*, like the antecedent theorems in PLANNER (Article VI.C3), automatically perform some knowledge-base maintenance function when the programmer specifies some change. This approach had a problem common to all *procedural-knowledge representations*, namely, that all of the triggers had to be carefully tailored as a set to avoid unintended infinite loops of adding and erasing database entries.

By allowing a global, static perspective on the actions of the program's inference procedures, explicit tracking of dependencies allows coherent treatment both of new inferences and of assumptions made on the basis of incomplete information. The techniques described below make it possible to adopt an assumption when necessary on the basis of incomplete information, to subsequently abandon the conclusions drawn from the assumption should it later be abandoned, and to recover the previously abandoned conclusions if the assumption is reinstated.

History

Dependency records were first employed, in robot problem-solving programs, to help clean up the consequential database entries following robot actions or failures. The effects of actions were typically represented in *ADD/DELETE* lists. Fikes (1975) kept track of derivations, so that all consequences of a database entry could be erased when that entry was deleted by order of a delete list (see Article II.D5, in Vol. I, on STRIPS). Hayes (1975) kept track of the dependence of each planning decision on other such decisions, so that all consequential decisions could be abandoned when some plan-execution error or independent worldly change invalidated the preconditions of a decision about some plan step.

The role of dependencies was then broadened by Stallman and Sussman (1977), who in the context of electronic circuit analysis employed dependencies in explanations of conclusions, in abandoning and retrieving consequences of abandoned or reinstated assumptions, and in *dependency-directed* (nonchrono-logical) backtracking. London (1978) developed similar techniques for use in robot planning, improved to conduct incremental revisions of conclusions.

Building on the work of Stallman and Sussman, Doyle (1979) introduced assumptions as dependency records of nonmonotonic inferences, such as THNOT in PLANNER (see Article XII.E, in Vol. III, on nondeductive reason-ing and nonmonotonic logic), and identified the role of such assumptions in dependency-directed backtracking. Doyle (1980) also illustrated the use of dependencies in explicitly guiding program actions through a process of decision-making based on *dialectical argumentation*. The survey and bibliog-raphy by Doyle and London (1980) should be consulted for descriptions of other papers concerned with these techniques.

Recording and Maintaining Dependencies

The fundamental data structures involved in dependency records are *nodes* and *justifications*. Nodes label database entries, inference rules, proce-dures, and so forth, for use in justifications. Justifications, in turn, represent inference steps from combinations of nodes to another node (more properly, from the referents of combinations of nodes to the referent of another node). The simplest sort of justification is a list of antecedent nodes. For example, suppose a program has the following entries in its knowledge base:

```
Node-1: The patient has a cold
Node-2: If the patient has a cold, he sneezes
Node-3: If A, and A implies B, then B,
```

where `Node-1` and `Node-2` are facts and `Node-3` is an inference rule. The program might then infer a new statement, The patient sneezes, labeled `Node-4`, and record the list (Node-1 Node-2 Node-3) as a justification of `Node-4`.

The currently active set of nodes can be defined in terms of the current set of justifications. A node is currently active if it has a valid justification, where a justification is valid if each of the nodes it mentions is currently active. Newly created nodes are thus inactive. Empty-list justifications are always valid, and the nodes they justify are called *premises* and are always active. Premises form a base from which all other currently active nodes may be explained in terms of valid justifications.

The currently active set of nodes controls the program actions. For example, instead of using procedures that are triggered when a database entry is added or erased, a program might use procedures that are triggered upon the inactive-to-active or active-to-inactive transitions of a node. While nothing prevents the justification of one node in terms of currently inactive nodes, the normal use is to draw conclusions from currently active nodes.

The currently active set of nodes is updated whenever justifications are added or erased by a revision procedure, which we will call RP. This use of

RP is sometimes referred to in the literature as *truth maintenance, dependency-network maintenance,* or *belief revision.* If a justification J for node N is added, RP checks to see if each node in J is active. If so, N is made active, and, recursively, all inactive nodes with justifications mentioning N are reexamined to see if they, too, can be made active. If a valid justification for N is erased, a list is made of N together with all the active nodes depending on N via other valid justifications. Each of these nodes is made inactive. Then, each node on the list is reexamined to see if it can be made active. This deactivation and reexamination is used to avoid making nodes active on the basis of circular arguments.

Erasing justifications is a bad idea for several reasons, however, not the least of which is that it needlessly discards valuable information about past inferences and adoption of premises (other reasons are discussed by Doyle, 1979, 1980). To avoid erasures, *nonmonotonic justifications* are used to create assumptions. A nonmonotonic justification is a pair (A, I) of lists of nodes and is valid only if each node in A is active and each node in I is inactive.

For example, the justification of the statement The patient has normal digestion, labeled Node-5, might rely on the fact that there is no reason to believe he has abnormal digestion (another fact, represented by, say, Node-6: The patient has abnormal digestion). The justification for Node-5 would be represented by the form (( ),(Node-6)). As long as there is no known justification for Node-6, Node-5 would be active. These justifications are called nonmonotonic because the set of active nodes—the facts that are believed to be true at any one time—can *shrink* upon the addition of a new justification. Nonmonotonic justifications allow the effect of defeating justifications without losing information. For example, if some indication of abnormal digestion were found, Node-6 could be activated, causing Node-5 to be deactivated, without changing in any way the form of its justification.

Although the extension of RP to handling nonmonotonic justifications may appear to be a simple task, the surprising subtlety of the many problems involved makes this extension a nest of traps for the unwary. Two key reasons for the delicacy of this matter are that inactive nodes have consequences and that ambiguities of revision must be settled by RP. On the first point, the very fact that a node is inactive may be used in the nonmonotonic justification of another node, as in our digestion example. Hence, changing a node from inactive to active may invalidate justifications, making inactive the nodes they support, and vice versa.

As for ambiguities, suppose, for example, that Node-7 has the justification (( ),(Node-8)) and Node-8 has the justification (( ),(Node-7)); that is, they are mutually exclusive nodes. If RP must choose one of Node-7 and Node-8 to be active, great care is required, since other nodes, possibly including other assumptions and contradictory nodes, may depend on the choice. RP must be able to sift through the *global* ramifications of such local ambiguities (see Doyle, 1979).

Assumptions enter dependency-directed backtracking by filling the role of *choice points* in chronological backtracking. For each active node, RP maintains a distinguished, noncircular explanation by picking one valid justification as the supporting justification. Thus, an assumption is properly an active node whose supporting justification is nonmonotonic. To reject a node, that is, to make it inactive, the program just traces through its supporting justification and chooses some underlying assumption as the culprit. This assumption is then defeated by creating a new node that is used to activate one of the inactive nodes mentioned in its supporting justification.

For example, let us suppose that Node-9 has the supporting justification (( ), (Node-10 Node-11)). This can be thought of as saying: Make Node-9 active first, and if that fails try Node-10 or Node-11. Backtracking might add the justification (( ), (Node-11)) for Node-10, thereby defeating the assumption Node-9 and setting up Node-11 as the next alternative. As this example shows, assumptions may be defeated without discarding justifications, thereby avoiding loss of information about past assumptions. In other words, the set of justifications always grows monotonically, while giving rise to a nonmonotonically changing set of active database entries.

Discussion

Many unanswered questions make the technique of dependencies and assumptions an active area of investigation in AI. One such question concerns the mechanisms that RP should use to resolve the ambiguities when several possible revisions present themselves. A second question is how the existing RP algorithms might be improved, since each has certain deficiencies. A third question, then, is how systems should be organized so that dependency information can be conveniently recorded and used (see, e.g., the proposals made by de Kleer et al., 1979).

In spite of these unanswered questions, the technique of tracking dependencies and assumptions is important because the solution of complex problems often demands making simplifying or heuristic assumptions, either about the problem itself or about the way to proceed in solving it. Later, these assumptions can be reasoned about in several ways. One way is to correct the assumptions leading to inconsistencies or to fruitless paths of investigation. Other ways are to extend the solution of the simplified problem to that of the complex original problem, to compare the importance of alternate collections of assumptions, and to index abstract solutions to problems.

References

See Doyle (1979, 1980) and de Kleer et al. (1979); also, the bibliography by Doyle and London (1980).

Chapter VII

Applications-oriented AI Research:
Science

CHAPTER VII: APPLICATIONS–ORIENTED AI RESEARCH: SCIENCE

A. OVERVIEW

OVER the past decade, many of the fundamental AI techniques described in the previous chapters on search, knowledge representation, and natural-language processing have been applied in the form of *expert systems*, that is, computer systems that can help solve complex, real-world problems in specific scientific, engineering, and medical specialties. These systems are most strongly characterized by their use of large bodies of *domain knowledge*—facts and procedures, gleaned from human experts, that have proved useful for solving typical problems in their domain. Expert-systems research promises to lead to AI applications of great economic and social impact. But far from being solely concerned with applying AI problem-solving techniques, the research described in this and the following two chapters has often addressed fundamental questions concerning the nature of knowledge, both in terms of formal representational systems and as an essentially social phenomenon—knowledge as something that must be shared and transferred among men and machines.

Evolution of Expert Systems

AI research in the 1960s identified and explored several general-purpose problem-solving techniques. This work introduced and refined the concept of heuristic search (see Chap. II, in Vol. I) as an important model of problem solving. Many of the AI systems developed during this period, like GPS, the Logic Theorist, REF-ARF, QA4, and PLANNER (all described elsewhere in the *Handbook*), dealt with problems in simple, constrained domains such as chess, textbook problems, robot planning, blocks-world manipulations, and puzzles like "Tower of Hanoi" and "Missionaries and Cannibals." But by the mid-1960s, some researchers in the DENDRAL project at Stanford and the MACSYMA project at M.I.T. had begun work on the first expert systems—organic chemical analysis in the case of DENDRAL and symbolic integration and formula simplification in MACSYMA.

These systems were designed to manipulate and explore symbolically expressed problems that were known to be difficult for human researchers to solve. The problems were characterized by the increasing number of solution possibilities that had to be examined as the problem specifications grew in complexity—the larger the size of the problem specification (e.g., the size of the molecule or the complexity of the expression to be integrated), the more difficult it was for human researchers to discover solutions or be confident that all valid solutions had been found. This *combinatorial explosion* in the solution search space often outstripped the abilities of human researchers. The capability of AI systems to deal with the larger solution spaces is important in that it extends the types of problems that can be solved with the same conceptual tools.

More recently, several other factors have motivated research on expert-systems development. Most notably, expert systems promise to be quite profitable because they can help solve hard problems that require the best (most expensive) human expertise. (See, e.g., Articles VII.C4 and VII.D3 on systems that may help design chemical-synthesis techniques and explore for mineral deposits.) In some domains, like medical diagnosis, the fact that the exhaustive nature of problem solving in expert systems ensures that remote possibilities are not overlooked is important. And often the very codification of expertise in suitable form for an expert system is an illuminating and valuable part of the expert-systems development. (This systematic reorganization of what is known can lead, e.g., to new insights into the structure of the domain or to new ideas about how to teach it.)

In a domain like medicine (and unlike symbolic integration) where the nature of the problem is not sufficiently understood to completely specify the search space, large amounts of domain-specific knowledge have to be represented and reasoned with. Thus, while heuristic-search management is still a major concern in the construction of any expert system, efficient implementation and automated maintenance of large knowledge bases must also be addressed. A particularly important design issue is devising effective means for acquiring such large amounts of knowledge from the human experts, who insist on "talking about" what they do rather than "dumping" what they know, as computers do.

The issue of acquiring knowledge from human experts is now seen as a part of the general problem of *transfer of expertise*. Since humans are both the *source* and the eventual *users* of expertise, current concerns in expert-systems design center on considerations of how humans talk about what they know. For an expert system to be truly useful, it should be able to learn what human experts know, so that it can perform as well as they do, understand the points of departure among the views of human experts who disagree, keep its knowledge up to date as human experts do (by reading, asking questions, and learning from experience), and present its reasoning to its human users in much the way that human experts would (justifying, clarifying, explaining, and even tutoring). These issues in the transfer of expertise can be seen as a microcosm of many of the central concerns of Artificial Intelligence.

Representing Expertise

Specialists are distinguished from laymen and general practitioners in a technical domain by their vast task-specific knowledge, acquired from their training, their subsequent readings, and especially their experience of many hundreds of cases in the course of their practice. Whether car mechanics or neurosurgeons, experts can solve problems that others cannot, because they know things that nonexperts do not. Sometimes this knowledge is in the form of specific facts about the domain that have, over the years, been committed to memory, and sometimes the expertise appears as hunches, "educated guesses" about the way to proceed in problem solving.

Representing and using the various types of knowledge that characterize expertise constitute one principal focus of expert-systems research. Among the things that might be useful for an expert system to know about are:

1. Facts about the domain: "The shin bone is connected to the ankle bone" or, more typical of human experts, "The automatic choke on '77 Chevys often gets stuck on cold mornings";

2. Hard-and-fast rules or procedures: "Always unplug the set before you stick a screwdriver into the back";

3. Problem situations and what might be good things to try to do when you are in them (heuristics): "If it won't start but you are getting a spark, check the fuel line";

4. Global strategies: differential diagnosis;

5. A "theory" of the domain: a causal explanation of how an internal-combustion engine works.

All of the knowledge-representation schemes described in Chapter III (in Vol. I) have been used in expert systems; in fact, much original work on knowledge representation has been done in the context of expert-systems design.

Note that much of the knowledge that characterizes human expertise is hunchlike, in the sense that it does not constitute definite consequences of actions or certainty of conclusions. Reasoning with such knowledge has been the key idea that made expert systems possible and constitutes the main problem in developing their power further. In particular, *inexact reasoning*, using hunches or *heuristics* to guide and focus what would otherwise be a search of an impossibly large space (see Articles II.C3 and II.C4, in Vol. I), has resulted in systems with human-level problem-solving abilities. Indeed, these systems have at times proved superior to the human experts, primarily because they consider a much larger set of possible solutions (as much as several orders of magnitude larger) and do not miss unlikely or unexpected possibilities, once these have been noted as worthy of consideration by the expert who built the knowledge base.

Transfer of Expertise

Solving real-world problems at human-expert levels of performance is only the beginning of expert-systems design. Most of the applications systems described in this chapter can be viewed as *consultants* that formulate opinions and give advice to their users. The tasks these consultants are designed to perform require the application of facts and relationships known only by specialists. The current systems emphasize the cognitive abilities that support interaction with the user during problem solving, such as the ability to explain lines of reasoning or to acquire new domain knowledge interactively.

Typically, such a system will be considered "intelligent" if it meets the following criteria: (a) The system gives correct answers or useful advice, and (b) the concepts and reasoning processes it uses to solve the problem resemble those that the user might employ. This last concern has led to the design of systems that can explain their reasoning about a case, maintain a focused dialogue with a user when pursuing relevant facts and inferences about his (or her) case, and employ knowledge at the conceptual level of the user when solving and explaining both the problem and the system's solution. Successfully addressing these primarily *human-engineering* concerns has required many advances in AI. These abilities and developments are detailed for each system in the following articles (see especially Article VII.B).

Explanation and the opacity of knowledge. As mentioned previously, a major design issue for some of these systems, for the consultants in particular, is whether the system needs to explain its reasoning to a user. This capability is implemented primarily to convince users that the system's reasoning is appropriate and that its conclusions about a case are reasonable.

Sometimes the problem-solving expertise of the system is in a form that is not at all similar to the expertise that a human expert would apply to obtain the solution. For example, in the case of the DENDRAL programs, the generator of chemical-structure candidates employs a procedure for exhaustively producing possible structures based on various graph-theoretic notions that organic chemists who use the system are unlikely to know or care about. Thus, a major portion of the DENDRAL expertise resides in a procedure that is conceptually *opaque* to the typical user. The generator was developed because it was discovered that the method used by chemists to find solutions for these problems is, in fact, incomplete, while the method used by the DENDRAL program has been mathematically proved to be complete. A similar situation exists in the MACSYMA system, which uses the Risch algorithm for evaluating various types of integrals. While mathematically correct, the algorithm is rarely employed by human mathematicians because of its complexity. The correctness and continuing success of these programs serve as their primary form of explanation: The user community is thereby convinced that the performing system is both acceptable and usable.

In contrast, *consultation systems* like MYCIN and PROSPECTOR have been designed to represent and explain the reasoning process of the system in a manner that is understandable to the knowledgeable user. These systems require a representational formalism capable of supporting the reasoning and explanation abilities that would closely approximate the conceptual framework of the expert and the user. Since most of these scientific and technical domains have a well-defined set of concepts that their practitioners use consistently, the systems' designers have capitalized on this consistency and have designed the programs to accept and reason with knowledge using these concepts.

Assuming that a system has an explanation facility, the system designer faces another issue: Should the system reason and apply the expertise in a manner that resembles the methods of human experts? In MYCIN, for example, no claim is made by the designers that the simple backward-chaining reasoning methodology has any resemblance to the methods actually employed by human physicians in diagnosing infectious diseases. Although the medical concepts employed by the system are familiar to most physicians, the method of inferring the infections and causal organisms, while understandable by physicians, bears little resemblance to their normal diagnostic reasoning. By contrast, the PIP and INTERNIST systems emphasize the similarities of their diagnostic procedures to those of physicians.

Knowledge acquisition. During the development of the knowledge base, experts are unlikely to present all of the relevant facts and relationships for expert performance in the domain. Being human, experts tend to forget or to simplify details about their knowledge, requiring the system to augment its knowledge at a later time. Since the knowledge imparted to the system is largely empirical and the domains are themselves developing rapidly, it is necessary for the system to make these changes easily and in an *incremental* or modular fashion. Thus, most of the recent applications systems have emphasized representation schemes that allow for the incremental construction of the knowledge base.

Most researchers have approached incremental construction by means of *production-rule* knowledge representation. Each rule, and rule set, represents a "chunk" of domain expertise that is communicable to the user and that can be added to or deleted from the system's knowledge base with relatively constrained changes in the system's behavior (see Article III.C4 and the discussion of *modularity* in knowledge representation in Article III.A, in Vol. I). Thus, the system can be improved by modifying the knowledge base with new rule sets that deal with new subdomains. Furthermore, the production-rule formalism can directly accommodate the knowledge of the domain experts in the form that they most often communicate it—for example, "In this situation I suspect this problem and perform these tests."

The Status of Applications Research

The major domains of expertise that have been developed as applications systems include the diagnosis and treatment of various diseases (see Chap. VIII), the design of computer assistants for both the analytic and the synthetic aspects of organic chemistry (Sec. VII.C), interactive tutoring systems in education (Chap. IX), and assistants for performing advanced mathematics

(Article VII.D1). A number of other notable applications have been developed, including applications of AI to database information-retrieval problems (see Article VII.D4) and a geological prospecting assistant (Article VII.D3).

Among the rapidly growing host of applications-oriented systems are SACON, a system for advising structural engineers in the use of a large, finite-element analysis program for modeling various mechanical structures (Bennett et al., 1978); PUFF, a system for diagnosing a patient with pulmonary dysfunctions (Feigenbaum, 1977); and HEADMED, a system for diagnosing and treating psychiatric patients (Heiser, Brooks, and Ballard, 1978). More recent are McDermott's (1981) R1 expert on computer-system configurations and Stefik's (1980) work on an aid in designing experiments in molecular genetics (see also Article XV.D2, in Vol. III, on MOLGEN). Current research in this area includes extensions of the expert-system paradigm to computer-based assistants for computer-system failure diagnosis, aids for VLSI circuit design, more sophisticated database-query systems, and systems that can act as tutors in their areas of expertise (see Article IX.C6).

One important development in current research on expert systems is the emergence in recent years of "expert-systems-building" systems, which facilitate the construction of expert systems in any domain. For example, the EMYCIN system (van Melle, 1980) consists of the basic control structure of MYCIN, but with MYCIN's infectious-disease knowledge base removed. With another knowledge base substituted in the same production-rule format as MYCIN's, this "Empty MYCIN" system retains the capability of interacting with the user during a case, to explain its reasoning, and to answer questions about a case in the new domain. EMYCIN has been used successfully to develop the applications in the treatment of pulmonary dysfunction, in structural analysis, and in the psychiatric diagnosis mentioned earlier. Several other expert-systems-building systems are being developed, including IRIS (see Article VIII.B6), AGE (Nii and Aiello, 1979), OPS (Forgy and McDermott, 1977), and ROSIE (Fain et al., 1981; Hayes-Roth et al., 1981). Systems such as these, which attempt to facilitate the construction of expert systems, are an important area of current research.

Another primary research activity in the near future will be the development of better facilities for acquiring the domain concepts and the empirical knowledge that expert systems must have. Feigenbaum (1977) suggests that the painful process of *knowledge engineering*, which involves domain experts and computer scientists working together to design and construct the domain knowledge base, is the principal bottleneck in the development of expert systems. Efficient interfaces for acquiring this domain-specific knowledge, along the interactive transfer-of-expertise lines explored in TEIRESIAS (Article VII.B) or the automatic *theory-formation* methods used by the Meta-DENDRAL system (Article VII.C2c), need to be developed before significantly larger expert systems can be constructed.

The size of current systems is typically given in terms of some convenient measure of the domain-specific knowledge contained by the system. For example, the MYCIN system has approximately 450 rules and a similar number of clinical parameters with which it diagnoses and prescribes treatments for patients with bacteremia, cystitis, and meningitis. The SYNCHEM system has approximately 390 transforms for constructing plausible organic-synthesis routes. The amount of expert knowledge contained in a system has been primarily a function of the level of involvement and effort of the human expert. These systems have the potential for supporting larger knowledge bases, but there has been no attempt yet to construct more comprehensive systems. At present, only selected subdomains are actually represented.

It is clear that researchers in AI and computer science will have to develop new techniques for handling the truly large-scale knowledge bases of the future. A step in this direction has been taken with the development of techniques for representing knowledge about knowledge, or *meta-knowledge* (see Article III.A, in Vol. I, and Article VII.B). This domain-specific knowledge provides a means for determining the consistency and appropriateness of various knowledge sources used by the system. Current research is examining the representation and application of meta-knowledge as a way to organize large amounts of domain knowledge so that it is used effectively by the program while remaining comprehensible to the human user and expert.

The Applications Chapters

Chapters VII, VIII, and IX describe research in expert-systems technology. The present chapter, with articles discussing some design issues in the context of the TEIRESIAS system and the important applications in analytic and synthetic chemistry, also presents an article about an expert system in mathematics, MACSYMA, and some articles on scientific-applications research that did not fit in anywhere else, including the geology consultant PROSPECTOR. Chapter VIII describes the research on medical applications, and, finally, Chapter IX discusses AI applications to tutoring systems, principally the work on what is called Intelligent Computer-assisted Instruction (ICAI).

Each article on an individual system will attempt to include:

1. A description of the problem domain (e.g., chemistry, infectious disease), the particular task the applications system was designed to perform (e.g., elucidate chemical structures, diagnose and recommend treatment for a patient with an infectious disease), and the major motivations for the system's design, both for AI and for the task domain;

2. A description of the task-specific knowledge used by the system to perform the problem-solving task (e.g., knowledge about probable bond breaks for a compound in a mass spectrometer, knowledge about possible infections and their causal organisms);

3. A description of the particular AI methods employed to represent this knowledge and a description of how the represented knowledge is used to reason about a particular case, sometimes including an annotated sample interaction between a user and the system;

4. An indication of the current level of expertise of the system and an indication of its present status and possible future development.

Throughout these articles, emphasis is placed on illuminating the major AI issues involved in the design of these systems.

References

Duda and Gaschnig (1981) present an excellent popular review of expert-systems technology. The forthcoming book edited by Hayes-Roth, Waterman, and Lenat is a thorough and up-to-date discussion of the issues and status of expert-systems research. The book edited by Waterman and Hayes-Roth (1979) is an earlier presentation of many of these issues. Feigenbaum (1977) gives a short review of expert-systems research, as does the textbook by Winston (1977). Also of interest is a special issue of the *Journal of Artificial Intelligence* (Sridharan, 1978) on AI applications in science and medicine.

B. TEIRESIAS

TEIRESIAS is a system that assists in entering and updating the large knowledge bases used in expert systems. Although TEIRESIAS is not itself an application of AI to some domain, it deals with many important issues in expert-systems design that are relevant to all of the programs described in this section of the *Handbook*. The system was developed by Randall Davis as part of his doctoral research with the MYCIN project at Stanford University, and this article assumes some familiarity with MYCIN's *rule-based* knowledge-representation scheme and its *backward-chaining* control structure (see Article VIII.B1). However, the ideas and techniques that TEIRESIAS uses are not necessarily limited to MYCIN's domain of infectious diseases or to its production-rule formalism.

Knowledge-based Programs

As discussed in Article VII.A, systems that attain expert-level performance in problem-solving tasks derive their power from a large store of task-specific knowledge. As a result, the creation and management of large knowledge bases and the development of techniques for the informed use of knowledge are now central problems of AI research. TEIRESIAS was written to explore some of the issues involved in these problems.

Most expert programs embody the knowledge of one or more experts in a field (e.g., infectious diseases) and are constructed in consultation with these experts. Typically, the computer scientist *mediates* between the experts and the program he (or she) is building to model their expertise. This is a difficult and time-consuming task, because the computer scientist must learn the basics of the field in order to ask good questions about what the program is supposed to do. TEIRESIAS's goal is to reduce the role of the human intermediary in this task of knowledge acquisition, by assisting in the construction and modification of the system's knowledge base.

The human expert communicates, via TEIRESIAS, with the *performance program* (e.g., MYCIN), so that he can discover, with TEIRESIAS's help, what the performance program is doing and why. TEIRESIAS offers facilities for modifying or adding to the knowledge base to correct errors: Through TEIRESIAS, the human expert can "educate" the program just as he would tutor a human novice who makes mistakes. Ideas about how this "debugging" process is best carried out are at the core of TEIRESIAS's success. As discussed in Chapter XIV (in Vol. III), TEIRESIAS can be viewed as a *learning* program, since it incorporates advice from the human expert. The expert, however, does much of the work, since he must state the advice in terms that the system understands (fully *operational*) and then must *evaluate* the system's performance and *assign credit* or blame to individual rules. (See especially Article XIV.C on learning by taking advice.)

TEIRESIAS recognizes the inexact, experiential character of the knowledge that is often required for knowledge-based systems and (as examples below will illustrate) offers the expert some assistance in formulating new "chunks of knowledge" of this sort. The system also provides a mechanism for embodying strategic information about how to proceed in problem solving (e.g., diagnosis in MYCIN). *Meta-rules* (also discussed below) help direct the use of object-level rules in the knowledge base and provide a mechanism for encoding problem-solving strategies.

Interactive Transfer of Expertise

It is an established result that an expert knows more about a field than he realizes or is capable of articulating completely. Thus, asking him a broad question like "Tell me everything you know about staph infections" will yield only a fraction of his knowledge on the subject. TEIRESIAS's approach is to present the expert with some errors made by an already established, but still incomplete, knowledge-based program and to ask a *focused* question: "What do you know that the program doesn't know that makes your expert diagnosis different in this case?"

This interaction is called *transfer of expertise.* TEIRESIAS incorporates into the performance program the capabilities of the human expert. It does not attempt to derive new information on its own but, instead, tries to "listen" as attentively and intelligently as possible, to help the expert augment or modify the knowledge base.

Interactive transfer of expertise between an expert and an expert program begins when the expert identifies an error in the performance of the program and invokes TEIRESIAS to help track down and correct the error. Errors are manifest as program responses that the expert would not have made or as lines of reasoning that the expert finds odd, superfluous, or otherwise inappropriate. The first kind of error might be, for example, a wrong conclusion about the identity of a bacterium. The second kind of error occurs when the performance program asks, during a consultation, a question that, in the expert's opinion, does nothing to resolve the identity of the bacterium.

Both kinds of errors are assumed, by TEIRESIAS, to be indicative of a deficit, or "bug," in the performance program's knowledge base. Transfer of expertise begins when TEIRESIAS is called upon to correct the deficit. TEIRESIAS fixes bugs in the knowledge base by:

1. Stopping the performance program when the human expert identifies an error;

2. Working backwards through the steps in the performance program that led to the error, until the bug is found;

3. Helping the expert fix the bug by adding or modifying knowledge.

To identify faulty reasoning steps in the performance program, the expert can use the WHY and HOW commands to ask TEIRESIAS to back up through previous steps, *explaining* why they were taken. Of course, the same explanatory abilities can also be employed when there is no bug, to help the user follow the system's line of reasoning. Since many large performance programs carry out very complex inferences that are essentially hidden from the person using the program, this is a valuable facility.

Meta-level Knowledge

One of the principal problems of AI is the question of appropriate representation and use of knowledge about the world (see Chap. III, in Vol. I). Numerous techniques have been employed to represent domain knowledge in various applications programs. A central theme of the research on TEIRESIAS is exploring the use of *meta-knowledge*. Meta-level knowledge is simply the representation in the program of knowledge about the program itself—about how much it knows and how it reasons. This knowledge is represented in the same formalism as the domain knowledge, yielding a program containing *object-level* representations that describe the external world and *meta-level* representations that describe the internal world of the program, its self-knowledge.

Meta-level knowledge takes different forms as it has been explored in AI and psychology (Barr, 1979), but it can be summed up as "knowing about what you know." In general, it allows the system both to use its knowledge directly and to examine it, abstract it, and direct its application. The attempt to construct capabilities for explanation, knowledge acquisition, and strategic reasoning in TEIRESIAS led directly to the incorporation of explicit meta-level knowledge. (The representation and importance of meta-knowledge are discussed in more depth in Article III.A, in Vol. I.)

Explanation

There are two important classes of situations in which expert systems should be able to explain their behavior and results. For the user of the system who needs clarification or reassurance about the system's output, the explanation can contribute to the *transparency*, and thus the *acceptance*, of the system. The second major need for explanation is in the debugging process described above, where a human expert, in order to locate some error in the knowledge base, makes use of the system's explanations of why it has done what it has done. The first of these applications of explanation has been explored in the question-answering facility of the MYCIN system; the explanation capability in TEIRESIAS has explored both uses but has concentrated on the latter.

The techniques in TEIRESIAS for generating explanations are based on two assumptions about the performance program being examined, namely, (a) that a recapitulation of program actions can be an effective explanation, as long as the correct level of detail is chosen, and (b) that there is some shared framework for viewing the program's actions that will make them comprehensible to the user. In the MYCIN-like expert systems that employ production-rule knowledge bases, these assumptions are valid, but it is easy to imagine expert systems in which one or both are violated. For example, the first assumption simplifies the explanation task considerably, since it means that the solution requires only the ability to record and play back a history of events. This assumption rules out, in particular, any need to simplify those events. However, it is not obvious, for instance, that an appropriate level of detail can always be found. Furthermore, this approach of recapitulation, which often offers an easily understood explanation in programs that reason symbolically, might not apply to expert systems that perform primarily numeric computations.

A simple recapitulation will be an effective explanation only if the level of descriptive detail is constrained. It must be *detailed* enough that the operations the system cites are comprehensible; the conceptual level must be *high* enough that the operations are meaningful to the observer, with unnecessary detail suppressed; and it must be *complete* enough that the operations cited are sufficient to account for all behavior.

The second assumption concerns the user's comprehension of the expert system's activity, which depends on the fundamental inference mechanism of the program and the level at which it is examined. Consider a program that does medical diagnosis using a statistical approach based on Bayes's theorem. It is difficult to imagine what explanation of its actions the program could give if it were queried about computed probabilities. No matter what level of detail is chosen, such a program's actions are not (nor were they intended to be) a model of the reasoning process typically employed by physicians. Although they may be an effective way for the computer to solve diagnosis problems, there is no easy way to interpret these actions in terms that will make them comprehensible to humans unacquainted with the program (see the discussion of the *opacity* of reasoning in Article VII.A).

Thus, the absence of mechanisms for simplifying or reinterpreting computation means that TEIRESIAS's approach is basically a first-order solution to the general problem of explanation. However, in the context of a MYCIN-like expert system, for which TEIRESIAS was designed, the simple AND/OR goal-tree control structure offers a basis for explanations that typically needs little additional clarification. (The operation of TEIRESIAS's explanation facility is illustrated in the lengthy sample protocol at the end of this article.)

The invocation of a rule is taken as the fundamental action of the system. This action, within the framework of the goal tree, accounts for enough of the system's operation to make a recapitulation of such actions an acceptable explanation.

In terms of the constraints noted earlier, TEIRESIAS's explanations are sufficiently detailed—the actions performed by a rule in making a *conclusion*, for instance, correspond closely enough to the normal connotation of that word—that no more detailed explanation is necessary. The explanation is still at a sufficiently high conceptual level that the operations are meaningful, and the explanation is sufficiently complete. There are no other mechanisms or sources of information that the observer needs to know in order to understand how the program reached its conclusions. See Swartout (1981) for a discussion of the explanation capabilities of expert systems in the context of the Digitalis Therapy Advisor (Article VIII.B5).

Knowledge Acquisition: Rule Models and Schemas

When the expert has identified a deficit in the knowledge base of the performance program, TEIRESIAS questions the expert in order to correct the deficit. This process relies heavily on meta-level knowledge about the performance program, encoded in *rule models* and *schemas*. In other words, TEIRESIAS uses these data structures to represent knowledge about what the performance program knows.

The meta-level knowledge about *objects* in the domain includes both structural and organizational information and is specified in *data-structure schemas*. Acquisition of knowledge about new objects takes place as a process of instantiating a schema—creating the required structural components to build the new data structure and then attending to its interrelations with other data structures. By making inquiries in a simple form of English about the values of the schema's components, this knowledge-acquisition process is made to appear to the expert as a natural, high-level inquiry about the new concept. The process is more complex, of course, but the key component is the system's description of its own representation.

TEIRESIAS's *rule models* are empirical generalizations of subsets of rules, indicating commonalities among the rules in that subset. For example, in MYCIN there is a rule model for the subset of rules that conclude affirmatively about *organism category*, indicating that most such rules mention the concepts of *culture site* and *infection type* in their premise. Another rule model notes that those rules that mention *site* and infection *type* in the premise also tend to mention the *portal of entry* of the organism.

The knowledge about the contents of the domain rules represented in the rule models is used by TEIRESIAS to build *expectations* about the dialogue. These expectations are helpful in translating the English statements into the performance program's internal representation and in identifying information missing from the expert's entry. An example of TEIRESIAS's use of rule models in its knowledge-acquisition dialogue is given in the sample protocol below.

Meta-rules and Performance Strategies

In performance programs with sufficiently small knowledge bases (like MYCIN's), exhaustive invocation of the relevant parts of the knowledge base during a consultation is still computationally feasible. However, with the inevitable construction of larger knowledge bases, exhaustive invocation will become unrealistic. In anticipation of this, *meta-rules* are implemented in TEIRESIAS as a means of encoding strategies that can direct the program's actions more selectively than exhaustive invocation can. The following meta-rule is from MYCIN's infectious-disease domain:

META-RULE 001

IF   (1) the infection is a pelvic-abscess, and
           (2) there are rules that mention in their
               premise Enterobacteriaceae, and
           (3) there are rules that mention in their
               premise gram positive rods,

THEN   There is suggestive evidence (.4) that the rules
           dealing with Enterobacteriaceae should be evoked
           before those dealing with gram positive rods.

This rule suggests that, since enterobacteria are commonly associated with a pelvic abscess, it is a good idea to try rules about them first, before the less likely rules mentioning gram positive rods. Note that this meta-rule does not refer to specific object-level rules. Instead, it specifies certain attributes of the rules it refers to, for example, that they mention in their premise Enterobacteriaceae.

An Example: TEIRESIAS in the Context of MYCIN

We now illustrate TEIRESIAS's operation in affiliation with the MYCIN system (see Article VIII.B1), paying particular attention to the explanation and knowledge-acquisition facilities of TEIRESIAS. MYCIN is intended to provide a physician with advice about the diagnosis and drug therapy for bacterial infections. The user interacts with TEIRESIAS, which in turn communicates with the MYCIN system, although the user is unaware of more than one program being involved. The system asks questions about the patient, the infection, the cultures grown from specimens from the patient, and any organisms (bacteria) growing in the culture. (Typically, of course, the exact identity of the organism is not yet known.)

MYCIN's knowledge base is composed of rules that specify a situation (involving information about the patient, culture, and organism) and the conclusions that can be drawn in that situation. For example, to conclude whether a patient suffers from a bacterium in the Enterobacteriaceae category, MYCIN invokes rule 95:

RULE 095

```
IF      The site of the culture is blood, and
        the gram stain is positive, and
        the portal of entry is gastrointestinal tract, and
        [A-the abdomen is the locus of infection, or
        B-the pelvis is the locus of infection]

THEN    There is strongly suggestive evidence that
        Enterobacteriaceae is the class of organisms
        for which therapy should cover.
```

MYCIN asks questions of the physician to determine which rules are applicable in the current case—that is, to determine the "situation." To determine if the organism is of type Enterobacteriaceae, MYCIN would inquire whether each clause in the IF-part of rule 95 were true.

The procedure of working backward from the conclusion to the situation that would make the conclusion true is called *backward chaining* and is MYCIN's fundamental reasoning mechanism. Backward chaining can go several levels deep, meaning that the clauses in a situation that must be true (for the conclusion to be true) might themselves be conclusions of other rules. For example, a condition on the identification of Enterobacteriaceae is that the infection be localized in the abdomen or the pelvis; but this condition is itself a conclusion, and it is only true if its conditions (that the culture from these places is recent and is therapeutically significant) are true. Furthermore, the condition of therapeutic significance has its own conditions, and so on. Here is a protocol showing MYCIN's basic style of interaction (the physician's responses are prefixed by **):

```
————————Patient 281————————

1) Patient's name:

** Albert Hall

2) Sex:

** Male
```

3) Age:

** 34

4) Have you been able to obtain positive microbiological
   information about a possible infection of Albert Hall?

** Yes

──────── Infection 1 ────────

5) What is the infection?

** Primary-Bacteremia

6) Please state when signs and symptoms of infection-1
   first appeared:

** 15-Dec-80 12:00

──────── Culture 1 ────────

7) From what site was the specimen for culture-1 taken?

** Blood

8) Please give the date and time when this blood culture was
   obtained:

** 16-Dec-80 12:00

The first significant organism from this blood culture will be
referred to as:

──────── Organism-1 ────────

9) Enter the identity of organism-1

** Unknown

10) Is organism-1 a rod, or coccus (etc.):

** Rod

11) The gram-stain of organism-1:

** Gram negative

12) Did organism-1 grow in the aerobic bottle?

** Yes

13) Did organism-1 grow in the anaerobic bottle?

** Yes

⋮

My therapy recommendations will be based on the following
probable infection(s) and potential causative organism(s):

INFECTION-1 is PRIMARY-BACTEREMIA
    <Item-1> E.COLI [ORGANISM-1]
    <Item-2> PSEUDOMONAS-AERUGINOSA [ORGANISM-1]

In sum, MYCIN constructs a *goal tree* (see Article II.B2, in Vol. I) of questions
that must be resolved in the course of the consultation to conclude the identity
of a bacterium. When it cannot resolve a question by inference from what it
already knows, it asks the respondent to provide an answer. Each node of the
goal tree has subnodes that result from the application of a rule, as shown in
Figure B–1.

Explanation: HOW and WHY. Suppose that during a consultation
with MYCIN the clinician wants an explanation of the reasoning behind some
question that MYCIN has asked. The explanation given by TEIRESIAS in
response to the physician's question, WHY, involves backing up the goal tree
to the previous node and presenting the rule used to derive the subnode from
its ancestor. (Again, the physician's responses are prefixed by **.)

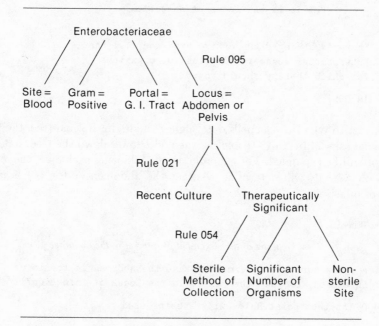

Figure B–1.   A MYCIN goal tree.

First, MYCIN's question:

```
What is the suspected portal of entry of organism-1 into this
sterile site?
```

The physician requests an explanation.

```
** WHY
```

Then TEIRESIAS proceeds to explain it's "reasoning."

```
[I.e., why is it important to determine the suspected portal
of entry of organism-1 into this sterile site?]

[3.0] ... in order to find out about an organism or class of
      organisms for which therapy should cover.

It has already been established that
    [3.1] The site of the culture is blood
    [3.2] The stain of the organism is gram positive

Therefore if:
    [3.3] The portal of entry of the organism is G.I.
    [3.4] [Abdomen is the locus of infection, or
          Pelvis is the locus of infection]

Then
    There is strongly suggestive evidence (.9) that
    Enterobacteriaceae is the class of organisms
    for which therapy should cover.

[Rule 095]
```

In contrast to WHY, which spells out "higher" nodes in the goal tree, the HOW command asks TEIRESIAS to explain the nodes lower down the tree that have been or will be expanded. For example, in the following exchange, the expert asks how MYCIN will determine whether the abdomen or the pelvis is the locus of infection:

```
** HOW [3.4]
```

Note: [3.4] is the prefix of the statement of interest in the exchange above.

```
[I.e., how were you determining that the Abdomen is the locus
of infection, or that the Pelvis is the locus of infection?]

[4.0] At that point Rule 021 was being used.
```

If the doctor now wants to see rule 21, he asks TEIRESIAS to explain HOW it was used, referring to the prefix [4.0] of the statement in which it was mentioned:

```
** HOW [4.0]

[I.e., how was Rule 021 used?]

    [5.0] It has already been established that
    [5.1] the culture is recent.

Therefore if:
    [5.2] There is therapeutically significant disease
          associated with the occurrence of this organism

Then
    It is definite (1.0) that the site of the culture
    is the locus of infection in the patient.
```

The explanation facilities of TEIRESIAS involve climbing up and down MYCIN's goal tree, explaining why questions are asked and how they are answered. If MYCIN makes a misdiagnosis, these same facilities are used to back up through the rules that achieved the diagnosis until the expert has found the faulty one or determined that one is missing. TEIRESIAS is then used to expedite the alteration or construction of rules by the expert. (See Article IX.C8 for a discussion of how a similar explanation facility is used in the tutorial system EXCHECK.)

Knowledge acquisition. TEIRESIAS can help an expert formulate rules in English because it has expectations about what rules "look like." These expectations are stored internally as *rule models* that are formed automatically by examining all the rules in the knowledge base. TEIRESIAS knows, for example, that there is a class of rules that have as their conclusions the probable identity of a bacterium and that these rules typically have as conditions (a) the site of the culture, (b) the stain of the culture, and (c) the probable portal of entry of the bacteria. These rule models help TEIRESIAS translate English versions of new rules into a machine representation acceptable to MYCIN.

To illustrate TEIRESIAS's debugging and correction facilities, we will continue with the consultation shown earlier. Suppose that after MYCIN presents the expert with its diagnosis, TEIRESIAS steps in and checks whether the expert agrees (the physician's response is indicated by **):

```
My therapy recommendation will be based on the following
probable infection(s) and potential causative organism(s):

INFECTION-1 is PRIMARY BACTEREMIA
    <Item-1> E.COLI [ORGANISM-1]
    <Item-2> PSEUDOMONAS-AERUGINOSA [ORGANISM-1]
```

    Now TEIRESIAS steps in.

Are all these identities correct?

** No.

Are there any identities missing?

** Yes.

Which ones?

** KLEBSIELLA-PNEUMONIAE, PROTEUS-NON-MIRABILIS

Are there any identities which shouldn't have appeared?

** Yes.

Which one(s)?

** PSUEDOMONAS-AERUGINOSA

Do you want to
    1] track down the problem yourself, or
    2] allow me to guide the debugging, or
    3] ignore it for now and fix it another time.
Type 1, 2, or 3.

** 2.

If the expert had typed 1, he would have used the HOW and WHY commands to debug the problem, as discussed above.

We'll start with PSEUDOMONAS-AERUGINOSA first:

TEIRESIAS starts debugging by trying to find out why an inappropriate diagnosis occurred. Frequently, solving one problem will make others "go away" as well.

The following rules were used in deducing that the identity of organism-1 is PSEUDOMONAS-AERUGINOSA:

RULE 184
  Since
    [1.1] The category of organism-1 is not known
    [1.2] The gram stain of organism-1 is gram negative
    [1.3] The morphology of organism-1 is rod
    [1.4] the aerobicity of organism-1 is facultative

  There is weakly suggestive evidence (.3) that the identity of organism-1 is PSEUDOMONAS-AERUGINOSA.

Is this rule correct?

Note that this rule, which resulted in the wrong conclusion, is not necessarily an incorrect rule. It might be (and in fact is) the case that it was incorrectly invoked because one or more of its conditions are true when they should be false.

** Yes.

Should its premise have failed for this case?

** Yes.

Which clause of the premise should have failed?

** Clause 1.

> *The expert believes that MYCIN should have known the category of
> ORGANISM-1. MYCIN failed to establish the category, causing rule 184
> to be used.*

Should it have been possible to conclude a category?

** Yes.

Which one?

** Enterobacteriaceae.

There were no rules successfully invoked in the attempt to
deduce that the category of organism-1 is Enterobacteriaceae.

The following (potentially applicable) rules were NOT executed
because the marked [++] clause failed:

RULE 116
     If
     1) The identity of organism-1 is not known
  ++ 2) The gram stain of organism-1 is not known
     3) The morphology of organism-1 is not known
     4) The site of culture-1 is CSF
     5) The infection is meningitis
     6) The age of Albert Hall is less than or
        equal to 2 months

     Then there is weakly suggestive evidence (.33) that the
     category of organism-1 is Enterobacteriaceae

RULE 050
     If
     1) The morphology of organism-1 is rod
     2) The gram stain of organism-1 is gramneg
     3) The aerobicity of organism-1 is facul
  ++ 4) The infection with organism-1 was acquired
        while the patient was hospitalized

     Then there is suggestive evidence (.7) that the category of
     organism-1 is Enterobacteriaceae.

Are all these rules correct?

** Yes.

Should any of them have been successfully invoked?

** No.

> *This would be the case if one of the marked premises was false because it was "stepped on" by yet another rule farther back in the chain.*

Is there a rule missing?

** Yes.

Would you like to give me such a rule now?

** Yes.

Good ...

> *The expert then proposes another rule to TEIRESIAS:*

If:
    1 ** THE PATIENT'S INFECTION IS PRIMARY-BACTEREMIA
    2 ** THE SITE IS ONE OF THE STERILE SITES
Then:
        ** THERE IS EVIDENCE (.8) THAT THE CATEGORY IS
           ENTEROBACTERIACEAE

> *TEIRESIAS parses this rule into its internal representation and then translates it back into English, so that the expert can check it. We pick up the dialogue after the expert has agreed on the parse. TEIRESIAS is applying its rule model.*

I hate to criticize, Dr. Davis, but did you know that most
rules about what the category of an organism might be,
that mention
    the site of a culture
    the infection

Also mention -
    [A] the portal of entry of the organism

Shall I try to write a clause to account for [A]?

** Yes.

> *Here we see one of the utilities of the rule model. TEIRESIAS prompts the expert to add a bit of knowledge that is typically found in rules like these and offers to fix the rule itself. This completion is accomplished by looking at other rules that fit the same rule model, to find the most likely portal-of-entry clause.*

How about -
    [A] The portal of entry is gastrointestinal. OK?

** Yes.

TEIRESIAS then does some finishing up: checking the complete rule with the expert for final approval and asking the expert to write a brief description (for bookkeeping purposes) of why the rule was needed. Finally, it runs the consultation again internally, using the responses from the early part of the dialogue, which it has stored. It turns out that adding the rule above did, in fact, correct the other problems with the first consultation, and this time the diagnosis is satisfactory to the expert.

Summary: TEIRESIAS and Expert Systems

TEIRESIAS aids a human expert in monitoring the performance of a knowledge-based system. When the human expert spots an error in the program's performance, in either the program's conclusions or its line of reasoning, TEIRESIAS assists in finding the source of the error in the database by *explaining* the program's conclusions—retracing the reasoning steps until the faulty (or missing) rule is identified. At this point, TEIRESIAS assists in *knowledge acquisition*, modifying faulty rules or adding new rules to the database. *Meta-level knowledge* about the kinds of rules and concepts in the database is applied to build expectations in TEIRESIAS's *model-based understanding* process. Meta-level knowledge is also used to encode problem-solving *strategies*, in particular, to order the invocation of rules so that those that are most likely to be useful (given the current knowledge of the program) are tried first.

References

The principal reference on TEIRESIAS is the doctoral dissertation by Davis (1976). Applications of meta-knowledge in expert systems are discussed in Davis and Buchanan (1977). See also Davis (1977, 1978, 1980).

C. APPLICATIONS IN CHEMISTRY

C1. Chemical Analysis

COMPUTER PROGRAMS have been developed as aids in almost every aspect of chemistry. As evidenced by recent articles in two journals devoted to uses of computers for chemical problems, *Computers and Chemistry* and *Journal of Chemical Information and Computer Science*, most of the computer programs have focused on numeric problems of data acquisition, data reduction, complex electronic-energy calculations, and the like. By contrast, AI methods have found application in two major classes of nonnumeric chemical-reasoning problems: (a) determining the molecular structure of an unknown organic compound—that is, the analysis or structure-determination problem; and (b) planning a sequence of reactions in order to synthesize organic chemical compounds—the synthesis problem.

Structure Elucidation

The elucidation of molecular structures is fundamental to the application of chemical knowledge to important problems in biology and medicine. Some of the areas in which chemists are actively interested include: (a) identification of naturally occurring chemical compounds isolated from terrestrial or marine organisms; (b) verification of the identity of new synthetic materials; (c) identification of drugs and their metabolites in clinical studies; and (d) detection of metabolic disorders of genetic, developmental, toxic, or infectious origins through the identification of organic constituents excreted in abnormal quantities in human body fluids.

In many circumstances, especially in the areas of interest mentioned above, the powerful analytic techniques of x-ray crystallography and x-ray fine-structure analysis may not be applicable (see Article VII.C3), and chemists must resort to structure elucidation from data obtained by various other methods. Foremost among them historically is mass spectrometry (discussed in detail below). If a chemist wants to determine the molecular structure of an unknown chemical compound, he (or she) first isolates a pure sample of the compound. Two questions must then be answered:

1. What are the atoms in the compound?

2. How are the atoms arranged (joined together) in a three-dimensional structure?

It is relatively simple to determine the constituents of the molecule, but the enormous number of possible three-dimensional arrangements makes the second question especially difficult to answer. It is this problem that is addressed by the structure-elucidation programs. If the unknown substance is a crystal, or can be crystallized, x-ray crystallography can be used to determine the exact locations and connections of atoms in space.

If x-ray crystallography and x-ray fine-structure analysis techniques cannot be applied, the chemist must take a more complicated approach to structure elucidation. No other tests are available to tell the chemist the *exact* molecule; at best, he can use tests that help him discover small, connected clusters of atoms, called *molecular fragments*, which are either present or absent in the compound. Therefore, although the chemist may not know the structure of the molecule, he can identify some of its subparts. From the fragments identified as present in the compound and those known to be absent, the chemist can derive a set of *constraints*. A constraint can be thought of as a piece of a graph that must either occur or not occur in the final graph representation of the molecule. This is how constraints are represented in the structure-elucidation programs we discuss.

From the known constraints for a given molecule under investigation, it is often possible to produce the graphs of all molecules that comply with those constraints. An algorithm was developed by Joshua Lederberg (1964b) to generate all possible acyclic (unringed) molecular structures from a set of atoms; Brown and Masinter (1974) developed an algorithm that worked for cyclic structures as well. Thus, it is now theoretically possible to generate every possible molecular structure containing known subparts, but it is often prohibitively expensive (computationally) to do so. However, the exhaustive generation algorithms can often be constrained to enumerate a relatively small set of candidate molecular structures, one of which is the unknown molecule.

If the number of atoms in an unknown molecule is relatively small, and the number of known constraints is large, a chemist can figure out the molecular structure by hand. However, the manual approach has been significantly augmented by computer programs developed in the DENDRAL project at Stanford University. These programs do not generate all the possible molecular structures and then discard structures according to the constraints. The computation required for the initial generation would be prohibitive. Instead, they use the constraints to ensure that only a small subset of the theoretically possible structures is ever actually generated.

Structure Elucidation with Constraints from Mass Spectrometry

Structure-elucidation programs are designed to help organic chemists determine the molecular structure of unknown compounds. Experimental data about the unknown compounds may be gathered by many different analytic techniques, including mass spectrometry (MS), nuclear magnetic resonance spectroscopy (NMR), infrared spectroscopy (IR), ultraviolet spectroscopy (UV), and "wet chemistry" analysis. The first method mentioned, mass spectrometry, is still a new and developing technique. It is particularly useful when the quantity of the sample to be identified is very small, for mass spectrometry requires only micrograms of a sample.

A mass spectrometer bombards the chemical sample with electrons, causing *fragmentations* and rearrangements of the molecules. Charged fragments are collected by mass. The data from the instrument, recorded in a histogram known as a mass spectrum, show the masses of charged fragments plotted against the relative abundance of the fragments at a given mass. Although the mass spectrum for each molecule may be nearly unique, it is still a difficult task to infer the molecular structure from the 100–300 data points in the mass spectrum. Partly, this is because a spectrum contains "noise peaks" and overlapping peaks originating from many parts of the molecule, but, what is more critical, the theory of mass spectrometry is not complete.

Throughout Section C, the following terms will be used to describe the actions of molecules in the mass spectrometer:

Fragmentation—the breaking of a connected graph (molecule) into fragments by breaking one or more edges (bonds) within the graph.

Atom *migration*—the detachment of nodes (atoms) from one fragment and their reattachment to other fragments. This process alters the mass of all of the fragments.

Mass spectral *process*—a fragmentation followed by zero or more atom migrations.

Other analytic techniques are commonly used in conjunction with, or instead of, mass spectrometry. There are some rudimentary capabilities in structure-elucidation programs for interpreting proton NMR and Carbon 13 (13C) NMR spectra. For the most part, however, interpretation of other spectroscopic and chemical data has been left to the chemist. The programs still need to provide a means for integrating the chemist's partial knowledge into the generation of structural alternatives.

Organization of the Chemistry-applications Section

The following five articles cover the most important research in applying AI to problems in chemistry. The first three articles describe the original DENDRAL system, the subsequent work on the CONGEN generator program, and the Meta-DENDRAL program, which attempts to formulate automatically rules of mass spectrometry from examples of actual molecule-spectrum pairs. Article VII.C3 describes the CRYSALIS system, which works in the domain of x-ray crystallographic analysis and has an interesting, *blackboard*-style AI architecture. Finally, Article VII.C4 describes three research systems, LHASA,

SECS, and SYNCHEM, all in the area of synthetic chemistry. Here, the goal is not to figure out the structure of an unknown molecule, but rather to find a technique for actually synthesizing a known substance in the laboratory.

C2. The DENDRAL Programs

C2a. Heuristic DENDRAL

THE HEURISTIC DENDRAL program finds the relatively small set of possible molecular structures of known constituent atoms that could account for the given spectroscopic analysis of an unknown molecule. In 1964, Joshua Lederberg developed the DENDRAL algorithm, which, given a set of constituent atoms, enumerates all possible acyclic (unringed) molecular structures that could be formed. This algorithm allowed an exhaustive approach to structure elucidation—the problem of specifying how a complex molecule is formed from its component atoms. In 1965, the DENDRAL project began at Stanford University, with one intent to show that algorithmic programs that produce results exhaustively but at enormous expense could be augmented by some of the heuristic knowledge of experts to produce much the same results with a fraction of the effort.

The Heuristic DENDRAL program achieved this objective by augmenting the use of the DENDRAL structure-enumeration algorithm with data from mass-spectrographic analysis of the unknown molecule and a set of rules used by expert chemists to infer constraints on molecular structures from such data. Pressing expert chemists to formulate rules about mass spectrometry, however, proved to be an arduous process—the theory of mass spectrometry was incomplete and the rules about it were inexact and difficult for experts to explicate. Therefore, in 1970, the Meta-DENDRAL project addressed the problem of automatically inferring these rules of mass spectrometry from examples of molecular structures that had been properly analyzed by humans (see Article VII.C2c).

In 1976, the CONGEN program became the center of attention in the DENDRAL project. The limitations of the DENDRAL algorithm were such that Heuristic DENDRAL could generate only acyclic structures: ketones, alcohols, ethers, thiols, thioethers, and amines. CONGEN replaced Lederberg's original acyclic structure generator with a generator that did not have the acyclic limitation. CONGEN has been used as a stand-alone system by research chemists and is discussed in Article VII.C2b.

DENDRAL has three functional parts, namely, PLAN, GENERATE, and TEST:

1. PLAN. Planning in this context means redefining the problem in terms that reduce the effort of the problem solver—for example, the problem of finding all possible combinations of a set of atoms is redefined

106

to the problem of finding all such combinations consistent with constraints derived from mass spectrometry. Automatic inference of these
constraints is the planning part of Heuristic DENDRAL. The constraints
are listed in two parts: molecular fragments (clusters of atoms) that *must*
be in the final molecular structure and fragments that *must not* appear
in the final structure.

2. GENERATE. Within PLAN's constraints, the DENDRAL algorithm generates only those structures that do not include forbidden subparts or
   exclude mandatory subparts. The generator was originally derived from
   Lederberg's algorithm. When CONGEN was implemented as a stand-
   alone system, these constraints were provided by the chemists using the
   program, not by the planning part.

3. TEST. This last part of the program ranks the resulting list of candidate
   structures by simulating their behavior in a mass spectrometer. The
   structures resulting in simulated spectra closest to the empirical one are
   ranked highest.

Heuristic DENDRAL thus has *two* sets of rules that encode the mass-
spectrometry knowledge: (a) rules applied during planning that interpret
mass-spectral data and infer molecular fragments and (b) rules applied during
testing that simulate the action of the mass spectrometer on the structure
or structures proposed by CONGEN and that predict peaks that should be
observed in the spectrum of the molecule.

Planning: Inferring Constraints from the Mass Spectrum

The Heuristic DENDRAL program is given the mass spectrum and the
atomic constituents of a molecule. From the latter it can infer the molecular
weight, M, of the molecule. Many of the rules for interpreting mass spectra
include M, for example, the following rule (see Fig. C2a–1):

> If the spectrum for the molecule has two peaks at masses
> x_1 and x_2 such that
>   a. $x_1 + x_2 = M + 28$, and
>   b. $x_1 - 28$ is a high peak, and
>   c. $x_2 - 28$ is a high peak, and
>   d. at least one of x_1 or x_2 is high,
> Then the molecule contains a ketone group.

This piece of knowledge about mass spectrometry allows Heuristic DENDRAL
to constrain its structure-generating algorithm to produce molecules with a
ketone group as a mandatory constituent. Many rules like this one significantly
constrain the number of molecules generated by the structure generator.
For example, given the spectrum for a molecule containing 8 carbons, 16
hydrogens, and 1 oxygen, the constraint-generating program can eliminate

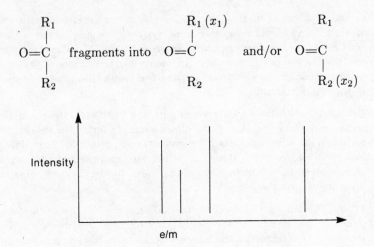

Figure C2a–1.   Mass spectrum data.

from consideration (i.e., place on a list of forbidden structures called BADLIST) all possible structures except those containing ethyl ketone 3, which reduces the number of generated molecular structures from the topologically possible 790 to a constrained set of three (called the GOODLIST).

The Generator

The algorithm for generating molecular structures is complicated and has no AI content; we discuss it only in general terms and refer the reader to Buchanan, Sutherland, and Feigenbaum (1969) for a more detailed presentation. Article VII.C2b discusses the more recently developed CONGEN generator.

There are several design characteristics of the generator that are related to the enormous number of molecules combinatorially possible in an analysis problem. First, the generator must be *proved* to be complete—it must be able to generate all topologically possible molecular structures. It should also be nonredundant; that is, it should generate each structure only once. Redundancy was a problem for structures with rings, because Lederberg's algorithm treated symmetrically identical candidate molecules as unique structures. A third characteristic is that the generator should be flexible enough to be focused by constraints from the planning part—it should not blindly generate all possible structures, but only those meeting the constraints. If GOODLIST and BADLIST are empty, it should generate all isomers (structural variants) of the given composition.

Some simple checks are made by the generator. The composition should be compatible with the constraints inferred from the spectrum, and the structures generated should have only the types and amounts of atoms specified in the composition. Finally, the generator should not produce a structure known to be unstable.

The structure generator essentially "grows" molecules, starting with a small fragment of the molecule and adding pieces of the composition to it. At any point in the growing process, there are numerous atoms or molecular fragments that can be added to the growing structure, and there are many places where these parts can be attached. But generally the constraints offered by GOODLIST and BADLIST limit the number of possible structures that might be grown at any point in the process.

The Testing and Ranking Routines

The programs MSPRUNE and MSRANK (Varkony, Carhart, and Smith, 1977) employ a large body of knowledge about the process of molecular fragmentation in a mass spectrometer to make testable predictions from each plausible candidate molecule. Predicted data are compared to the data from the unknown compound, and some candidates are thrown out (by MSPRUNE) while others are ranked (by MSRANK).

MSPRUNE works with (a) a list of candidate structures from the structure generator and (b) the mass spectrum of the unknown molecule. It uses a fairly simple model of mass spectrometry (encoded in rules) to predict commonly expected fragmentations for each candidate structure. Predictions that deviate greatly from the observed spectrum are considered prima facie evidence of incorrectness, and the corresponding structures are pruned from the list. MSRANK then uses more subtle rules of mass spectrometry to rank the remaining structures according to the number of predicted peaks found (and not found) in the observed data, weighted by measures of importance of the processes producing those peaks.

Research Results

The Heuristic DENDRAL project, from 1968 to the present, and including CONGEN, has produced a number of results of significance to chemists. The work has shown that it is possible for a computer program to equal the performance of experts in some very specialized areas of science. Published papers on the program's analysis of aliphatic ketones, amines, ethers, alcohols, thiols, and thioethers (Duffield et al., 1969; Schroll et al., 1969; Buchs et al., 1970) make the point that although the program does not know more than an expert (and, in fact, knows far less), it performs well on the structure-elucidation task because of its systematic search through the space of *possible* molecular structures and its systematic use of what it does know to constrain the list of possibilities.

A paper on the program's analysis of estrogenic steroids notes that the program can solve structure-elucidation problems for complex organic molecules (Smith et al., 1972). Another paper, on the analysis of mass spectra of mixtures of estrogenic steroids (without prior purification), establishes the program's ability to do better than experts on some problems (Smith et al., 1973). With mixtures, the program succeeds where people fail; the task of correlating data points with each possible fragmentation of each possible component of the mixture is too difficult for humans to do. Several articles based on results from CONGEN demonstrate its power and utility for solving problems of medical and biochemical importance (Smith, 1975; Smith and Carhart, 1976; Buchanan, 1976; Mitchell and Schwenzer, 1978; Varkony, Carhart, and Smith, 1977).

DENDRAL programs have been used in determining the structures of the following kinds of molecules:

1. terpenoid natural products from plant and marine animal sources,

2. marine sterols,

3. organic acids in human urine and other body fluids,

4. photochemical rearrangement products,

5. impurities in manufactured chemicals,

6. conjugates of pesticides with sugars and amino acids,

7. antibiotics,

8. metabolites of microorganisms, and

9. insect hormones and pheromones.

CONGEN (discussed in the next article) has also been applied to published structure-elucidation problems by students in organic chemistry classes to check the accuracy and completeness of published solutions. In several cases, the program found structures that were plausible alternatives to the published structures (based on problem constraints that appeared in the article). This kind of information served as a valuable check on conclusions drawn from experimental data.

References

See Lindsay et al. (1980) for a thorough and current treatment of the DENDRAL programs. Buchanan and Feigenbaum (1978) is a shorter description of the programs. Also see Buchanan, Sutherland, and Feigenbaum (1969, 1970) and Lederberg (1964b).

C2b.   CONGEN and Its Extensions

CONGEN (for CONstrained GENerator) is a program that was designed in 1976 to replace the old DENDRAL generator of acyclic (unringed) structures. It has proved to be a powerful stand-alone program to assist the chemist in determining the molecular structure of unknown compounds. The purpose of CONGEN was twofold: (a) to allow the user to specify interactively certain types of structural information determined from any of several sources (e.g., spectroscopy, chemical degradation, isolation) and (b) to generate an exhaustive and nonredundant list of structures consistent with this information. Unlike the original Heuristic DENDRAL program, it does not infer *constraints* from mass spectra but allows the chemist to specify them. Another difference between CONGEN and Heuristic DENDRAL is that the newer program can generate *cyclic* as well as acyclic molecular structures. The generation is a stepwise process, and the program allows interaction at every stage so that, based on partial results, the chemist may be reminded of additional information he (or she) can specify, thus limiting further the number of structural possibilities.

CONGEN breaks down the problem statement given by the chemist in several different ways; for example, (a) hydrogen atoms are omitted until the final steps of processing, (b) parts of the graph containing no cycles are generated separately from cyclic parts (and combined at the end), (c) cycles containing only unlabeled nodes are generated before the nodes are labeled with the names of chemical atoms (e.g., carbon or nitrogen), and (d) cycles containing only three-connected nodes (e.g., nitrogen or tertiary carbon) are generated before two-connected nodes (e.g., oxygen or secondary carbon) are mapped onto the edges. At each step, several constraints may be applied to limit the number of emerging chemical graphs (Carhart et al., 1975).

There are two algorithms at the heart of CONGEN whose validity in producing nonredundant structures has been mathematically proved (Brown and Masinter, 1974; Masinter et al., 1974) and whose computer implementation has been well tested. Combined, they are designed to determine all topologically unique ways of assembling a given set of atoms, each with an associated valence, into molecular structures. The atoms may be chemical atoms with standard chemical valences, or they may be names representing molecular fragments (superatoms) of any desired complexity, where the valence corresponds to the total number of bonding sites available within the superatom. The algorithms can be thought of as performing *problem reduction* and *reconstruction*, or *subproblem recomposition*, on molecular structures.

The first, *partitioning*, algorithm breaks down the problem of finding a complete molecular structure into subproblems, for example, to determine the structures of the ringed and unringed components of the molecule. The second, *embedding*, algorithm combines the substructures, found by partitioning, into complete molecular structures. Clearly, because of the combinatorics involved, neither partitioning nor reconstruction can be unconstrained. There are simply too many possible subproblems to solve, and each of them may have many solutions. Consequently, combining subproblem solutions exhaustively is not feasible. In both algorithms, constraints are brought to bear to limit the size of the problem. There are three types of these constraints:

1. *Graph theoretic.* Symmetric structures are not considered unique.

2. *Syntactic.* Structures are constrained by the valences of the constituent atoms. For example,

$$C \atop | \atop C - O - C$$

   is impossible because oxygen is bivalent; that is, it has only two bonding sites.

3. *Semantic.* The chemist provides additional information about the molecule that will help to determine its structure.

Substantial work has gone into modifying the two basic procedures, particularly the structure-generation algorithm, allowing it to accept a variety of other structural information (constraints) and using it to prune the list of structural possibilities. Current capabilities include specification of good and bad substructural features, good and bad ring sizes, proton distributions, and connectivities of isoprene units (Carhart and Smith, 1976). Usually the chemist has additional information (if only some general rules about chemical stability), of which the program has little knowledge but which the chemist can use to limit the number of structural possibilities. For example, the chemist may know that the chemical procedures for isolating the compound would change organic acids to esters; thus, the program would not need to consider structures with unchanged acid groups. In CONGEN, the chemist is given the facilities to impart this knowledge interactively to the program.

To make CONGEN easy for research chemists to use, the program has an interactive "front end." This interface contains EDITSTRUC, an interactive structure editor; DRAW, a teletype-oriented structure-display program; and the CONGEN "executive" program, which ties together the individual subprograms and assists the user in various tasks such as defining superatoms (small groups of connected atoms) and substructures, creating and editing lists of constraints or superatoms, and saving and restoring superatoms, constraints, and structures. Recently, CONGEN was rewritten to search *depth first*, so that examples could be produced right from the beginning of the computation. This often allows the chemist to see that a particular problem has been poorly or incorrectly constrained and to stop the computation early.

The current system is running on the SUMEX computing facility at Stanford University and is available nationwide over the TYMNET network. It has recently been completely rewritten in the BCPL programming language to run on various other machines.

Limitations and Extensions

Although there are now computer programs, including CONGEN, that assist chemists in constructing structural isomers from information about partial structures, the programs have one serious, common limitation. Each program must use nonoverlapping structural fragments as building blocks. This limitation leads to at least two important problems. First, the chemist using such a program must select nonoverlapping partial structures; otherwise, an incomplete set of structures will result. This procedure, done manually, is time-consuming and prone to error. Second, as a consequence of the first step, problems are solved less efficiently by the programs because a detailed environment of fewer atoms has been specified (to ensure that there are no overlaps).

The GOODLIST INTERPRETER is a first attempt to remove this limitation by simulating the manual procedure that the chemist follows to arrive at a set of nonoverlapping constraints. It is designed to make more efficient use of information about required structural features (GOODLIST plus superatoms) of an unknown compound. Some early successes have demonstrated that new problems are brought within the realm of solution by the GOODLIST INTERPRETER that are impossible in CONGEN alone, due to the constraints on computational resources.

Stereochemistry

One of the most important new additions to CONGEN deals with the problem of enumerating all the stereoisomers of a given compound.

The mathematical problem of enumerating stereoisomers was solved by James Nourse. Considerations of symmetry as embodied in the mathematical theory of groups were critical to the solution. Coupled with the stereoisomer generator, and given an empirical formula and some constraints, CONGEN can generate all the stereoisomers that are possible solutions to the unknown target molecule to be elucidated.

While this approach to the enumeration of stereoisomers involves very few, if any, AI techniques, it solves a problem that human beings find very difficult to solve. Chemists usually learn to solve this problem through visual intuition. The mathematics involved is deep enough so that many chemists will not have the patience to learn enough about the algorithm to apply its insights in enumerating stereoisomers. One of the central problems for AI work in chemistry now is how to use this new facility in structure elucidation.

EXAMINE

Often in the course of a structure-elucidation problem, a large number of candidate structures, perhaps a hundred or more, are generated, and additional constraints must be derived, either from further data analysis or from new experiments. The EXAMINE function, written by Neil Gray, works from within CONGEN to survey, classify, display, or discard structures. This function is very useful to the chemist who is searching for features common to a large number of the structures or for features that are unique to certain structures. The insights gained from EXAMINE can be used in planning new experiments or in further data analysis. In pursuit of these objectives, the chemist can define functional groups and other structural features or can work with a predefined library of them. The EXAMINE function is then called, and it examines the list of candidate structures for the presence or absence of these features.

For example, the chemist can ask EXAMINE to look for all structures with exactly one labile proton. (A labile proton is a hydrogen atom attached to a nitrogen atom or to an oxygen atom.) The chemist can represent this structure in EXAMINE as an exclusive-OR statement: exactly one hydrogen attached to an oxygen atom in the structure OR (exclusive) exactly one hydrogen attached to a nitrogen atom in the structure. The user can then request EXAMINE to draw those structures that have this characteristic and those that do not, to produce summary statistics on its frequency of occurrence, or to discard those structures with or without it. While CONGEN is always able to discard or prune away structures that do not satisfy certain constraints, EXAMINE provides the interactive ability to develop Boolean combinations of constraints for pruning, substructure search, or subsequent classification.

REACT

Before spectroscopy became a major tool of the structural chemist, all structure elucidation had to be done by means of reaction chemistry, which is still a major tool in solving structures. REACT is an interactive program written by Tomas Varkony, Dennis Smith, and Carl Djerassi (1978). Although it is a close relative to the synthetic programs described in Article VII.C4, its purpose is to aid chemists in the structure-elucidation task rather than in finding new synthetic routes.

To show how REACT works to reduce the number of candidate structures found by CONGEN, consider the following example. A dehydration reaction can be expressed as a production rule of the form: "If you see the pattern C—C—O, convert it to the pattern C=C." We now suppose that a dehydration reaction was applied to the unknown in question and yielded three distinct structures, because the pattern C—C—O occurred in the molecule in three different places. This information can be used to eliminate structures from those under consideration. The structure list generated by CONGEN is passed to REACT, the dehydration reaction is defined by the user and then applied to all the candidate structures, and those that do not yield exactly three products can be eliminated from consideration as candidate structures.

Although REACT does not contain stereochemical, conformational, or electronic information (the electronegativities of its atoms and groups), it still performs reliably in its structure-elucidation function. Reactions used for structure determination tend to have high yield, to be reliable, and to involve simple separations. The reactions operate under a wide variety of conditions and usually involve rather simple changes to the unknown molecule. Thus, the perception routines do not need the sophisticated stereochemical, conformational, and electronic information of the organic-synthesis programs discussed above.

Summary

Research in the DENDRAL project has followed two themes: to build a performance program for analysis of molecular structures and to explore some problems of scientific inference with AI methods. The performance of Heuristic DENDRAL has been evaluated in the same way as that of a research chemist—by publications. In addition, CONGEN is used daily by chemists to help solve structure-elucidation problems.

Because of the combinatoric size of analysis problems, exhaustive problem-solving methods were not an option, and much thought was given to what knowledge enabled chemists to solve these problems. DENDRAL was one of the first programs to demonstrate the power of encoding domain-specific, heuristic expertise and was therefore one of the first projects to recognize knowledge acquisition as a major problem in AI (Buchanan, Sutherland, and Feigenbaum, 1969; Davis, 1976). The next article (VII.C2c) discusses automatic inference of rules as one solution to the problem of knowledge acquisition.

References

In addition to the DENDRAL references in the previous article, the following may be of interest: Brown, Masinter, and Hjelmeland (1974), Brown and Masinter (1974), Carhart et al. (1975), Carhart and Smith (1976), Masinter et al. (1974), Sheikh et al. (1970), and Smith and Carhart (1978).

C2c. Meta–DENDRAL

THE domain-specific rules that constitute DENDRAL's knowledge about mass spectrometry were derived from consultation with experts in that field. Since the consultation process is time-consuming, two alternatives to handcrafting knowledge bases have been explored. One is *interactive transfer of expertise*, as described in Article VII.B. The other is *automatic theory formation*. Meta-DENDRAL is a program of the latter type. The rule-formation task that Meta-DENDRAL performs is similar to grammatical inference, sequence extrapolation, and concept formation and is classified in AI as learning (see Chap. XIV, in Vol. III). Programs that perform these tasks can all be thought of as "induction" programs, because they formulate general rules (or concepts, or patterns) from examples.

Meta-DENDRAL is designed to infer theories (rule sets) for the Heuristic DENDRAL program (Article VII.C2a), which represents knowledge about mass spectrometry as production rules. Automatic rule formation was chosen as a paradigm for Meta-DENDRAL for two general reasons. First, this design poses interesting epistemological questions, and, second, as mentioned before, it is an arduous task to derive rules from human consultants, especially when the task domain has only a small number of experts (as is the case in mass spectrometry).

Representation of Knowledge About Mass Spectrometry

In DENDRAL, knowledge about the fragmentation processes in a mass spectrometer is represented in the form of production rules. Each rule specifies a bond fragmentation in a particular context in a molecule. These rules are used by DENDRAL during its TEST phase to predict mass-spectral data points, given a certain molecular structure. For example, one simple rule is:

R1. N—C—C—C $\rightarrow$ N—$C * C$—C .

Rules are interpreted for each molecule in the following way:

1. Find all places in the molecule that match the subgraph expressed by the left-hand side of the rule.

2. For each match, break the molecule at the bond marked with an asterisk in the right-hand side of the rule and save the fragment associated with the atoms to the left of the asterisk.

3. Record the mass of all saved fragments.

Note that no *migration* of atoms between fragments is predicted by rule R1.

The language of processes (right-hand sides of rules) is relatively simple: One or more bonds from the left-hand side may break, and zero, one, or more atoms may migrate between fragments. The interpretation of rule R1 in the example above is straightforward: If a molecule contains a nitrogen atom and three carbon atoms bonded as N—C—C—C, then it will fragment in the mass spectrometer between the middle two carbon atoms, and the N—C fragment will be recorded in the spectrometer as a peak at the point in the spectrum corresponding to the molecular weight of this fragment.

Formation of Mass-spectral Rules

The task of Meta-DENDRAL is to infer rules, like R1 above, from empirical data. Meta-DENDRAL is provided with descriptions of the structures of a related set of molecules, and with the set of peaks produced by the fragmentation of each molecule in the mass spectrometer. From these data it infers a small and fairly general set of mass-spectral rules to account for the fragmentations of the molecules and the corresponding spectral peaks.

Training instances. In order to learn rules, the Meta-DENDRAL program is presented with many examples of actual input-output pairs from the mass spectrometer. Each pair represents a molecular graph structure, together with a single data point from the mass spectrum for that structure. The rules to be learned constitute a representation of the relevant fragmentations in the mass spectrometer. Typically, the program starts with a training set of 6–10 related molecules and their associated spectra, each containing 50–150 data points—peaks marking the masses of recorded fragments (and the relative abundance of fragments at those masses).

In a large molecule, rule R1 may apply more than once. For example, the spectrum of $CH_3—CH_2—CH_2—NH—CH_2—CH_2—CH_2—CH_3$ will contain data points at masses 72 and 86 corresponding to the two fragments derived from the application of this rule:

$$CH_3—CH_2—CH_2—NH—CH_2$$

and

$$CH_2—NH—CH_2—CH_2—CH_2—CH_3 \ .$$

For a number or reasons, data points are not associated uniquely with a single fragmentation and atom-migration process (rule). For example, a single process may occur more than once in a molecule (as above), or more than one process may produce identical fragments, producing peaks at the same mass points in the spectra.

Spectral Data Points and Mass-spectral Processes:
Statistical and Semantically Constrained Associations

Purely statistical learning programs (Jurs, 1974) find associations indicated by the data without judging the meaningfulness of these associations. This feature can be advantageous; at times, investigators' biases inhibit their seeing important associations. But it is a disadvantage when the number of associations is so large that the meaningful ones, unmarked, get lost in the crowd.

In contrast to statistical approaches, Meta-DENDRAL utilizes a *semantic model* of the domain. This model has been included for two important reasons. First, it provides guidance for the rule-formation program in a space of rules that is much too large to search exhaustively and in a domain in which input data are often ambiguous. Second, it provides a check for the meaningfulness of associations produced by the program in a domain in which the trivial or meaningless associations far outnumber the important ones.

Semantic model of the domain. The base-level, or zero-order, theory of mass spectrometry states that every subset of bonds within a molecule may break and that the resulting fragments, plus or minus migrating atoms, will all be recorded. This zero-order model of mass spectrometry is not specific enough to constrain effectively the rule search. Therefore, some general guidelines have been imposed on it, the so-called *half-order* theory.

The half-order theory asserts that bonds will break and atoms will migrate to produce data points. This theory orders the break-and-migrate process according to the following constraints:

Constraints on fragmentations:

1. Double bonds and triple bonds do not break.

2. No aromatic bonds break.

3. Only fragments larger than two carbon atoms show up in the data.

4. Two bonds to the same carbon atom cannot break together.

5. No more than three bonds break in any one fragmentation.

6. No more than two complete fragmentations occur in one process.

7. At most two rings fragment in a multiple-step process.

Constraints on atom migration:

1. At most two hydrogen atoms can migrate after a fragmentation.

2. At most one H_2O unit is lost after any fragmentation.

3. At most one CO unit is lost after any fragmentation.

One of the most helpful features of this model is its *flexibility:* Any of the parameters can be easily changed by a chemist to fit his model of the process; any of these assumptions can be removed and, as discussed in the following section, additional statements substituted or added. This power to guide rule formation results in the program's discovering only rules within a well-known framework; on the other hand, it also results automatically in rules that are meaningful to the domain.

A chemist will often know more about the mass spectrometry of a class of molecules than is embodied in the half-order theory. It is important, then, to be able to augment the program's model by specifying class-specific knowledge to the program. This capability provides a way of forming new rules in the context of additional intuitions or biases about mass spectrometry. A chemist can thus see the most interesting rules (as defined by the augmentations) before the other rules. For example, one might be interested in rules that mention at least one nitrogen atom before one looks at the numerous (and generally less interesting) rules that mention only carbon and hydrogen substructures.

Learning strategy. The Meta-DENDRAL program is based on a generator of production rules that uses predetermined syntax operating under the constraints of a semantic world model. The operation of Meta-DENDRAL can be summarized as follows.

Input. Recall that Meta-DENDRAL is not a structure-elucidation program but infers rules of mass spectrometry, which associate molecular structures and their mass spectra. Thus, the input to the program is

    a. the structure of each of a set of related molecules,

    b. the spectral data points (peaks) for each of the molecules, and

    c. the half-order theory (or some semantic theory to constrain the generation of rules).

Step 1: *INTSUM*. For each molecule, explain each peak in its spectrum by finding one or more fragmentation process that would account for the peak. The number of plausible fragmentation processes is limited by

    a. considering only the fragmentations that are allowed by the half-order theory (e.g., no spectral peak can be explained by a fragmentation process that involves breaking a double bond) and

    b. considering only fragmentations that produce fragments with a molecular weight corresponding to the weight represented by the peak. (Recall that each peak in a mass spectrum represents a number of molecular fragments of a given mass.)

For example, if the total weight of the molecule under inspection is M, and the spectrum has a large peak associated with a molecular weight of $M - 47$ mass units, then the only fragmentation processes considered as explanations for this point would be those that produce a fragment with a molecular weight of $M - 47$. The tens, or hundreds, of other processes that produce fragmentations consistent with the half-order theory, like cleaving off a hydrogen atom, are not even considered. After each data point in the spectrum for each molecule has been explained by a plausible fragmentation process, the list of processes is summarized, since the same fragmentation processes will often be found to account for many spectral data points. The final product of INTSUM is a list of fragmentation processes with the total evidence for each such process.

Step 2: *RULEGEN.* The rules provided by INTSUM each account for a single fragmentation process in the context of a single molecule. As such, they are not general. The problem with general rules, on the other hand, is that a single one may subsume several of INTSUM's very specific fragmentations, *but also* fragmentations not represented in the set produced by INTSUM. That is, a general rule may correctly explain many data points in mass spectra (positive evidence) but may also predict points that do not occur in any of the spectra (negative evidence). The purpose of RULEGEN is to find a set of rules that are more general than those of INTSUM, using positive evidence as a criterion of success. Negative evidence introduced by these rules is handled by a later step, called RULEMOD.

RULEGEN works by "growing" a tree of fragmentation rules, starting with one that is overly general and adding features to it so that it becomes more constrained. The rule that RULEGEN starts with is $X * X$, that is, the bond between any atoms will break, and the mass of fragment X will be recorded in the mass spectrometer as a peak. Obviously, every fragmentation rule is a specialization of this one, and it is too general to be interesting. But by specifying values for four features—the identity of X, the number of nonhydrogen neighbors of X, the number of hydrogen neighbors of X, and the number of doubly bonded neighbors of X—the general rule $X * X$ can be grown into something more interesting.

Step 3: *RULEMOD.* RULEGEN can generate rules that predict nonexistent data points in the mass-spectral data. This negative evidence is the cost of the coarse method used by RULEGEN for finding general rules. RULEMOD "tidies up" the rules produced by RULEGEN by merging rules, eliminating redundancies, and making rules more specific or more general. In addition, if a rule has been used successfully for a time, but an instance is found in which it is inappropriate, RULEMOD can modify the rule accordingly.

Output. The output of Meta-DENDRAL is a set of mass-spectral fragmentation rules that are specialized enough to be interesting, but general enough to be efficient and nonredundant.

The Meta-DENDRAL Program

The program itself is organized as a series of plan-generate-test steps, as found in many AI systems (Feigenbaum, Buchanan, and Lederberg, 1971). After scanning a set of several hundred molecular structure/spectral data-point pairs, the program searches the space of fragmentation rules for plausible explanations and then modifies its rules on the basis of detailed testing. When rules generated from a training set are added to the model and another block of data is examined, the rule set is extended and modified further to explain the new data. The program iteratively modifies rules formed from the initial training set (adding to them), but it is currently unable to "undo" rules.

Integrating subsequent data. A requirement for any practical learning program is the ability to integrate newly acquired data into an evolving knowledge base. New data may dictate that new rules be added to the knowledge base or that existing rules be modified or eliminated. Rules may be *added* to the rule base by running RULEGEN on the new data and then running RULEMOD on the combined set of new and previously generated rules.

When an existing rule is *modified*, it is important to maintain the integrity of the modified rule over past training instances. Consider the following example: A new training instance is acquired and, after questions of *credit assignment* are resolved, it is decided that rule R was incorrectly "triggered" by some situation S. The left-hand side of rule R must be modified so that it no longer matches S. In general, there would be many changes possible to R that would kill the match to S, but some are better than others. The correct changes to R are those that do not alter past correct applications of R. Of course, there is no way of knowing which of the possible changes to R will turn out to be correct for future data, and once a change is selected, there is still the possibility of backtracking at some future point.

Mitchell (1977) developed a method for representing all versions of the left-hand side of a rule that are consistent with the observed data for all iterations thus far. This representation is referred to as the *version space* of the rule. By examining the version space of R, one can answer the question "Which of the recommended changes to R will preserve its performance on past instances?" The answer is, simply, "Any changes that yield a version of the rule contained in the version space." Using version spaces avoids the problem of selecting a single unretractable modification to R and therefore eliminates the need for backtracking. For example, all the elements of the version space that match some negative instance S are eliminated. Similarly, when new data are encountered in which a situation S' is found to correctly trigger R, only those elements of the version space that match S' are retained (see Article XIV.D3a, in Vol. III, for a complete discussion).

Results

One measure of the proficiency of Meta-DENDRAL is the ability of a DENDRAL program using the learned rules to predict correct spectra of new molecules. One of the DENDRAL performance programs ranks a list of plausible hypotheses (candidate molecules) according to the similarity of their predictions (predicted spectra) to observed data. The rank of the correct hypothesis (i.e., the molecule actually associated with the observed spectrum) provides a quantitative measure of the "discriminatory power" of the rule set.

The Meta-DENDRAL program has successfully rediscovered known, published rules of mass spectrometry for two classes of molecules. What is more important, it has discovered new rules for three closely related families of structures for which rules had not previously been reported. These are the mono-, di-, and tri-keto androstanes, which share the common structural skeleton shown in Figure C2c–1.

Meta-DENDRAL's rules for these classes have been published in the chemistry literature (Buchanan et al., 1976). Evaluations of all five sets of rules are discussed in that publication. This work demonstrates the utility of Meta-DENDRAL for rule formation in mass spectrometry for classes of structures.

The most recent application of Meta-DENDRAL has been to a second spectroscopic technique—*13C–nuclear magnetic resonance* (13C–NMR) spectroscopy (Mitchell and Schwenzer, 1978). This version provides the opportunity to direct the induction machinery of Meta-DENDRAL under a model of 13C–NMR spectroscopy. It generates rules that associate the resonance frequency of a carbon atom in a magnetic field with the local structural environment of the atom. Note that for 13C–NMR spectroscopy there is no requirement for a half-order theory, since there is no equivalent to the fragmentation processes that occur in mass spectroscopy. Each data point is assigned to a unique atom in the molecule prior to the Meta-DENDRAL run. Thus, there is no analogue of the INTSUM phase required by the mass-spectroscopy version. Instead, an assigned spectrum (atoms to data points) is given directly to RULEGEN.

The 13C–NMR rules have been generated and applied in a candidate-molecule-ranking program similar to the one described above. Also, 13C–NMR rules formulated by the program for two classes of structures have been successfully applied to identify the spectra of additional molecules (of the same classes, but outside the set of training data used in generating the rules). The

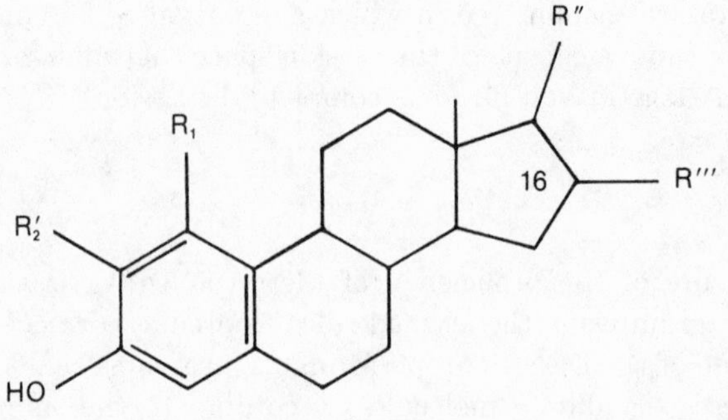

Figure C2c–1.   Structural skeleton for three classes of androstanes.

rule-based molecule-ranking program performs at the level of a well-educated chemist in both the mass-spectral and the 13C–NMR domains.

References

See Lindsay et al. (1980) for a thorough and current treatment of the DENDRAL programs, including Meta-DENDRAL. The thesis by Mitchell (1978) is the principal source on this system. Article XIV.D4b in the chapter on learning and inductive reasoning (in Vol. III) is a description of Meta-DENDRAL as a learning program.

C3. CRYSALIS

THE CRYSALIS system is an attempt to apply AI methodology to the task domain of protein crystallography. Although the computer has been an essential tool in x-ray crystallography research for many years, nearly all its applications have been in data collection, data reduction, Fourier analysis, graphics, and other essentially numerical tasks (Feigenbaum, Engelmore, and Johnson, 1977). Those aspects of molecular-structure inference that require symbolic reasoning or that use a significant amount of judgmental knowledge have traditionally been performed manually. A prime example is the task of *electron-density-map* interpretation.

In the course of deriving a protein structure, the crystallographer generates an electron density map, a three-dimensional description of the electron density distribution of a molecule. Due to the resolution imposed by the experimental conditions, the electron density map is an indistinct image of the structure and does not reveal the positions of individual atoms. The crystallographer must interpret the map in light of auxiliary data and general principles of protein chemistry in order to derive a complete description of the molecular structure. The goal of the CRYSALIS system is to integrate these diverse sources of knowledge and data to try to match the crystallographer's level of performance in electron-density-map interpretation. Automation of this task would shorten the time taken for protein-structure determination by several weeks, to months, and would fill in a major gap in the construction of a fully automated system for protein crystallography.

Description of the Problem

When crystallographers refer to an electron density map, they usually have in mind some pictorial representation of the electron density defined over a certain region of space. The most common representation is a three-dimensional contour map, constructed by stacking layers of conventional two-dimensional contour maps drawn on transparent sheets. By carefully studying the map, the experienced protein crystallographer can find features that allow him (or her) to infer approximate atomic locations, molecular boundaries, groups of atoms, the backbone of the polymer, and so on. After several weeks (or months), he has built a model of the molecular structure that conforms to the electron density map and is also consistent with his knowledge of protein chemistry, stereochemical constraints, and other available chemical and physical data (e.g., the amino acid sequence). Figure C3–1a shows a portion of a protein structure and Figure C3–1b shows the associated electron density map from which it was inferred.

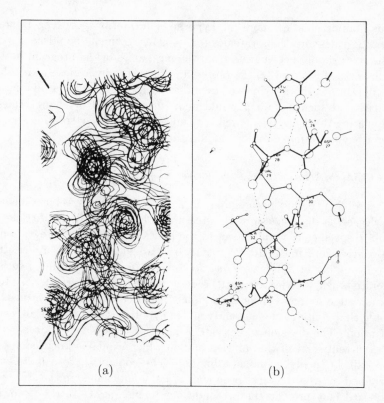

Figure C3–1.   (a) A portion of the molecular structure of lysozyme; (b) a
view of the electron density at 2.8 Å of an α–helix in lysozyme,
corresponding to the structure in (a) (Snape, 1974).

The automation of this task would require a computational system that
could generate its own structural hypotheses, as well as display and verify
them. This capability requires: (a) a representation of the electron density
function suitable for machine interpretation, (b) a substantial chemical and
stereochemical knowledge base, (c) a wide assortment of model-building algorithms and heuristics, (d) a collection of rules and associated procedures for
using this knowledge to make inferences from the experimental data, and (e) a
problem-solving strategy for applying these *knowledge sources* effectively, so
that the appropriate procedures are executed at the times that they are most
productive.

Protein crystallographers who build models move continually across a
large field of basic facts, special features of the data, and implications of
the partial model already built, looking for any and all opportunities to add
another piece to their structure. There are several desiderata to working

in this "opportunistic" mode of hypothesis formation: (a) The inference-generating rules and the strategies for their deployment should be separate, (b) the rules should be separate from the mechanics of the program in which they are embedded, and (c) the representation of the hypothesis space should be compatible with the kinds of hypothesis-generating rules available. The modularity of such a system would allow users to add or change rules for manipulating the database, as well as to investigate different solution strategies without having to make major modifications to the system.

The CRYSALIS Architecture: The Blackboard

A problem-solving paradigm that meets the above specifications, to a large degree, is the *blackboard* architecture of HEARSAY–II (see Article V.C1, in Vol. I), specifically with respect to the issues of knowledge integration and focus of attention. In HEARSAY–II, an "iterative guess-building" process takes place: A number of different *knowledge sources* (facts, algorithms, heuristics) cooperate when working on various descriptions of the hypothesis. To use the knowledge sources efficiently, a global database—the blackboard—is constructed that contains the currently active hypothesis elements at all levels of description. The decision to activate a particular knowledge source depends on the current state of the solution and on which available knowledge source is most likely to make further progress. The control is, to a large extent, determined by what has just been learned: A small change in the state of the blackboard may provide the preconditions to instantiate further knowledge sources (an illustration of this process in the context of electron-density-map interpretation is given below).

Figure C3–2 shows the types of data and hypotheses that are found in CRYSALIS. As in HEARSAY–II, the hypotheses are represented in a hierarchical data structure. In our case, the different information levels can be partitioned into three distinctly different "panels," but the concept of a globally accessible space of hypotheses is essentially the same for both systems. This figure also illustrates how knowledge sources (only a small subset is shown) play the same role as in HEARSAY–II: adding, changing, or testing hypothesis elements on the blackboard. Further explanation of these diagrams is given in Engelmore and Nii (1977). The processes of generating or modifying hypotheses and of invoking knowledge sources are nearly identical to those for the AGE system (Nii and Aiello, 1978).

Representation of Knowledge in CRYSALIS

As mentioned above, there are many diverse sources of information in protein-structure inference. The problem of representing all the knowledge in a form that allows its cooperative and efficient use in the search for plausible hypotheses is of central concern to the developers of CRYSALIS. The system

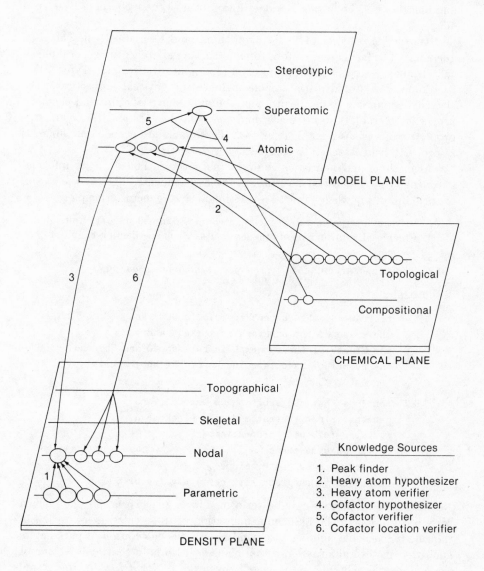

Figure C3–2.   Panels of the CRYSALIS blackboard and examples of the application of knowledge sources.

as currently developed draws upon many concepts that have emerged in the design of other large knowledge-based systems—for example, production rules and blackboards. Following is a description of how these concepts have been adapted.

Knowledge consists of facts, algorithms, and heuristics (rules of good guessing). The facts required for protein-structure inference are general physical, chemical, stereochemical, and crystallographic *constraints*. Typical factual knowledge stored in the system includes the physical properties of the elements commonly found in proteins, the molecular structure and chemical properties of the 20 amino acids, and the bond lengths and the symmetry properties of various crystal structures. These facts are encoded as tables or as property lists attached to specific structural entities.

Algorithms and heuristics comprise both the formal and the informal knowledge that generates or verifies hypothesis elements. The representation of this kind of knowledge in CRYSALIS follows two general principles:

1. Identifiable areas of knowledge are decomposed into elementary units, in which each unit increments the hypothesis when specified preconditions are met.

2. The elementary units are represented as *situation-action rules*.

To illustrate:

```
IF     the name of the current-residue is GLU, and
       the shape of the subgraph is forked, and
       the length of the subgraph is between 40 and 75, and
       the number of associated peaks of the subgraph is
          greater than 1

THEN   conclude that the subgraph is matched, and
       generate a new superatom on the blackboard,
       with the following properties:
       Type is side-chain
       Belongs to current-residue
       Data-link to subgraph with certainty factor 500.
```

Note that several actions may be performed for a given situation. Not shown here, but present in the LISP implementation of these rules, is a position in the rule for variable bindings, to avoid repetitious calculation of parameters appearing in several situation-action clauses. Also note that at least one of the actions of each rule is to place a token on an *event list*. In the actual implementation, the syntax of the "action" clause is represented as a single function. An example follows:

Syntax: (⟨inference type⟩ ⟨element being changed⟩ ⟨att-value pairs⟩)

Example: (SUBGRAPH.MATCHED (GENSUPATOM) ((TYPE SIDECHAIN)
           (BELONGSTO CURRENT.RESIDUE) (DATALINK (SUBGRAPH.500))))

In this example, an event, SUBGRAPH.MATCHED, will be generated and queued on the event list. The event list is used by the interpreter (discussed below) to determine what to do next, that is, which set of knowledge sources to invoke after the current event has been processed.

Event-driven Control

The CRYSALIS system uses an *event-driven control structure*. In this scheme, the current state of the hypothesis space determines what to do next. The monitor continually refers to a list of current events—the event list—that triggers the knowledge sources most likely to make further headway. As a knowledge source makes a change in the current hypothesis, it also places an item on the event list to signify the type of change made. Thus, as events are drawn from the event list for processing, new events are added, so that under normal conditions the monitor always has a means for choosing its next move.

The normal iterative cycle of problem solving uses the event list to trigger knowledge sources, which create or change hypothesis elements and place new events on the event lists. The system's behavior is *opportunistic:* It is guided primarily by what has been most recently discovered, rather than by the requirement to satisfy subgoals. An event-driven control structure was chosen partly to be efficient in selecting appropriate knowledge sources and partly to conform with the opportunistic structure-modeling process normally employed by protein crystallographers.

Rules

The formal and informal procedures that comprise the knowledge sources are expressed as rules, as discussed above. These rules are collected into sets, each set being judged appropriate to use when particular kinds of events occur. The events generally reflect the level at which the inference is being made, which in turn reflects the model's level of detail. The correspondence between *event classes* and rule sets is established by another set of rules, the *task rules*. The task rules are used to decide which knowledge source or sequence of knowledge sources to call in order to perform one of the typical tasks in building the structure—for example, tracing the protein backbone between two anchor points. The decision is based on the state of the blackboard and the items on the event list. The task rules thus form a second layer of rules that directs the system's choice of knowledge sources for a given event, reflecting the system's knowledge of what it knows.

Once a task either is completed or fails, the system looks to a higher level of control to determine what to do next. At this higher level—the strategy level—the structure-building process can either try to solve the current subproblem by another method or shift attention to another region of the structure. Strategy-level decisions are also expressed as rules and make use of the current state of the blackboard and event list. One such strategy rule is:

```
IF      the initialization task is complete, and
        the locations of two or more atoms are known
          (called toeholds), and
        these toeholds are separated by less than six
          residues in the amino acid sequence, and
        none of the intervening residues is identified
          from the data,

THEN    select the two-point chain-tracing task and focus
        on the sub-sequence bounded by the toeholds.
```

The part of the monitor that interprets and obeys the event rules may be likened to a middle-level project manager who knows which specialists to call in as new, partial solutions to a particular problem are discovered. Continuing the analogy, the middle-level manager occasionally gets stuck and needs help from higher level management. As mentioned earlier, some high-level decision (such as merging two or more events to produce a new event or shifting attention to another part of the blackboard) is required. This level of decision making is embodied in a set of strategy rules, which are used to direct the top-level flow of control.

We thus have a completely rule-based control structure that employs three distinct levels of rules (or knowledge): the specialists, commonly called the knowledge sources; the task rules, representing knowledge about the capabilities of the specialists; and the strategy rules, which know when to use all available knowledge to solve the problem. Although this pyramidal structure of rules and meta-rules could continue indefinitely, the flexibility of knowledge deployment offered by our three-tiered system appears sufficient for this problem-solving system. Similar ideas in a simpler context have been explored by Davis (1976) in his TEIRESIAS system (see Article VII.B).

System Performance—An Example

To give some indication of the system's current level of performance, we present a typescript in which a typical hypothesis-formation task is completed. The example is the subproblem of extending the model from an "island of certainty," or anchor point, by using the crytallographic data to determine where to extend the model in space and by using the amino acid sequence to generate expectations of features that ought to be present in that region.

The knowledge sources invoked in this example use an abstraction of the density map called a *subgraph*. A subgraph is a collection of segments obtained from a skeletonized density map, which, one hopes, matches an identifiable substructure in the protein—for example, a sidechain. The amino acid sequence assumed here is METhionine, LYSine, LYSine, TYRosine, and so forth (the example uses data from the protein Rubredoxin). The example starts after passing control to a knowledge source called ANCHOR.TOEHOLD. The toehold of interest in this case is the sulphur atom in the methionine sidechain. This toehold is just a point in space and must be connected to the skeleton.

```
INFERENCE:  EVENT-1  BY RULE 1  IN RULESET  ANCHOR.TOEHOLD
   EVENT NAME: TOEHOLD.ANCHORED
   CURRENT HYPOTHESIS ELEMENT: SA2
   NEW PROPERTIES:  ((TYPE SIDECHAIN) (BELONGSTO (MET .1))
      (SEGS (((1 SEG240) .100) ((1 SEG238) .100))) (MEMBERS (A3)))
```

The ANCHOR.TOEHOLD knowledge source has found subgraphs of the skeleton, but its limited knowledge cannot assign much certainty to the inference. The "real" matching of skeleton parts with expected residue is accomplished by MATCH.SDCHN. This knowledge source uses the shape of the subgraph, its length, the number of peaks associated with the candidate subgraph, and their heights. If a certainty factor (CF) of 500 or more is assigned, the sidechain is considered to be located (CFs have a range of -1000 to 1000, with the CF combining function the same as that used by MYCIN; see Article VIII.B1).

```
INFERENCE:  EVENT-2  BY RULE 3  IN RULESET  MATCH.SDCHN
   EVENT NAME: TOEHOLD
   CURRENT HYPOTHESIS ELEMENT: SA3
   NEW PROPERTIES: (SEGS (((1 SEG238) .823) ((1 SEG240) .555)))
```

If a sidechain is found, the trace tries to find the alpha carbon location by finding a peak of a certain type near the root of the sidechain. The knowledge source used to propose an alpha carbon position is called POSSIBLE.CALPHA. The system assumes that the location of this peak is a more accurate guide than the skeleton for locating this class of atom.

```
INFERENCE:  EVENT-3  BY RULE 5  IN RULESET  POSSIBLE.CALPHA
   EVENT NAME: C.ALPHA
   CURRENT HYPOTHESIS ELEMENT: A4
   NEW PROPERTIES: ((TYPE C) (NAME CA) (BELONGSTO (MET .1))
      (D.PEAKS ((PKO76 .500))))
```

Once the toehold has been anchored, this trace becomes essentially a generate-and-test search, heavily constrained by the sequence. The basic control cycle for the trace is, first, propose a sidechain and match it; next, propose a peptide and match that; and, finally, loop until a match fails. Sometimes the carbonyl group present in each peptide will appear as a small sidechain. If this happens, the proposed peptide will extend only from the last sidechain up to this pseudo sidechain, and the peptide will fail to match. This failure prompts the system to try matching the "sidechain" as a carbonyl.

Success of this match would mean that only half of the peptide has been found; the system can then propose a larger peptide, which contains the old one, and proceed as before.

```
INFERENCE:  EVENT-4  BY RULE 4  IN RULESET  MATCH.PEPTIDE
   EVENT NAME: PEPTIDE
   CURRENT HYPOTHESIS ELEMENT: SA4
   NEW PROPERTIES: ((TYPE PEPTIDE) (BELONGSTO (MET .1))
      (SEGS (((SEG6 SEG8) .84))) (PEAKS (PKO76 PKO78)))

INFERENCE:  EVENT-5  BY RULE 5  IN RULESET  MATCH.CARBONYL.SC
   EVENT NAME: CARBONYL.FOUND
   CURRENT HYPOTHESIS ELEMENT: A5
   NEW PROPERTIES: ((TYPE CO) (NAME CARBONYL)
      (BELONGSTO (MET .1))
      (SEGS (((1 SEG5) .581))) (PEAKS (PKO36)))

INFERENCE:  EVENT-6  BY RULE 4  IN RULESET  MATCH.PEPTIDE
   EVENT NAME: PEPTIDE
   CURRENT HYPOTHESIS ELEMENT: SA4
   NEW PROPERTIES: ((SEGS (((SEG6 SEG8 SEG10) .420)))
      (PEAKS (PKO76 PKO78 PKO36)))

INFERENCE:  EVENT-7  BY RULE 7  IN RULESET  MATCH.SDCHN
   EVENT NAME: SIDECHAIN
   CURRENT HYPOTHESIS ELEMENT: SA6
   NEW PROPERTIES: ((TYPE SIDECHAIN) (BELONGSTO (LYS .2))
      (SEGS (((1 SEG242) .527))))

INFERENCE:  EVENT-8  BY RULE 5  IN RULESET  POSSIBLE.CALPHA
   EVENT NAME: C.ALPHA
   CURRENT HYPOTHESIS ELEMENT: A6
   NEW PROPERTIES: ((TYPE C) (NAME CA) (BELONGSTO (LYS .2))
      (D.PEAKS ((PKO78 .500))))

INFERENCE:  EVENT-9  BY RULE 4  IN RULESET  MATCH.PEPTIDE
   EVENT NAME: PEPTIDE
   CURRENT HYPOTHESIS ELEMENT: SA6
   NEW PROPERTIES: ((TYPE PEPTIDE) (BELONGSTO (LYS .2))
      (SEGS (((SEG232 SEG16) .600))) (PEAKS (PKO17 PK125)))
```

(Three more events, similar to the preceding ones, have been omitted.)

```
INFERENCE:  EVENT-13  BY RULE 6  IN RULESET  MATCH.SDCHN
   EVENT NAME: SIDECHAIN
   CURRENT HYPOTHESIS ELEMENT: SA9
   NEW PROPERTIES: ((TYPE SIDECHAIN) (BELONGSTO (TYR .4))
      (SEGS (((6 SEG212 SEG40 SEG36 SEG35 SEG228) .502))))
```

The matching cycle terminates in one of two ways. If the skeleton becomes so overconnected that the access function cannot propose the next subgraph (sidechain or peptide), the trace fails; or if the certainty of a match is too low and there are no rules to save the situation, the trace fails. Upon termination, one final knowledge source is called to link together hypothesis elements belonging to the same residue, creating an organizing "backbone."

```
INFERENCE:  EVENT-14  BY RULE 3  IN RULESET  TRACE.CLEANUP
   EVENT NAME: LINK-CA-TO-PEPTIDE
   CURRENT HYPOTHESIS ELEMENT: SA4
   NEW PROPERTIES: ((MEMBERS (A4)))
```

(Two more events like the preceding one are omitted here.)

```
INFERENCE:  EVENT-17  BY RULE 7  IN RULESET  TRACE.CLEANUP
   EVENT NAME: BACKBONE
   CURRENT HYPOTHESIS ELEMENT: ST1
   NEW PROPERTIES: ((TYPE BACKBONE) (CF 511) (DIRECTION 1)
      (RANGE (1 .4)) (MEMBERS (SA1 SA2 SA3 SA4 SA5 SA6 SA7 NIL)))
```

Summary

At the present time, CRYSALIS is capable of performing only a small portion of the total task of interpreting electron density maps. The development and implementation of all the knowledge sources required for the complete task is a long-term effort. CRYSALIS currently contains a relatively small knowledge base that permits the interpretation of portions of high-quality, high-resolution (2.0 Ångströms or better) electron density maps. The system is expected to evolve toward an extensive knowledge-based problem solver capable of complete interpretation of medium-quality, medium-resolution (2.0 to 2.5 Å) electron density maps. Although CRYSALIS is not yet worthy of serious attention by the protein-crystallographic community, its defects lie primarily in its relatively meager knowledge base and not in its design. As new knowledge sources are added to the system, its level of performance is expected to rise to the point where it will be a significant aid in the determination of new protein structures.

References

See Engelmore and Terry (1978, 1979), Engelmore and Nii (1977), and Feigenbaum, Engelmore, and Johnson (1977).

C4. Applications in Organic Synthesis

THE SYNTHESIS of organic compounds is central to the creation of new chemical products and to the development of more efficient processes for manufacturing old products. However, the synthesis process for a particular product is typically expensive to run and hard to design. Hence, there is great interest among both academic and industrial chemists in new tools for finding synthetic routes.

A synthesis problem begins with the structural description of a compound that someone wants synthesized, often because the compound has useful properties (e.g., a drug or a vitamin). Synthesis can also help confirm a postulated structure for an unknown compound, since the synthesized compound and the unknown compound will, if identical, produce identical test results.

Chemists use the computer and AI techniques to explore systematically the synthesis tree and to help organize the immense body of available knowledge about chemical reactions. This approach of exhaustively exploring the interesting branches of the synthesis tree was called the logic-centered approach by E. Corey and W. T. Wipke (1969), who first explored computer-aided organic synthesis. Interesting branches are those most likely to produce the desired result. "Interesting" is an extremely difficult concept to define and to cast into an algorithm; therefore, for now, the search for interesting branches must be guided interactively by the chemist. Some of the relevant considerations are the efficiency of a reaction, the cost of materials, and the difficulty of meeting the experimental conditions that support a reaction.

The chemist represents the target structure graphically and relates it to simpler chemicals via known chemical reactions. He (or she) relates those to still simpler ones, until he reaches a set of commands, comparable to starting materials that are readily available from chemical supply houses or that can be easily synthesized in a few steps in the laboratory. A plan for synthesizing the compound, called a synthetic route, may involve dozens of separate reactions. If the molecule is at all complicated, there is an immense number of distinct synthesis routes. For example, a simple steroid composed of about 20 atoms has over 10^{18} possible direct routes.

Synthesis routes can be viewed in terms of an AND/OR tree (discussed in Article II.C4, in Vol. I). The tree descends from the goal node, representing the target molecule, to the terminal nodes, equivalent to the starting materials. The branches connecting the nodes are chemical reactions. Since a synthesis plan involves combining compounds in reactions, the AND-links of the tree are present in any one synthesis route; alternative ways of making a compound anywhere within the plan are represented by OR-nodes.

The Three Major AI Synthesis-research Programs:
LHASA, SECS, and SYNCHEM

There are three major programs in computer-aided organic synthesis. The earliest is LHASA (Logic and Heuristics Applied to Synthetic Analysis), which was written by Corey and Wipke at Harvard and is maintained at Harvard by Corey and his research group. SECS (Simulation and Evaluation of Chemical Synthesis) is an outgrowth of LHASA and was written by Wipke and maintained by him and his research group at the University of California at Santa Cruz. It extended the LHASA paradigm by the inclusion of stereochemical and conformational information into all aspects of the computer program. The third major program is SYNCHEM (SYNthetic CHEMistry), written and maintained by H. L. Gelernter and his research group at the State University of New York at Stony Brook. The main features of these three programs are summarized in Table C4-1.

Since SECS was designed to extend the methods in LHASA, much of the discussion of SECS applies to both programs. Of the three, only SECS is demonstrably transportable to computers other than the one on which it was developed.

Two Approaches

A major distinction between SECS (and LHASA) and SYNCHEM is that SECS is oriented toward high performance while SYNCHEM is oriented more toward AI issues involving search. Because of this, and because chemists' intuitions about interesting pathways are hard to define, SECS relies on a

TABLE C4-1

Chemical Synthesis Programs

Program	Principal designer	Main features
LHASA	E. J. Corey	Large procedural knowledge base of transforms; interactive; high performance.
SECS	W. T. Wipke	Separate knowledge base of many transforms with special interactive language for defining new ones (ALCHEM); interactive graphics; high performance.
SYNCHEM	H. Gelernter	Motivated by AI search problems; evaluation during search done by the program, not by a chemist.

chemist's interacting with the program. SYNCHEM, on the other hand, searches the space of possible synthetic routes without interactive guidance from a chemist. In operational terms, the main difference is whether the evaluation function for the search procedure is explicitly given to the program and used without guidance from the chemist (as in SYNCHEM) or it is not explicitly given to the program (as in SECS and LHASA). In the following, these are called the noninteractive and interactive approaches, respectively. SECS can be reconfigured to run noninteractively, although with the chemist's guidance the system tends to give better results.

The Chemical Knowledge Base

The primary item of knowledge in chemical synthesis is the chemical reaction—a rule describing a situation in which a change can occur (to a molecular structure) plus a description of that change. For example, the reaction shown in Figure C4–1 describes a change to a molecule containing the substructure $O=C—C—C=O$ in the presence of the reagent oxalyl chloride. To design a synthesis route from starting materials to target molecule, knowledge of reactions can be used in either of two ways:

1. *Forward direction:* Apply known reactions to starting materials, then to the products of those reactions, to the products of products, and so forth, until the target is reached. The combinatorics of this approach make it impossible in practice, because there are thousands of possible starting compounds and only one target.

2. *Reverse direction:* Starting with the target molecule, determine which reactions might produce it. Then look for ways to make the precursors, the precursors of precursors, and so forth, until the starting materials are reached. Storing the reactions in the reverse direction makes it easier to search the tree of possible pathways.

All three programs have a large knowledge base of reverse chemical reactions called *transforms*—production rules of the condition-action form (see Article III.C4, in Vol. I). The left-hand side of each rule represents a substructure pattern to be matched in the target structure (or intermediate structure) and the right-hand side is a description of precursors that will produce the goal structure under specified reaction conditions. Each of the three projects has dealt with the problems of constructing a knowledge base in very different ways. (Fig. C4–2 shows the representation in the SECS knowledge base for

$$O=C—C—C=O + \text{Oxalyl Chloride} \longrightarrow O=C—C=C—CL$$

Figure C4–1. Graphical representation of a chemical reaction.

the reverse reaction of the one shown in Fig. C4-1, plus all the associated information.)

1. The LHASA knowledge base is a set of procedures. Although it contains very sophisticated chemistry knowledge, it is difficult to modify (see Article III.C2, in Vol. I).

2. The SECS knowledge base contains about 400 separate transforms. New transforms can be defined by users and entered into the knowledge base without changes to the program. Because of its clarity, it is useful for illustration and is discussed in detail below.

3. The SYNCHEM knowledge base is a library of reactions that can be updated by chemists without reprogramming. Each reaction is compiled automatically into a reverse reaction. In addition, the knowledge base contains a large library of starting compounds that are available commercially. (In a newer version, SYNCHEM2, the catalogue of starting materials has been replaced by a set of stopping criteria for synthesis routes.)

Each of the SECS transforms is stored external to the SECS program; this allows the knowledge base to be tailored to a specific problem domain. Further, the number and complexity of the transforms are not limited by the size of core memory. A simple, flexible language, called ALCHEM, is provided in which chemists can enter new transforms into the knowledge base.

ALCHEM embodies a model of what information is needed to describe a reaction adequately. According to this model, a transform consists of the following six sections:

1. Transform name;

2. Substructure key or pattern to be matched;

3. Character—used to help judge the relevance to strategic planning;

4. Scope and limitations;

5. Reaction conditions—not to be violated by the remainder of the molecule containing the substructure key;

6. Manipulation statements—describing the graph transformations to be performed.

This will be clarified below with an example.

In the reaction shown in Figure C4-1, one of the oxygens double-bonded to carbon is replaced by a single bond to a chlorine. To go from a graphical representation of a synthetic *reaction* to the graphical representation of a SECS *transform*, we reverse the left- and right-hand sides and specify additional important conditions. Using the ALCHEM language, the chemist could interactively enter the representation of this transform as shown in Figure C4-2.

In the manipulation statements, **BREAK BOND 3** refers to the third bond from the left in the substructure key; the double bond between the two carbons

---

Comment: Chloroenones, O=C—C—C=O goes to O=C—C=C—CL
Reagent: Oxalyl Chloride
Ref: Heathcock and Clark (1976).

Transform name: **CHLOR-ENONE**
Substructure key: O=C—C=C—CL ⟨1 = 2 — 3 = 4 — 5⟩
Priority: 100

Character: CHARACTER ALTERS GROUP

Scope   IF ACID IS OFF PATH THEN KILL
and limitations: IF ESTER IS OFF PATH THEN KILL
                     IF HYDROGEN IS ALPHA TO ATOM 4 THEN
                         BEGIN
                         IF HYDROGEN IS ALPHA TO ATOM2
                         THEN SUBTRACT 75 FROM PRIORITY
                         DONE

Manipulation   BREAK BOND 3
statements: DELETE ATOM 5
                     ADD O OF ORDER 2 to ATOM 4

In the actual reaction, of course, the chlorinated compound comes from the precursor.

Figure C4–2. ALCHEM representation of a SECS transform.

is reduced to a single bond. Similarly, **DELETE ATOM 5** refers to the chlorine atom CL, the fifth atom from the left. When the program is actually run, a compiler called SYNCOM translates the ALCHEM statements into machine-readable form before SECS reads the knowledge base.

A Brief Description of SECS

SECS and LHASA have been designed to divide the work between the chemist and the computer in an optimal way. Wipke and his associates (1977) explain their philosophy as follows:

Our performance goal for the program was that the program should be able to help a chemist find many more good and innovative syntheses than the chemist could working alone. Because of the complexity of the problem domain, we felt the chemist and computer working together with each assigned tasks for which they are best suited, and with efficient interaction between the two, would be more effective than either working alone. Our goal was not to replace the chemist, but to augment the chemist's problem solving capabilities. (p. 174)

Graphics. To communicate with the SECS program, the chemist uses a graphics terminal with a CRT, a minicomputer, a keyboard, and a light pen. With the pen, the chemist draws on the screen the graphical structure of the target molecule to be synthesized. Much work has gone into the human-engineering aspects of the program, so that the SECS graphics routines are designed to be as near as possible to the chemist's normal ways of thinking in terms of the structure diagram or the molecular model. There are similar facilities in LHASA. By convention, hydrogen atoms are suppressed. Also by convention, only noncarbon atoms (called heteroatoms) are labeled. This is useful, since the majority of nonhydrogen atoms in organic molecules are carbon.

Application of a transform. Applying a transform is not simply a matter of matching the substructure key to a molecule and, if the subgraph fits, executing the graph-manipulation statements. The scope and limitations determine much of the context in which the transform will be applicable. Also, it is necessary to check three-dimensional information and electronic-environment information (i.e., the tendency of the atoms in the molecule to be positively or negatively charged) to make an accurate assessment of whether a transform is applicable.

A situation commonly encountered in chemical synthesis is that there is a functional group to be modified and a reagent available that would normally bring about the appropriate change, but access to the functional group is hindered (spatially) by another functional group or another portion of the molecule, and the reagent does not have the desired effect. Without the three-dimensional information given by the so-called model-building routines, the program has no way of knowing that the transform cannot apply. After the spatial modeling has been done, the program can perceive that even though the required functional group is present, the transform cannot be applied directly because it is inaccessible to the reagent molecules. If the transform is very high priority, a *means-ends analysis* can be done to find ways of altering the molecule, so that the given functional group is accessible.

A Brief Description of SYNCHEM

The aims of Gelernter's group on SYNCHEM are stated very clearly by Gelernter and his associates (1977):

Extraordinarily rapid progress during the early stages of an attack on a new problem area is a rather common occurrence in AI research; it merely signifies that the test cases with which the system has been challenged are below the level of difficulty where combinatorial explosion of the number of pathways in the problem space sets in. . . . It is the goal of AI research to move

that threshold higher and higher on the scale of problem complexity through
the introduction of heuristics—heuristics to reduce the rate of growth of the
solution tree, heuristics to guide the development of the tree so that it will
be rich in pathways leading to satisfactory problem solutions, and heuristics
to direct the search to the "best" of these pathways. (p. 1044)

SYNCHEM is noninteractive. The molecule to be synthesized is input,
and the program uses heuristic search to look for the best synthetic route.
The program decides which node of the tree to develop further, by estimating
the "cost" of reaching the goal from that node plus the cost of reaching that
node from starting materials. One of the interesting AI issues here is that
the program's definition of cost depends on the context of the problem as
well as on static features such as efficiency of reactions, the monetary cost
of materials, and so forth. For example, costs are measured differently in an
exploratory research context than in an industrial production context.

The long-range hope of the SYNCHEM group is that the study of AI in this
domain will lead to new insights into AI and also eventually to a noninteractive
system that will be of use to chemists.

SYNCHEM2. The first version of SYNCHEM, written largely by N. S.
Sridharan, was operational between 1971 and 1974. Gelernter's SYNCHEM2
supersedes it and contains many improvements, some of which are discussed
below. SYNCHEM2 has been designed so that further changes in the representation can be made easily, with minimal reprogramming. A major drawback of
the original SYNCHEM was that it entirely neglected stereochemistry. SYN-
CHEM2 now incorporates stereochemistry into its representation of molecules
and into its transform-evaluation rules. The representation is flexible enough
to include electronic and conformational information (roughly, bond lengths,
bond angles, and other three-dimensional information). The format for specifying a transform, which had been a simple fixed-field input form, was
redesigned to be similar to the ALCHEM facility in SECS.

Transforms were always applied serially in SYNCHEM, that is, to one
functional group at a time in a molecule. A new feature in SYNCHEM2, called
multiple match, allows the program to apply transforms more intelligently to
all the appropriate functional groups in a molecule. More specifically, the
new program now recognizes that multiple occurrences of a functional group,
under certain circumstances, can all be transformed by a reaction.

SYNCHEM solution evaluation. The following quotation (Gelernter
et al., 1977) illustrates the difference between organic synthesis and a more
familiar domain like theorem proving:

> Unlike much of the earlier work in problem solving ... where any formally
> valid sequence of transformations from premises to goal provided an accept-
> able solution, we were not to be satisfied by an indicated synthesis route
> of very low yield, or one requiring difficult or inefficient separations of goal
> molecules from by-products along the way, at least not before the machine
> had tried and failed to find a more efficient procedure of higher yield. ... It

is the question of relative merit of proposed solutions under the constraints of the problem that represents a substantial departure from most of the work reported in the literature of artificial intelligence. (p. 1042)

The complexities of the domain are highlighted by the fate of one of the most significant results produced by the program. SYNCHEM proposed a synthetic route for a naturally occurring antibiotic that was at that time under development by A. R. Rinehart's group at the University of Illinois. The route was considered interesting enough to merit a laboratory investigation. However, the laboratory attempt failed. One of the crucial steps in the synthesis route could not be accomplished in the laboratory and the proposed route had to be reluctantly abandoned. No successful routes to the molecule have yet been found. All synthetic routes, whether proposed by a computer program like SYNCHEM or by a person, are provisional until they can be verified by experiment.

SYNCHEM's Search Strategy

SYNCHEM's search algorithm first expands the goal node to find all its precursors. Next, it computes the cost of reaching the target molecule from the precursors, taking into account the efficiency and difficulty of the reactions. It also estimates the difficulty of synthesizing the precursor nodes from the available starting materials. Subgoal selection criteria are a function both of the accumulated heuristic estimates of reaction merit and yield along the path from subgoal to goal and of a prediction of the probable reaction merit and yield along the best path from starting materials to the subgoal. SYNCHEM updates the merit ratings with information associated with each intermediate structure. Merit, as mentioned above, is based on most recent estimates of compound complexity (i.e., difficulty in synthesizing it) and reaction-path merit (yield, cost, etc.) after each cycle of subgoal generation.

The selection of a new subgoal always begins with a new scan of the tree from the top. Thus, the search is performed in a *best-first* manner: If newly acquired information changes the ratings for subgoals, the next subgoal selected can lie on a completely different branch of the tree. In this way, the program will never develop an unfortunate choice (pathway down to starting materials) before backtracking and exploring more fruitful branches.

Summary

Computer-aided chemical synthesis is a potentially powerful new tool for both research and industrial chemists. The utility of any of the programs discussed here depends critically on the size and accuracy of their knowledge base of organic chemical reactions. Although far from complete, the knowledge bases now contain highly detailed descriptions of numerous synthetic reactions. All of the programs have convincingly demonstrated their ability to find plausible synthetic routes for important organic materials, often in less time than chemists working alone. The SECS program has a user community of chemists in Europe and North America, who add new transforms as well as use the program for synthesis planning. The effort spent on human engineering for chemists has made it possible for chemists to use the program effectively (and to want to use it) and independently of the program's designers. One of the long-range hopes of chemists and computer scientists working in computer-aided organic synthesis is that this work on knowledge bases will lead to an improved classification of chemical reactions.

Because the heuristic-search paradigm fits the synthesis-planning problem well, AI research has had much to offer. In addition, current AI work on knowledge-based expert systems provides concepts and tools for representation and management of these large, ever-changing sets of chemical facts and relations.

References

See Corey and Wipke (1969), Gelernter et al. (1977), Gund, Andose, and Rhodes (1977), and Wipke et al. (1977).

D. OTHER SCIENTIFIC APPLICATIONS

D1. MACSYMA

MACSYMA is a large, interactive computer system designed to assist mathematicians, scientists, and engineers in solving mathematical problems. It has a wide range of algebraic-manipulation capabilities, all working on symbolic inputs and yielding symbolic results, as well as an extensive numerical subroutine library (IMSL) and plotting package. (Other mathematics-oriented AI research projects are discussed in Articles II.D3 and II.D4, in Vol. I, and XIV.D4c, in Vol. III.)

MACSYMA is used extensively by hundreds of researchers from government laboratories, universities, and private companies throughout the United States. Many of these users spend a substantial portion of every day logged in to the system. Currently, MACSYMA runs exclusively on a Digital Equipment Corporation KL–10 at M.I.T. and is accessed through the ARPA Network; however, there are plans to distribute it to other sites in the near future. MACSYMA's funding is provided almost exclusively by its user community.

The original design for MACSYMA was laid out in 1968 by Carl Engleman, William Martin, and Joel Moses. They built on their previous experience with the Mathlab 68 system and on the doctoral projects of Martin and Moses. Martin had constructed an algebraic-manipulation system to solve certain problems in applied mathematics. Moses had produced a program, called SIN, that was able to perform indefinite integration as well as a typical graduate student could (see Article II.D4, in Vol. I). MACSYMA had its first users in 1971 and has undergone continuous development since then, for a total of about 45 man-years of effort.

The implementation of MACSYMA is based on the belief that the way to produce a high-performance program for general mathematics is to build in a large amount of knowledge. This approach to system construction is often called knowledge-based programming (see Article VII.A). MACSYMA is an extremely large system. It can perform at least 600 distinct mathematical operations, including differentiation, integration, solution of equations and systems of equations, Taylor series expansions, matrix operations, vector algebra, and order analysis. The current system consists of about 230,000 words of compiled LISP code and an equal amount of code written in the MACSYMA programming language. About half of this code was written by the staff of the MACSYMA project; the rest was contributed by various users.

The primary goal of research on algebraic manipulation has been to invent and analyze new mathematical algorithms and to extend previously known numerical algorithms to symbolic manipulation. While most of the algorithms incorporated into MACSYMA were known to mathematicians prior to its construction, a substantial number came about as a result of this research. The last decade brought the discovery of new algorithms for finding the greatest common divisors of polynomials (Brown and Traub, 1971; Moses and Yun, 1973), factoring rational expressions (Musser, 1975; Wang and Roth-schild, 1975), sum simplification (Gosper, 1977), symbolic integration (Moses, 1971; Norman, 1975; Risch, 1969; Rothstein, 1977; Trager, 1978), and asymptotic analysis (Fateman, 1976; Norman, 1975; Zippel, 1976). The nature of this work has been largely mathematical and, although AI was instrumental in providing the environment in which MACSYMA was created, it has made little direct contribution since then.

Knowledge-based programming does, however, engender a number of difficulties for which AI techniques offer partial answers. Two general classes of difficulties are discussed here: (a) user education and (b) the handling of mathematical problems not amenable to algorithmic solution.

Nonalgorithmic Procedures in MACSYMA

One of the most pressing problems in algebraic manipulation is simplification. Symbolic algorithms often generate large, unwieldy expressions that must be simplified into smaller, more meaningful forms. (Generally, the size of expressions is the most important criterion for simplicity, with standard formats and particularly revealing forms taking precedence.) To help users simplify their results, MACSYMA provides a variety of explicit expression-transformation commands (such as expansion, factorization, and partial fraction decomposition) and a simplifier that automatically applies a set of mathematical rules to every new expression as it is constructed. Examples of these rules are:

$$x \cdot x \rightarrow x^2$$
$$\sin(x + \pi/2) \rightarrow \cos x$$
$$\log(ab) \rightarrow \log a + \log b$$

The user can, of course, define new commands and new rules.

Semantic Pattern Matching

In applying a simplification rule, MACSYMA utilizes a semantic pattern matcher to find instances of the rule's pattern. The matcher is semantic in that it applies knowledge about the operators and constants in an expression to find nonsyntactic matches. For example, the pattern $ax^2 + bx + c$, where a, b, and c are pattern variables free of x, will match the expressions $4x^2 + 4x + 1$, $2x^2 + x + 1$, x^2, and $(x+1)^2$. In defining a rule, the user may specify arbitrary conditions (in the form of procedural predicates) on the pattern variables. For example, determining whether an expression matches the above pattern, MACSYMA would call a user-specified function to check that any tentative assignments for a, b, and c are free of x. As a result, the pattern would not match $4x^2 + 3x + \sin x$.

One problem with this pattern matcher is that the user cannot control how much "semantics" the system uses in finding a match. A recently completed pattern matcher allows the user to specify a set of identities to use in attempting to identify instances of patterns. For example, while it is often desirable that the matcher use inverses, in some situations a user might prefer a simpler matcher, lest the rule $ab \rightarrow c$ apply to every lone a and b, as in $b \rightarrow c/a$. With the new pattern matcher, the user will be able to specify when the inverse axioms are to be used.

Simplification by Hill Climbing

While the size of an expression is not the sole criterion for its simplicity, it is a useful guideline. For those applications in which the user desires the smallest possible form for an expression, MACSYMA provides a search-oriented simplifier called SCSIMP. Given an expression and a set of rules, SCSIMP applies each of the rules to the expression, in turn, and retains the smallest result. If any such substitution leads to an expression smaller than the original, the process is repeated. For example, given the identities below, SCSIMP will convert the first expression into the last.

Given: $\qquad K^2 + L^2 = 1 \qquad\qquad N^2 - M^2 = 1$

First expression: $\quad K^2 N^2 + K^2 M^2 N^2 - K^2 L^2 N^2 - K^2 L^2 M^2 N^2$

Intermediate: $\qquad K^4 M^2 N^2 + K^4 N^2 \qquad$ (substituting for L)

Final expression: $\; K^4 N^4 \qquad\qquad\qquad$ (substituting for M)

Note, however, that because SCSIMP is a *hill-climbing* algorithm, it is not guaranteed to produce the smallest answer. For example, it would not perform the simplification shown below, since the intermediate expression is *larger* than the initial expression.

First expression: $\qquad K^2 N^2 + L^2 M^2$

Intermediate form: $\quad K^2 N^2 - K^2 M^2 + M^2 \quad$ (substituting for L)

Simplest form: $\qquad\quad K^2 + M^2 \qquad\qquad$ (substituting for N)

Due to the combinatorics involved in generating arbitrarily large intermediate forms, this technique has not been incorporated into the current version of SCSIMP.

The Relational Database and Inference

In certain problems, the symbols in mathematical expressions have restrictions on their ranges or on other properties that are useful in simplification. To allow the user to specify such properties, MACSYMA maintains a relational database of facts about symbols, stored in the form of a semantic network. For example, a user can declare (with the DECLARE command) that the symbol n is restricted to integer values, and MACSYMA can then simplify $\cos((2n + 1)/\pi)$ to 0. Similarly, one can specify (with the ASSUME command) that $x \leq y$, $y \leq z$, and $z \leq x$, and MACSYMA can then deduce that $x = y = z$ (using the CPM algorithm described below).

The database retrieval routines are supplemented by a fast but limited inference algorithm called CPM (Genesereth, 1976), which performs taxonomic deductions, property inheritances, set intersections, and other simple inferences. For example, given the facts that x is an integer, integers are rational, and the real numbers are partitioned into rationals and irrationals, CPM automatically deduces that x is not an irrational. Given the fact that a rational can be written as an integral numerator over an integral denominator, CPM automatically deduces that x can be so written.

The CPM inference algorithm was developed to enhance the retrieval capabilities of a high-level database system organized as a semantic network. It is an elaboration of Grossman's work (1976) on constraint expressions but has been carefully restricted so that it can be implemented on parallel hardware. The algorithm is a highly compiled form of domain-independent constraint propagation, in which constraints, represented by labels on the nodes of the network, propagate across links to other nodes according to the laws of logic. It can perform certain inferences much more efficiently than their straightforward implementation in procedural problem-solving languages like CONNIVER. Fahlman (1977) has described how such a constraint-propagation algorithm can be implemented in parallel hardware for even greater efficiency.

Heuristic Problem Solving

MACSYMA also includes a number of specialized procedural problem-solvers, for example, the first phase of the integration routine (Moses, 1971), the commands for performing root contraction and logarithmic contraction, and the inequality theorem prover.

User Education

The advantage of a large, knowledge-based system like MACSYMA over a smaller, sparer system like REDUCE (Hearn, 1973) is that MACSYMA has more mathematical knowledge built in. As a consequence, the users are not forced to communicate as much mathematical knowledge to the system. The disadvantage is that MACSYMA can be more difficult to understand and to use. For example, users might be unaware of the capabilities available or not know the commands, or they might get unexpected results that they cannot explain.

To minimize these difficulties, MACSYMA offers a wide variety of on-line user aids (Genesereth, 1977; Lewis, 1977), including a *frame-oriented* interactive primer, an information network, and a program for searching the reference manual. In addition, some of MACSYMA's commands are designed to be able to explain their progress. For example, if the VERBOSE option is selected, the POWERSERIES command prints out the goals and subgoals that it generates while working on an expansion.

Even with such provisions, users occasionally encounter difficulties because they do not know the system. Furthermore, such users are often unwilling to learn more about MACSYMA than is necessary for solving an immediate problem. The simplest way for such users to acquire just the information they need is to ask a consultant for help. With the consultant's advice, they can surmount the difficulty and solve the problems.

Consultation is a method widely used in computer centers as well as in business, law, and medicine; furthermore, as computer technology becomes more pervasive and computer systems become more complex, the need for consultation grows. Unfortunately, human consultants are a scarce resource and quite expensive. An experimental version of an automated consultant for MACSYMA novices, called the Advisor, has recently been implemented. It is a program with its own database and expertise, distinct from MACSYMA. The Advisor accepts a description of a difficulty from its user and tries to reconstruct the user's plan for solving his (or her) problem. Based on this plan and its knowledge of MACSYMA, the Advisor then generates advice tailored to the user's specific need. For a description of the Advisor's operation, see Genesereth (1978).

Future Plans

In addition to the features described above, several other AI-related capabilities are under development in MACSYMA. Two of these are mentioned here, namely, a new representation for algebraic expressions using data abstractions and a knowledge-based, plan-based mathematician's (or physicist's, or engineer's) "apprentice."

David Barton has designed a radically new scheme for representing algebraic expressions. MACSYMA has two major representations, the general one that uses LISP's traditional prefix format and the rational one that uses a canonical form for polynomials and rational functions. The rational representation has become unwieldy over the years, as extensions to the system have changed its specifications. For example, coefficients of polynomials were originally assumed to be integers and were later generalized to include floating-point numbers. A new representation was desired to handle Taylor series that contains rational-number exponents, since the former representation, while relatively close to the rational representation, could not be retrofitted onto the rational representation. Barton's approach alleviates these difficulties and provides a capability for future generalization. His approach is, furthermore, a natural one for abstract algebra.

Consider, for example, a 2×2 matrix whose elements are Laurent series in y (truncated at y^2), whose coefficients are polynomials in x, with rational coefficients. In order to add such a 2×2 matrix to another 2×2 matrix, one needs to know how to add the elements. One approach would be to design a general addition routine that would check the types of each argument and perform the appropriate addition. This approach is similar to the one previously taken by the rational-function representation. In a symbolic system, and, in fact, in most applications, the type of object is intimately related to a set of operations that can be performed on it. In the MACSYMA context, these operations include addition, subtraction, multiplication, division, differentiation, substitution, coefficient extraction, and computation of greatest common denominator. Barton's approach is to attach a tree of vectors to each expression. The tree corresponds to the gross structure of the expression. For example, each subexpression, an element in the matrix, has a vector corresponding to it. The vector's elements are in a fixed order and contain pointers to the procedures that perform the corresponding operation on the type of the subexpression.

Barton's approach permits expressions to be composed of arbitrarily nested types. This is a critical requirement in an interactive symbolic system. Preliminary tests of expressions represented in this manner indicate that common manipulations are usually not much slower, and often even faster, than in the former implementation. (The reason for a speed-up is that less type-testing is needed in this approach.)

Work has also begun on the design of an apprentice for the MACSYMA user. At present, MACSYMA is used mostly as a "symbolic calculator," with the user directing its actions line by line and keeping track of the meaning of each result. The goal of the apprentice is to relieve the user of much of this bookkeeping. The approach being taken involves two components, namely, knowledge about the user's domain and the use of a high-level, problem-solving plan formalism.

Currently, most symbols in MACSYMA have no special meaning, and they can take on arbitrary values. In particular problem areas, however, certain symbols have particular interpretations and range restrictions. For example, the symbol MASS has a very special meaning to physicists and an obvious range restriction (nonnegative). A physicist's apprentice should know this range restriction and be able to use it, for example, in discarding negative roots or performing integrations. Similarly, practitioners in certain fields like to see their expressions written in standard formats, determined by the interpretation of the constituent symbols. For example, electrical engineers usually prefer resistance (R_i) and capacitance (C_i) expressions written as $f(R_1, R_2, \ldots, R_n) \cdot g(C_1, C_2, \ldots, C_n)$, rather than having the R_i and C_i intermixed.

Another way that an apprentice could be of use in MACSYMA is by keeping track of the user's *plan* for solving his problem. If the apprentice knows the steps involved and the significance of various results, it could inform the user of potential errors, make suggestions, and in many cases carry out steps by itself. The apprentice can gain familiarity with the user's plan in various ways: It may be a well-known mathematical procedure (e.g., some standard technique for solving partial differential equations or perturbation problems), the user may have described his intentions before beginning his MACSYMA session, or the user may reapply some previous plan. It is expected that this notion of a problem-solving plan will play an extremely important role in the next generation of algebraic-manipulation systems.

References

Unfortunately, there is no good introductory reference on the structure of MACSYMA. The reader is referred to the MACSYMA manual (Mathlab Group, 1977) and the primer (Moses, 1975) for an introduction to its use.

D2. The SRI Computer-based Consultant

A COMPUTER–BASED CONSULTANT (CBC) is a computer system that contains a body of specialized knowledge about a particular task domain and makes that knowledge conveniently available to users working in that domain. This article describes some research done at SRI International in the early 1970s on a computer-based consultant designed to help a novice mechanic work with electromechanical equipment. The goal of this research is to build a system that approximates a human consultant in its communication and perceptual skills, as well as in its reasoning and problem-solving skills.

The consultant was designed to answer the user's spoken questions and to monitor his (or her) progress on the task, offering advice and reminders where necessary. To fit the needs of a particular user, it is essential that the system be able to provide advice about the task at several levels of detail. To determine the appropriate level of detail, the CBC must form a model of the user, monitor his performance as he executes the task, and update internal models to reflect the current state of the task environment.

Design of the Computer-based Consultant

The particular task of the SRI computer-based consultant is to help an inexperienced mechanic repair and modify complex electromechanical equipment. The mechanic works on a piece of equipment at a special work station where he is provided with a headset that allows him both to talk to the system and to receive spoken replies in English. The system has a commercial phoneme-synthesizer for giving spoken responses to the user and a commercial phrase-recognizer for understanding his speech. A television camera and a laser range-finder provide the visual component for the system. The laser range-finder can also work as a visual pointer, so that the system can respond to requests such as "Show me the pressure switch" by illuminating it with the laser beam.

Requests for information by the user are translated into an internal representation, or *model*, by the natural-language and visual components of the system. These models are used to structure communications with the mechanic as he performs the task. For example, a question about the location of a part ("Where is the pump brace?") is answered by reference to a stored geometric model that keeps track of the spatial relations between the parts. Other models are necessary for the natural-language components of the system; for instance, a discourse model is needed to understand a spoken utterance.

150

Planning a Sequence of Constructions

The user of the CBC can request that it *plan* a sequence of assembly steps and relate this sequence to him for execution. The CBC has a state-of-the-art planning component for composing assembly and disassembly sequences (see Chap. XV, in Vol. III). There are several kinds of knowledge that are important in the planning process. First, there is the model of the equipment itself, in this case, an air compressor, which is essentially a graph whose nodes correspond to the parts of the compressor and whose arcs correspond to the mechanical connection between the parts. Second, each type of connection has associated with it a set of procedures that tells how that connection is physically established. Third, each of these procedures may contain calls to other procedures that elaborate how a job is done.

This hierarchy of procedural knowledge forms the basis for producing plans that can be presented to the user at several levels of detail. The procedural model is used by the planning program to determine the order in which parts should be assembled. The planning program initially assumes that the parts can be connected in any order. By checking preconditions and the effects of performing each step, it reorders the steps in the plan to eliminate conflicts. For example, the pump can be installed only if there is no pulley on its shaft. The planner recognizes this fact and imposes an order on the plan so that the pump will be installed before its pulley is placed on the shaft. When all the conflicts have been resolved, the remaining steps of the plan can be solved in any order. This ability—to recognize alternative orderings in a plan—is important for a computer-based consultant: The user may take the initiative and proceed with certain steps of the assembly on his own, and the planner must recognize that the steps being taken are valid.

The plan is represented as a data structure called a *procedural net* (see Article XV.D1, in Vol. III). A sample net is shown in Figure D2–1. Each node corresponds to an assembly step at some level of detail. The procedural net is actually a hierarchy of plans, all of which accomplish the same task but at varying levels of detail. The ith row in the net corresponds to a plan specified at the ith level of detail. Notice that the plan splits into two paths at level 2, indicating that the two subplans can be performed in either order. The branching vertical lines indicate the expansion of a step into a more detailed subplan.

The procedural net is useful for the specification of plans at the various levels of detail required by the user. The net is also used during planning to represent partially formed plans, so that the planning component of the system can be restarted during execution to modify an existing plan if, for example, new information requiring replanning is discovered as the assembly proceeds.

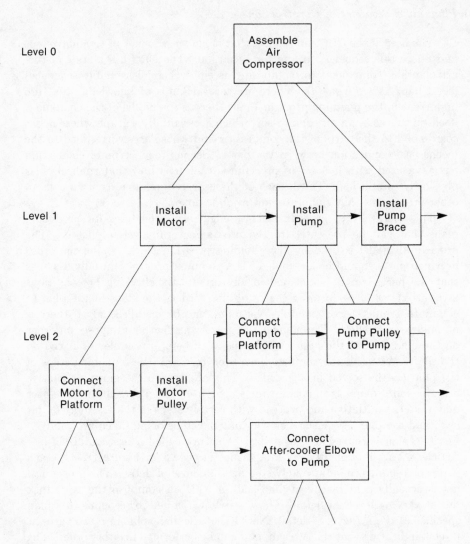

Level 0

Level 1

Level 2

Figure D2–1.   A fragment of a procedural net (after Hart, 1975).

The system keeps an internal model of the connectedness of the different components of the air compressor as it is being assembled or disassembled. It also keeps a "graphical" model of the locations of the different components of the air compressor. For example, the graphical model knows about the pump, motor, pressure switch, and so forth, and the connectivity model knows about all the visible components.

Interfacing to the Real World: Vision and Dialogue

Visual processing is especially difficult in the domain of electromechanical machinery because the components usually have only a limited range of color and texture for a great variety of possible shapes. Shadows and highlights also depend on the stage of the assembly process. For these reasons, an approach has been taken that capitalizes on prior knowledge of visual appearances and geometric relations: There is a "tool recognizer" that accepts a limited semantic description of a tool, builds a model of the tool from this description, and uses this model to differentiate the tool's image from those of the probable alternatives.

There are two other visual modules, both of which rely on stored geometric models of the equipment. The first module allows the CBC to respond to requests of the form "Show me the X." It points to X with the laser range-finder, which is accomplished by locating the outline of the visible surface of X. The final module allows the user to ask, "What part is this?" while he is pointing at the unknown part with a special wand equipped with a small light at its tip.

The following is a portion of a dialogue between a novice mechanic (whose input is preceded by **) and the CBC on the task "Assemble the air compressor." The example is taken from Hart (1975).

```
Try to achieve assembled aircompressor.

** How?

The top level plan is ... install pump ...
install pumpbrace ... install pumppulley ...
install belt ... install belthousingcover ...
Ready for questions.

** Show me the pump.

    Laser beam moves to point at pump.

Ready for questions.
                    ⋮

** What is this?

    User points with wand at tank platform.

Tank platform.
Ready for questions.

** None.

Install pump.
```

```
** How?
```

Connect pump to platform.

```
** How?
```

Get 4 1&1/4-inch 5/16 hexagonal bolts and 4 9/16 flat washers and 4 size 5/16 hexagonal nuts.

```
** OK.
```

Summary

The main goal of the research on the SRI computer-based consultant was to create the fundamental technology needed to build such consultant systems. Much of this technology is independent of the domain chosen and of the details of the task environment.

Work on the electromechanical CBC described here was stopped in April 1975. Since then, a new consultant project has been under way at SRI International extending many of the ideas from the 1975 system and adding new features. The new consultant system is being used in two entirely different domains: mineral exploration (see Article VII.D3) and agricultural pest management. It appears that computer consultants are likely to remain both a fruitful area for AI research and a practical means of deploying knowledge to people working in the specific task domains.

References

See Hart (1975) and Nilsson (1975).

D3. PROSPECTOR

PROSPECTOR (Duda et al., 1978) is a computer-based consultation system that is being developed at SRI International to assist geologists working on certain problems in "hard-rock" mineral exploration. Like other expert systems, such as MYCIN (see Article VIII.B1) and INTERNIST (Article VIII.B3), PROSPECTOR attempts to represent a significant portion of the knowledge and the reasoning processes of experts working in a specialized domain. The intended user of this program is an exploration geologist who is in the early stages of investigating an exploration site, or "prospect." We assume that he (or she) has a professional understanding of geology but, nonetheless, wants the assistance of a specialist in evaluating the findings.

In an attempt to keep the PROSPECTOR system domain-independent, a clear separation is maintained between the geological knowledge base and the mechanisms that employ this knowledge (although characteristics of the problem domain have certainly influenced the design of the system). Expressed abstractly, the main function of PROSPECTOR is to match data from a particular situation against *models* that describe a moderately large number of disjoint classes of situations. In PROSPECTOR's domain, the models are formal descriptions of the most important types of ore deposits, and the data are primarily surface geological observations. The available data are assumed to be uncertain and incomplete, so that the conclusion is expressed as a probability or a degree of match. In addition, the program alerts the user to different possible interpretations of the data and identifies additional observations that would be most valuable for reaching a more definite conclusion.

A typical consultation session with PROSPECTOR begins with the user giving the system the information about the most significant features of his prospect: the major rock types, minerals, and alteration products. The program matches these observations against its models and, when the user has finished volunteering information, proceeds to ask the user for additional information that will help confirm the best matching model. At any time during the consultation, the user can interrupt to volunteer new information, change previous statements, or request an evaluation.

The following edited excerpt from a PROSPECTOR session illustrates many of these ideas. The data for the run describe a fictitious porphyry copper deposit that has some, but not all, of the desired characteristics. We begin at the point where the user (indicated by **) starts volunteering information to the system.

```
** There is quartz monzonite

Quartz monzonite (5)
```

** There is a cretaceous dike

Cretaceous dike (5)

** There is sericite and pyrite

Sericite (5) pyrite (5)

** There may be biotite

Biotite (2)

** Done

> *These simple assertions describe the most prominent rocks, minerals, and alteration products in the target area. The system indicates its recognition of each statement by echoing the statement and appending an assigned certainty. Certainty factors range from −5 (positive that a situation does not hold) to 5 (positive that it does hold). All assertions made by PROSPECTOR have associated certainty factors. The program now enters the consequent mode of reasoning.*

Presently, the models in PROSPECTOR and their scores are:
  1. Komatiitic nickel sulfide deposit -- KNSD (0.0)
  2. Type-A porphyry copper deposit -- PCDA (0.0)
     ++current hypothesis++
  3. Kuroko-type massive sulfide deposit -- MSD (.001999)
  4. Western-states-type sandstone uranium deposit -- WSSU (0.0)
  5. Mississippi-Valley-type lead/zinc deposit -- MVTD (-4.8)
Which of the above would you like to rule out?

** None

> *The volunteered information was sufficient to rule out one of the models but was not nearly specific enough to establish any of the others. The choice of the second model as the current hypothesis was based not on its certainty but on the number and types of connections between it and the volunteered statements. To avoid a possibly fruitless investigation of unpromising models, the system gives the user the opportunity to exclude models of lesser interest. In this case, the user allows all of the models to be explored, and the system begins with the current hypothesis.*

I am considering the possibility of a
(Type-A porphyry copper deposit -- PCDA)
in the target area.

The following questions are intended to establish the nature of the petrotectonic setting.

1--To what degree do you believe that:
(the target area is in a continental margin mobile belt) ?

** -2

> *This is a discouraging answer for the PCDA model, and it removes a context needed for the investigation of other properties of the continental-margin mobile belt.*

The following questions are intended to determine the nature of the regional environment.

2--To what degree do you believe that:
(there are granitic intrusives in the region) ?

** 5

3--To what degree do you believe that:
(the region contains an abundance of small stocks) ?

** -3

        ⋮

8--To what degree do you believe that:
(igneous rocks in the region have porphyritic texture) ?

** Why

I am trying to establish whether some of the intrusive rocks in your area have textures suggestive of a hypabyssal to subvolcanic environment. Porphyry textures resulting from the rapid cooling and crystallization of a silicate melt which contains large mineral grains are suggestive of relatively shallow levels of emplacement.

> *Like MYCIN, PROSPECTOR provides a variety of commands for such things as requesting a summary, changing previous answers, or volunteering additional information. The above response to a WHY command is not automatically generated from the rule but is merely stored text associated with the space.*

8---To what degree do you believe that:
(igneous rocks in the region have porphyritic texture) ?

** 5

My certainty in (the texture and morphology of the intrusive system suggest a subvolcanic (hypabyssal) regional environment) is now: 4.924

Do you want to pursue this further?

** No

> *At this point the system noted that the certainty for the hypothesis about a hypabyssal environment was above 4.5, and it also noted that if the remaining rules were answered in the most unfavorable way possible, the certainty could not fall below 4.5. To save time, it let the user decide whether or not to continue working on this subgoal.*

The questioning continues as above until it becomes necessary to consider properties that vary within the target area. Thus, for the first time it becomes necessary to be able to use the rules more than once, and a communication convention must be established to distinguish different spatial locations.

Porphyry copper deposits are often composed of characteristic zones of alteration and mineralization. (In some cases these can be looked upon as different stages superimposed upon one another.) I shall call the most prominent such zone Zone 1. Even though you may have already identified this zone as, say, the propylitic zone or the sericitic zone, I need to consider other possibilities as well. Thus, the following questions are intended to determine the possibilities for Zone 1.

25--To what degree do you believe that:
(there are fresh-looking feldspars in Zone 1) ?

** -5

Questioning continues in this manner. Eventually, PROSPECTOR establishes that two zones exist in the region of interest and, after examining each in detail, it concludes that their geologic makeup supports the hypothesis that Type-A porphyry copper exists in the region.

On a scale from -5 to 5, my certainty that (there are alteration zones that are favorable for a Type-A porphyry copper deposit) is now 4.833

There are two favorable factors; in order of importance:
    2.3.1: 1. there is a sericitic zone in Zone 1 (4.834)
                ++ establishes 2.3.1 ++
    2.3.1: 2. there is a potassic zone in Zone 2 (4.499)

There are many factors that would have been unfavorable had no favorable factor existed to override them; in order of importance:

    2.3.1: 3. there is a barren-core zone in Zone 1 (-5.0)
    2.3.1: 4. there is a potassic zone in Zone 1 (-5.0)
    2.3.1: 5. there is a propylitic zone in Zone 1 (-5.0)
    2.3.1: 6. there is a sericitic zone in Zone 2 (-5.0)
    2.3.1: 7. there is a propylitic zone in Zone 2 (-4.989)
    2.3.1: 8. there is a barren-core zone in Zone 2 (-4.495)

For which of the above do you wish to see additional information?
        ⋮

Knowledge Representation

The data structure for representing the geological knowledge embodied in PROSPECTOR is called the *inference network* and guides the plausible reasoning performed by the system. The nodes in this network correspond to various assertions, such as *There is pervasively biotized hornblende* or *There is alteration favorable for the potassic zone of a porphyry copper deposit.* In a particular run, any assertion may be known to be true, known to be false, or suspected to be true with some probability.

Most of the arcs in the inference network define *inference rules* that specify how the probability of one assertion affects the probability of another assertion. For example, the presence of pervasively biotized hornblende suggests the potassic zone of a porphyry copper deposit, and the absence of any biotized hornblende is very discouraging for that conclusion. These inference rules correspond to the production rules used in MYCIN. The remaining arcs indicate that an assertion is the context for another assertion, preventing conclusions from being drawn until the right contexts are established. For example, one should establish that hornblende has been altered to biotite before asking about the degree of alteration.

The primary task confronting a geologist who wants to prepare a new model for PROSPECTOR is the representation of his model as an inference network. The current system contains models of five different types of deposits, developed in cooperation with five different consulting geologists. The statistics in Table D3–1 give a rough indication of the size and complexity of these models.

To allow certain kinds of logical reasoning by the system, each assertion is represented as a *space* in a *partitioned semantic network* (see Article III.C3, in Vol. I). A typical space asserts the hypothetical existence of physical entities having specific properties (such as being composed of biotite) and participating in specific relations (such as an alteration relation). In addition, a large taxonomic network describes important element-subset relations among the terms mentioned, such as the fact that biotite is a mica, which in turn is a silicate, which in turn is a mineral.

The articulation of assertions as a set of relations allows the system to recognize subset-superset connections between pairs of assertions. For example, the assertion *There is pervasively biotized hornblende* is clearly related to the assertion *There is mica;* assertion of the first also asserts the second,

TABLE D3–1

Size of Knowledge Base of Five PROSPECTOR Models

Model	Number of assertions	Number of rules
Koroko-type massive sulfide	39	34
Mississippi-Valley-type lead/zinc	28	20
Type A porphyry copper	187	91
Komatiitic nickel sulfide	75	49
Roll-front sandstone uranium	212	133
Total	541	327

and denial of the second denies the first. This kind of recognition is used in two main ways. First, it provides important intermodel and intramodel connections beyond those given explicitly by the inference rules. Second, it allows the system to recognize connections between information volunteered by the user and the coded models.

Probabilistic Reasoning

Some of the logical constraints that hold between spaces have probabilistic implications. In particular, if A is an instance (i.e., subset) of B, then the probability of A can never exceed the probability of B. We maintain this constraint by automatically generating certain inference rules. For example, if evidence E could raise the probability of A above the probability of B, we generate a rule from E to B that will increase the probability of B sufficiently to just satisfy the constraint. The exact procedure used here is described in Duda et al. (1977).

The various inference rules connect to form an inference network; thus, when the user provides some evidence, this information can change the probabilities of several hypotheses, which in turn can change the probabilities of hypotheses that depend on them. The probability formulas determine exactly how these probability changes propagate through the inference net. (The reader might also refer to Articles VIII.B2 and VIII.B6, on CASNET and IRIS, for alternative methods of propagation.)

Control

PROSPECTOR is a mixed-initiative system that begins by allowing the user to volunteer information about the prospect. This volunteered information is currently limited to simple statements in constrained English about the names, ages, and forms of the rocks and the types of minerals present. These statements are parsed by LIFER, a natural-language interface facility (see Article IV.F7, in Vol. I), and represented as partitioned semantic networks. A network-matching program compares each of these volunteered spaces against the spaces in the models, noting any subset, superset, or equality relations that occur.

If a volunteered space is exactly equal to a space in a model, the probability of the model space is updated and that change is propagated through the inference network. If a volunteered space is a subset of a space in a model and if it has a higher probability than the model space, once again the probability of the model space is updated and that change is propagated through the inference network.

Unfortunately, if the volunteered space matches a superset of a model space (which is usually the case), no probability change can be made unless the user expresses doubt about the situation. For example, if the user mentions biotite, the probability of the space that asserts that there is pervasively biotized hornblende is unchanged, unless the user has said that he doubts that there is any biotite. However, it is obvious that the system may want to follow up this observation, and the existence of the connection to the model is recorded.

When the user has finished the initial volunteering, PROSPECTOR scores the various models on the basis of the number and types of connections that have occurred and selects the best matching model for further investigation. Here, the basic control strategy is MYCIN-like backward chaining or consequent reasoning. At any given time, there is a current goal space whose existence is to be determined. The initial goal space is the one that corresponds to the best matching model. The various spaces in the models represent either evidence that can be sought from the user (are "askable") or internal hypotheses that are to be deduced from evidence (are "unaskable"). Naturally, the initial goal space is always unaskable. If the current goal space has any unestablished context spaces, they are pushed on the goal stack and one of them becomes the new current goal.

If the current goal is askable and has not been asked before, the user is asked about it, the effects of the answer are propagated through the inference network, and the process is repeated. If it is unaskable, it must be either the consequence of one or more inference rules or a logical combination of one or more other spaces. In the former case, the rules are scored to determine their potential effectiveness in influencing H, and the antecedent of the best scoring rule becomes the next goal. In the latter case, a predetermined supporting space becomes the next goal. In either case, the same procedure is repeated until (a) the top-level goal becomes so unlikely that another top-level goal is selected, (b) all of the askable spaces have been asked, or (c) the user interrupts with new volunteered information.

Summary

This brief overview covers the basic knowledge-representation and inference mechanisms used in PROSPECTOR. Many aspects of the system have not been discussed, such as the treatment of quantitative evidence, the matching procedure, the use of graphical input, the inference-network compiler, the explanation system, model-acquisition aids, and the test and evaluation effort.

The five models in the current system are but a fraction of what is needed for comprehensive coverage of the prospecting domain, and even these models have only recently reached the degree of completeness required for doing meaningful evaluations. Limited initial tests have shown very close agreement between the evaluations provided by the system and the evaluations of the model designers, using data from actual deposits of the types modeled. And, in fact, PROSPECTOR recently made a prediction about the location of molybdenum ore at an exploration site in the state of Washington that was substantially confirmed by subsequent drilling. More information on the system, the extent of its geological knowledge, its performance on known deposits, and its possible applications can be found in Duda et al. (1978).

References

Duda, Gaschnig, and Hart (1979) is a brief description of PROSPECTOR. See also Duda et al. (1977, 1978).

D4. Artificial Intelligence in Database Management

A DATABASE MANAGEMENT SYSTEM (DBMS) is a computer system that provides for the storage and retrieval of information about some domain. Typical examples are airline reservation systems, payroll systems, and inventory systems. This article presents a simplified definition of a DBMS and examines a number of applications of AI to database management.

A database management system consists of (a) an organized collection of *data* about some subject and (b) a *data-manipulation language* for querying and altering the data. Besides the above essentials, a DBMS may also include (c) a *database schema*, which describes the organization of the data; (d) *constraints*, for ensuring the integrity of the database; (e) *views*, for presenting individual users with a "customized" version of the database; and (f) provisions for *concurrency* (simultaneous access by several users), *backup* (recovery in the event of a system crash), and *security* (restricting the access of various users in terms of which parts of the database they may access and which operations they may perform).

Consider, for example, a database of personnel records. Assume that the records are split into two files: the ESD file with one record for each employee, containing his (or her) name, salary, and department, and the DM file with one record for each department, indicating its manager (see Fig. D4–1).

A *schema* for this database would explicate which files are in the database, what information is in each file, and what form the entries in each record take. For example:

```
Relation ESD   (Name: string; Salary: integer; Dept: string);
Relation DM    (Dept: string; Manager: string);
```

A query like *Who is the manager of John Doe?* might be expressed in the DBMS's data-manipulation language as

```
Retrieve DM.MANAGER where DM.DEPT=ESD.DEPT and ESD.NAME="JOHN DOE",
```

	ESD		DM	
Name	Salary	Dept.	Dept.	Manager
John Doe	$30K	Sales	Sales	J. Brown
Al Smith	$40K	Sales	Marketing	F. Lamont
H. Macken	$25K	Marketing	Inventory	K. L. Tang

Figure D4–1. A database composed of two files.

163

which means: In the DM file, find all records in which the DEPT field matches the DEPT field in a record in the ESD file that also has "John Doe" in its NAME field. A typical constraint for this database would be that employee salaries must always be greater than zero, which might be expressed as:

FOR ALL ESD: ESD.SAL > 0.

AI methodology has been applied to DBMSs in three ways. First, AI techniques have been employed to improve the user interface—to make it easier for the user to interact with the system. Second, AI techniques have made it possible to increase the efficiency of the DBMS system—to find the best expression in the data-manipulation language for what the user wants to know, considering how the data are distributed among files in the database. Finally, the similarities between AI and database management, both of which involve representation of information, may be exploited to extend the capabilities of a DBMS, allowing it to answer different kinds of questions about the data and about itself. Each of these will now be considered in turn.

The User Interface

Improved user interfaces have been developed to provide a degree of *data independence*, allowing the user to interact with the system without considering the manner in which the database is actually organized. In the following paragraphs, we discuss a number of ways this can be accomplished.

Natural language. The dominant aspect of the user interface is the *data-manipulation language* for accessing the database. One possibility in this regard is to allow the user to access the database in a natural language (NL) such as English. Although NL processing is a major subarea of AI research (see Chap. IV, in Vol. I), its use in database management introduces new problems, including the following:

1. Users of DBMSs, once they become familiar with the system, will often express their requests in a very abbreviated and not necessarily grammatical form.

2. Users will often misspell words.

3. The DBMS's *parser* may not have a complete lexicon of the words the user might use in his queries, since the information in the database is always changing.

4. The user, while aware of the structure of the application domain, is often ignorant of the structure of the database and of the connection between the two.

Several NL systems focusing on database access have been implemented, including LADDER (Sacerdoti, 1977), PLANES (Waltz, 1978), ROBOT (Harris,

1977), and TQA (Damerau, 1979). These systems have explored such features as the ability to handle *elliptic* input, to correct spelling errors, to handle pronouns, and to use the database to look up unknown terms in the query. (Not all systems provided all features.) The systems functioned in different ways, but all used a *grammar* of the particular language and a *parser* to process the input in terms of the grammar.

The LADDER system, for example, was designed to interrogate a database of naval information. The LADDER grammar was designed to be interpreted by the parser of the LIFER natural-language system (Article IV.F7, in Vol. I). The following segment illustrates LADDER's handling of ellipsis and spelling errors (the user's input is preceded by **):

```
** Where is the Kennedy

Parsed!
(PTP '6000N03000W' PTD 7601171200)
```

> *The ship was at 60 degrees north latitude, 30 degrees west longitude, at noon on January 17, 1976.*

```
** Pecos

Trying ellipsis: Where is Pecos
```

> *The parser was unable to make sense of "Pecos" as a sentence, so it tried a substitution into the previous sentence.*

```
Parsed!
(PTP '2131S00234E PTD 7601171200)

** Who commands the Biddle

Parsed!
(RANK 'CAPT' CONAM 'J.TOWNES')

** What is his lineal number

His => ((NAM EQ 'BIDDLE') (? RANK) (? CONAM))
```

> *The interpretation of "his" is the commander of the Biddle.*

```
Parsed!
(LINEAL 4850 RANK 'CAPT' CONAM 'J.TOWNES')

** What ships faster than the Kennedy are within 500 miles
of Naples

Parsed!
None

** How far is the Kitty Hwk from Gibralter

Spelling --> Hawk
```

Parsed!
(GCDIST 1087)

The distance is 1,087 nautical miles.

Automatic derivation of a natural-language front end. A number
of other DBMS systems have been designed, not to provide a general NL
interface but, rather, to explore the usefulness of specific NL features in the
front end. For instance, the TED system (Hendrix and Lewis, 1981) functions
in a similar manner to LADDER, except that the NL front end is *derived
semiautomatically*. Instead of requiring extensive programming to build the
NL interface, TED uses the database schema and a dialogue it conducts with
the user; the result of this process is a grammar similar to the one used by
LADDER.

The dialogue may include questions about the English expression of concepts from the database, connections between files in the database, ranges
of certain attributes, and so forth. The following are simplified examples of
questions asked in formulating a front end for a database of naval information
like the one for LADDER:

> *Assume a file named SHIP*, with attributes NAME, TYPE, MCS, and
> MED, and a file named UNIT*, with attributes CONAM and HOGEO.*

MCS is 1. arithmetic 2. feature (yes/no) 3. symbolic ?

** 1

Please type in the minimum and maximum values for MCS.

** 0 999

If there are other names for the attribute MCS, please list
them.

** Speed

If there is a word wwww such that the question "HOW wwww IS
THE SHIP?" is equivalent to "WHAT IS THE MCS OF THE SHIP?",
please type wwww.

** Fast

$\vdots$

UNIT* has links to or from which of the following files:
(SHIP* UNIT*)

** SHIP*

$\vdots$

The current link associates with each SHIP of file SHIP* a UNIT
of file UNIT*. Which properties of the UNIT (from file UNIT*)
are inherited through this link as properties of the associated
SHIP (from file SHIP*)?

```
** CONAM HOGEO
```

> *At the completion of this dialogue, TED could answer questions such as*
> List the ships.
> *What are the home ports of the fastest medical ship?*
> *Which ships have home port = NewY?*

The language capability produced in this way is slightly more restricted than the manually created one for LADDER.

Cooperative responses. The direct, literal response to a user's natural-language query may not be what he wants and might even be misleading. For example, if a user asks, "Which students failed Computer Science 301 last spring?" but the course is offered only in the fall, a simple answer of "none" is misleading, although correct. A better response would be to inform the user that the course was not offered in the spring. The COOP system (Kaplan, 1979) was designed to provide exactly this kind of response. If the state of the database violated the user's *presumptions*, as inferred by COOP from the user's query, the system would formulate a *corrective, indirect response* that was more informative than the formally correct response.

Incremental query formulation. Instead of specifying the query in full, complex detail, the user may expect help from the system in constructing it. Such interactive query-formulation was the goal of the RENDEZVOUS system (Codd, 1978). RENDEZVOUS operated by passing the initial query through a *parser*, which converted it to a logical form. The parser then initiated a *clarification dialogue* to resolve parts of the query that were ambiguous or unclear. The output from this phase was processed by a *menu driver*, which offered a list of choices at each point in the dialogue, attempting to fill in any gaps in the query specification by interrogating the user. Finally, the completed query was passed to a *generator*, which printed out an English translation of the final form for the user's approval.

Thus, RENDEZVOUS was designed to accept a partially specified query in rather rough form and to attempt to complete it by (a) entering into a clarification dialogue with the user to resolve parts of the query that were unclear and (b) attempting to fill in "gaps" in the initial query specification, by initiating a dialogue such as the following:

```
Please type in your query:

** nonexcellent non Detroit suppliers shipping part P37

What kind of response to your query are you expecting?
     1.  A list of items of information to be printed from the
         database
     2.  A yes/no or true/false answer
     3.  A count of items from the database

** 1
```

On which of the following items do you want information printed?
1. Suppliers
2. Shipments
3. Parts
4. None of the above

** 1

Which of the following items of information on suppliers do you
want printed?
1. Number
2. Name
3. Location
4. Rating
5. None of the above

** 1, 2, 3, 4

This is what the system understands your query to be:

> Print the serial number, name, location, and rating
> of every supplier not rated excellent and not located
> in Detroit who sent a shipment of part number P37.

Is the system's understanding
1. Correct & complete
2. Not yet complete
3. Incorrect ?

** 2

Does the interpretation fail to mention any specification(s) on
suppliers, parts, or shipments?

** Yes

What information do you want to specify for (or add to) your
query?
1. Supplier(s) (e.g., one named Acme, etc.)
2. Part(s) (e.g., one with quantity on hand 10, etc.)
3. Shipment(s) (e.g., one sent on June 23, 1976, etc.)
4. None of the above

** 3

Which particular item(s) of the following information on
shipments do you want to specify?
1. Serial number of parts shipped
2. Serial number of suppliers making shipment
3. Quantity shipped
4. Date shipped
5. None of the above

** 4

```
Please enter the date of shipment you wish to specify

** Aug75

This is what the system understands your query to be:

    Print the serial number, name, location, and rating
    of every supplier not rated excellent and not located
    in Detroit who, during August 1975, sent a shipment
    of part number P37.
```

More sophisticated interfaces. Ideally, the user of a DBMS should be able to interact with the system in terms of the enterprise being modeled, not confining his questions to concepts and terminology covered by the database per se. He should also be able to ask questions *about* the database—for example, about the kinds of information stored in it. Such concerns, and others, are the goals of the KLAUS system currently under development at SRI International (Haas and Hendrix, 1980). Eventually, KLAUS is intended to assist users in the management of information in various forms by serving as an interface between the user's need and the resources of the computer system.

A pilot implementation, NanoKLAUS, can build a model of the domain by engaging the user in an interactive dialogue in natural language. Following is an example of NanoKLAUS learning about a naval domain like the one used by LADDER and TED:

```
    The following demonstrates acquiring a hierarchy of classes:

** A submarine is a ship

You're saying that anything that is a SUBMARINE is also a SHIP.
OK, now I have assimilated SUBMARINE.

** A destroyer is a ship

You're saying that anything that is a DESTROYER is also a SHIP.
Is SUBMARINE a proper subclass of DESTROYER?

** No

Is SUBMARINE necessarily composed of entirely different members
from DESTROYER?

** Yes

Do SUBMARINE and DESTROYER span the set of all SHIPS?

** No

    The following demonstrates learning about verbs and actions:

** An officer can assign a unit
```

```
Give the -ed and -en form of ASSIGN (e.g., for GO: WENT, GONE):

** assigned, assigned

If an OFFICER can ASSIGN something a UNIT, type the most general
description of that something.

** a task group

Can an OFFICER ASSIGN a UNIT TO a TASK GROUP?

** Yes
```

> Note that, unlike TED, KLAUS concerns itself with the domain being
> represented, rather than just the structure of the database.

Query Optimization

AI techniques can also be used in ways that are not noticeable to the user but that result in an improvement in the behavior of the system. The QUIST system (King, 1981) uses *semantic-constraint* information available in the database schema to improve the execution of queries. For example, a typical piece of semantic-constraint information from a database about shipping might be a statement like *The only ships over 600 feet long are tankers.* Applying this constraint, QUIST can transform a query like *Which ships are more than 700 feet long?* into *Which tankers are more than 700 feet long?* The latter query might be much more efficient to process if, for example, the information about tankers were stored in a separate file in the database. QUIST contains a *cost model* that enables it to estimate the cost of executing a particular query. Different, but semantically equivalent, formulations of a query can thus be compared with respect to the cost of processing them.

The tanker example above illustrated a constraint on the value of a particular attribute. Another type of semantic constraint involves limitations on the number of entities that can be related to other entities in a particular way. For example, the number of ships that can be docked at a port may be bounded by the number of berths at the port. With this constraint, the query *What ports have more than 15 French ships docked at them?* can be transformed into the query *What ports with more than 15 berths have more than 15 French ships docked at them?*

Furakawa (1977) developed a deductive database-query system, DBAP, that used a theorem prover to plan its access to the database. The theorem prover was designed to make the access efficient by observing a number of heuristics like the following:

1. Do not access the (logically) same record in a relation more than once.

2. Get all records that satisfy the given conditions to a certain relation at one time.

3. When more than one record is to be accessed, plan the access order to minimize the database accesses (this was accomplished by operating on an *association graph* listing the connections between the relations in the database).

Note that the heuristics used by DBAP are *syntactic*, referring only to the structure of the database, as compared to the information about the actual contents of the database (e.g., the lengths of different kinds of ships) in King's QUIST system. These methods are therefore differentiated as *syntactic query optimization* and *semantic query optimization*.

Enhancing DBMS Capabilities

Database management, like AI, is concerned with the representation, retrieval, and use of information. Recognition and formalization of the similarities between the two fields have exposed some shortcomings in database systems. Two issues, in particular, concern extensions of the *data model*, which describes the structure of the database in the database schema, and the use of formal logic to reveal restrictions on the ability of database systems to represent certain kinds of information or to perform certain operations.

Improved data models. As mentioned above, DBMSs typically incorporate a database *schema* that describes the organization of the database. The schema includes a description of the objects in the database, the operations permitted on them (for both retrieval and update), and the *constraints* that the database must satisfy. The schema is actually expressed by means of a descriptive language called a *data model*, which provides a set of constructs for describing aspects of the database. The idea of a language for encoding knowledge about the database corresponds closely to the AI concept of a *knowledge-representation language* that provides the appropriate structure for encoding some knowledge used by an AI system (see Chap. III, in Vol. I). The knowledge to be encoded with the data model concerns the structure of the database itself, which will in turn be used by the DBMS for reasoning about queries.

Sowa (1976) and Roussopoulos (1977) independently developed data models based on the semantic-network knowledge-representation formalism (see Article III.C3, in Vol. I). The models were capable of representing such aspects of DBMSs as semantic constraints, generalized inference for query processing, and inheritance of properties between classes of objects. The network notation could be used both for specifying the data model and for stating queries. For example, Sowa's (1976) conceptual graph model would represent a relation HIRE, with attributes MANAGER, EMPLOYEE, and DATE, as follows, and the query *Who is the manager of Lee?* as follows,

$$\boxed{\texttt{PERSON: ?}} \longrightarrow \boxed{AGT} \longrightarrow \boxed{\texttt{HIRE}} \longrightarrow \boxed{PTNT} \longrightarrow \boxed{\texttt{PERSON: LEE}} \; .$$

Special algorithms were specified for answering queries by matching the graph encoding the query against the graph representing the data model. This provided the system with powerful capabilities for question answering, including the use of inferencing, the ability to use a procedure instead of the database, and the ability to answer queries phrased in a high-level form.

TAXIS (Mylopolous, Bernstein, and Wong, 1980) is a language for the design of information systems such as databases. It covers both the description of the structure of the database and the formal specification of the procedures for operating on the data. TAXIS uses the semantic-net representation formalism and also implements the principles of *data abstraction* and *exception handling* from programming-language research.

The semantic data model, SDM (Hammer and McLeod, 1978), allows more precise specification of semantic information than in a traditional data model. In particular, the relationships between the entities in the domain could be characterized as relationships of *restriction, abstraction,* and *aggregation.* The SDM was intended to facilitate representation of information about the domain of application, as well as about the database.

Logic as a conceptual framework. First-order logic offers a standard notation with an explicit semantics and mechanizable inference methods, which accounts for its popularity in AI applications (Article III.C1, in Vol. I). Logic also provides a clear standard within which different ideas can be expressed and compared. A recent trend has been to use logic to express certain aspects of a database. Reiter (1978) points out that a typical database is merely a collection of *well-formed formulas,* containing only ground literals (formulas containing constants but no variables), augmented with types and various other restrictions. This characterization indicates a number of restrictions present in DBMSs as compared to AI systems; two such restrictions will be described here.

First, current databases are incapable of representing many kinds of *quantified* information (e.g., facts about the existence of an unspecified entry, like *There is an employee who works in Montreal*), and *disjunctive* information (e.g., *Either John or Peter is a teacher*). These sorts of statements can be handled in the query language, but not represented in the database.

Second, databases typically do not contain extensive capabilities for *inference.* An example of deductive inference would be the use of a fact such as *John works in the sales department* and a general rule such as *All employees in the sales department work on commission* to infer the fact *John works on commission.* Certain forms of deduction are performed by means of *constraints* and *views,* but general inferencing capabilities do not exist in current DBMSs. There have been a number of proposals to incorporate deduction into databases, for purposes such as query processing (Shaw, 1980; Reiter,

1978; Minker, 1978; Chang, 1978; Kellogg, Klahr, and Travis, 1978) and query optimization (King, 1981; Furakawa, 1977).

References

The entertaining survey article on the state of natural-language processing by Hendrix and Sacerdoti (1981) discusses the issues in natural-language front ends for data bases. More advanced discussions of AI applications in database management systems can be found in the articles in the collection edited by Gallaire and Minker (1978).

Chapter VIII

Applications-oriented AI Research: Medicine

CHAPTER VIII: APPLICATIONS–ORIENTED AI RESEARCH: MEDICINE

A. OVERVIEW

THIS CHAPTER reviews the research on AI "consultation" systems designed as aids to medical decision making. (We do not cover the other major AI application in medicine, namely, the use of AI techniques in x-ray and ultrasound image analysis; see Preston, 1976, for a discussion of this application.) The motivation for the development of expert computer-based medical consultation systems is twofold. First, there are obvious benefits to society from providing reliable and thorough diagnostic services—perhaps even at a reduced cost. It has been observed (Ledley and Lusted, 1959) that most of the errors made by clinicians are errors of omission. That is, in trying to identify the disease that a patient is suffering from, the physician does not consider all possibilities, thereby missing the correct diagnosis. Assuming that adequate patient data are available to it, a computer program can be designed to consider exhaustively the diseases in its domain. Furthermore, there are some tasks that computers can perform more rapidly and accurately than the clinician can, such as calculating doses of medicines, particularly in cases where dosage is critical and many factors must be taken into account in the calculation (as in digitalis therapy; see Article VIII.B5). There are also some tasks that physicians are notoriously poor at and that are routine enough for the computer to do, such as the prescription of antimicrobial therapy.

The second motivation for development of these systems is found in current interests in computer science. Clinical medicine has been a fertile area for the study of cognitive processes, and diagnosis as a cognitive process has been studied extensively (e.g., Jacquez, 1964). It involves a highly developed medical taxonomy; a large, relatively well-organized knowledge base; and a number of human experts in the domain whose performance is significantly better on difficult problems than that of the average practitioner (i.e., there is identifiable expertise). Furthermore, the kind of problem solving that takes place in the domain is repetitive. These attributes reflect some of the prerequisites for applications of the developing subfield of AI known as *knowledge engineering*—taking AI beyond the stage of "toy" problems to confront large, real-world problems (see Article VII.A).

The development of computer-based consultation systems brings with it many formidable social, psychological, and ethical problems that must be addressed by the builders of the systems. These problems include validating the systems, exporting them to hospitals and clinics, getting physicians and patients to accept them, and deciding the responsibility for clinical decisions made with the help of these systems.

Medical Decision Making

There are three principal parts to medical decision making: data gathering, diagnosis, and treatment recommendation. Data gathering consists of obtaining the patient's history and clinical and laboratory data. The clinical data include the *symptoms*, which are the subjective sensations reported by the patient (such as headache and chest pain), and the *signs*, which are objective and observable by the physician (Feinstein, 1967). Laboratory results generally are referred to as *findings*. *Manifestation* refers to any symptom, sign, or finding. Diagnosis, then, is the process of using these data to determine the illness. The three phases of medical decision making are not independent; disease hypotheses are used to direct further information-gathering, while treatment recommendation depends on the diagnosis and generally requires more information gathering. Often, the decision to do a test includes a physician's estimate of the cost, in terms of both money and danger to the patient, which is weighed against the value of the information gained. Gathering information, diagnosing the disease, and deciding on a treatment regimen constitute a *consultation*. Figure A–1 illustrates this process in relation to the course of the disease.

Etiology refers to the original causes of the disease; *pathogenesis*, to the way in which the disease developed from its causes. Ideally, a diagnosis involves determining the etiology. A treatment is then formulated for the identified diseases and their causes. Often, however, medical knowledge is incomplete, and it is not possible to determine the causes of a disease. In these cases, treatments must be based on the empirical associations of disease characteristics and how they are known to respond to treatment.

There are some parts of consultations that computers cannot do, such as the physical examination. The physician gains much information from general appearance, facial expressions, and so forth, which are inaccessible to the computer. And, of course, the computer cannot talk with the patient to get

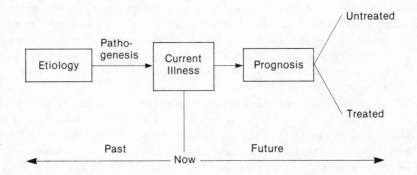

Figure A–1.   Consultation process depicting a time-specific interpretation of a medical problem.

information, explain therapy, or administer therapy. The design of computer consultation systems must, therefore, take these factors into account and offer mechanisms for acquiring some of this information indirectly.

The History of Computers in Medicine

The use of computers in medical decision making began in the early 1960s with the implementation of programs that performed well-known statistical analyses. These programs focused on the diagnosis part of the consultation: They accepted a set of findings and selected one disease from a fixed set, using methods such as pattern recognition through discriminant functions, Bayesian decision theory, and decision-tree techniques (Croft, 1972; Nordyke, Kulikowski, and Kulikowski, 1971). Somewhat more complex programs performed *sequential diagnosis.* Here, when sufficient information is not available for a reliable diagnosis, the next test to be given the patient (to get more information) is determined by a strategy that selects the best test based on three factors: the cost of the test, the danger to the patient, and the amount of discriminating information the test would supply.

The appeal of statistical methods is that the decisions based on such methods are optimal according to specified criteria. Unfortunately, these statistical systems proved unsatisfactory as medical decision-making aids. The mathematics they were based on assumed that the patient had only one disease and that the data were not erroneous. More fundamentally, certain assumptions and simplifications concerning the independence and mutual exclusivity of various disease states, required to make the statistical techniques practical, were found to be unjustified. Furthermore, many prior and conditional probabilities needed for complete analysis were simply not available.

Since the early 1970s, AI techniques have been applied increasingly to medical decision making. However, some of the classical AI problem-solving and knowledge-representation techniques (see Chaps. II and III, in Vol. I) were not directly applicable. Consider, for example, a simple application of state-space search to the determination of treatment. If one assumes that the *initial state* is the diseased patient, that the *final state* is the healthy patient, and that the *operators* for changing states are the various drugs, physical therapies, surgical procedures, and so forth, it would appear that simple search methods would find a path between the initial and final states. But there are two fundamental problems with this simpleminded approach. First, the initial state, the disease of the patient, is rarely known with certainty. Second, the application of an operator—that is, a treatment—is not guaranteed to result in an expected state. To deal with these problems, methods for representing *inexact knowledge* and for performing *plausible reasoning* have been developed in each of the consultation systems described in this chapter.

Medical diagnosis can be viewed as a problem of *hypothesis formation* (see Article VIII.B4). The diagnosis task involves using clinical findings to form a consistent set of disease hypotheses (not to select one disease from a fixed set of possible diseases). These hypotheses are typically related to each other in various ways. Each of the experimental medical consultation systems described in this chapter demonstrates a different approach to this hypothesis-formation problem.

The State of the Art

The state of the art in computer-based medical decision making is represented by the programs described in the following articles. These experimental programs are MYCIN (Shortliffe, 1976), CASNET (Weiss et al., 1978), INTERNIST (Pople, 1975), PIP (Szolovits and Pauker, 1978), the Digitalis Therapy Advisor (Silverman, 1975; Swartout, 1977b), IRIS (Trigoboff and Kulikowski, 1977), and EXPERT (Weiss and Kulikowski, 1979). There are several other experimental programs under development, including:

1. PUFF, a pulmonary-function program (Kunz et al., 1978);

2. HODGKINS, a system for performing diagnostic planning for Hodgkins disease (Safrans, Desforges, and Tsichlis, 1976);

3. HEADMED, a psychopharmacology advisor (Heiser, 1978);

4. VM, an intensive-care monitor (Fagan, 1979);

5. RX (Blum and Wiederhold, 1978); and

6. ONCOCIN, a program for monitoring the treatment of oncology out-patients on experimental treatment regimens (Shortliffe et al., 1981).

The major issues addressed during the development of all these programs concerning their construction and their acceptance by the medical community are discussed in the remainder of this article.

Representation of knowledge. Two distinct types of medical knowledge must be represented in these programs: (a) general knowledge of diseases, including manifestations, causal mechanisms, and diagnostic procedures, and (b) specific knowledge about the patient, including the current medical history and therapies. The usual representation formalisms of AI—semantic nets, production rules, frames, and predicate calculus (all discussed in Chap. III, in Vol. I)—are not directly applicable because of the inexact nature of medical knowledge. In all the consultation systems that have been developed, these representations have been augmented to incorporate some way of expressing strength of belief or strength of association.

Medical knowledge is represented in MYCIN, for example, as a set of production rules augmented by *certainty factors;* these factors express the strength of belief in the conclusion of a rule, given that all of the premises are true. (Extensive revisions of the MYCIN knowledge base are discussed in Article IX.C6 on GUIDON.) CASNET uses a *causal-network* representation (a semantic network with one relation, CAUSES) in which each CAUSES link is qualified by a number representing the strength of causality. In INTERNIST, a taxonomy of diseases is stored as a huge tree with each node representing a disease. Associated with each disease node is a list of manifestations, with numerical weights reflecting the strength of association between the disease and the manifestation. In PIP, the *frame* formalism is augmented by numbers that reflect both the strength of belief in a slot filler and the degree to which the frame itself applies to this patient. IRIS, in which the semantic-net and production-rule formalisms have been combined, provides a facility for incorporating an arbitrary representation of strength of belief.

Clinical reasoning. Clinical reasoning involves weighing different pieces of evidence for particular hypotheses. Each system has a different approach, but most employ the technique of *thresholding;* if the numerical score of a hypothesis exceeds a certain preset threshold (defined by the expert physician who builds the knowledge base), the hypothesis is believed to be true. The clinical reasoning of MYCIN, for instance, uses a production-rule-based inference mechanism (see Article III.C4) to determine parameters (e.g., the patient's infections and the causative organisms). The premises of a rule are considered true if the combined value of the associated certainty factors exceeds a predefined threshold. If several rules contribute to a conclusion about a parameter, their certainty factors are functionally combined to form a composite certainty factor for this conclusion. These confidence-factor-combining functions can be shown to be related to probability theory.

In CASNET, a status measure is associated with each state in the causal network. Weights are propagated in both forward and backward directions depending on disease causality. A state is considered confirmed if its status exceeds a specified threshold.

In INTERNIST, disease hypotheses are scored by a procedure that takes account of the strength of association among (a) the manifestations exhibited by the patient and the disease, (b) the manifestations associated with the disease that are not present in the patient, and (c) the confirmed diseases causally related to this disease. Disease hypotheses are ranked, and the top-ranked diseases are investigated further. When the difference between the scores of the top two disease hypotheses reaches a criterion, the top-ranking disease is confirmed.

PIP combines two methods of reasoning: categorical and probabilistic. Categorical decisions are based on logical criteria rather than on numerical values. The probabilistic reasoning involves scoring the disease. The applicability of a disease frame to a particular patient can be confirmed on either logical or probabilistic criteria.

In IRIS, an attempt is made to confirm nodes of a semantic net as being true for the patient. Information is passed between the nodes of the semantic net via sets of production rules associated with the links. These production rules can encode both logical and probabilistic decisions.

Explanation and justification. The explanation and justification of a system's line of reasoning are important factors for the acceptance of consultation systems by physicians. Explanation shows the user the line of reasoning in a particular diagnosis; justification is concerned with the medical accuracy and the reliability of the knowledge and the reasoning strategies used.

Only two research projects currently address the issue of explanation. MYCIN explains a diagnosis by printing out an English version of the chain of rules used. More complex explanation facilities are provided by Davis's TEIRESIAS system (see Article VII.B), an explanation and knowledge-acquisition system developed in the context of MYCIN.

The OWL Digitalis Therapy Advisor provides English explanations of its reasoning that are generated directly from the OWL code. The detail of the explanation can be controlled by the program (Swartout, 1981). Both the INTERNIST and CASNET systems are able to summarize the consultation by displaying the scores of the hypotheses and the status measures of states in the causal network; however, they are unable to explain the methods by which they arrived at these scores. CENTAUR (Aikins, 1980), a reconfiguration of the PUFF system designed in part to provide better explanations, can summarize its hypothesis-directed reasoning.

The issue of justification is a complex one. Both CASNET and MYCIN can cite references to the research literature in support of diagnoses and treatment recommendations. One aspect of justification is the accuracy and reliability of the expert's knowledge and whether this knowledge has been accurately captured in the representation formalism. Often, medical experts have differing opinions, and it is not clear whether a consensus should be sought or whether the different opinions should all be represented. Another aspect of justification is relating the program's reasoning steps to deeper causal models, that is, justifying the associations represented in the system's knowledge base. Little work has been done on this problem.

Validation. Just as the effectiveness of the various instruments and drugs used by physicians must be validated, so the accuracy, utility, and dependability of consultation programs must eventually be assessed. CASNET and MYCIN have undergone extensive clinical trials and have been rated, in experimental evaluations, as performing at human-expert levels in their respective domains (Yu, Buchanan, et al., 1979; Yu, Fagan, et al., 1979).

Acquisition of knowledge. Knowledge acquisition is the transfer of the expert's knowledge to a program. Currently, the only successful way of doing this is through a computer-scientist intermediary, although eventually experts should be able to communicate directly with the consultation program.

Concluding Remarks

Despite the extensive work that has been done, none of these systems is in routine clinical use, except for PUFF, mentioned above. Constructed with

EMYCIN (a system for building expert systems in any domain, with MYCIN's representation and control structure), PUFF employs a set of about 55 rules on pulmonary dysfunction. The program offers treatment recommendations that can be overridden by the physician.

The main reason that other expert systems have not been put to use in medical practice is that they have yet to satisfy the indispensability criterion: They are not indispensable to the practice of medicine, and physicians perform adequately without them. For AI programs to make a significant impact on health care, at least in the short term, it appears that PUFF's example should be followed. Thus, the ingredients for a successful application in medicine appear to be (a) a careful choice of the medical problem and (b) the cooperation of interested experts. The domain must be narrow and relatively self-contained, the computer should provide substantive assistance to the physician, and the task should be one that the physician either cannot do or is willing to let a computer do.

To summarize, the main focuses of AI research activity in medical decision-making aids today are: knowledge engineering, for acquiring knowledge from experts; knowledge representation, for building and maintaining the large medical knowledge bases; strategy design, for reasoning with the medical knowledge; and explanation capabilities as part of program designs, for presenting their reasoning to users.

References

Shortliffe, Buchanan, and Feigenbaum (1979) is an up-to-date overview of medical computing, including AI applications in this area. Feigenbaum (1977) gives a short review of this research. Most of the work on medical systems is discussed in detail in the AIM Workshop proceedings (AIM, 1975–81). Work on some of the most important systems is described in a special issue of the *Journal of Artificial Intelligence* (Sridharan, 1978). The article by Szolovits in that issue is an excellent overview of AI applications in medicine.

B. MEDICAL SYSTEMS

B1. MYCIN

THE MYCIN system (Shortliffe, 1976) was designed to provide consultative advice on diagnosis and therapy for infectious diseases. Such advice is often required in hospital care because the attending physician may not be an expert on infectious diseases that show themselves during hospitalization—for example, an infection that develops in a cardiology patient after heart surgery. Time considerations compound the problem. A specimen (blood, urine, etc.) from a patient can show some evidence of bacterial growth within 12 hours, but generally it takes 24 to 48 hours (or more) for positive identification. The physician must, therefore, often decide in the absence of complete information whether or not to start treatment and what drugs to use if treatment is required. Both of these may be difficult questions.

The MYCIN protocol that follows shows the initial and final parts of a sample interaction between a physician and the system. MYCIN, in effect, interviews the doctor about the patient, collecting information from which it infers the diagnosis and selects an appropriate therapy.

————————PATIENT-1————————

1) Patient's name: (first-last)

** Fred Smith

MYCIN collects some background data about the patient. The physician's response follows the double asterisks.

2) Sex:

** Male

3) Age:

** 55

4) Have you been able to obtain positive cultures from a site at which Fred Smith has an infection?

** Yes

————————INFECTION-1————————

5) What is the infection?

** Primary-bacteremia

184

6) Please give the date and approximate time when signs or
symptoms of the primary-bacteremia (infection-1) first appeared.
(mo/da/yr)

** May 5, 1980

The most recent positive culture associated with the
primary-bacteremia (infection-1) will be referred to as:

————————CULTURE-1————————

7) From what site was the specimen for culture-1 taken?

** Blood

8) Please give the date and time when this blood culture
(culture-1) was obtained.   (mo/da/yr)

** May 9, 1980

The first significant organism from this blood culture
(culture-1) will be referred to as:

————————ORGANISM-1————————

9) Enter the identity of organism-1:

** Unknown

> *Typically, the identity of the organism is not known and, hence, must be
> inferred by MYCIN from various other pieces of laboratory and clinical
> information. MYCIN proceeds to ask questions that could help to deter-
> mine the identity of the organism.*

10) Is organism-1 a rod, or coccus (etc.):

** Rod

11) The gram stain of organism-1:

** Gramneg

12) Have there been positive cultures from sites which are NOT
associated with infections about which you are seeking advice?

** No

13) Did organism-1 grow aerobically?

** Yes (.8)

14) Did organism-1 grow anaerobically?

** Yes

15) What is the suspected portal of entry of organism-1 into
this sterile site?

** GI (.6)

*More questions follow, to gather sufficient information for inferring pos-
sible identities of the infecting organisms.*

My therapy recommendation will be based on the following
probable infection(s) and potential causative organism(s):

INFECTION-1 is PRIMARY-BACTEREMIA
<Item 1> The identity of organism-1 may be PSEUDOMONAS-AERUGINOSA
<Item 2> The identity of organism-1 may be KLEBSIELLA-PNEUMONIAE
<Item 3> The identity of organism-1 may be E.COLI
<Item 4> The identity of organism-1 may be BACTEROIDES-FRAGILIS
<Item 5> The identity of organism-1 may be ENTEROBACTER
<Item 6> The identity of organism-1 may be PROTEUS-NON-MIRABILIS

46) On a scale of 0 to 4, where higher numbers indicate
increasing severity, how would you rate Fred Smith's degree
of sickness?

** 3

47) Does Fred Smith have a clinically significant allergic
reaction to any antimicrobial agent?

** No

48) Fred Smith's weight in kilograms (or <number> pounds):

** 70

Note that two drugs cover for six potential organisms.

[Rec 1] My preferred therapy recommendation is as follows:

In order to cover for Items <1 2 3 5 6>:
    Give: GENTAMICIN
    Dose: 119 mg (1.7 mg/kg) q8h IV [or IM] for 10 days
    Comments: Modify dose in renal failure

In order to cover for Item <4>:
    Give: CLINDAMYCIN
    Dose: 595 mg (8.5 mg/kg) q6h IV [or IM] for 14 days
    Comments: If diarrhea or other GI symptoms develop,
              patient should be evaluated for possible
              pseudomembranous colitis.

Do you wish to see the next-choice therapy?

Alternative choices are available.

** Yes

Which, if any, of the above drugs do you wish eliminated
from consideration?

** Clindamycin

[Rec 2] Next best therapy recommendation:

In order to cover for Items <2 3 4 5 6>:
    Give: CHLORAMPHENICOL
    Dose: 1 gm (15 mg/kg) q6h IV for 14 days
    Comments: Monitor patient's white count

In order to cover for Item <1>:
    Give: GENTAMICIN
    Dose: 119 mg (1.7 mg/kg) q8h IV [or IM] for 10 days
    Comments: Modify dose in renal failure

MYCIN's Knowledge Base

The medical knowledge in MYCIN is encoded as *production rules* of the sort shown in Figure B1–1 (see Article III.C4, in Vol. I, on production-system knowledge representation). The rules are stored internally in the LISP form shown, from which the English version is generated. Each rule is a single "chunk" of domain-specific information indicating an *action* (in this case, a conclusion) that is justified if the conditions specified in the *premise* are fulfilled. Since the rule employs a vocabulary of concepts common to the domain, it forms, *by itself*, a comprehensible statement of some piece of domain knowledge. As will become clear, this characteristic is useful in many ways.

Each rule is highly stylized—with an IF . . . THEN format and a specified set of admissible *primitives*. In fact, the internal form, as illustrated, is executable LISP code. Furthermore, this tightly structured form makes it possible for a program to be designed to *examine the rules* as well as execute them.

RULE 050

PREMISE: (AND (SAME CNTXT INFECT PRIMARY-BACTEREMIA)
                  (MEMBF CNTXT SITE STERILESITES)
                  (SAME CNTXT PORTAL GI))
ACTION: (CONCLUDE CNTXT IDENT BACTEROIDES TALLY .7)

MYCIN's English translation:

IF   1) the infection is primary-bacteremia, and
            2) the site of the culture is one of the sterile sites, and
            3) the suspected portal of entry of the organism is
               the gastrointestinal tract,
THEN   there is suggestive evidence (.7) that the identity of the
            organism is bacteroides.

Figure B1–1. A MYCIN production rule.

For example, the rules can be translated into a readable English format, as in Figure B1–1. This translation capability has been used in MYCIN to *explain* the program's inferences to the expert. (The importance of the system's ability to explain a line of reasoning leading to a conclusion and to justify why the program is asking a particular question in a given case is discussed in Articles VII.A, VII.B, and VIII.A.) The current knowledge base contains 450 such rules that allow MYCIN to diagnose and prescribe therapy for bacteremia (infections of the blood) and meningitis.

The premise of each rule is a Boolean combination of one or more *clauses*, each of which is constructed from a predicate function with an associative triple—(attribute, object, value)—as its argument. Thus, each premise clause typically has the following four components:

⟨predicate function⟩ ⟨object⟩ ⟨attribute⟩ ⟨value⟩ .

For example, the second clause in rule 50, above, is:

```
The site of the culture is one of the sterile sites;
```

or, in LISP:

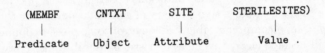

```
(MEMBF        CNTXT        SITE        STERILESITES)
  |             |           |             |
Predicate     Object     Attribute      Value .
```

MEMBF is a predicate, and the triple says that the site of the current object (an organism, in this case) is a member of the class of sterile sites. A standardized set of some 24 domain-independent predicate functions (e.g., SAME, KNOWN, DEFINITE) and a range of domain-specific attributes (e.g., IDENTITY, SITE), objects (e.g., ORGANISM, CULTURE), and associated values (e.g., E.COLI, BLOOD) form the vocabulary of conceptual primitives for constructing rules.

A rule premise is always a conjunction of clauses, but it may contain arbitrarily complex conjunctions or disjunctions nested within each clause. (Instead of writing rules whose premise would be a disjunction of clauses, a separate rule is written for each clause.) The action part indicates one or more conclusions that can be drawn if the premises are satisfied, making the rules purely inferential.

Certainty Factors

Note that the rules are judgmental; that is, they make inexact inferences on a confidence scale of −1.0 to 1.0, where −1.0 represents complete confidence that a proposition is false and 1.0 represents complete confidence that it is true. In the case of the rule in Figure B1–1, the evidence cited in the premise is enough to assert the conclusion shown with a mild degree of confidence: .7. This number is called the *certainty* or *confidence factor* (CF) and embodies a model of confirmation described by Shortliffe (1976).

MYCIN uses CFs rather than other, more standard statistical measures to decide among alternatives during a consultation session. Standard statistical measures were rejected in favor of CFs because experience with clinicians had shown that clinicians do not use the information comparable to implemented standard statistical methods. However, the concept of CFs did appear to fit the clinicians' reasoning patterns—their judgments of how they weighted factors, strong or weak, in decision making.

The CFs are a measurement of the association between the premise and action clauses of each rule. When a production rule succeeds because its premise clauses are true in the current context, the CFs of the component clauses that indicate how strongly each clause is believed are combined, and the resulting CF is used to modify the CF specified in the action clauses. Thus, if the premise was only weakly believed (low, positive total CF), any conclusions that the rule might make would be modified (reduced) to reflect this weak belief that the patient was in a particular situation. In questions 13 and 15 in the preceding transcript, the user shows lack of complete confidence. Also, since the conclusion of one rule may be the premise of another, reasoning from premises with less than complete confidence factors is commonplace.

Medical facts about the patient are represented as 4-tuples made up of an associative triple and its current CF. Positive CFs indicate that the evidence confirms the hypothesis; negative CFs indicate disconfirming evidence. The following are examples of such 4-tuples:

```
(IDENT ORGANISM-2 KLEBSIELLA .25)
(IDENT ORGANISM-2 E.COLI .73)
(SENSITIVS ORGANISM-1 PENICILLIN -1.0)
(IMMUNOSUPPRESSED PATIENT-1 YES 1.0)
```

MYCIN's model of inexact reasoning permits the coexistence of several plausible values for a single attribute, if this is suggested by the evidence. For example, after attempting to deduce the identity (IDENT) of an organism, MYCIN may have concluded (correctly) that there is evidence of both *E.coli* and *Klebsiella*.

To summarize, there are two major forms of knowledge representation in use in the performance program: (a) the attributes, objects, and values, which form a vocabulary of domain-specific conceptual primitives, and (b) the inference rules expressed in terms of these primitives.

Reasoning: The Inference Engine

The mechanism used to draw conclusions based on the rules in the knowledge base and the data for the current case is the system's reasoning process, or *inference engine*. In MYCIN, rules are invoked in a simple *backward-chaining* fashion that results in an exhaustive *depth-first* search of an AND/OR goal tree (see Article II.B2, in Vol. I). For example, assume that the program is attempting to determine the identity of an infecting organism. It retrieves all the rules that make a conclusion about the topic (i.e., that mention the *identity of bacteria* in their action clause) and invokes each one in turn, evaluating each premise clause to see if the conditions specified have been met. For the sample rule in Figure B1–1, this process would begin with the first clause, determining whether the *type of the infection* is primary bacteremia. Since the type of the infection is unknown, it is set up as a subgoal and the process recurs—the system then looks for rules that conclude about this new topic, the type of the infection.

The subgoal that is set up is a *generalized* form of the original goal. In other words, the subgoal is always of the form *Determine the value of* ⟨attribute⟩ rather than *Determine whether the* ⟨attribute⟩ *is equal to* ⟨value⟩. Thus, for the first clause in rule 50 (*the infection is primary-bacteremia*), the subgoal set up is *Determine the type of infection.* By setting up the generalized goal of collecting all evidence about an attribute, the performance program effectively exhausts each subject as it is encountered and thus tends to group together all questions about a given topic. This feature results in a system that displays a much more focused, methodical approach to the task, which is a distinct advantage when human-engineering considerations are important. The cost is the effort of deducing or collecting information that is not strictly necessary. However, since this unnecessary effort occurs rarely—only when the ⟨attribute⟩ can be deduced with certainty to be the ⟨value⟩ named in the original goal—it has not proved to be a problem in practice.

The search is thus *depth first* (because each premise condition is thoroughly explored in turn), the tree that is sprouted is an AND/OR goal tree (because rules may have OR conditions in their premise), and the search is exhaustive (all of the rules that are applicable are "fired" and their conclusions are rank-ordered by certainty factors). Since the rules are inexact—leading to conclusions of less than total certainty—it is a wisely conservative strategy to continue to collect all evidence about the subgoal from other applicable rules even if one rule succeeds; MYCIN considers *all* the possibilities every time.

If, after trying all relevant rules to resolve a subgoal, the total weight of the evidence about a hypothesis falls between $-.2$ and $.2$ (an empirically determined threshold value), the answer is regarded as still unknown. This result would occur if no rules were applicable (because their premises did not match the available data), if the applicable rules were too weak, if the effects of several rules offset each other, or if there were no rules for this subgoal at all. In any of these cases, when the system is unable to deduce the answer, it asks the user for the value of the subgoal (using a phrase that is stored along with the attribute itself).

This strategy, of always attempting to deduce the value of a subgoal and asking the user only when deduction fails, ensures a minimum of questions. It could also mean, however, that work might be expended searching for a subgoal, arriving perhaps at a less than definite answer when the user might already know the answer with certainty. To prevent this inefficiency, some of the attributes have been labeled "laboratory data" to indicate that they represent information available as results of quantitative tests. In these cases, the deduce-then-ask procedure is reversed, and the system attempts to deduce the answer only if the user cannot supply it. Given the desire to minimize both tree search and the number of questions asked, there is no guaranteed optimal solution to the problem of deciding when to ask for information and when to try to infer it, but the distinction described here has worked well and seems to embody an appropriate criterion.

Two other additions to straightforward tree search increase the inference engine's efficiency. First, before the entire list of rules for a subgoal is retrieved, the program attempts to find a sequence of rules that would establish the goal with certainty, based only on what is currently known. Since this is a search for a sequence of rules with $CF = 1$, the result is termed a *unity path*. In addition to efficiency, this process offers the advantage of allowing the program to make commonsense deductions with a minimum of effort (rules with $CF = 1$ are largely definitional). Because there are few such rules in the system, the search is typically very brief.

Second, the inference engine performs a partial evaluation of rule premises. Since many attributes are found in several rules, the value of one clause (perhaps the last) in a premise may already have been established while the rest are still unknown. If this clause alone would make the premise false, there is clearly no reason to do all the search necessary to establish the others. Each premise is thus previewed by evaluating it on the basis of currently available information. The result is a Boolean combination of TRUEs, FALSEs, and UNKNOWNs, and straightforward simplification (e.g., $F \times U = F$) indicates whether the rule is guaranteed to fail.

Therapy Selection

After MYCIN determines the significant infections and the organisms that cause them, it proceeds to recommend an antimicrobial regimen if this is appropriate. The MYCIN therapy selector (Clancey, 1978) uses a description of the patient's infections, the causal organisms, a ranking of drugs by sensitivity, and a set of drug-preference categories (such as *Propose two drugs: one second-choice drug and one third-choice drug*) to recommend a drug regimen. The algorithm will also modify dosages in the case of renal failure in the patient. The program can provide detailed explanations of how it made a regimen choice and can accept and critique a regimen proposed by the physician.

Acquisition and Use of New Knowledge

The representation of knowledge as production rules and the ability to explain specific rules allow MYCIN to interact with an expert clinician in a

manner that permits the system to acquire and apply new knowledge. Davis's
TEIRESIAS system (see Article VII.B) works in conjunction with MYCIN and
allows the expert to inspect faulty reasoning chains and then add and modify
any rules or clinical parameters required to augment and repair the medical
knowledge of MYCIN.

When the expert is dissatisfied with the system's performance on a particular case, MYCIN is able to explain how it made the erroneous conclusions
and to guide the expert while he (or she) is determining the source of the
reasoning "bug." To correct the reasoning, the expert may elect to enter new
rules or alter existing ones. He enters his requests through a "nearly natural
language" interface. These requests to add or modify a rule are parsed by
the system and used to create a new rule in MYCIN's internal (LISP) format,
which is then translated back into English (as in Fig. B1–1) and presented to
the user for inspection. This interaction helps minimize any misunderstanding
between the clinician and MYCIN.

Once this new rule is accepted and understood by the system, the next
consultation will make use of it and alter its recommendations accordingly.
This ability permits the system to interact directly with the domain experts
without the intervention of a programmer.

Concluding Remarks

Formal evaluations of the MYCIN system have been made that indicate
that MYCIN compares favorably with experts in infectious disease in diagnosing and selecting therapy for patients with bacteremia and meningitis (Yu,
Buchanan, et al., 1979; Yu, Fagan, et al., 1979). At present, however, the system is not used on the wards, primarily because of its incomplete knowledge
of the full spectrum of infectious diseases.

MYCIN was one of the first of a new breed of computer systems—systems
that step out of the toy worlds of AI into the real world. These systems must
deal with many of the social and psychological problems of man-machine
interactions. Issues such as modularity and representation of knowledge,
reasoning in specific domains, explanation of a system's logic, and the ability
to accumulate and use new information must be considered, with attention
given both to programming and to interfacing problems. MYCIN has been
designed with these issues in mind and has consequently shown promise as a
real-world aid to the clinician.

References

See Shortliffe (1976) and Davis (1976).

B2.   CASNET

THE Causal ASsociational NETwork (CASNET) program (Weiss, Kulikowski, and Safir, 1977) is a computer system developed at Rutgers University for performing medical diagnosis. The major application of CASNET has been in the domain of glaucoma. The system represents a disease not as a static state but as a *dynamic process* that can be modeled as a network of causally linked pathophysiological states. The system diagnoses a patient by determining the pattern of pathophysiological causal pathways present in the patient and identifying this pattern with a *disease category*. Once the disease category is explicitly identified, the most appropriate treatments can be prescribed. The causal model also makes possible a prediction of the likely course of a disease both if treated and if untreated.

Representation of Medical Knowledge

A CASNET model consists of three planes of knowledge, parts of which are shown in Figure B2–1. The *plane of pathophysiological states* is the heart of the model. The nodes in this plane represent elementary hypotheses about the disease process, and arcs here represent a causal connection between two elementary hypotheses; for example, INCREASED INTRAOCULAR PRESSURE ... CAUSES ... CUPPING OF THE OPTIC DISK. Associated with each link is a forward weight or *confidence factor*, a number on a scale of 1 through 5, where 1 corresponds to "rarely causes" and 5 to "(almost) always causes." The determination of these weights and their utility in confirming or disconfirming the presence of a pathophysiological state are discussed later in this article.

The *plane of observations* contains nodes representing evidence gathered from the patient—signs, symptoms, and laboratory tests. During a consultation, some or all of these nodes will be instantiated. Nodes in this plane are linked to nodes in the pathophysiological plane. The links have associated confidences, again on a scale of 1 through 5, reflecting the degree to which the particular test, symptom, or sign *supports* the associated state. For example, a scotoma (a perimetry measurement) strongly indicates VISUAL FIELD LOSS, so it has a confidence value of 5. The same test, however, could have a different confidence value depending on the results; for example, 15 mm of Hg could be considered evidence for INCREASED INTRAOCULAR PRESSURE, but a result of 30 would be definite evidence and would carry a greater confidence value. The confidence values with which observations are linked to pathophysiological states are predetermined by the designers of CASNET.

In general, there is usually more than one test for a particular state, and the same test might indicate more than one state. Each test also has an

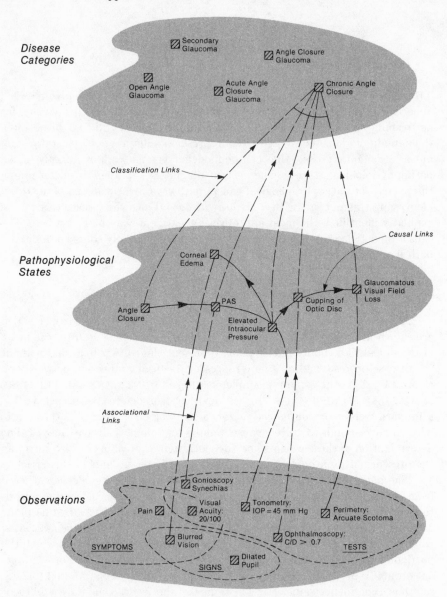

Figure B2–1. Three-level description of a disease process (Weiss et al., 1978).

associated *cost* that reflects both monetary cost and danger to the patient. Some states may not have a corresponding test, since such a test may not exist or may be judged too difficult or costly to use for a particular pathology.

The third plane contains the *classification tables* for the disease. A classification table defines a disease as a set of confirmed and denied pathophysiological states. It also contains a set of treatment statements for that disease. For example, the classification table in Figure B2–2 indicates that if a patient is found to have ANGLE CLOSURE and INCREASED INTRAOCULAR PRESSURE but neither CUPPING nor VISUAL FIELD LOSS, then he (or she) has ANGLE CLOSURE GLAUCOMA; if he has ANGLE CLOSURE, INCREASED INTRAOCULAR PRESSURE, CUPPING, and VISUAL FIELD LOSS, then he has CHRONIC ANGLE CLOSURE GLAUCOMA. The concept represented in the classification tables is that a disease is dynamic with respect to time and that confirmed states farther down a *pathway* represent more advanced stages of the disease. The states in a classification table will generally be on the same pathway. A starting state is a state with no causes in the network (also called a basic disease mechanism). Inadequate understanding of disease mechanisms or incomplete models sometimes lead to classification tables containing states from more than one pathway.

Reasoning

Figure B2–2 illustrates how CASNET defines a disease as a conjunction of causally related pathophysiological states. Diagnosis in CASNET is a matter of finding one or more causal pathways between these states. Reasoning in CASNET is designed to maximize the likelihood of finding these pathways, given a set of signs, symptoms, and test results.

A diagnostic session begins with the program's asking the user (physician) a series of questions about the patient. The physican answers with values for any tests, signs, and symptoms, or he answers UNKNOWN. These values, together with the confidences associated with the tests and the weights associated with the causal arcs, are used to compute a *status*, or confidence factor, for each node in the causal net.

The STATUS of a state is affected both by the results of its associated tests and by the STATUS values of the states around it. For example, if *A* causes *B* and *B* is confirmed by observation, then there is strong evidence for *A*. A general algorithm is used to propagate these weights on a state, both in the forward direction (i.e., along the direction of the causal link) and in the backward direction. A state is marked *confirmed* if its STATUS is greater than a preset threshold, and it is marked *denied* if its STATUS is less than a second

STATE	DISEASES	TREATMENTS
ANGLE CLOSURE		
INCR IOP	ANGLE CLOSURE GLAUCOMA	TREATMNT1
CUPPING		
VFL	CHRONIC ANGLE CLOSURE GLAUCOMA	TR1, TR2

Figure B2–2.   A classification table.

threshold; otherwise, it is *undetermined.* The program employs a strategy for selecting the next question that is based on the cost of the test and on the likelihood that it will lead to the confirmation or denial of a state.

After all available symptoms and findings have been entered and after the STATUS values have been computed, the classification tables are used to determine diagnoses and treatments. The tables are selected to cover all confirmed nodes. The strategy for selecting the tables is to find the starting states for which causal pathways can be generated that reach the largest number of confirmed states without traversing a denied state. This procedure is repeated until all of the confirmed states are covered.

The treatment statements of the selected classification tables are then used to select a therapy for the indicated diseases. Like a state, a treatment has an associated STATUS that is interpreted as its confidence in its success as a treatment. The treatment with the highest STATUS is selected. This assessment is repeated for all selected classification tables. A final algorithm decides whether some treatments are subsumed by others, and then the final treatment recommendations are printed. If desired, a short summary of research justifying the diagnosis and treatment can also be printed. The current glaucoma model contains about 150 states, 350 tests, and 50 classification tables.

Summary

CASNET adopts a strictly bottom-up approach to the problem of diagnosis, working from the tests, through the causal pathways, to a diagnosis. The separation of medical knowledge (encoded in the causal network) from reasoning strategies (embodied in the program) will make the expansion of the disease model, when new research discoveries are made, a simple matter. The program is continually being tested and updated by a computer-based network of collaborators.

The model also provides a convenient way of following the progress of a patient's disease over multiple visits—the causal net can be used to view the disease progression, both forward and backward, along the pathways. Although CASNET has been used primarily for glaucoma, the representational scheme and decision-making procedures are applicable to other diseases that are understood well enough to make the process of disease known. The program's performance has been evaluated by opthalmologists and is considered close to expert level.

References

See Weiss et al. (1978).

B3. INTERNIST

INTERNIST is a consultation program in the domain of internal medicine developed jointly by H. Pople, a computer scientist, and J. Myers, a specialist in internal medicine, both at the University of Pittsburgh. The program is presented with a list of *manifestations* of disease in a patient (e.g., symptoms, physical signs, laboratory data, and history), and it attempts to form a diagnosis. The diagnosis consists of a list of diseases that would account for the manifestations. Using information presented during the course of the consultation, the program is able to discriminate between competing *disease hypotheses*. The current version of the program only formulates diagnoses and does not recommend treatments.

One of the major goals of the INTERNIST project has been to model the way clinicians do diagnostic reasoning. The program has been used to explore the way that certain symptoms evoke particular disease hypotheses in the minds of clinicians, how hypothesized diseases give rise to expectations of other symptoms, how clinicians focus on particular disease areas and temporarily ignore certain other symptoms that they judge irrelevant, and how they decide between competing disease hypotheses.

From the standpoint of computer science, INTERNIST is solving a *theory-formation* or *hypothesis-formation* problem (see Chap. XIV, in Vol. III). Determining a satisfactory diagnosis involves inferring a set of hypotheses to explain the patient data. In INTERNIST, the data are manifestations and the hypotheses are diseases.

Diagnosis in internal medicine is complicated because a patient may suffer from a number of diseases simultaneously. Although some diseases are more likely to be associated than others, the possible combinations are too numerous to encode a priori. (Pople, 1977, suggests that a conservative estimate of this number is 10^{40}.) Clearly, diagnosis of a set of diseases present in a patient is nontrivial. INTERNIST–I accomplished this diagnosis by establishing sequentially the diseases that best fit the data. INTERNIST–II is an improvement over its predecessor in that it establishes the set of diseases in parallel and therefore avoids some of the annoying artifacts of sequential processing, such as considering a number of incorrect diagnoses before "focusing in" on the correct one.

For INTERNIST–I, a *problem* is defined as a set of mutually exclusive disease hypotheses. If a patient has a number of diseases, INTERNIST–I must solve that number of problems. In brief, INTERNIST–I finds a set of diseases that account for some or all of a set of symptoms. Then it selects one disease from the set on the basis of a scoring schema, which is the solution for one of the problems. Then it finds another set of diseases that account for some or all of any remaining symptoms and again selects the most likely of these alternatives. It continues in this manner until all symptoms have been accounted for.

Representation of Medical Knowledge

INTERNIST's knowledge of diseases is organized into a *disease tree*, or taxonomy, using the "form-of" relation (see Fig. B3–1). For example, hepato-cellular disease is a form of liver disease. The top-level classification in this tree is by organs—heart disease, lung disease, liver disease, and so on. A *disease node*'s offspring are refinements of that disease, terminal nodes being individual diseases. A nonterminal node and its subtree are referred to as a *disease area*, while a terminal node is referred to as a *disease entity*. The disease hierarchy is predetermined and fixed in the system.

Diseases and their manifestations are related in two major ways: (a) a manifestation can *evoke* a disease and (b) a disease can *manifest* certain signs and symptoms. These relations can be thought of as probabilities: $p(D \mid M)$ (the conditional probability of D given M) and $p(M \mid D)$, respectively. The strength of these relations is given by a number on a scale of 0 through 5, where 0 means that no conclusions can be drawn about the disease and the manifestation and 5 means that the manifestation is always associated with the disease. Each disease in the tree is associated with its relevant manifes-tations. Several other relationships are superimposed on the disease tree to capture causal, temporal, and other association patterns among diseases.

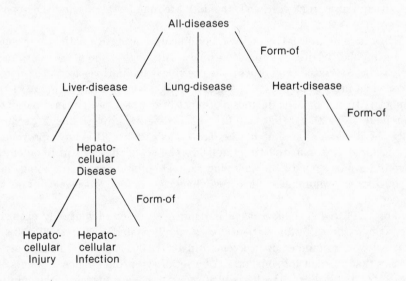

Figure B3–1.   INTERNIST's disease tree.

The disease tree and its associated manifestations are constructed and maintained separately from the diagnosis program. All known EVOKE and MANIFEST relations are entered for the terminal nodes (diseases) of the tree. A list of manifestations is then computed for each nonterminal node of the tree by taking the intersection of the manifestation lists of that node's offspring. In this way, the manifestations "percolate" up through the tree to the most general disease with which they are associated and are stored only with this node. This means that manifestations associated with a nonterminal disease node are, by implication, also associated with every node (terminal or nonterminal) beneath it in the tree. As well as providing storage economy, this information is used during the consultation for selecting disease areas on which to focus. For example, jaundice (yellowing of the skin) will be associated with some nonterminal disease (e.g., hepatitis) under liver diseases, and its presence in a patient will cause the consultation program to investigate diseases in that disease area.

Various properties are associated with each manifestation. The most important ones are TYPE and IMPORT. The TYPE property is a measure of how expensive it is to test for a manifestation, in terms of both financial cost and physical risk to the patient. TYPE is used to order the questions asked by the consultation program: Questions about less expensive manifestations are asked first. The IMPORT of a manifestation is a measure of how easily it can be ignored in a diagnosis. The manifestation "Shellfish ingestion" can easily be ignored, but a liver biopsy showing caseating granulomas must be explained.

Reasoning

At the beginning of a consultation, a list of manifestations is entered. As each manifestation is entered, it evokes one or more nodes of the disease tree. A *model* is created for each evoked disease node. The model consists of four lists:

1. Observed manifestations that this disease cannot explain (this list is called the *shelf*);

2. Observed manifestations that are consistent with the disease;

3. Manifestations that should be present if this disease is the correct diagnosis but that have not been observed in the patient;

4. Manifestations consistent with this disease but that have not yet been observed in the patient.

After the initial entry of manifestations, the disease tree consists of nodes that have been "lit up" (evoked) and those that have not. A diagnosis corresponds to a set of lit terminal nodes that account for all of the symptoms. In general, at this stage very few of the terminal nodes will be lit up, so the program must ask for further information. To get this further information, the program will focus on a disease area and formulate a problem.

Each disease model is *scored*, receiving a positive score for each manifestation it explains and a negative score for each manifestation that it cannot explain. Both are weighted by IMPORT. It receives a bonus if it is linked causally to a disease that has already been confirmed. The disease models are partitioned into two sets: (a) the top-ranked model and the diseases that are mutually exclusive to it (alternatives) and (b) the diseases that are complementary to the top-ranked model. For example, if the top-ranked node is hepatocellular injury, then other evoked liver diseases will be alternatives to it, while lung or heart diseases will be complementary.

Having formulated a problem by partitioning the disease models, the system follows one of several strategies, depending on the number of candidate diseases in the problem set. If there are many (more than four) alternative hypotheses, it attempts to rule out as many as possible. Questions about manifestations that strongly indicate a disease (high $p(M \mid D)$) are selected first. If these manifestations are not present, this disease can be ruled out. If there are between two and four possibilities, the program attempts to discriminate between them. Then questions about manifestations that strongly indicate one disease, D_1 (high $p(M \mid D_1)$), and weakly indicate another disease, D_2 (low $p(M \mid D_2)$), are selected. These questions are used to discriminate between the two diseases. If there is only one candidate, questions that have a good chance of confirming this disease are asked. Sometimes, if there are not enough data, it will not be possible to confirm one of the terminal nodes, and a more general diagnosis is given (e.g., "liver disease").

After a disease is confirmed, its manifestations are marked "accounted for," bonus scores are given to previously manifested diseases that are causally linked to this one, and focus shifts to the new top-ranked disease and the formulation of a new problem.

INTERNIST–II

There was a major problem with INTERNIST–I: In complex cases, the program had a tendency to begin the analysis by focusing first on totally inappropriate areas. While the final diagnosis was usually correct, the initial meandering was annoying to clinicians. The cause of the problem was traced to the sequential method of problem formulation. In INTERNIST–II, the simultaneous formulation of several problems is being investigated.

Representation of medical knowledge. INTERNIST–II uses the same knowledge base as INTERNIST–I, but it is augmented by a set of *constrictor* relations. These are manifestations that do not evoke a particular disease but, rather, a general area of infirmity. For example, jaundice alerts clinicians to the presence of liver disease. It does not discriminate between liver diseases, but it does delimit this disease area. Formally, a disease area constrained by a constrictor manifestation is a subtree of the disease tree, in this case, the subtree of liver diseases.

Reasoning. A problem for INTERNIST–I is to find a set of terminal nodes on the disease tree that accounts for a set of manifestations. It then chooses one node from the set and formulates another problem. INTERNIST–II does not start a diagnosis by formulating a set of terminal nodes, because the number of combinations of terminal disease-nodes that may account for a set of manifestations is enormous. Instead, INTERNIST–II partitions the disease tree into disease areas, which collectively account for all the manifestations. Constrictor manifestations are used to make the partitions. If a patient manifests more than one constrictor, the disease tree will be partitioned into more than one disease area. The conjunction of all the disease areas is called the *root structure* and is formally a set of subtrees of the disease tree. A root structure accounts for all the patient's manifestations. The problem for INTERNIST–II is to decide which terminal nodes (actual diseases) within the root structure best account for the manifestations. This is accomplished by partitioning the root structure into smaller subtrees exactly as the disease tree was partitioned into the root structure, namely, by using manifestations that strongly suggest a disease area (this time, however, the disease area is smaller). The process of partitioning the root structure into smaller areas continues until all the manifestations are accounted for.

This is a summary account of the operation of INTERNIST–II. In actuality, it is more complicated (see Pople, 1977, for a complete explication). The main point of INTERNIST–II is that it diagnoses a patient's diseases by dividing the disease tree into smaller and smaller subtrees, until it achieves a set of terminal nodes that accounts for all the manifestations.

Summary

The two INTERNIST programs have successfully combined a bottom-up and top-down approach to medical diagnosis. The patient data evoke certain disease hypotheses (bottom-up) that are then used to predict (top-down) other manifestations that should be present if the hypothesis is to be confirmed. The system is purely associational. It does not attempt to model any disease processes but considers a disease as a static category and diagnosis as the task of assigning a patient to one or more categories. INTERNIST–I has a large knowledge base, currently containing over 500 of the diseases of internal medicine (about 75% complete). It has displayed expert performance in complex cases involving multiple diseases. Pople and Myers expect that the system will eventually be in clinical use.

References

See Pople (1975, 1977).

B4.   Present Illness Program

THE PRESENT ILLNESS PROGRAM (PIP) is being developed at M.I.T. (see Pauker et al., 1976; Szolovits and Pauker, 1976, 1978). One application of it thus far has been to take present illnesses of patients with renal (kidney) disease. Taking a present illness is different from performing a complete diagnosis—it is the typical consultation a patient has with a general practitioner. The patient usually presents a *chief complaint* that becomes the initial focus of the consultation, and diagnosis is based on only very low cost sources of information (such as patient history, physical examination, and routine laboratory tests). High-cost or high-risk procedures that may be necessary for a complete diagnosis are not used.

The medical knowledge in PIP is represented as a network of *frames* (see Article III.C7, in Vol. I). The frames are centered around diseases, clinical states, and physiological states (hereafter called the patient situation) and contain data such as typical findings, relationships to other patient situations, and rules for judging how well a set of *findings* exhibited by a patient matches the situation described by the frame. *Matching* is the key strategy in the diagnosis, which involves comparing findings to those indicated in the disease frames and then selecting a set of frames that covers all of the findings. There are, at present, 36 frames for dealing with renal disease.

Currently, the program does not make treatment recommendations. The system was originally written in CONNIVER (see Article VI.C2), but that version was too slow and it has been recoded to run in MACLISP.

Representation of Medical Knowledge

The general medical knowledge in PIP, as mentioned above, is knowledge about diseases, the patient situation (findings, results of the physical examination, and reported symptoms), and the relationships between these entities. This medical knowledge is organized as a *frame system.* Shown in Figure B4–1 is part of a typical frame.

The slots in the frame are grouped into categories as shown. The *typical findings* are those that are expected in a patient having this disorder. However, patients with the disorder need not exhibit all of the typical findings. The job of the matching algorithm is to compute the "goodness of fit" between the findings and a frame. Some of the typical findings have the special status TRIGGER, and they are key elements of the clinical decision-making strategy. A TRIGGER is a finding that is so strongly related to a disorder that the presence of the finding in the patient makes the PIP system attend to the disorder frame as an *active hypothesis.* For example, FACIAL EDEMA is listed in Figure B4–1 as a TRIGGER for ACUTE GLOMERULONEPHRITIS, meaning that PIP will consider this disease as an active hypothesis if a patient displays facial edema.

The *logical decision criteria* are rules that permit the confirmation or rejection of a hypothesis on the basis of a small number of key findings. Findings that are strongly correlated with a disease will be listed in the slot IS–SUFFICIENT. If any of these findings are reported, they will be sufficient to confirm the presence of the disease.

The relations between frames reflect the ways in which disorders are related in medicine. Sometimes disease mechanisms are well understood and it is possible to say that one disorder CAUSES another or is a COMPLICATION–OF another. If mechanisms are poorly understood, the disorders may simply be ASSOCIATED. The latter frames are *complementary;* they represent disorders

```
                    ACUTE-GLOMERULONEPHRITIS

     Typical Findings
        TRIGGERS            (EDEMA with LOCATION=FACIAL ...  )
        FINDINGS            (ANOREXIA ...  )

     Logical Decision Criteria
        IS-SUFFICIENT       (None)
        MUST-HAVE           (None)
        MUST-NOT-HAVE       (None)

     Complementary Relations to Other Frames
        CAUSED-BY           (STREPTOCOCCAL-INFECTION, ...  )
        CAUSE-OF            (SODIUM-RETENTION, ...  )
        COMPLICATED-BY      (ACUTE-RENAL-FAILURE, ...  )
        COMPLICATION-OF     (CELLULITIS)

     Differential Diagnosis
        CHRONIC-HYPERTENSION implies CHRONIC-GLOMERULONEPHRITIS
        RECURRING-EDEMA implies NEPHROTIC-SYNDROME

     Scoring
        (((PATIENT WITH AGE=CHILD) → 0.8)
         ((PATIENT WITH AGE=MIDDLE-AGED) → -0.5)
         ...)
        (((EDEMA with SEVERITY = not MASSIVE) → 0.1)
         ((EDEMA with SEVERITY = MASSIVE) → -1.0)
         ...)
```

Figure B4–1. Part of the frame for acute glomerulonephritis (kidney stones).

that the patient might have in addition to the initial disorder. In contrast, the *differential diagnosis* slots indicate mutually exclusive disorders—the patient may have one of them and not the disorder represented by the current frame.

The final slot indicates how the findings are scored for the disorder represented by the frame. This score indicates the goodness of fit of this disorder to the findings. The statements comprising this slot are sets of clauses that are evaluated in turn. Within a clause, evaluation terminates when one of the conditions in the clause is true; its score will be used. The local score for a frame is the sum of the values of the clauses, normalized by the maximum total score possible. Thus, 1 denotes complete agreement, while arbitrarily large negative numbers denote complete disagreement.

Reasoning

The clinical reasoning strategy used by PIP is based on the manipulations of hypotheses and findings. Knowledge about findings is stored separately from the frame system, since a finding can be applicable to many frames. A hypothesis is an instantiation of a disorder frame. There are three kinds of hypotheses: confirmed, active, and semiactive. Hypotheses with ratings (as computed by the scoring process) that are higher than a preset threshold are considered *confirmed hypotheses*. *Active hypotheses* are those with at least one confirmed TRIGGER finding, and they contend for the focus of attention. *Semiactive hypotheses* are the immediate neighbors of the active hypotheses in the frame system. They correspond to hypotheses that, although not strong enough to be investigated, are "at the back of the consulting physician's mind."

The consultation begins with the physician telling the system the main symptoms and signs of a patient. The program then takes the initiative and tries to determine the validity of any active hypotheses by selecting and asking appropriate questions.

The program works through the following cycle:

1. *Acquire a new finding.* This task is accomplished by asking a sequence of questions that characterizes the finding according to its possible descriptions.

2. *Process the finding.* All of the frames in which this finding is relevant are located.

3. *Update the list of active hypotheses.* Several actions can be taken at this point: Remove an active hypothesis if the finding matches a MUST–NOT–HAVE rule; confirm a hypothesis if the premise of an IS–SUFFICIENT rule is now true; activate a hypothesis if the new finding is one of the hypothesis TRIGGERs or if the finding allows the premise of a differential diagnosis link to succeed; or revise the score of the hypothesis if the finding matches a scoring rule. If a new hypothesis is activated, then all of its immediate relatives are made semiactive.

4. *Select the next finding to query.* The highest rated hypothesis becomes the focus of attention, and a question is generated for the next unexplored finding. If there are no hypotheses, a question about a finding for the highest rated, causally related frame is asked. Questioning terminates when there are no more active hypotheses or causal relatives with findings to be determined.

If the logical decision criteria are insufficient to confirm or deny a hypothesis, the score of the hypothesis is computed by combining (a) the value of a function that measures the fit of observed findings and typical (expected) findings for the frame (called the *matching score*) and (b) the value of a function that is the ratio of the number of findings accounted for by the hypothesis to the total number of findings (the *binding score*). The matching score, in turn, consists of two parts, a local score for the frame (described above) and a score propagated from causally related frames.

Summary

Like INTERNIST (see Article VIII.B3) and unlike MYCIN (Article VIII.B1), PIP is intended to simulate the clinical reasoning of physicians (see, however, the work on NEOMYCIN discussed in Article IX.C6). The way in which the general medical knowledge has been represented as a system of hypothesized-disorder frames and clinical findings reflects this intent, as do the strategies used to select questions for confirming a hypothesis.

The system employs two types of reasoning, *categorical* and *probabilistic*. Decisions about the applicability of a hypothesis are determined using the logical decision criteria (the IS–SUFFICIENT, MUST–HAVE, and MUST–NOT–HAVE rules) that a physician applies. When these are insufficient, the probabilistic methods (the computation of matching scores and binding scores) are used. Both kinds of reasoning feature a combination of local and global decision strategies. Local strategies decide how well the findings fit a particular frame, while global strategies determine how well a set of frames fits the findings.

There are several difficulties with the program. One problem is that the questioning can be erratic, since the top-ranked hypotheses tend to alternate rapidly. This oscillation is unlike a physician's line of reasoning, which tends to concentrate on questions that resolve one hypothesis at a time. There is also the problem of when to stop the questioning. The current approach is to stop questioning only when all questions about all possibly relevant hypotheses have been exhausted. This strategy seems too conservative; many irrelevant questions tend to get asked.

References

See Pauker et al. (1976) and Szolovits and Pauker (1976, 1978).

B5. Digitalis Therapy Advisor

THERE has been considerable work by the Clinical Decision Making Research Group at M.I.T. to develop a system that advises physicians on the administration of the drug *digitalis* (Gorry, Silverman, and Pauker, 1978; Silverman, 1975; Swartout, 1977a, 1977b). These programs are not concerned with diagnosing the need for the drug in a patient; rather, they determine an appropriate treatment regimen and its subsequent management for patients known to require digitalis. This system differs from most other medical AI systems in that it concentrates primarily on the problem of continuing patient management and integrates both quantitative and qualitative models. (One other system emphasizing continuing patient management, in the context of monitoring respiratory function in the intensive-care ward, is the VM system described by Fagan, 1979.)

Digitalis is administered to slow and stabilize the cardiac rhythm of patients who are experiencing or are likely to experience various arrhythmias and to strengthen the heartbeat of patients who are in heart failure. Digitalis is difficult to administer properly for several reasons. One is that the difference between the amount of drug required for the desired therapeutic results and the amount resulting in toxic manifestations is small. Some of the early toxic manifestations can easily be mistaken for therapeutic manifestations. Moreover, the appropriate amount of digitalis varies from patient to patient, depending on the changing disease state of the patient and the patient's recent history of digitalis administration. Finally, digitalis is widely administered, even by physicians with little training in cardiology.

The therapeutic effect of digitalis is achieved by maintaining an appropriate amount of the drug in the heart. However, since digitalis is distributed throughout the body and the digitalis in the heart cannot be measured, the typical distribution among the heart, the bloodstream, and the rest of the body must be used to *estimate* the amount in the heart. The digitalis leaves the body primarily through the kidneys (in the case of digoxin, the most common digitalis preparation) and also through the liver, with the amount excreted being proportional to the amount in the bloodstream. The normal strategy in administering digitalis is to give the patient a relatively large amount of the drug over a period of one to four days to reach a drug level sufficient for the desired therapeutic result in the heart and then to give a smaller daily dose to replace the digitalis that is excreted.

Various mathematical models have been in existence for some time that provide an approximation of the relation of digitalis history, body weight, renal function, and level of digitalis in the body (e.g., Jelliffe, 1967). Based on these pharmacokinetic models, computational aids for administering digitalis

206

have been constructed (with and without the additional information provided by serum drug levels). Unfortunately, such aids provide information only on how much drug is in the body, while physicians are really interested in the amount needed to achieve the desired therapeutic results without toxicity. To make use of such an aid, physicians must be able to make the difficult transformation between their clinical goals (e.g., slowed heart rate, decreased arrhythmias, increased cardiac output) and the drug-level information offered by these clinical aids. They must take into account all of the clinical aspects of giving the drug, such as recognizing toxic signs, adjusting for factors that make the patient sensitive to digitalis, and determining the level of digitalis necessary to compensate for the patient's disease state.

The research group at M.I.T., comprised of G. Gorry, W. Long, S. Pauker, H. Silverman, W. Swartout, and P. Szolovits, has been developing a program directed at the continuing management of each specific patient's digitalis therapy, guided by the response of the patient to the drug and the changing disease state. The important points about this program are the following:

1. It combines qualitative models of the patient's needs and responses with the quantitative model of digitalis pharmacokinetics to make recommendations directed at the same goal as the physician's.

2. It tailors these models to the specific conditions that exist in the patient, taking into account such factors as increased likelihood of toxicity or damage in some states (e.g., a low serum-potassium level or an acute myocardial infarction), increased requirement for digitalis (e.g., in atrial fibrillation), and malabsorption syndromes.

3. It utilizes an adaptive feedback process to reach and maintain a good state of therapeutic management of the patient.

4. It requires only the kind of information that a cardiologist would require to make the same decisions.

5. It utilizes concepts and reasoning that a physician would understand and relate to.

The Digitalis Therapy Advisor interacts with the physician to select and parameterize the models appropriate to the patient. This interaction involves asking about the current disease state and all of the factors that might influence the way that digitalis should be administered. The program then proposes a dosage schedule to achieve the desired goals and asks the physician to interact with the program again after a suitable time has elapsed, for an assessment of the patient's progress. At a follow-up session, the program assesses the changes in the state of the patient, looking for therapeutic effects, possible signs of toxicity, changes in potential sensitivities, and signs of possible noncompliance or malabsorption of the drug. These follow-up sessions continue until this feedback process adjusts the dosage schedule to the particular characteristics of the patient.

The Patient-specific Model

The following is an annotated transcript of the first session for a patient being treated for atrial fibrillation (a type of fast, irregular rhythm of the heart muscle). This transcript begins after the name, time, age, weight, height, and sex have been recorded. (The physician's responses are preceded by **.)

What is the cardiac rhythm?

The possibilities are:
1. Normal sinus rhythm
2. Paced-rhythm
3. Atrial fibrillation
4. Atrial flutter
5. Pat
6. Pat with block
7. Nonparoxysmal junctional tachycardia

Enter single value

** 3

Is there regularization of ventricular rhythm?

The possibilities are:
1. Present
2. Absent

Enter single value

** 2

> *Regularization of the rhythm would imply that the rhythm is probably actually nonparoxysmal junctional tachycardia, which is not treatable with digitalis and is usually a sign of digitalis toxicity.*

What is the ventricular rate?
Enter numerical value

** 138

What is the status of PVCs?

The possibilities are:
1. Present
2. Absent

Enter single value

** 1

Is the patient really having PVCs or aberrantly conducted supraventricular beats (Ashman beats)?

The possibilities are:
1. PVCs
2. Ashman beats

Enter single value

** 2

If they were actually PVCs, they should be closely watched because an increase in the number of PVCs is an early sign of digitalis toxicity. At this point, the program assesses the present status of digitalis use, assesses the renal function, and starts checking for possible increased sensitivity to digitalis.

What is the level of serum potassium? Units: MEQ per liter
Enter numerical value

** 3.4

Is the patient being given or about to be given diuretics?

The possibilities are:
1. Given
2. Not given

Enter single value

** 2

Most diuretics would further deplete the potassium.

It is generally agreed that patients with low serum potassium levels are more prone to develop dig toxicity. Please watch this patient carefully and administer potassium supplements.

The program continues to query the user about cardiomyopathy, possible acute myocardial infarctions (heart attacks), oxygen level, thyroid condition, and upcoming procedures (cardioversion, catheterization, and surgery), omitted here. In this case, the user indicates that cardiac surgery is anticipated in two days, requiring that the digitalis level be fairly low at the time of surgery. After asking all of these questions, the program prints the parameters it will use in making its recommendations.

Parameters used to make recommendations:
Reduction factor due to hypokalemia → 0.800
Total alteration sensitivity factor → 0.800

The program will aim for four-fifths of what it normally would, because of the low potassium level.

Body store goal → 0.551 mg

This is the desired average amount of digitalis in the body. It is computed from the basic requirements of the disease state (atrial fibrillation requires more digitalis than heart failure), the patient's weight, and the patient's sensitivity (and, in later sessions, the response) to the previous level of digitalis.

Projected average amount on board → 0.000 mg
Projected current amount on board → 0.000 mg
Body stores shift → 0.637 mg

This amount would have to be given now for the average over the next 24 hours to be .551 mg.

Remaining time to reach goal → 24.0 hrs.
Half life → 55.8 hours 2.3 days
Daily loss at equilibrium → 0.164 mg

Once the goal is reached, this amount per day will be required to maintain that level.

Absorption factor → 0.75

Unless the program discovers otherwise, it is assumed that 75% of an oral dose reaches the bloodstream. Next, the program asks how often digitalis is to be administered and, being told "twice daily," provides the following dosage recommendations:

The dosage recommendations are:

Date	Time	Oral	IV
11/10/79	9:00	.5 mg	0.4375 mg (or 1.75 cc)

Report back after the first dose.

The effects of the first dose will be assessed and adjustments made in the schedule.

| | 21:00 | .25 mg | 0.125 mg (or 0.5 cc) |
| 11/11/79 | 9:00 | .0625 mg | 0.0625 mg (or 0.25 cc) |

Hold the digitalis for the cardiac-surgery.

When the physician consults the program again about this patient (ideally just before the second dose is scheduled), the program will assess the therapeutic results. Since the patient is being treated for atrial fibrillation, the primary therapeutic result the program will look for is a decrease in the heart rate. The program judges the therapeutic results to be in one of three categories: none, partial, or complete. A decrease in the heart rate is considered a partial therapeutic result. If the heart rate has dropped into the range 60 to 100 or the rhythm has been converted to the normal sinus rhythm, the program will consider the therapeutic effect to be complete. Similarly, the program checks the possible signs of toxicity and judges the level of toxicity to be none, partial, or definite. The nine possible combinations of therapeutic and toxic states provide a basis for adjusting the therapy. The goal of this feedback process is to maintain the highest level of therapeutic effect with the minimum dosage without letting the patient become significantly toxic.

Status of the Digitalis Therapy Advisor

The original program was evaluated by comparing its recommendations to the actual treatment given to 19 patients. The program did quite well, anticipating the toxic episodes without falsely suspecting any. In 1977, William Swartout added an explanation capability to the program, which explains the actions of the program by examining the actual code. In 1978, the program underwent an extensive evaluation involving the case histories of 50 patients from the Veterans Administration Hospital in Houston. The results of this evaluation were judged by a panel of five experts. On the average, they had a preference for the recommendations of the attending physician over those of the program when there was a difference, but the program's recommendations were judged to be the same or better in 60% to 70% of the cases (see Long, 1980). More recently, new qualitative and quantitative models are being developed for the program to account more accurately for the various phenomena involved in adjusting the therapy.

References

See Gorry, Silverman, and Pauker (1978) and Silverman (1975). The explanation capability is described by Swartout (1977a, 1981).

B6. IRIS

THE DESIGN GOALS for IRIS (Trigoboff and Kulikowski, 1977; Trigoboff, 1978) are different from those for the other consultation systems constructed to be expert clinical decision-making systems in a particular medical domain. IRIS was designed to be a tool for building and experimenting with such systems. Developed at Rutgers University and written in INTERLISP, it was intended to permit easy experimentation with alternative representations of general medical knowledge, clinical strategies, and modes of interaction and to be used by a computer specialist in collaboration with a domain expert. A consultation system for glaucoma has been developed with IRIS.

The IRIS system employs a combination of two well-established knowledge-representation formalisms, namely, *semantic nets* and *production rules* (see Articles III.C3 and III.C4, in Vol. I). The semantic net consists of nodes representing patient information and uses a large and extendable set of *link types* to build associations in this medical knowledge base. A set of production rules associated with each link of the network controls the transmission of information between the nodes of the semantic network. This process, called *propagation*, is the basis of any clinical strategy implemented in IRIS.

Representation of Medical Knowledge

Like the other medical consultation systems, IRIS makes a very sharp distinction between general medical knowledge and patient-specific knowledge. The general medical knowledge is represented partly as a semantic net and partly as production rules. The nodes of the net represent clinical concepts such as pathophysiological states, diseases, symptoms, findings, and treatments. Examples of nodes in the glaucoma application are OPEN ANGLE GLAUCOMA, SCOTOMA, and PILOCARPINE THERAPY. The links represent relations between the nodes—for example, CAUSES, TREATMENT–FOR, SYMPTOM–OF, and ASSOCIATED–WITH.

The patient-specific knowledge gathered during a consultation is represented as a set of knowledge structures called Information SPECifications (ISPECs), which are associated with nodes of the semantic net and are created, deleted, and modified during the course of the consultation. An ISPEC is an assertion about the patient and is essentially a *frame* (see Article III.C7, in Vol. I) with the following slots:

1. NODE. This slot is the name of the associated node in the semantic net. The node represents the concept being asserted about this patient.

2. SIDE. This slot indicates the half of the body to which this ISPEC refers. Its possible values are LEFT, RIGHT, and NIL. Some nodes in the net will

be applicable to a left organ and a right organ (e.g., eye), while others are not (e.g., headache, diabetes). The use of SIDE provides an economical representation, since many nodes might otherwise be duplicated in the net.

3. MB. This slot is a "measure of belief" reflecting the degree of certainty in the assertion represented by the ISPEC. Any numerical method of representing degrees of belief can be implemented here. In the glaucoma application, the confidence factor mechanism of MYCIN (Article VIII.B1) has been implemented. The MB is a pair of numbers: SB (strength of belief) and SD (strength of disbelief). The actual MB is the difference of these two numbers and ranges from total belief to total disbelief.

4. TIME. The time slot is a list of two dates, the date the ISPEC became true of the patient and the date the ISPEC ceased to be true. The system can also work with a "coarser" view of time: PAST, PAST–OR–PRESENT, and FUTURE. This time representation is part of the mechanism for dealing with multiple visits and for following a patient through a course of therapy.

5. MODIFIERS. These are further specifications and qualifications of the basic ISPEC. Examples of modifiers are VALUE, DEGREE, COLOR, and WIDTH. These modifiers do not appear in all ISPECs, but only in those to which they are applicable. These modifiers allow further patient-specific specifications of the concept in the semantic net. For example, *severely increased intraocular pressure* is represented as an ISPEC for INCREASED INTRAOCULAR PRESSURE with a modifier, DEGREE: SEVERE.

6. TYPE. The type slot of an ISPEC determines how it is interpreted. An arbitrary number of types is possible. Currently implemented TYPEs are NIL (the standard and default), FAMILYHISTORY, PATIENTHISTORY, and several others that are used by the diagnosis strategy—CHOSEN, COVERED–BY, SUBSUMED–BY, and TREATED–BY.

The statement *The pressure is 10 in the right eye* is equivalent to the ISPEC:

```
NODE  =  INTRAOCULAR PRESSURE
SIDE  =  RIGHT
MB    =  (1,0)
TIME  =  PRESENT
MODS  =  VALUE: 10
TYPE  =  NIL
```

Reasoning

IRIS makes no commitment to any particular strategy of question selection. Currently, a questionnaire strategy has been implemented. At the beginning of a consultation, the program runs through a set of questions and the user answers them.

In the applications of IRIS in which consultation and diagnosis are the goal, ISPECs are associated first with the set of symptoms displayed by the patient. In IRIS's knowledge base, symptom nodes are linked to disease nodes, among other things. Thus, a set of disease nodes can be "activated" by the symptoms; a disease node is said to explain the symptom nodes that characterize it. (See also the discussion of manifestations *evoking* disease nodes in INTERNIST's knowledge base, Article VIII.B3.) Disease nodes are also linked to treatment nodes, and when IRIS has determined which disease holds for a patient, it will activate the appropriate (linked) treatment nodes.

The process of nodes evoking each other in IRIS is called *propagation of ISPECs*, because an ISPEC is associated with a symptom, disease, or treatment node relevant to a patient. When symptoms evoke a disease or when a disease evokes a treatment, an ISPEC is created. This propagation of information and generation of inferences between any linked nodes in the semantic net is controlled by a set of production rules associated with the link. If the ISPECs associated with the node at the tail of the link satisfy the precondition pattern of a rule, the actions specified by the rule will be performed at the node at the head of the link. Typical actions include the creation or deletion of ISPECs and the modification of MBs. Thus, IRIS uses a *forward-chaining* reasoning process.

An important propagation pattern is that of the propagation cone. Consider the rule:

$$\text{If SYMPTOM}_1 \text{ and SYMPTOM}_2 \text{ and SYMPTOM}_3 \text{ then DISEASE}_1$$

In the semantic net, the nodes in this rule would be represented as follows:

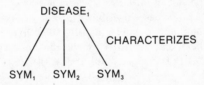

Clearly, an ISPEC should propagate only to DISEASE_1 if all three symptoms are present. In the case depicted above, propagation should be from the base of the cone to the apex. This propagation pattern is achieved by associating the same decision table with all three CHARACTERIZES links (essentially "ANDing" SYM_1, SYM_2, and SYM_3 into one production to ensure that *all* symptoms are present before a disease node is evoked). In some cases, the direction of propagation will be from apex to base, for example, when propagating COVERED–BY ISPECs from a treatment node to each of the diseases it treats.

The production rules are encoded as *decision tables* to make their execution more efficient. Consider the following set of production rules:

```
R1:   if A and B then D
R2:   if B and (not C) then (not E)
R3:   if A and B and (not C) then F
```

In evaluating these rules, A and C are evaluated twice and B is evaluated three times. A decision table encoding these three rules is:

	R1	R2	R3
A	+		+
B	+	+	+
C		−	−
	*	*	* *
D	+		
E	−		
F			+

A column of the decision table corresponds to a rule. A condition is evaluated only once, and the result is used in each applicable column.

The IRIS claim is that any clinical strategy can be implemented with the available medical primitives. In fact, the propagation of weights in CASNET, therapy selection in MYCIN, and the formation of composite hypotheses in INTERNIST-II were implemented with very little effort (Trigoboff, 1978).

Clinical Strategy of IRIS for Glaucoma Diagnosis

The clinical strategy for the glaucoma application is implemented via six special nodes in the semantic net: CHOSEN-DIAGNOSIS, CHOSEN-TREATMENT, POSSIBLE-DIAGNOSIS, POSSIBLE-TREATMENT, UNEXPLAINED-SYMPTOM, and UNTREATED-PATHOLOGY. The goal of the consultation is (a) to have one or more ISPECs associated with the nodes CHOSEN-DIAGNOSIS and CHOSEN-TREATMENT and (b) to have all ISPECs associated with UNEXPLAINED-SYMPTOMS and UNTREATED-PATHOLOGY be TYPE=COVERED-BY. As the findings are entered, they propagate ISPECs to the node UNEXPLAINED-SYMPTOMS. Propagation across SYMPTOM-OF links will result in ISPECs with varying CFs (certainty factors) associated with a number of disease nodes.

Any disease with a sufficiently high CF will propagate an ISPEC to the node POSSIBLE-DIAGNOSIS. After all data have been entered, the diseases associated with POSSIBLE-DIAGNOSIS are then investigated in turn. Each diagnosis temporarily receives TYPE=CHOSEN, and TYPE=COVERED-BY propagates to each symptom explained by this disease. The number of explained symptoms is used as a measure of the explanatory power of a disease. This process, of temporary assignment, is repeated for each possible diagnosis, and the disease that explains the most symptoms is given a permanent TYPE=CHOSEN. If there are any unexplained symptoms, the process is repeated. A similar strategy using the nodes POSSIBLE–TREATMENT, CHOSEN–TREATMENT, and UNTREATED–PATHOLOGY is applied to select treatments.

Summary

IRIS has been explained in the context of its glaucoma application, but it was designed to represent medical knowledge from *any* domain and to implement a variety of clinical strategies. (Recall that aspects of CASNET, MYCIN, and INTERNIST–II have been implemented in IRIS.) This generality is feasible because the representation of knowledge is itself very general (augmented semantic nets). In principle, knowledge from any domain—medical or nonmedical—can be represented.

A second characteristic of IRIS that makes it very general is the separation of clinical strategy, both conceptually and operationally, from medical knowledge. Note that to implement the consultation strategy, IRIS needed to know about only six nodes in the knowledge base: chosen diagnosis, chosen treatment, possible diagnosis, possible treatment, unexplained symptom, and untreated pathology. These six concepts are inherent to the clinical strategy of consultation; every other node in the knowledge base is conceptually and operationally independent of the implementation of the clinical strategy.

References

See Trigoboff and Kulikowski (1977) and Trigoboff (1978).

B7. EXPERT

THE EXPERT system developed at Rutgers University is a general facility for helping investigators design and test consultation models (Weiss and Kulikowski, 1979). It was designed independently of any specific application but has been influenced by the experiences of the Rutgers Resource Group in building consultation models in medicine, including rheumatology, ophthalmology, and endocrinology. Experimental models have been developed in other areas, such as chemistry, oil-well log analysis, laboratory-instrument interpretation, and automobile repair.

The consultation problems best suited for EXPERT are classification problems, which have a predetermined list of possible conclusions from which the program may choose. PROSPECTOR and EMYCIN are similar knowledge-based systems that specialize in forms of classification problems.

Some of the major themes in the design of EXPERT include:

1. A relatively simple language and notation for representing expert knowledge. The representation is consistent with the traditional two-level view of a diagnostic problem: (a) selecting appropriate hypotheses or conclusions by (b) interpreting a set of findings or observations.

2. An emphasis on categorical reasoning instead of on suboptimal scoring functions.

3. Efficient operation through compilation and ordering of rules.

4. An emphasis on decision methods that tend to yield predictable and correctable results. This may in some cases require that the expert provide more explicit statements of correlations among findings and a greater number of decision rules than would otherwise be called for. Since the interaction between rules and the associated classification strategies is usually predictable, it is not difficult to trace the changes in program behavior that will result from modifying individual rules. A novel feature of EXPERT is that it detects automatically just such changes in the reasoning about cases stored in its database. This is an important tool for incrementally generating and testing a consultation model.

The process of creating and running an EXPERT model is similar to writing and running a computer program. A standard text editor is used to create a file that will contain statements to describe a model in a special-purpose programming language. The model is checked for syntactic errors and translated into an efficient internal representation by the compiler program. The model may then be executed, and cases may be entered for consultation. The system is programmed in FORTRAN and is therefore relatively efficient

and transferrable between machines. There are versions available for both
DEC and IBM equipment.

EXPERT has many facilities that have proved useful for designing consultation models, such as explanations of the program's interpretations and the
capability to accept volunteered information from the user. All consultation
facilities of EXPERT are fully sequential; for example, one may ask for the
system's interpretation at any point in a consultation session. Extensive work
has been done on interfacing EXPERT models to databases of stored cases.
Many utilities are available for the empirical analysis of cases, including a
complete database system for searching through cases for patterns of both
model interpretations and user-entered data.

Representation of Medical Knowledge

An EXPERT consultation model consists of three sections: hypotheses,
findings, and decision rules. Findings are the facts about a patient elicited during a consultation—the history, symptoms, signs, and laboratory test results.
Findings are reported in the form of true, false, unavailable, or numerical
responses to questions from EXPERT. Hypotheses are the conclusions that
may be inferred by the system. They include diagnostic and prognostic
decision categories and therapy recommendations, as well as intermediate
hypotheses about pathophysiological states, expected causes of illness, or typical aggregates of findings. A measure of uncertainty is usually associated with
a hypothesis.

Within the three sections of the model, several subsections are possible.
The representation used in building a model divides the sections as follows
(two asterisks indicate one of the major sections, a single asterisk indicates a
subsection, and brackets indicate optional statements):

```
**HYPOTHESES
 *TAXONOMY
[*CAUSAL AND INTERMEDIATE HYPOTHESES]
[*TREATMENTS]
**FINDINGS
**RULES
[*FF RULES]
 *FH RULES
```

The major hypotheses are structured into a taxonomic classification
scheme. Contained within the *TAXONOMY subsection shown above are the
possible diagnostic and prognostic conclusions and the useful set-subset relationships between general diagnostic categories and intermediate interpretations. As an example, we show part of a thyroid-disease classification:

```
*TAXONOMY

EU          .Euthyroid (.75)
THO         .Thyroid Dysfunction (.25)
HYPER       ..Hyperthyroidism (.05)
HYPO        ..Hypothyroidism (.20)
NOP         .No Pathology (.70)
GRAV        .Graves' Disease (.25)
```

The mnemonic (EU, THO, etc.) for each hypothesis becomes a shorthand for specifying its place in the production rules. The optional weight (e.g., .75) associated with some hypotheses indicates their frequency of occurrence relative to the higher level hypotheses in which they are included. The indentation (shown by dots) indicates the set-subset relationship among hypotheses.

Findings are represented as attributes that can be present, absent, or undetermined in the patient or as a numerical variable that, when measured, adopts a value within a prespecified range. In those cases in which uncertainty is associated with an observation, the uncertainty must be described explicitly in terms of additional modifying findings. For example, the accuracy of a test result can be requested and decision rules then written to modify inferences about the original test. To acquire information about a patient, several question types—multiple choice, checklist, numerical, and yes-no—may be employed.

There are three types of rules for describing logical relationships among findings and hypotheses:

1. FF—finding-to-finding rules,
2. FH—finding-to-hypothesis rules,
3. HH—hypothesis-to-hypothesis rules.

The FF rules specify truth values of findings that can be deduced directly from an already established finding. They are processed in the fixed order specified by the model designer and are used to establish local control over the sequence of questions in a fashion consistent with medical practice. FH rules are logical combinations of findings that indicate confidence in the confirmation or denial of hypotheses. The general format for FH rules is:

$$X_1 \ \& \ X_2 \ldots X_i \to H(\text{MNE, CF}), \qquad -1 \leq \text{MNE} \leq 1,$$

where

$$X_i = F(\text{MNE, TVAL})$$
$$= [n : F(\text{MNE}_1, \text{TVAL}), F(\text{MNE}_2, \text{TVAL})\ldots].$$

If the logical combination of findings on the left side of the rule is satisfied, the hypothesis, MNE, is assigned a confidence value, CF. The selector argument,

n in $[n : F(\text{MNE}_1, \text{TVAL}), \ldots]$, indicates that if n of the listed findings are satisfied, the bracketed condition is evaluated as true. An example of an FH rule is:

$$F(\text{RHP}, t) \ \& \ F(\text{FFT}, t) \rightarrow H(\text{HYPER}, .5),$$

which can be stated as:

```
IF:   RHP is true (rapid heart palpitation) and
      FFT is true (fine finger tremor)
THEN: Conclude hyperthyroidism with a confidence of .5.
```

The HH rules allow the model builder to specify inferences among hypotheses and treatment selections that follow from other (diagnostic and prognostic) hypotheses. Since such higher level inferences may be sometimes modified by the presence or absence of a finding, the left-hand side of HH rules may also contain assertions about findings. In addition, each HH rule must have a context defined in terms of a set of findings or hypotheses, which makes possible the application of efficient rule-evaluation strategies over the compiled model. The context specifies a set of necessary conditions among the findings to permit evaluation of the HH rule. HH rules are evaluated in the order of specification in the model. Hypotheses are specified with a range of confidence that must be satisfied for the HH rule to be invoked. The HH rules are implemented in a table of the following form:

```
*HH rules
*If there are eye and thyroid dysfunctions
F(EENO, F) and (HXTH, T)
*Then consider Graves' disease:
F(ETHO, T) and H(EYE, .5:1.) → H(GRAV, .9)
*End
```

Reasoning Strategies

When an assertion about a finding is made to the system, the rules in which this result appears are evaluated. The results are usually received in batches, as in the form of responses to a multiple-choice or checklist question. The rules are evaluated in the following order to produce weights that rank the hypotheses:

1. FF rules are evaluated. They take simple responses of true, false, or unknown and merely enlarge the set of new results of findings. They are handled in the same way as results received directly in response to questions.

2. FH rules are then evaluated. Only those FH rules in which new results of findings appear need be evaluated. FH rules have the property that, when the left-hand side of a rule is evaluated as true or false, it remains

true or false for the remainder of the consultation session, unless an erroneous response is received.

3. Finally, HH rules are evaluated. The IF part of each HH rule table is evaluated at the same time as the FH rules. Only HH rules found in tables that have their IF part evaluated as true are considered. All such HH rules must be reevaluated sequentially. The premises and consequents of HH rules may include hypotheses and associated intervals of confidence. Unlike findings that remain true or false, these intervals can change not only directly from results of findings, but also indirectly from other rules (both FH and HH) that affect the confidence measure of a hypothesis. HH rules are evaluated in the order of their appearance in the model. There is no backward chaining, because the order of evaluation is determined beforehand by the model builder. Self-referencing rules are therefore acceptable. Because HH rules and tables are evaluated in sequence, by their order of appearance in the model file, it is important to order the HH rules carefully. An HH rule implying a hypothesis, H_1, that is later needed to establish another hypothesis, H_2, should appear in the model file before H_2 is referenced in the left side of another HH rule. The confidence ranges in the HH rules are those that have been directly set by other FH or HH rules. They are not the adjusted weights implied by the taxonomy.

The preceding procedures result in the assignment of the confidence measures, CF_i, that can be determined directly from the rules of evidence and hypothesis weight propagation: the FH and HH rules. When more than one rule is applicable, the maximum absolute value of confidence is used. Another procedure is invoked that is helpful both in question selection and as a simple heuristic to adjust weights slightly. Each hypothesis that has some positive evidence, in the form of a satisfied rule or a partially satisfied rule (with unknown truth value), is marked. The count of such rules that apply to each hypothesis is kept. This corresponds approximately to the number of positive indicators of a hypothesis.

A different set of weights is derived from the taxonomy and causal network structure. Forward weights are propagated from predecessor to successor, and inverse weights are propagated from successor to predecessor. A taxonomy contains implied relationships between hypotheses that can be treated in a manner similar to causal connections. The procedures for generating weights are similar to those used in CASNET. After all FH and HH rules have been evaluated, the measures of confidence, CF_i, may be modified or propagated according to their taxonomic or causal relationships.

A final weight is derived from both the rule-based and the taxonomic-causal-net weights. It is taken as the maximum absolute value from all the indicated directions (with the appropriate sign). A small bonus may be awarded to the final weights.

The general procedure for sequential test selection may be specified as follows:

1. Consider those rules (FH or HH) such that:

   a. they set confidence measures for marked hypotheses—they are related to current evidence;

   b. the confidence of the rule is greater than the current confidence in H_j, so that it provides useful additional information.

2. Select an unasked finding F_i, belonging to the set of rules found in part 1, such that:

   a. the cost is minimal;

   b. the current weight $W(H)$ is greatest, indicating that the finding pertains to the most likely hypothesis;

   c. the potential $CF(H)$ is greatest for F_i, so that this finding F_i is one that can yield greater confidence in H_j than another F_k.

Applications

Several applications of the EXPERT system are in progress. Consultation models are being developed in rheumatology, ophthalmology, and endocrinology (thyroid diseases). A consultation system in rheumatic diseases appears to have strong potential for acceptance by the medical community. There is a shortage of rheumatologists in the United States, and keeping up to date on the interpretation of many new immunological tests can be difficult for nonspecialist physicians. In collaboration with investigators at the University of Missouri, the EXPERT formalism is being used to develop a prototype consultation system for rheumatic diseases (Lindberg et al., 1980). Initially, the set of problems considered has been confined to fewer than 10 important, yet complex, diagnostic categories. The model is currently being expanded to cover additional problem areas.

References

See Weiss, Kulikowski, and Safir (1977), Weiss et al., (1978), and Weiss, Kulikowski, and Galen (1981).

Chapter IX

Applications-oriented AI Research: Education

CHAPTER IX: APPLICATIONS–ORIENTED

AI RESEARCH: EDUCATION

A. OVERVIEW

EDUCATIONAL APPLICATIONS of computer technology have been under development since the early 1960s. These applications have included scheduling courses, managing teaching aids, and grading tests. The predominant application, however, has been to use the computer as a device that interacts directly with the student, rather than as an assistant to the human teacher. For this, there have been three general approaches.

The "ad lib," or *environmental*, approach is typified by Seymour Papert's LOGO Laboratory (Papert, 1980; Abelson and diSessa, 1981), which allowed the student more or less free-style use of the machine. In this case, the student is involved in programming. It is conjectured that learning problem-solving methods takes place as a side effect of working with tools that are designed to suggest good problem-solving strategies to the student. The second approach uses games and simulations as instructional tools. Once again, the student is involved in an activity—for example, doing simulated genetics experiments—for which learning is an expected side effect. The third computer application in education is computer-assisted instruction (CAI). Unlike the first two approaches, CAI makes an explicit attempt to instigate and control learning (Howe, 1973), although this may take place while the student is involved in some activity like a simulation or a game. Applications of AI techniques to this third use of computer technology in education are the focus of the systems described in this chapter (see Article IX.D for a description of work by AI researchers in a more environmental vein).

The goal of CAI research is to build instructional programs that incorporate well-prepared course material in lessons that are optimized for each student. Early programs were either electronic "page-turners," which printed prepared text, or drill-and-practice monitors, which printed problems and responded to the student's solutions using prestored answers and remedial comments. In the Intelligent CAI (ICAI) programs of the 1970s, course material was represented independently of teaching procedures, so that problems and remedial comments could be generated differently for each student. Research today focuses on the design of programs that can offer instruction in a manner that is sensitive to the student's strengths, weaknesses, and preferred style of learning. The role of AI in computer-based instructional applications is seen as making possible a new kind of learning environment.

This article surveys how AI techniques have been applied in research attempting to create intelligent computer-based tutors. In the next article, some design issues are discussed and typical components of ICAI systems are described. Subsequent articles describe some important applications of AI techniques in instructional programs.

Frame-oriented CAI Systems

The first instructional programs took many forms, but all adhered to essentially the same pedagogical philosophy. The student was usually given some instructional text (sometimes "on line," sometimes not) and asked a question that required a brief answer. After he (or she) responded, the student was told whether his answer was right or wrong. His response was sometimes used to determine his "path" through the curriculum, that is, the sequence of problems he was given (see Atkinson and Wilson, 1969; Barr and Atkinson, 1975). When the student made an error, the program branched to remedial material.

The *courseware author* attempts to anticipate every wrong response, pre-specifying branches to appropriate remedial material based on his ideas about what the underlying misconceptions might be that would cause each wrong response. Branching on the basis of response was the first step toward *individualization of instruction* (Crowder, 1962). This style of CAI has been dubbed ad-hoc, frame-oriented (AFO) CAI by Carbonell (1970b) to stress its dependence on author-specified units of information. (The term *frame* as it is used in this context predates the more recent usage in AI research on knowledge-representation—see Article III.C7, in Volume I—and refers to a page or unit of text.) Design of ad-hoc frames was originally based on Skinnerian stimulus-response principles. The branching strategies of some AFO programs have become quite involved, incorporating the best learning theory that mathematical psychology has produced (Atkinson, 1972; Fletcher, 1975; Kimball, 1973). Some of these systems have been used successfully and are available commercially.

Intelligent CAI

In spite of the widespread use of ad-hoc, frame-oriented CAI in diverse educational applications, many researchers believe that most AFO courses are not the best use of computer technology:

> In most CAI systems of the AFO type, the computer does little more than what a programmed textbook can do, and one may wonder why the machine is used at all....When teaching sequences are extremely simple, perhaps trivial, one should consider doing away with the computer, and using other devices or techniques more related to the task. (Carbonell, 1970b, pp. 32, 193)

In this pioneering paper, Carbonell goes on to define a second type of CAI that is known today as knowledge-based or Intelligent CAI. ICAI systems and the earlier CAI systems both have representations of the subject matter they teach, but ICAI systems also carry on a dialogue with the student and use the student's mistakes to diagnose his misunderstandings.

Early uses of AI techniques in CAI were called *generative CAI* (Wexler, 1970), since they stressed the ability to generate problems from a large database representing the subject they taught. (See Koffman and Blount, 1975, for a review of some early generative CAI programs and an example of the possibilities and limitations of this style of courseware.) However, the kind of courseware that Carbonell was describing in his paper was to be more than just a problem generator—it was to be a computer *tutor* that had the inductive powers of its human counterparts. ICAI programs offer what Brown (1977) calls a *reactive learning environment*, in which the student is actively engaged with the instructional system and his interests and misunderstandings drive the tutorial dialogue. This goal was expressed by other researchers trying to write CAI programs that extended the medium beyond the limits of frame selection (Koffman and Blount, 1975):

> Often it is not sufficient to tell a student he is wrong and indicate the correct solution method. An intelligent CAI system should be able to make hypotheses based on a student's error history as to where the real source of his difficulty lies. (p. 218)

The Use of AI Techniques in ICAI

The realization of the computer-based tutor has involved increasingly complicated computer programs and has prompted CAI researchers to apply AI techniques. AI work in natural-language understanding, knowledge representation, and methods of inference, as well as specific AI applications such as algebraic simplification, symbolic integration, medical diagnosis, and theorem proving, have been applied by various researchers toward making CAI programs increasingly intelligent and effective. Early research on ICAI systems focused on *representation* of the subject matter. Benchmark efforts include SCHOLAR, the geography tutor of Carbonell and Collins (see Article IX.C1); SOPHIE, the electronics troubleshooting tutor of Brown and Burton (Article IX.C3); and EXCHECK, the logic and set theory tutor by Suppes and his associates (Article IX.C8). The high level of domain expertise in these programs permits them to be responsive in a wide range of problem-solving interactions.

These ICAI programs are quite different from even the most complicated frame-oriented, branching program:

> The traditional approaches to this problem using decision theory and stochastic learning models have reached a dead end due to their oversimplified representation of learning. . . . It appears within reach of AI methodology to develop CAI systems that act more like human teachers. (Laubsch, 1975, pp. 124–125)

However, an AI system that is expert in a particular domain is not necessarily an expert *teacher* of the material—"ICAI systems cannot be AI systems warmed over" (Brown, 1977, p. 255). A good teacher must understand what the student is doing, not just what he is supposed to do. AI programs often employ very powerful problem-solving methods that do not resemble those of humans. In some cases, CAI researchers borrowed AI techniques for representing subject-domain expertise but had to modify them, often making the inference routines *less powerful*, in order to force them to follow human reasoning patterns, to make the line of reasoning more understandable to the student, and to model his problem-solving progress more closely (Goldberg, 1973; Smith, 1976). Even AI representations designed to replicate human reasoning steps at some level of detail, such as *production rules*, may be inadequate for use in teaching if important organizational and strategic concepts are not represented explicitly (Clancey and Letsinger, 1981; see also the discussion of NEOMYCIN in Article IX.C6 on GUIDON).

In the mid-1970s, a second phase in the development of ICAI tutors was characterized by the inclusion of additional expertise in the systems regarding (a) the student's learning behavior and (b) tutoring strategies (Brown and Goldstein, 1977). AI techniques were used to construct models of the learner that represent his knowledge in terms of issues (see Article IX.C4) or skills (Barr and Atkinson, 1977) that should be learned. This model then controls tutoring strategies for presenting the material. Finally, some ICAI programs are now using AI techniques to represent explicitly these *tutoring strategies*, gaining the advantages of flexibility and modularity of representation and control (Burton and Brown, 1979a; Goldstein, 1977; Clancey, 1979b).

References

The best general review of research in ICAI is Brown and Goldstein (1977). Several papers are collected in a special issue of the *International Journal of Man-Machine Studies*, Volume 11 (1979), an expanded version of which is to be published as a book (Sleeman and Brown, in press).

B. ICAI SYSTEMS DESIGN

THE MAIN COMPONENTS of an Intelligent CAI (ICAI) system are *problem-solving expertise*, the knowledge that the system tries to impart to the student; the *student model*, indicating what the student does and does not know; and *tutoring strategies*, which specify how the system presents material to the student. (See Self, 1974, for an excellent discussion of the differences and interrelations of the types of knowledge needed in an ICAI program.) Not all of these components are fully developed in every system. Because of the size and complexity of ICAI programs, most researchers tend to concentrate their efforts on the development of a single part of what would constitute a fully usable system. The issues that have been discussed in the design of each component are described briefly below.

The Expertise Module

The "expert" component of an ICAI system is charged with the task of generating problems and evaluating the correctness of the student's solutions. The CAI system's knowledge of the subject matter was originally envisioned as a huge, static database that incorporated all the facts to be taught. This idea was implicit in the early drill-and-practice programs and was made explicit in *generative CAI* (see Article IX.A). Representation of subject-matter expertise in this way, for example, with *semantic nets* (see Article III.3, in Vol. I), has been useful for generating and answering questions involving causal or relational reasoning (Carbonell and Collins, 1973; Laubsch, 1975; see also Articles IX.C1 and IX.C2 on the SCHOLAR and WHY systems).

Recent systems have employed *procedural representation* of domain knowledge, for example, in the form of methods for taking measurements and making deductions (see Article III.C2, in Vol. I). This knowledge is represented as *procedural experts* that correspond to subskills that a student must learn in order to acquire the complete skill being taught (Brown, Burton, and Bell, 1975). *Production rules* (Article III.C4, in Vol. I) have been used to construct modular representations of skills and problem-solving methods (Goldstein, 1977; Clancey, 1979b). *Problem-solving grammars* have been explored as a representation of the expertise involved in writing computer programs (Miller and Goldstein, 1977). In addition, Brown and Burton (1978) have pointed out that *multiple representations* are sometimes useful for answering student questions and for evaluating partial solutions to a problem (e.g., a semantic net of facts about an electronic circuit and procedures simulating the functional behavior of the circuit). Stevens and Collins (1978) considered an evolving

229

series of simulation models for reasoning metaphorically about the behavior of causal systems.

It should be noted that not all ICAI systems can actually solve the problems they pose to a student. For example, BIP, the BASIC Instructional Program (Barr, Beard, and Atkinson, 1975), cannot write or analyze computer programs: BIP uses sample input/output pairs (supplied by the course authors) to test the student's programs. Similarly, the procedural experts in SOPHIE–I could not debug an electronic circuit (see Article IX.C3). In contrast, the production-rule representation of domain knowledge in WUMPUS and GUIDON allows these programs to solve problems independently, as well as to criticize student solutions (see Articles IX.C5 and IX.C6). Being able to solve the problems, ideally in any of several possible ways, is necessary if the ICAI program is to make fine-grained suggestions about the completion of partial solutions.

The expert component of an ICAI system is called an *articulate expert* (Goldstein, 1977) if it can explain each problem-solving decision in terms that correspond (at some level of abstraction) to those of a human problem-solver. In contrast, typical expert AI programs have data structures and processing algorithms that do not necessarily mimic the reasoning steps of humans and are therefore considered "opaque" to the user. For example, the electronic-circuit simulator underlying SOPHIE–I, which is used to check the consistency of a student's hypotheses about failed circuit elements and to answer some of his (or her) questions, is an opaque expert on the functioning of the circuit. It is a complete, accurate, and efficient model of the circuit, but its mechanisms are never revealed to the student, since they are certainly not the mechanisms that he is expected to acquire. In WEST, on the other hand, while a complete, efficient, opaque expert is used to determine the range of possible moves that the student could have made with a given roll of the dice, a different, *articulate* expert, which models only pieces of the game-playing expertise, helps determine possible causes for less than optimal moves by the student.

ICAI systems are distinguished from earlier CAI approaches by the separation of teaching strategies from the subject expertise to be taught. However, the separation of subject-area knowledge from instructional planning requires a structure for organizing the expertise that captures the difficulty of various problems and the interrelationships of course material. Modeling a student's understanding of a subject is closely related conceptually to figuring out a representation for the subject itself or for the language used to discuss it.

Trees and lattices showing prerequisite interactions have been used to organize the introduction of new knowledge or topics (Koffman and Blount, 1975). In BIP, this lattice took the form of a *curriculum net* that related the skills to be taught to sample programming tasks that exercised each skill (Barr, Beard, and Atkinson, 1976). Goldstein (1979) called the lattice a *syllabus* in the WUMPUS research and emphasized the developmental path that a learner takes in acquiring new skills. For arithmetic skills needed in WEST, Burton and Brown (1976) employ curriculum units called *issues* at several levels, for example, the use of arithmetic operators, strategies for winning the game, and meta-level considerations for improving performance. Burton and Brown suggest that when the skills are "structurally independent," the order of their presentation is not particularly crucial. This representation is useful for modeling the student's knowledge and coaching him on different levels of abstraction. Stevens, Collins, and Goldin (1978) have argued further that a good human tutor does not merely traverse a predetermined network of knowledge in selecting material to present. Rather, it is the process of the tutor's ferreting out student misconceptions that drives the dialogue.

The Student-model Module

The modeling module represents the student's understanding of the material to be taught. Much recent ICAI research has focused on this component. The purpose of modeling the student is to make hypotheses about his misconceptions and suboptimal performance strategies so that the tutoring module can point them out, indicate why they are wrong, and suggest corrections. It is advantageous for the system to be able to recognize alternative ways of solving problems, including the incorrect methods that the student might use as a result of systematic misconceptions about the problem or inefficient strategies.

Some early frame-oriented CAI systems employed mathematical *stochastic learning models*, but this approach failed because it modeled only the probability that a student would give a specific response to a stimulus. In general, knowing the probability of a response has little diagnostic power (Laubsch, 1975)—it is not the same as knowing what a student understands.

Typical uses of AI techniques for modeling student knowledge include (a) simple *pattern recognition* applied to the student's response history and (b) flags in the subject-matter semantic net or in the rule base representing areas that the student has mastered. In these ICAI systems, a student model is formed by comparing the student's behavior to that of the computer-based "expert" in the same environment. The modeling component marks each skill according to whether evidence indicates that the student knows the material or not. Carr and Goldstein (1977) have termed this component an *overlay model*—the student's understanding is represented completely in terms of the expertise component of the program (see Article IX.C5).

Another approach is to model the student's knowledge not as a subset of the expert's knowledge, but rather as a perturbation of or deviation from the expert's knowledge—a "bug." (See, e.g., the SOPHIE and BUGGY systems—Articles IX.C3 and IX.C7.) There is a major difference between the overlay and bug approaches to modeling: In the bug approach, it is not simply assumed that the student reasons as the expert does, except for knowing less; the student's reasoning can, in fact, be substantially different from expert reasoning.

Other information that might be accumulated in the student model includes the student's preferred modes for interacting with the program, a rough characterization of his level of ability, a consideration of what he seems to forget over time, and an indication of what his goals and plans seem to be for learning the subject matter.

Major sources of evidence for maintaining the student model can be characterized as: (a) implicit, from student problem-solving behavior; (b) explicit, from direct questions asked of the student; (c) historical, from assumptions based on the student's experience; and (d) structural, from assumptions based on some measure of the difficulty of the subject material (Goldstein, 1977). Historical evidence is usually determined by asking the student to rate his level of expertise on a scale from beginner to expert. Early programs, like SCHOLAR, used only explicit evidence. Recent programs have concentrated on inferring implicit evidence from the student's problem-solving behavior. This approach is complicated in that it is limited by the program's ability to recognize and describe the strategies applied by the student. Specifically, when the expert program indicates that an inference chain is required for a correct result and the student's observable behavior is wrong, how is the modeling program to know which of the intermediate steps are unknown or wrongly applied by the student? This is the *apportionment of credit or blame problem;* it has been an important focus of WEST research (Article IX.C4).

In his work on the MACSYMA Advisor, Michael Genesereth (1979) built a system that interprets the MACSYMA user's activity in terms of a *problem-solving grammar* (Miller and Goldstein, 1977b). MACSYMA is a powerful and complex computer-based tool for mathematical problem solving used by scientists and engineers across the country (see Article VII.D1). The analysis by the MACSYMA Advisor allows the user's efforts to be modeled in terms of a "standard set" of problem-solving operations. The Advisor's *plan-recognition* procedure attempts to interpret, or parse, the user's solution steps in terms of the grammar, building a model of what the user is trying to do, called the *plan.* The plan is used to infer the user's beliefs and misconceptions.

The SPADE–0 system (Miller, 1979; Miller and Goldstein, 1977a, 1977b) explored the relation between expert knowledge and student modeling in the context of a LOGO-graphics programming tutor. Since a complete expert module for programming tasks is beyond the state of the art, SPADE–0 focused on providing an *instructional programming environment* in which an articulate program-planning dialogue could take place. *Plans* for LOGO programs were displayed as treelike hierarchies of design choices; programming-language "code" was at the leaves of these tree structures. Each node in a SPADE–0 plan could be annotated according to purpose (what it was to do) and rationale (why it was chosen). Although only rudimentary tutorial and modeling capabilities were actually implemented in SPADE–0, its design provided a test case for exploring potential AI contributions along these lines. The insight of human tutors apparently results from recognizing the student's plan and analyzing its differences from the most similar "expert" plan; underlying misconceptions are inferred from sequences of "buggy" student plans. SPADE–0's attempt to interact with the student in terms of an explicit vocabulary of high-level planning and debugging ideas represented a radical departure from conventional programming instruction (which is typically organized around specific language constructs).

Because of inherent limitations in the modeling process, it is useful for a "critic" in the modeling component to measure how closely the student model actually predicts the student's behavior. Extreme inconsistency or an unexpected demonstration of expertise in solving problems might indicate that the representation in the program does not capture the student's approach. Finally, Goldstein (1977) has suggested that the modeling process should attempt both to measure whether or not the student is actually learning and to discern what teaching methods are most effective. Much research is needed in this area.

The Tutoring Module

The tutoring module of ICAI systems must integrate knowledge about natural-language dialogues, teaching methods, and the subject area. This is the module that communicates with the student, selecting problems for him to solve, monitoring and criticizing his performance, providing assistance upon request, and selecting remedial material. The design of this module involves issues such as when it is appropriate to offer a hint or how far the student should be allowed to go down the wrong track:

> These are just some of the problems which stem from the basic fact that teaching is a skill which requires knowledge additional to the knowledge comprising mastery of the subject domain. (Brown, 1977, pp. 256–257)

This additional knowledge, beyond the representation of the subject domain and of the student's state of understanding, is knowledge about how to teach.

Most ICAI research has explored teaching methods based on *diagnostic modeling*, in which the program debugs the student's understanding by posing tasks and evaluating his response (Collins, 1976; Brown and Burton, 1978; Koffman and Blount, 1975). From the program's feedback, the student is expected to learn which skills he uses wrongly, which skills he does not use (but could use to good advantage), and so forth. Recently, there has been more concern with the possibility of saying just the right thing to the student so that he will realize his own errors and switch to a better method (Carr and

Goldstein, 1977; Burton and Brown, 1979a; Norman, Gentner, and Stevens, 1976). This new direction is based on attempts to make a bug *constructive* by establishing for the student that there is something suboptimal in his approach, as well as giving enough information for the student to use what he already knows to focus on the bug and characterize it so that he avoids this failing in the future.

However, it is by no means clear how "just the right thing" is to be said to the student. We do know that it depends on having a very good model of his understanding process (the methods and strategies he uses to construct a solution). Current research is focusing on means for representing and isolating the bugs themselves (Stevens, Collins, and Goldin, 1978; Brown and Burton, 1978).

Another approach is to provide an environment that encourages the student to think in terms of debugging his own knowledge. In one BIP experiment (Wescourt and Hemphill, 1978), explicit debugging strategies for computer programming were conveyed in a written document and then a controlled experiment was undertaken to see whether this training fostered a more rational approach for detecting faulty use of programming skills.

Brown, Collins, and Harris (1978) suggest that one might foster the ability to construct hypotheses and test them (the basis of understanding in their model) by setting up problems in which the student's first guess is likely to be wrong, thus "requiring him to focus on how he detects that his guess is wrong and how he then intelligently goes about revising it."

The Socratic method used in WHY (Stevens and Collins, 1977) involves questioning the student in a way that will encourage him to reason about what he knows and thereby modify his conceptions. The tutor's strategies are constructed by analyzing protocols of real-world interactions between student and teacher.

Another teaching strategy that has been successfully implemented on several systems is called *coaching* (Goldstein, 1977). Coaching programs are not concerned with covering a predetermined lesson plan within a fixed time (in contrast to SCHOLAR). Rather, the goal of coaching is to encourage skill acquisition and general problem-solving abilities by engaging the student in some activity like a computer game (see Articles IX.A and IX.D). In a coaching situation, the immediate aim of the student is to have fun, and skill acquisition is an indirect consequence. Tutoring comes about when the computer coach, "observing" the student's play of the game, interrupts the student and offers new information or suggests new strategies. A successful computer coach must be able to discern what skills or knowledge the student might acquire, based on his playing style, and to judge effective ways to intercede in the game and offer advice. WEST and WUMPUS (Articles IX.C4 and IX.C5) are both coaching programs.

Socratic tutoring and coaching represent different styles for communicating with the student. All mixed-initiative tutoring follows some dialogue strategy, which involves decisions about when and how often to question the student and methods for the presentation of new material and review. For example, a coaching program, by design, is nonintrusive and only rarely lectures. On the other hand, a Socratic tutor questions repetitively, requiring the student to pursue certain lines of reasoning. Recently, ICAI research has turned to making explicit these alternative *dialogue-management* principles. Collins (1976) has pioneered the careful investigation and articulation of teaching strategies. Recent work has explored the representation of these strategies as *production rules* (see Articles IX.C2 and IX.C6 on WHY and GUIDON).

For example, the tutoring module in the GUIDON program, which discusses MYCIN-like case-diagnosis tasks with a student, has an explicit representation of discourse knowledge. Tutoring rules select alternative dialogue formats on the basis of economy, domain logic, and tutoring or student-modeling goals. Arranged into procedures, these rules cope with various recurrent situations in the tutorial dialogue, for example, introducing a new topic, examining a student's understanding after he asks a question that indicates unexpected expertise, relating an inference to one just discussed, discussing the next plan of attack after the student completes a subproblem, and wrapping up the discussion of a topic.

Conclusion

In general, ICAI programs have only begun to deal with the problems of representing and acquiring teaching expertise and of determining how this knowledge should be integrated with general principles of discourse. The programs described in the articles to follow have all investigated some aspect of this problem, and none offers an answer to the question of how to build a computer-tutor. Nevertheless, these programs have demonstrated potential tutorial skill, sometimes showing striking insight into students' misconceptions. Research continues toward making viable AI contributions to computer-based education.

References

Goldstein (1977) gives a clear discussion of the distinctions between the modules presented here, concentrating on the broader, theoretical issues. Burton and Brown (1976) also discuss the components of ICAI systems and their interactions and provide a good example. Self (1974) is a classic discussion of the kinds of knowledge needed in a computer-based tutor.

C. INTELLIGENT CAI SYSTEMS

C1. SCHOLAR

IN ADDITION to responding to the student's questions, the tutor should be able to take the initiative during an instructional dialogue by generating good tutorial questions. These questions can be used by the tutor to indicate the relevant material to be learned, to determine the extent of a student's knowledge of the problem domain, and to identify any misconceptions that he (or she) might have. SCHOLAR is one such *mixed-initiative,* computer-based tutoring system; both the system and the student can initiate conversation by asking questions. SCHOLAR was the pioneering effort in the development of computer tutors capable of handling unanticipated student questions and of generating instructional material in varying levels of detail, according to the context of the dialogue. Both the student's input and the program's output are English sentences.

The original SCHOLAR system, created by Jaime Carbonell, Allan Collins, and their colleagues at Bolt Beranek and Newman, Inc., tutored students about simple facts in South American geography (Carbonell, 1970b). It has a number of *tutoring strategies* for composing relevant questions, determining whether or not the student's answers are correct, and answering questions from the student. Both the knowledge-representation scheme (see below) and the tutorial capabilities are applicable to domains other than geography. For example, NLS–SCHOLAR was developed to tutor people unfamiliar with computers in the use of a complex text-editing program (Grignetti, Hausmann, and Gould, 1975).

In addition to investigating the nature of tutorial dialogues and of human plausible reasoning, the SCHOLAR research project explored a number of AI issues, including:

1. How can real-world knowledge be stored effectively for the fast, easy retrieval of relevant facts needed in tutoring?
2. What general reasoning strategies are needed to make appropriate *plausible inferences* from the typically incomplete database of the tutor program?
3. To what extent can these strategies be made independent of the domain being discussed (i.e., dependent only on the *form* of the representation)?

The Knowledge Base—Semantic Nets

In SCHOLAR, knowledge about the domain being tutored is represented in a *semantic net* (see Article III.C3, in Vol. I). Each node, or unit, in the net,

236

corresponding to some geographical object or concept, is composed of the name associated with that node and a set of properties. These properties are lists of attribute-value pairs. For example, Figure C1–1 shows a representation of the unit for Peru. (For a discussion of the LISP notation, see Article VI.B.)

Attributes can be English words (other units) that are defined elsewhere in the net; one of several special attributes such as SUPRA for superattribute, SUPERC for superconcept or superordinate, SUPERP for superpart; or case-structure attributes used in parsing (see below). An example of SUPRA might be the fact that *fertile* refers to *soil* and *soil* refers to *topography*; of SUPERC, that Peru is a country; and of SUPERP, that Peru is part of South America. Values can also be *importance tags*, like the expressions (I 0) after LOCATION in Figure C1–1 and (I 1) after EASTERN: the lower the number, the more important the property. SCHOLAR uses these tags to measure the relevance of a node with respect to the topic under discussion.

Tutorial Dialogue

An important part of the SCHOLAR research has been an emphasis on the nature of tutorial dialogue, in particular, the Socratic style of tutoring, where the tutor first attempts to diagnose the student's misconceptions and then presents material that will force the student to see his own errors (Collins, Warnock, and Passafiume, 1974). As part of the SCHOLAR research, human

---

```
PERU:
     ((EXAMPLE-NOUN PERU))

     (I 0)                           "Importance" of unit is high

     (SUPERC (I 0) COUNTRY)
     (SUPERP (I 6) SOUTH/AMERICA)    Link to superordinate units

     (LOCATION (I 0)                 Values of LOCATION attribute follow:

          (IN (I 0) (SOUTH/AMERICA (I 0) WESTERN))
          (ON (I 0) (COAST (I 0) (OF (I 0) PACIFIC))
          (LATITUDE (I 4) (RANGE (I 0) -18 0))
          (LONGITUDE (I 5) (RANGE (I 0) -82 -68))
          (BORDERING/COUNTRIES (I 1)
                  (NORTHERN (I 1) (LIST COLUMBIA ECUADOR))
                  (EASTERN (I 1) BRAZIL)
                              ⋮
```

Figure C1–1. The unit for PERU.

tutorial protocols were analyzed to see what strategies people follow, in an attempt to incorporate these strategies into the system (see also Article IX.C2 on the groups continuing research in this direction). The following example is an excerpt from a session with the South American geography tutor. The student's questions and answers are preceded by ** and annotations are shown in italics:

What is the language of Argentina?

** Probably Spanish

Very good.
Approximately what is the area of Argentina?

> *Student changes topic...*

** Tell me something about Peru

Peru is a country.
It is located in South America.
The capital of Peru is Lima.
Now answer the question you didn't answer before.

> *...finally answers the question.*

** The area of Argentina is 1,100,000 square miles

Approximately true, but a more exact value is 1,200,000.
The eastern bordering country of Peru is ---.

> *Student makes an error and is corrected...*

** Catholicism

Wrong. Catholicism is not a country but a religion.
The correct answer is: Brazil
Where is Peru?

> *...and once again changes topic.*

** Is Asuncion hot?

Since Asuncion is part of Paraguay, yes.

** What is the most important difference between
Peru and Paraguay?

The primary difference is: The population of Peru
is larger by a factor of 7.8.

The natural-language processing used by SCHOLAR is based on a *case grammar* system (Article IV.C4, in Vol. I), and the semantic interpretation of a student's response is heavily guided by the geography knowledge in the semantic net. Natural-language processing is important in SCHOLAR because it allows the student to take the initiative and ask questions that were not anticipated by the program. However, comprehension of English input is facilitated by a taxonomy of expected question types. The case grammar is also used by the system to construct questions and presentations of new material from the semantic network. English output is composed of short, simple sentences, with no embedded clauses and a limited repertoire of verbs— generally some form of the verb *to be*.

A simple *agenda* keeps track of topics that are being discussed. Timing considerations and relevance (importance tags) affect the generation and pruning of topics on this agenda. Continuity between questions is weak, however, since SCHOLAR does not plan a series of questions to make a point. SCHOLAR is capable of diagnosing a student's misunderstanding only by following up one question with a related question.

Making Inferences

SCHOLAR's inference strategies, for answering student questions and evaluating student answers to its questions, are designed to cope with the incompleteness of the information stored in the semantic-net knowledge base. Some of the important strategies for reasoning with incomplete knowledge are given below. These abilities have been explored further in current research dealing with *default reasoning* (Reiter, 1978) and *plausible reasoning* (Collins, 1978).

Intersection search. Answering questions of the form "Can X be a part of Y?" (e.g., "Is Buenos Aires in Argentina?") is done by an intersection search: The superpart (SUPERP) arcs of both nodes for X and Y are traced until an intersection is found (i.e., a common superconcept node is found). If there is no intersection, the answer is "No." If there is an intersection node Q, SCHOLAR answers as follows:

$$\text{If } Q = Y, \text{ then "Yes";}$$
$$\text{If } Q = X, \text{ then "No, } Y \text{ is an } X\text{."}$$

For example, the question "Is Buenos Aires in Agentina?" is answered "Yes" because Argentina is a SUPERP of Buenos Aires in the net ($Q = Y$):

South America

/(Superpart)

Argentina (*Y*)

/(Superpart)

Buenos Aires (*X*)

But the question "Is Argentina in Buenos Aires?" receives the response "No, Buenos Aires is in Argentina."

South America

(Superpart)

Argentina (X)

(Superpart)

Buenos Aires (Y)

Common superordinate. If the common superpart node, Q, is neither X nor Y, the program focuses on the two elements that have Q as a common superordinate. If they are contradictory (i.e., contain suitable CONTRA properties) or have distinguishing, mutually exclusive properties (e.g., different LOCATIONs), the answer is, "No"; otherwise, the system answers, "I don't know." Answering "Is X a Y?" questions is similar, except SUPERC (superconcept) arcs are used for the intersection process.

Open and closed sets. In order to look for all objects in the system that satisfy some condition (e.g., "How many cities in Columbia are on the Atlantic?"), a distinction must be made about whether the resulting set of these objects is *closed* (explicitly contains all such objects) or *open* (contains some and need not contain all such objects). In SCHOLAR's net, sets are tagged by the courseware author as either open or closed, thus giving an indication of the *incompleteness* of the system's knowledge.

While it is easy for SCHOLAR to answer questions such as "Is France a country in South America?" about closed sets (i.e., the set of countries in South America), similar questions about open sets require the use of special techniques—SCHOLAR must be able to reason about the *extent* of its knowledge. For example, if we ask SCHOLAR whether or not rubber is a product of, say, Guyana and if there is no explicit information about Guyanese rubber production in the semantic net, SCHOLAR starts to reason with what it knows: It compares the importance tags (I-tags) of the agricultural products of Guyana with the importance tags for rubber in countries that it knows produce rubber. It happens that Peru is a known rubber producer. SCHOLAR looks at the I-tag of rubber for Peru and compares this tag to the largest (least important) I-tags associated with Guyana. If it finds that these are comparable, SCHOLAR infers that it knows as much about Guyana (up to some large I-tag value) as it knows about Peru. Therefore, SCHOLAR infers that it would know about rubber production in Guyana if it were important. Since rubber is not listed for Guyana, SCHOLAR makes the plausible (though uncertain) conclusion that rubber is not produced there. At this point, SCHOLAR answers that it does not know for certain and gives the information about rubber and Peru.

SCHOLAR's use of knowledge about the extent of its knowledge in this kind of *plausible reasoning* is unique in AI research and represents an application of *meta-level knowledge* (see Article III.A, in Vol. I).

Summary

The inferencing strategies of SCHOLAR are independent of the *content* of the semantic net and are applicable in different domains. The inferences produced are fairly natural; that is, they handle incomplete knowledge by employing reasoning processes similar to those that people use. The SCHOLAR project as a whole provides an ongoing environment for research on discourse, teaching strategies, and plausible reasoning (see Article IX.C2 on recent research, including the WHY system).

References

Carbonell (1970a) is a classic paper, defining the field of ICAI and introducing the SCHOLAR system. Collins (1976) is an illuminating study of human tutorial dialogues. Collins (1978) discusses inference mechanisms, and Collins (1978) reports extended research on plausible reasoning. Grignetti, Hausmann, and Gould (1975) describe NLS–SCHOLAR.

C2. WHY

RECENT RESEARCH by Allan Collins, Albert Stevens, and their ICAI research group at Bolt Beranek and Newman (BBN) has focused on developing computer-based tutors that can discuss complex systems. Their previous research on SCHOLAR (Article IX.C1), a system that offers tutoring in facts about South American geography, led them to investigate the nature of tutorial dialogues about subject matter that was not just factual—where the causal and temporal interrelations between the concepts in the domain were of interest and where students' errors could involve not only forgotten facts, but also misconceptions about why processes work the way they do. Stevens and Collins (1977) describe a new system, called WHY, that tutors students in the causes of rainfall, a complex geophysical process that is a function of many interrelated factors (no single factor can be isolated that is both necessary and sufficient to account for rainfall).

In their research on tutorial dialogue of this type, the BBN group has focused on three questions that are central themes throughout ICAI research (Stevens, Collins, and Goldin, 1978):

1. How can a good tutor's use of questions, statements, and examples be characterized? What is the "goal structure" of a Socratic tutor?

2. What types of misconceptions do students have? How do tutors diagnose these misconceptions from the errors students make?

3. What are the abstractions and viewpoints that tutors use to explain physical processes?

By analyzing tutorial dialogues between human experts and students, Collins and Stevens identify elements of a theory of tutoring. These are incorporated into a tutorial program, which is then used to find the weak points of the theory for further investigation. The current version of the WHY system is the first of a series of iterations of this sort. The work so far has concentrated on the first topic above, the nature of Socratic tutoring.

Socratic Tutoring Heuristics

Collins (1976) argues that learning to reason about and understand complex processes is best accomplished by dealing with specific problems and cases and trying to generalize from them. Socratic dialogue is especially appropriate for tutoring complex subjects in which factors interact and in which their interaction accounts for the phenomenon under consideration. In an effort to model explicitly the nature of the Socratic dialogue, the current version of WHY incorporates 24 *heuristics* that control the student/system interaction.

A sample heuristic is:

> *If*   the student gives as an explanation of causal dependence one or more factors that are not necessary,
>
> *then* select a counterexample with the wrong value of the factor and ask the student why his causal dependence does not hold in that case.

This rule forces the student to consider the necessity of a particular factor. For example, if the student gives rainfall as a reason for growing rice, then the computer-generated counterexample "Why do they grow rice in Egypt, where there isn't much rainfall?" challenges the student's explanation of rice growing. These heuristic rules are designed to facilitate tutorial dialogues in which the student must consider combinations of factors that are necessary for rainfall, eliminate irrelevant factors, and attempt to generalize from specific cases to general conditions. (See Collins, 1976, for a complete discussion of the tutoring rules; this subject is also discussed in Article IX.C6 on GUIDON.)

WHY's knowledge base about rainfall is represented in *script*-like data structures (see Article III.C7, in Vol. I), which encode temporal relations in the rainfall process; for example, *First water evaporates from an ocean or sea, then the water-laden air mass is carried over land by winds, which in turn causes the air mass to cool, which causes precipitation.* This knowledge representation is adequate for capturing many of the characteristics of a tutorial dialogue, but there are other kinds of knowledge about rainfall that are not represented here but that are discussed below.

The following excerpt is from a dialogue with the current version of the WHY system. The system prompts the student to suggest causes of rainfall, to look for prior or intermediate causes, and finally to suggest a general rule. When such a rule is proposed, the system finds a counterexample and forces revision of the rule to account for it. The system proceeds in this way until a rule of sufficient generality is found. The protocol is annotated with the heuristics employed by the system at each juncture in the conversation.

Heuristic 1: Ask for a prediction about a particular case.

```
Do you think the Amazon jungle has heavy rainfall
or light rainfall?

** Heavy rainfall
```

Heuristic 2: Ask for prior causes.

```
Why does the Amazon jungle have heavy rainfall?

** Because it's near the Atlantic

Yes, the Amazon jungle is near the equatorial Atlantic.
```

Heuristic 3: Ask for intermediate causes.

```
How does that affect rainfall in the Amazon jungle?
```

** The water in the current is warm

   ⋮

 Heuristic 4: Ask for subsequent causes.

What happens after the moisture-filled air reaches the land?

** I don't know

 Heuristic 5: Suggest a factor and ask if it is a cause.

Do you think the Andes mountain range has any effect on the
rainfall in the Amazon jungle?

** Yes

 Heuristic 3: Ask for intermediate causes.

How?

** The prevailing wind hits the Andes and the air cools

 Heuristic 3: Ask for intermediate causes.

How does the fact that the prevailing wind hits the Andes
lead to air cooling?

   ⋮

 Heuristic 6: Form a general rule for an insufficient cause.

Do you think that any place with mountains has heavy rainfall?

** Yes

 Heuristic 7: Pick a counterexample for an insufficient cause, and
 Heuristic 2: Ask for prior causes.

Southern California has mountains.
Why doesn't Southern California have heavy rainfall?

Current Research

Tutorial goals. One of the shortcomings of the existing system is that
it does not have long-term "goals" for the tutorial dialogue. Implicit in
the tutorial rules is some idea about local management of the interaction,
but a global strategy about the tutoring session is absent. Human tutors,
however, admit to having goals like *Concentrate on one particular part of the
causal structure of rainfall at a time* or *Clear up one misconception before
discussing another.* Stevens and Collins (1977) set about codifying these
goals and strategies for incorporation into the WHY system. They analyzed
tutoring protocols in which human tutors commented on what they thought
the students did and did not know and on why they responded to the students
as they did. From this analysis, two top-level goals became apparent:

1. Refine the student's causal structure, starting with the most important factors in a particular process and gradually incorporating more subtle factors.

2. Refine the student's procedures for applying his causal model to novel situations.

Student misconceptions. The top-level goals involve subgoals of identifying and correcting the student's misconceptions. Stevens and Collins classified these subgoals into five categories of bugs and provided directions for correcting them, as follows:

1. *Factual bugs.* The tutor deals with these by correcting the student. Teaching facts is not the goal of Socratic tutoring; interrelations of facts are more important.

2. *Outside-domain bugs.* These are misconceptions about causal structure, which the tutor chooses not to explain in detail. For example, the "correct" relationship between the temperature of air and its moisture-holding capacity is often stated by the tutor as a fact, without further explanation.

3. *Overgeneralization.* When a student makes a general rule from an insufficient set of factors (e.g., *Any place with mountains has heavy rainfall*), the tutor will find counterexamples to probe for more factors.

4. *Overdifferentiation.* When a student counts factors as necessary when they are not, the tutor will generate counterexamples to show that they are not.

5. *Reasoning bugs.* Tutors will attempt to teach students skills such as forming and testing hypotheses and collecting enough information before drawing a conclusion.

If a student displays more than one bug, human tutors will employ a set of heuristics to decide which one to correct first:

1. Correct errors before omissions.
2. Correct causally prior factors before later ones.
3. Make short corrections before longer ones.
4. Correct low-level bugs (in the causal network) before correcting higher level ones.

Functional relationships. The bugs just discussed are all domain independent; that is, they would occur in tutorial dialogues about other complex processes besides rainfall. But some bugs are the results of specific misconceptions about the functional interrelationships of the concepts of the specific domain. For example, one common misconception about rainfall is that *Cooling causes air to rise.* This is not a simple factual misconception, nor is it domain independent. It is best characterized as an error in the student's functional model of rainfall.

In fact, the script representation in the WHY system that captures the temporal and causal relations of land, air, and water masses in rainfall proved inadequate to get at all of the types of student misconceptions. Recent work has investigated a more flexible representation of *functional relationships*, which allows the description of the processes that collectively determine rainfall from multiple viewpoints—for example, the *temporal-causal-subprocess* view captured in the scripts and the *functional* view emphasizing the roles that different objects play in the various processes (Stevens, Collins, and Goldin, 1978). Misconceptions about rainfall are represented as errors in the student's model of these relationships. A functional relationship has four components: (a) a set of actors, each with a role in the process; (b) a set of factors that affect the process, all of which are attributes of the actors (e.g., water is an actor in the evaporation relationship and its temperature is a factor); (c) the result of the process, which is always a change in an attribute of one of the actors; and (d) the relation that holds between the actors and the result, or how an attribute gets changed. These functional relationships may be the result of models from other domains that are applied metaphorically to the domain under discussion (Stevens and Collins, 1978).

Summary

The WHY system started as an extension of SCHOLAR by the implementation of rules that characterize Socratic tutoring heuristics. Subsequently, an effort was made to describe the global strategies used by human tutors to guide the dialogue. Since these were directed toward dispelling students' misconceptions, five classes of misconceptions, as well as means for correcting them, were established. Many misconceptions are not domain independent and the key to more versatile tutoring lies in continuing research on knowledge representation.

References

The major reference on the research reported here is Stevens, Collins, and Goldin (1978). The tutorial rules are discussed fully in an excellent article by Collins (1976). The later work on the goal structure of a tutor is reported in Stevens and Collins (1977). Finally, research on conceptual models and multiple viewpoints of complex systems is discussed in Stevens and Collins (1978).

C3. SOPHIE

SOPHIE (a SOPHisticated Instructional Environment) is an ICAI system developed by John Seely Brown, Richard Burton, and their colleagues at Bolt Beranek and Newman, Inc., to explore broader student initiative during the tutorial interaction. The SOPHIE system provides the student with a learning environment in which he (or she) acquires problem-solving skills by trying out his ideas, rather than by instruction. The system has a model of the problem-solving knowledge in its domain, as well as numerous heuristic strategies for answering the student's questions, criticizing his hypotheses, and suggesting alternative theories for his current hypotheses. SOPHIE allows the student to have a one-to-one relationship with a computer-based "expert" who helps him come up with his own ideas, experiment with these ideas, and, when necessary, debug them.

Figure C3–1 illustrates the component modules of the original SOPHIE–I system (Brown, Rubenstein, and Burton, 1976) and the capabilities added for the SOPHIE–II system, discussed later in this article.

SOPHIE–I

SOPHIE teaches problem-solving skills in the context of a simulated electronics laboratory. The problem facing the student is to find the faults in a malfunctioning piece of equipment whose characteristics he obtains by taking measurements. Thus, the student takes a sequence of measurements (such as voltages, currents, and resistances) to determine what is wrong with the equipment and asks questions about the measurements and about what fault hypotheses he should consider, given the information he has discovered so far. SOPHIE evaluates the hypotheses by considering all of the information that the student should have been able to derive from his current set of measurements. The system also judges the merits of a student's suggestion for a new measurement in light of the prior sequence of measurements. SOPHIE can decide if a measurement is valuable, based on whether it eliminates or isolates a fault, and will inform the student when a proposed measurement provides no new information.

The following portion of a sample protocol (from Brown and Burton, 1975) illustrates some of the linguistic and inferential capabilities of the SOPHIE system. SOPHIE randomly selects a fault (in the performance of a circuit component), inserts it into a model or simulation of the circuit, and tells the student how the controls are set. The student is given a schematic diagram of the circuit, and the dialogue refers to components in the schematic diagram (e.g., resistor 8 [R8], node connection 1 [N1], transistors [Q1] and [Q6]). The

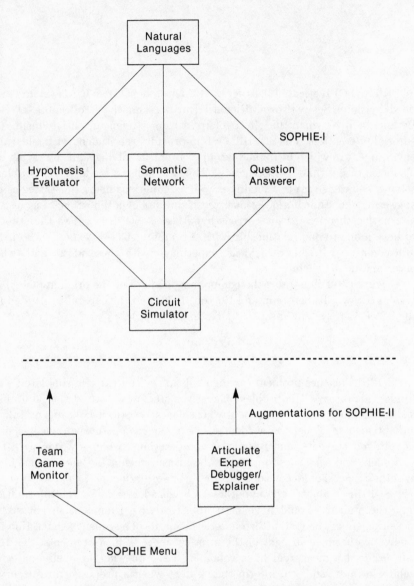

Figure C3–1.   SOPHIE–I and SOPHIE–II (Brown, Rubenstein, and Burton, 1976).

student begins his troubleshooting by performing measurements in the faulted circuit.

```
Welcome to SOPHIE, a reactive learning environment.
The piece of equipment you are studying is a regulated
```

power supply. Would you like to start with a faulted
instrument that needs fixing?

** Yes

The instrument has a fault and its present
control settings are:

CC	1.0	CURRENT CONTROL
CR	HIGH	CURRENT RANGE SWITCH
LOAD	20	LOAD RESISTANCE IN OHMS
VC	1.0	VOLTAGE CONTROL
VR	HIGH	VOLTAGE RANGE SWITCH

** What is the output?

The output voltage is 11.7 volts.

Notice that "output" was disambiguated as "output voltage."

** What is it in a working instrument?

In a working circuit the output voltage is 19.9 volts.

*In case the student does not know what the required value of measurement
should have been, he can ask for any measurement in a properly functioning instrument. The student then requests an internal measurement.*

** What is the voltage between R8 and Q1?

The voltage at N1 is 47.6 volts.

$\vdots$

** Replace Q6

*The student believes that he has discovered the problem (in transistor Q6)
and tries to fix it. Before a component is replaced, however, the system
queries him as to how he thinks it is faulted.*

I am going to ask you some questions about how Q6 is faulted.
Are any junctions shorted?

** I don't know

Are any terminals open?

** Yes

Which terminal(s) are open?

** The base

Q6 is not faulted in that manner. Q6 not replaced.

*After learning that Q6 does not have an open base, the student asks if
this was at least a reasonable hypothesis.*

** Is it possible that Q6 has an open base?

Before the system's evaluation procedures can be applied to the student's idea or hypothesis, the hypothesis must be completely specified. To help the student out, the system suggests a plausible complete specification of it in an abbreviated form familiar to the student.

Is the complete fault mode EB/EC/BC = Open/Ok/Open
what you intended?

** Sure

That fault is consistent with all of the measurements
you have made.

The hypothesis is reasonable, but other measurements will indicate that another component is faulty.

Natural-language Processing—Semantic Grammar

In an instructional setting, it is important that the student be provided with a convenient way to communicate his ideas to the system. The student will quickly become frustrated if he has to try several ways of expressing an idea before the system can understand it. SOPHIE's natural-language understander copes with various linguistic problems such as *anaphoric references*, context-dependent deletions, and *ellipses*, which occur frequently in natural dialogues.

SOPHIE's natural-language capabilities are based on the concept of a *performance* or *semantic grammar*, in which the usual syntactic categories such as noun, verb, and adjective are replaced by semantically meaningful categories (Burton, 1976b; Burton and Brown, 1979b). These categories represent concepts known to the system—measurements, circuit elements, transistors, hypotheses, and so on. For each concept there is a grammar rule that gives the alternate ways of expressing that concept in terms of its constituent concepts. Each rule is encoded as a LISP procedure that specifies the order of application of the various alternatives in each rule.

A grammar centered around semantic categories allows the parser to deal with a certain amount of "fuzziness," or uncertainty, in its understanding of the words in a given statement; that is, if the parser is searching for a particular instantiation of a semantic category, and the current word in the sentence fails to satisfy this instantiation, it skips over that word and continues searching. Thus, if the student uses certain words or concepts that the system does not know, the parser can ignore these words and try to make sense of what remains. To limit the negative consequences that may result from a misunderstood question, SOPHIE responds to the student's question with a full sentence that tells him what question is being answered. (See Chaps. IV

and V, in Vol. I, especially Articles IV.F7 and V.C4, for other systems using
semantic grammar parsers.)

Inferencing Strategies

To interact with the student, SOPHIE performs several different logical
and tutorial tasks. First, there is the task of answering *hypothetical questions*.
For example, the student might ask, "If the base-emitter junction of the
voltage-limiting transistor opens, then what happens to the output voltage?"

A second task SOPHIE must perform is that of *hypothesis evaluation*, in
which the student asks, "Given the measurements I have made so far, could
the base of transistor Q3 be open?" The problem here is not to determine
whether the assertion *The base of Q3 is open* is true, but whether this assertion is logically consistent with the data that have already been collected by
the student. If it is not consistent, the program explains why it is not. When
it is consistent, SOPHIE identifies which information supports the assertion
and which information is independent of it.

A third task that SOPHIE must perform is *hypothesis generation*. In its
simplest form, this involves constructing all possible hypotheses consistent
with the known information. This procedure permits SOPHIE to answer
questions like "What could be wrong with the circuit (given the measurements
that I have taken)?" The task is solved using *generate and test* with the
hypothesis-evaluation task described above performing the test function.

Finally, SOPHIE can determine whether a given measurement is *redundant*, that is, if the results of the measurement could have been predicted
from a complete theory of the circuit, given the previous measurements.

SOPHIE accomplishes all of these reasoning tasks through an *inference
mechanism* that relies principally on a general-purpose simulator of the circuit
under discussion. For example, to answer a question about a changed voltage
resulting from a hypothetical modification to a circuit, SOPHIE first interprets
the question with its parser and then, applying this interpretation, simulates
the desired modification. The result is a voltage table that represents the
voltages at each terminal in the modified circuit. The original question is
then answered in terms of these voltages.

The tasks of hypothesis evaluation and hypothesis generation are handled
in a similar manner, using the simulator. In evaluating hypotheses, SOPHIE
attempts to determine the logical consistency of a given hypothesis. To accomplish this task, a simulation of the hypothesis is performed on the circuit
model and measurements are taken of the result. If the values of any of these
measurements are not equivalent to the measurements taken by the student,
a counterexample has been established, which is used to critique the student's
hypothesis.

When generating hypotheses, SOPHIE attempts to determine the set of possible faults or hypotheses that are consistent with the observed behavior of the faulted instrument. This task is performed by a set of specialist procedures that propose a possible set of hypotheses to explain a measurement and then simulate them to make sure that they explain the output voltage and all of the measurements that the student has taken. Hypothesis generation can suggest possible paths to explore when the student has run out of ideas for what could be wrong with the circuit or when he wishes to understand the full implications of his last measurement. It is also used by SOPHIE to determine when a measurement is redundant.

SOPHIE-II: The Augmented SOPHIE Laboratory

Extensions to SOPHIE include (a) a *troubleshooting game* with two teams of students and (b) the development of an *articulate expert debugger/explainer*. The simple reactive learning environment has also been augmented by the development of frame-oriented CAI lesson material, to prepare the student for the laboratory interaction (Brown et al., 1976). The articulate expert not only locates student-inserted faults in a given instrument but also can articulate exactly the deductions that led to its discovery, as well as the more global strategies that guide the troubleshooting scenario.

Experience with SOPHIE indicates that its major weakness is an inability to follow up on student errors. Since SOPHIE is to be reactive to the student, it will not take the initiative to explore a student's misunderstanding or suggest approaches that he does not consider. However, the competitive environment of the troubleshooting game, in which partners share a problem and work it out together, was found to be an effective means of exercising the student's knowledge of the operation of the instrument being debugged. Finally, an experiment involving a minicourse—and exposure to the frame-based texts, the expert, and the original SOPHIE laboratory—indicated that long-term use of the system is more effective than a single, concentrated exposure to the material (Brown et al., 1976).

Summary

The goal of the SOPHIE project was to create a learning environment in which students would be challenged to explore ideas on their own and to come up with conjectures or hypotheses about a problem-solving situation. The students receive detailed feedback as to the logical validity of their proposed solutions. In cases where the students' ideas have logical flaws, SOPHIE can generate relevant counterexamples and critiques. The SOPHIE system combines domain-specific knowledge and powerful domain-independent inferencing mechanisms to answer questions that even human tutors might find extremely difficult to answer.

References

The most thorough discussion of SOPHIE is in Brown, Burton, and de Kleer (in preparation). Brown, Burton, and Bell (1975) give a complete description of the early work on SOPHIE; and Brown, Rubenstein, and Burton (1976) report on the later work. Also see Brown and Burton (1978).

C4. WEST

DEVELOPMENT of the first *computer coach* was undertaken by Richard Burton and John Seely Brown at Bolt Beranek and Newman, Inc., for the children's board game called "How the West Was Won." The term *Coach* describes a computer-based learning environment in which the student is involved in an activity, like playing a computer game, and the instructional program operates by "looking over his shoulder" during the game and occasionally offering criticisms or suggestions for improvement (Goldstein, 1977). This research focused on identifying (a) *diagnostic strategies* required to *infer* a student's misunderstandings from his observed behavior and (b) various explicit *tutoring strategies* for directing the tutor to say the right thing at the right time (Burton and Brown, 1976, 1979a).

The intention of the WEST research project was to use these strategies to control the interaction so that the instructional program took every possible opportunity to offer help to the student without interrupting so often as to become a nuisance and destroy the student's fun at the game. By guiding a student's learning through discovery, computer-based coaching systems hold the promise of enhancing the educational value of the increasingly popular computer games.

Philosophy of the Instructional Coach

The pedagogical ideas underlying much of the computer-coaching research in WEST can be characterized as *guided discovery learning.* It assumes that the student *constructs* his (or her) understanding of a situation or a task based on his prior knowledge. According to this theory, the notion of misconception, or *bug*, plays a central role in the construction process. Ideally, a bug in the student's knowledge will cause an erroneous or suboptimal behavior, which the student will notice. If the student has enough information to determine what caused the error and can then correct it, the bug is referred to as *constructive.* The role of a tutor in an informal environment is to give the student extra information in situations that would otherwise be confusing to him, so that he can determine what caused his error and can convert nonconstructive bugs into constructive ones (see Fisher, Brown, and Burton, 1978, for further discussion).

However, an important constraint on the Coach is that it should not interrupt the student too often. If the Coach immediately points out the student's errors, there is a danger that the student will never develop the necessary skills for examining his own behavior and identifying the causes of his mistakes. The Coach must be perceptive enough to make relevant comments but not be too intrusive, destroying the fun of the game. The research on the WEST system examined a wide variety of tutorial strategies that must be included to create a successful coaching system.

"How the West Was Won"

"How the West Was Won" was originally a computer-simulated board game, designed by Bonnie Anderson of the Elementary Mathematics Project, on the PLATO computer-based education system at the University of Illinois (Dugdale and Kibbey, 1977). The purpose of this original (nontutorial) program was to give elementary-school students drill and practice in arithmetic. The game resembles the popular "Chutes and Ladders" board game and, briefly, goes something like this: At each turn, a player receives three numbers (from spinners) with which he constructs an arithmetic expression using the operations of addition, subtraction, multiplication, and division. The numeric value of the completed expression is the number of spaces the player can move, the object of the game being to get to the end first.

However, the strategy of combining the three numbers to make the largest valued expression is not always the best strategy, because there are several special features on the game board that have a bearing on the outcome. Towns occur every 10 spaces, and if a player lands exactly on one, he skips ahead to the next town. There are also shortcuts, and if the player lands on the beginning of one, he advances to the other end of the shortcut. Finally, if the player lands on the space that his opponent is occupying, the opponent is bumped back two towns. The spinner values in WEST are small, so these special moves are encouraged (i.e., landing on towns, on shortcuts, or on the opponent).

Differential Modeling

There are two major related problems that must be solved by the computer Coach. They are (a) when to interrupt the student's problem-solving activity and (b) what to say once the Coach has interrupted. In general, solutions to these problems require techniques for determining what the student knows (procedures for constructing a *diagnostic model*) as well as explicit tutoring principles about interrupting and advising. These, in turn, require theories about how a student forms abstractions, how he learns, and when he is apt to be most receptive to advice. Unfortunately, few, if any, existing psychological theories are precise enough to suggest anything more than caution.

Since the student is primarily engaged in a gaming or problem-solving activity, diagnosis of his strengths and weaknesses must be unobtrusive to his main activity. This objective means that the diagnostic component cannot use prestored tests or pose a lot of diagnostic questions to the student.

Instead, the computer Coach must restrict itself mainly to inferring a student's shortcomings from what he does in the context of playing the game or solving the problem. This objective can create a difficulty—just because a student does not use a certain skill while playing a game, one cannot conclude that he does not *know* that skill.

Although this point seems quite obvious, it poses a serious diagnostic problem: The absence of a possible skill carries diagnostic value if and only if an expert in an equivalent situation would have used that skill. Hence, apart from outright errors, the main window a computer-based Coach has on a student's misconceptions is through a *differential-modeling* technique that compares what the student is doing with what an expert would do in his place. These differences suggest hypotheses about what the student does not know or has not yet mastered. (See the related discussion of *overlay models* in Articles IX.C5 and IX.C6.)

Constructing the differential model requires that two tasks be performed by the Coach with the computer *Expert* (the part of the program that is expert at playing the game WEST):

1. *Evaluate* the student's current move with respect to the set of possible alternative moves that the Expert might have made in exactly the same circumstances.

2. Determine what *underlying skills* were used to select and compose the student's move and each of the "better" moves of the Expert.

To accomplish the evaluative task, the Expert need only use the results of its knowledge and reasoning strategies—its better moves. However, for the second task the Coach has to consider the "pieces" of knowledge involved in making those moves, since the absence of one of these pieces of knowledge might explain why the student failed to make a better move.

Tutoring by Issue and Example—A General Paradigm

The Coach's comments should be both relevant to the situation and memorable to the student. The *Issues and Examples* tutoring strategy provides a framework for meeting these two constraints. *Issues* are concepts used in the diagnostic process to identify, at any particular moment, what is relevant. *Examples* provide concrete instances of these abstract concepts. Providing both the description of a generic Issue (a concept used to select a strategy) and a concrete Example of its use increases the chance that the student will integrate this piece of tutorial commentary into his knowledge. In the Issues and Examples paradigm, the Issues embody the important concepts underlying a student's behavior. They define the space of concepts that the Coach can address—the facets of the student's behavior that are monitored by the Coach.

In WEST, there are three levels of Issues on which a Coach can focus: At the lowest level are the basic mathematical skills that the student is practicing (the use of parentheses, the use of the various arithmetic operations, and the form or pattern of the student's move as an arithmetic expression). The second level of Issues concerns the skills needed to play WEST (like the special moves: bump opponent, land on town, take shortcut) and the development of a *strategy* for choosing moves. At the third level are the general skills of game playing (like watching the opponent to learn from his moves), which are not addressed by the WEST program.

Each of the Issues is represented in two parts, a *recognizer* and an *evaluator*. The Issue recognizer is *data driven;* it watches the student's behavior for evidence that he does or does not use a particular concept or skill. The recognizers are used to construct a *model* of the student's knowledge. The Issue evaluators are goal directed; they interpret this model to determine the student's weaknesses. The Issue recognizers of WEST are fairly straightforward but are, nevertheless, more complex than simple pattern-matchers. For example, the recognizer for the PARENTHESIS Issue must determine not only whether or not parentheses are present in the student's expression, but also whether or not they were necessary for his move, or for an optimal move.

Figure C4–1 is a diagram of the modeling-tutorial process underlying the Issues and Examples paradigm. The top part of Figure C4–1 shows the process of constructing a model of the student's behavior. It is important to observe that without the Expert it is impossible to determine whether the student is weak in some skill or whether the skill has not been used because the need for it has arisen infrequently in the student's experience.

The Coaching Process

The lower part of Figure C4–1 illustrates the top level of the coaching process. When the student makes a less than optimal move (as determined by comparing his move with that of the Expert), the Coach uses the evaluation component of each Issue to create a list of Issues on which it has assessed that the student is weak. From the Expert's list of better moves, the Coach invokes the Issue recognizers, to determine a second list of Issues that are illustrated by these better moves. From these two lists of Issues, the Coach selects an Issue and the move that illustrates it (i.e., creates an example of it) and decides, on the basis of *tutoring principles*, whether or not to interrupt the game. If the two lists have no Issues in common, the reason for the student's problem lies outside the collection of Issues, and the Coach says nothing.

If the Coach decides to interrupt, the selected Issue and Example are then passed to the *explanation* generators, which provide the feedback to the student. Currently, the explanations are stored in procedures, called

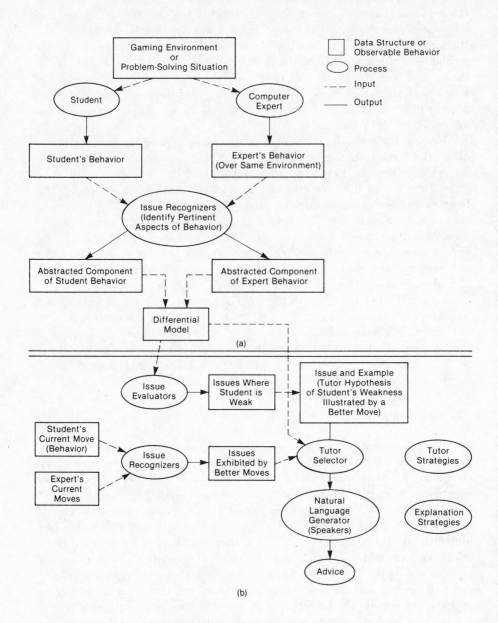

Figure C4–1.   Diagram of the modeling-coaching process (Burton and
              Brown, 1979a).

*SPEAKER*s, attached to each Issue. Each SPEAKER is responsible for presenting a few lines of text explaining its Issue.

Tutoring Principles

General tutoring principles dictate that, at times, even when relevant Issues and Examples have been identified, it may be inappropriate to interrupt. For example, what if there are two competing Issues, both applicable to a certain situation? Which one should be selected? The Issues in WEST are sufficiently independent that there is little need to consider their prerequisite structure, for example, whether or not the use of parentheses should be taught before division (see, however, the description of the *syllabus* in WUMPUS in Article IX.C5). Instead, additional tutoring principles must be invoked to decide which one of the set of applicable Issues should be used.

In WEST, experiments have been conducted using two alternate principles to guide this decision. The first is the Focus Strategy, which ensures that, everything else being equal, the Issue most recently discussed is chosen—the Coach will tend to concentrate on a particular Issue until evidence is present to indicate that it has been mastered. The alternate principle is the Breadth Strategy, in which Issues that have not recently been discussed tend to be selected. This strategy minimizes a student's boredom and ensures a breadth of concept coverage.

The rest of WEST's strategies for deciding whether to raise an Issue and what to say can be placed in the four categories listed below, with sample rules of each:

1. *Coaching philosophy.* Tutoring principles can enhance a student's likelihood of remembering what is said. For example, *When illustrating an Issue, use an Example* (an alternate move) *only when the result or outcome of that move is dramatically superior to the move made by the student.*

2. *Maintaining interest in the game.* The Coach should not destroy the student's inherent interest in the game by interrupting too often. For example, *Never tutor on two consecutive moves* or *If the student makes an exceptional move, identify why it is good and congratulate the student.*

3. *Increasing chances of learning.* Four levels of hints are provided by the WEST tutor, at the student's request: (a) Isolate a weakness and directly address that weakness, (b) delineate the space of possible moves at this point in the game, (c) select the optimal move and tell why it is optimal, and (d) describe how to make the optimal move.

4. *Environmental considerations.* The game-playing environment should be considered by the Coach. For example, *If the student makes a possibly careless error, one for which there is evidence that the student knows better, be forgiving.*

Noise in the Model

When the student does not make an optimal move, the program knows only that at least one of the Issues required for that move was not employed by the student. Which of these Issues blocked the student from making the move is not known. In practice, blame is apportioned more or less equally among all of the Issues required for a missed better move. One effect of this is the introduction of *noise* into the model; that is, blame will almost certainly be apportioned also to Issues that are, in fact, understood. A second source of noise in the differential model is that the system does not account for the entire process that a person goes through in deriving a move, so the set of Issues is, by definition, incomplete. A third source of noise is the difficulty of modeling human factors such as boredom or fatigue that cause inconsistent behaviors. For example, students are seldom completely consistent. They often forget to apply techniques that they know, or they get tired and accept a move that is easy but that does not reflect their knowledge.

Another source of noise is inherent in the process of learning. As the student plays the game, he acquires new skills. The student model, which has been building during the course of his play, will not be up to date; that is, it will still show the newly learned issues as weaknesses. Ideally, the old pieces of the model should decay with time. The costs involved in this computation are prohibitive. To avoid this particular failing of the model, the WEST Coach removes from consideration any Issues that the student has used recently (in the last three moves), assuming that they are now part of his knowledge.

To combat the noise that arises in the model, the Evaluator for each Issue tends to assume that the student has mastery of the Issue. Some coaching opportunities may be missed, but eventually, if the student has a problem addressed by an Issue, a pattern will emerge.

Experience with WEST

WEST has been used in elementary-school classrooms; in a controlled experiment, the coached version of WEST was compared to an uncoached version. The coached students showed a considerably greater variety of patterns in the mathematical expressions they used, indicating that they had acquired many of the more subtle patterns and had not fallen permanently into "ruts" that prevented them from seeing when such moves were important. Perhaps most significant of all, the students in the coached group enjoyed playing the game considerably more than did the uncoached group (Goldstein, 1979).

References

A good discussion of the WEST coach is Burton and Brown (1979a).

C5. WUMPUS

THIS ARTICLE describes a *computer coach* for WUMPUS, a computer game
in which the player must track down and slay the vicious Wumpus while
avoiding pitfalls that result in certain, if fictional, death (Yob, 1975). The
coach described here is WUSOR–II, one of three generations of computer
coaches for WUMPUS developed by Ira Goldstein and Brian Carr at M.I.T.
(Carr and Goldstein, 1977; for discussions of WUSOR–I and WUSOR–III, see
Stansfield, Carr, and Goldstein, 1976, and Goldstein, 1979, respectively). To
be a skilled Wumpus-hunter, one must know about logic, probability, decision
theory, and geometry. A deficit in one's knowledge may result in being eaten
by the Wumpus or falling to the center of the earth. In keeping with the
philosophy of computer coaching, students are highly motivated to learn these
fundamental skills.

The design of the WUSOR–II system involves the interactions of the
specialist programs shown in Figure C5–1. There are four modules: the
Expert, the Psychologist, the Student Model, and the Tutor. The Expert tells
the Psychologist if the player's move is nonoptimal and which skills are needed
for him (or her) to discover better alternatives. The Psychologist employs this
comparison to formulate hypotheses concerning which domain-specific skills
are known to the student. These hypotheses are recorded in the Student
Model, which represents the student's knowledge as a subset of the Expert's
skills—an *overlay model* (see Article IX.B). The Tutor uses the Student Model
to guide its interactions with the player. Basically, it chooses to discuss skills
not yet exhibited by the player in situations where their use would result in
better moves. Goldstein (1977) provides a more detailed discussion of the
structure and function of these coaching modules. (See also the discussion of
the WEST computer coach in Article IX.C4.)

The central box of Figure C5–1 contains a representation for the problem-
solving skills of the domain being tutored. It is, in essence, a formal representation of the syllabus. The Expert is derived from the skills represented
therein, as is the structure of the student model. The Psychologist derives
expectations from this knowledge regarding which skills the student can be
expected to acquire next, based on a model of the relative difficulty of items in
the syllabus. The Tutor derives relationships *between* skills such as analogies
and refinements, which can be employed to improve its explanations of new
skills (see Goldstein, 1979).

Theoretical Goals: Toward a Theory of Coaching

The approach to the design of computer coaches in WUSOR–II is to
construct a *rule-based representation* (see Article III.C4, in Vol. I) for the skills

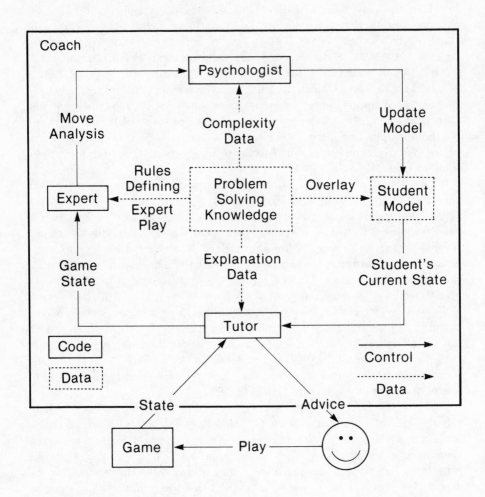

Figure C5–1.   Diagram of a computer coach (Goldstein, 1979).

needed by the Expert to play the game, for the modeling criteria used by the Psychologist, and for the alternative tutoring strategies used by the Tutor. Each is expanded below.

The *Expert* uses rules that embody the knowledge or skills required to play the game in order to analyze the player's behavior. The virtue of a rule-based representation of expertise is that its *modularity* both allows tutoring to focus on the discussion of specific skills and permits modeling to take the form of hypotheses regarding which rules are known by the player.

The *Psychologist* applies *rules of evidence* to make reasonable hypotheses about which of the Expert's skills the player possesses. Typical rules of evidence are:

1. Increase the estimate that a player possesses a skill if the player explicitly claims acquaintance with the skill, and decrease the reliability if the player expresses unfamiliarity.

2. Increase the estimate that a player possesses a skill if the skill is manifest in the player's behavior, and decrease the estimate if the skill is not manifest in a situation in which the Expert believes it to be appropriate; hence, implicit as well as overt evidence plays a role.

3. Decrease the estimate that a player possesses a skill if there is a long interval since the last confirmation was obtained (thereby modeling the tendency for a skill to decay with less use).

The *Tutor* uses *explanation rules* to select the appropriate topic to discuss with the player and to choose the form of the explanation. These rules include:

1. *Rules of simplification* that take a complex statement and reduce it to a simpler assertion. Simplification rules are essential if the player is not to be overwhelmed by the Tutor's explanations.

2. *Rules of rhetoric* that codify alternative explanation strategies. The two extremes are explanation in terms of a general rule and explanation in terms of a concrete instance.

The WUMPUS Expert

In WUMPUS, the player is initially placed somewhere in a randomly connected warren of caves and is told which caves adjoin his cave. His goal is to find the horrid Wumpus and slay it with an arrow. Each move to a neighboring cave yields information regarding that cave's neighbors. The difficulty in choosing a move arises from the various dangers in the warren—bats, pits, and the Wumpus itself. If the player moves into the Wumpus's lair, he is eaten. If he walks into a pit, he falls to his death. Bats pick the player up and randomly drop him elsewhere in the warren.

The player can minimize risk and find the Wumpus by making the proper logistic and probabilistic inferences from warnings that he is given. These warnings are provided whenever the player is near a danger. The Wumpus can be smelled within one or two caves. The squeak of bats can be heard one cave away, and the breeze of a pit can be felt one cave away. The game is won by shooting an arrow into the Wumpus's lair. If the player exhausts his set of five arrows without hitting the creature, all is lost.

The WUMPUS Expert uses a rule-based representation, consisting of about 20 rules, to infer the risk of visiting new caves. Five of these rules are shown below:

L1. *Positive Evidence Rule.* A warning in a cave implies that a danger exists in a neighboring cave.

L2. *Negative Evidence Rule.* The absence of a warning implies that no danger exists in any neighbors.

L3. *Elimination Rule.* If a cave has a warning and all but one of its neighbors are known to be safe, the danger is in the remaining neighbor.

P1. *Equal Likelihood Rule.* In the absence of other knowledge, all of the neighbors of a cave with a warning are equally likely to contain a danger.

P2. *Double Evidence Rule.* Multiple warnings increase the likelihood that a given cave contains a danger.

A Sample Protocol with the WUSOR–II Computer Coach

A transcript of an interaction with the WUSOR–II Coach is presented below. The player's responses are preceded by **.

```
Hello, Timmy.  There are 15 caves, 2 bats, 2 pits,
and 1 Wumpus.  You are now at cave 15 with neighbors 4,
14, and 0.  Brrr!  There is a draft.  You are near a pit.
What a stench!  The Wumpus is near.  What now?

** 4

You are now at cave 4 with neighbors 15, 14, and 2.
Brrr!  Squeak!  A bat is near.  What now?
```

The goal of the Coach is to tutor a beginner in the relevant logical, probabilistic, and strategic knowledge needed to play the game. For example, the Expert informs the Tutor that cave 14 should be treated as more dangerous than cave 0 or 2, since there is multiple evidence (from the drafts in caves 15 and 4) that cave 14 contains a pit. If the player now moved to cave 14, coaching might take place as follows:

```
** 14

Timmy, it isn't necessary to take such large risks with pits.
One of caves 2 and 14 contains a pit.  Likewise one of
```

```
caves 0 and 14 contains a pit.  This is multiple evidence
of a pit in cave 14, which makes it quite likely that cave 14
contains a pit.  It is less likely that cave 0 contains a pit.
Hence, we might want to explore cave 0 instead.
Do you want to take back your move?
```

Although it is not apparent from these simple remarks, every module of the Coach contributed to the dialogue. These contributions are summarized below.

The *Expert* analyzes all possible moves, using its set of skills. The outcome of its analysis is a ranking of possible moves with an attached list that associates the skills that would be needed to make each move. For example, using the five skills listed earlier, the Expert recognizes that cave 14 is the most dangerous move and cave 0 is the safest move.

Essentially, the Expert provides the following proof for use by the Psychologist and Tutor modules. (The proof is given here in English for readability; the Expert's actual analyses are in the programming language LISP.)

Lemma 1:   The Wumpus cannot be in cave 0, 2, or 14 since there is no smell in 4. (Application of the Negative Evidence Rule, L2, for the two-cave warning of Wumpus.)

Lemma 2:   Caves 0 and 2 were better than 14 because there was single evidence that caves 0 and 2 contained a pit, but double evidence for cave 14. (Application of the Double Evidence Rule, P2.)

Lemma 3:   Cave 2 is more dangerous than cave 0, since 2 contains a bat, and the bat could drop you in a fatal cave. (We know this fact because the squeak in 4 implied a bat in 14 or 2, but the absence of a squeak in 15 implies no bat in 14. Hence, by the Elimination Rule, L3, there is a bat in 2.)

The *Psychologist*, after seeing Timmy move to cave 14, decreases the Student Model weight indicating familiarity with the Double Evidence Rule, P2, since the Expert's proof indicates that this heuristic was not applied. Table C5–1 presents the Psychologist's hypotheses regarding which skills of the Expert the student possesses.

Modeling raises many issues. One subtlety is that the move to cave 14 above may be evidence of a more elementary limitation—a failure to understand the logical implications of the draft warning—that is, that a pit is in a neighboring cave. The current state of the Student Model is used by the Psychologist to determine, in the event of a nonoptimal move, which skill is, in fact, missing. The Student Model indicates the level of play that can be expected from this player—the player might be a beginner with incomplete knowledge of the basic rules of the game, a novice with an understanding of the logical skills, an amateur with knowledge of the logical and the more elementary probability skills, and so on. The Psychologist would attribute

TABLE C5–1

A Typical Student Model Maintained by the Coach

Rules	Appropriate	Used	Percent	Known
L1	5	5	100	Yes
L2	4	3	75	Yes
L3	4	2	50	?
L4	5	5	100	Yes
L5	4	1	25	No

the student's error in the current situation to unfamiliarity with a skill at his current level of play; in this case, Timmy is a player who has mastered the logical skills and is learning the basic probability heuristics. Hence, the Coach's explanation focused on explaining the double-evidence heuristic.

The *Tutor* is responsible for abridging the Coach's response to the player's move to cave 14. (The complete explanation generated by the Expert was the three lemmas shown above.) Such pruning is imperative if the Coach is to generate comprehensible advice. Hence, the Tutor prunes the complete analysis using simplification rules that delete those parts of the argument that are already known to the player (on the basis of the Student Model) and those portions that are too complex. Here, the coach deleted Lemma 1, the discussion of the Wumpus danger, because it is based on the negative-evidence skill that the Student Model attributes to the player. Lemma 2, the elimination argument for bats, is potentially appropriate to discuss, but a simplification strategy directs the Coach to focus on a single skill. Additional information will be given by the Coach if requested by the player.

Conclusions

The novelty of this research is that in a *single system* there is significant domain expertise, a broad range of possible interaction strategies available to the tutor, and a modeling capability for the student's current knowledge state. Informal experience with over 20 players of various ages has shown WUSOR–II to be a helpful learning aid, as judged by interviews with the players. The short-term benefit from this research is an improved understanding of the learning and teaching processes. The long-term benefit may be the development of a practical educational technology, given the expected decrease in hardware costs.

References

Carr and Goldstein (1977) describe WUSOR, the overlay model, and related theory. Also see Goldstein (1977, 1979) and Stansfield, Carr, and Goldstein (1976).

C6. GUIDON

GUIDON, a program for teaching diagnostic problem-solving, is being developed by William J. Clancey and his colleagues at Stanford University. Using the rules of the MYCIN consultation system (Article VIII.B1) as subject material, GUIDON engages a student in a dialogue about a patient suspected of having an infection. In this manner, it teaches the student about the relevant clinical and laboratory data and about how to use that information for diagnosing the causative organism. GUIDON's mixed-initiative dialogue differs from that of other ICAI programs in its use of prolonged, structured teaching interactions that go beyond responding to the student's last move (as in WEST and WUMPUS) and repetitive questioning and answering (as in SCHOLAR and WHY).

MYCIN's infectious-disease diagnosis rules constitute the skills to be taught. As applied to a particular problem, the rules provide GUIDON with topics to be discussed and with a basis for evaluating the student's behavior. GUIDON's teaching knowledge is wholly separate from MYCIN. It is stated explicitly in the form of 200 tutorial rules, which include methods for guiding the dialogue economically, presenting diagnostic rules, constructing a student model, and responding to the student's initiative. Because of the separation of teaching and domain knowledge, MYCIN's infectious-disease knowledge base can be replaced by diagnostic rules for another problem domain.

GUIDON is designed to explore two basic questions: First, how do the problem-solving rules, which perform so well in the MYCIN consultation system, measure up to the needs of a tutorial interaction with a student? Second, what knowledge about teaching might be added to MYCIN to make it into an effective tutorial program? MYCIN's rules have not been modified for the tutoring application, but they are used in new ways, for example, for forming quizzes, guiding the dialogue, summarizing evidence, and modeling the student's understanding.

Several design guidelines for the rules make it plausible that the rules would be a good vehicle for teaching. First, they are designed to capture a significant part of the knowledge necessary for good problem solving. Formal evaluation of MYCIN demonstrated that its competence in selecting antimicrobial therapy for meningitis and for bacteremia is comparable to that of the members of the infectious-disease faculty at the Stanford University School of Medicine (where MYCIN was developed; see Yu, Buchanan, et al., 1979). Second, flexible use of the rule set is made possible by the provision of *representational meta-knowledge*, which allows a program to take apart rules and to reason about the components (see Article III.A, in Vol. I). Finally, MYCIN's rules, in contrast with Bayesian programs, are couched in terms familiar to human experts, so it seems likely that reading back MYCIN's line of reasoning to a student might be helpful to him (or her).

This article discusses the following aspects of a GUIDON tutorial dialogue:

1. The nature of the interaction
2. The components of the student model
3. The organization of teaching knowledge into discourse procedures
4. The use of the student model
5. Opportunistic tutoring
6. Pedagogical principles behind the tutoring rules.

The capability of GUIDON to tutor from a library of cases and for domains outside of medicine is also discussed. The final section outlines the lessons learned about knowledge representation that are being applied to reconfigure the MYCIN rule base for its use in teaching.

Interaction with GUIDON

An essential part of tutorial *dialogue management* is allowing the student to express himself. In a mixed-initiative program, provision must be made for every *kind* of initiative on the part of the student. This includes referring back to an earlier topic to provide more details, changing the topic, and so on. We might summarize this by saying that we must allow the student to specify what he knows, what he wants to know more about, and what he wants to ignore. The annotated protocol excerpted below illustrates GUIDON's flexibility in responding to the student's initiative.

> *The student asks for the data and subgoals relevant to the topic being discussed. These are extracted from MYCIN's rules.*

** Factors

The following factors will be useful to determine the type of the infection:

    3a. whether the meningitis is partially treated

    3b. whether a lumbar puncture has been performed on Pt538

    3c. the duration of the neurological signs

    3d. the CSF protein

(*)3e. whether Pt538 has a rash consistent with Herpes Zoster

> *GUIDON keeps track of what has been discussed, MYCIN's use of data, and conjectures about what the student knows.*

Factors marked with (*) have already been stated. Based on what we have already mentioned, you should be able to conclude about: 3b.

The student asks how a particular datum is useful. He is given the case-specific information, and then a summary of its use in the rule or rules that apply in this case (negative conclusions are omitted here because the choices are mutually exclusive).

** Use 3c

The duration of the neurological signs is 7.2 hours.

Using other information available to you now, the duration of the neurological signs enables you to conclude that the type of the infection is bacterial (.2) viral (.2) [RULE524].

The student indicates that he has determined a particular subgoal. As described in this article, a "discourse procedure" is invoked to respond to the student. If the student model were not consistent with his claim, he would be asked to state his conclusion and then possibly support it.

** IKNOW 3b

Good. MYCIN has also made a decision.

The site of CULTURE-1 is evidence that a lumbar puncture has been performed on Pt538 [RULE112].

Back to our discussion of the type of the infection ...

At this point, the topic of discussion is completed, and the student is receiving a summary of the relevant conclusions. The program is automatically extracting the "key factor" from each rule and displaying only the "interesting" (useful) conclusions.

Summary of evidence that the type of the infection is bacterial (.98):

29a. The fact that the meningitis is partially treated (.95)
     is evidence that the type of the infection
     is bacterial (.19) [RULE148]

29b. The WBC from the CSF and the percent of PMNs in the CSF
     is evidence that the type of the infection
     is bacterial (.9) [RULE501]

The student requests more information about one of the inferences. The program reasons that because several subgoals have not been discussed, these are the details to offer first.

** Details 29a

For which of the following factors would you like to see a review of the evidence?

(Select from the following):

1. the infection which requires therapy

2. the fact that the meningitis
   is partially treated (.95)

** 2

```
Summary of evidence that the meningitis
is partially treated (.95):
```

32a. The infection which requires therapy, the fact that
     organisms were not seen on the stain of the pending
     CSF culture, and the time since therapy with the
     cephalothin was started are evidence that the
     meningitis is partially treated (.95) [RULE145]

   *Given this information, perhaps the student would like to see the details
   of how it is used.*

Do you want to see RULE148?

** No

GUIDON provides a menu of options for requesting case data, asking for
MYCIN's evaluation of the problem (e.g., "What subgoals are PENDING?"
"Give me DETAILS"), determining dialogue context (e.g., "What RULE are
we discussing?"), changing the topic, requesting assistance (the options HELP,
HINT, and TELLME), and conveying what is known (e.g., "I want to make a
HYPOTHESIS"). The menu of over 30 options allows for input to be terse,
while defining clearly for the student what the program can understand. As
arguments to the options, the student can use phrases (e.g., "IKNOW about
the lumbar puncture"), keywords (e.g., "IKNOW LP"), or indices of remarks
made by the program (e.g., "IKNOW 3B").

The Student Model

Before a session with the student begins, GUIDON uses MYCIN to "solve"
the case to be presented to the student. The results of this background
consultation, consisting of MYCIN's rule conclusions and its records of why
rules did not apply, are reconfigured into a complete *AND/OR tree* of goals
and rules, so the rules are indexed both by the goals they conclude about and
the subgoals or data needed to apply them. During the tutorial session, as
the student inquires about the patient and receives more case data, this same
information is used to drive MYCIN's rules in a forward direction. Thus, at
any time, some of the rules MYCIN uses for determining, say, the type of
the infection, will have led to a conclusion, while others will require more
information about the patient before they can be applied.

This record of what the expert (i.e., MYCIN) "knows" at any time during
the student-run consultation forms the basis for evaluating a student's partial
solutions and providing assistance. Such an *overlay model* (see Articles IX.B
and IX.C5) assumes that the student's knowledge is a subset of MYCIN's
knowledge and that there are unique reasoning steps for making any particular

deduction. Neither assumption is always correct; the rule set nevertheless provides a first-order approximation to the student-modeling problem.

The three components of the student model are shown in Figure C6–1. The cumulative record of which rules the student knows is called the USE–HISTORY. It is the program's belief that, if the student were given the premise of the rule, he would be able to correctly, in the abstract, draw the proper conclusion. USE–HISTORY is primed by the student's initial indication of his level of expertise, which is matched against "difficulty ratings" associated with each rule. Like the other components, USE–HISTORY is represented as a *certainty factor* (see Article VIII.B1) that combines the background evidence with the implicit evidence stemming from needs for assistance and verbalized partial solutions, as well as the explicit evidence stemming from a direct question that tests knowledge of the rule.

The second component, called STUDENT–APPLIED?, records the program's belief that the student is able to apply the rule to the given case, that is, that the student would refer to this rule to support a conclusion about the given goal. Thus, there is a distinction between knowing a rule (USE–HISTORY) and being able to apply it, since the student may know which subgoals appear in the rule but be unable to achieve them. STUDENT–APPLIED? is determined once for each rule during a case, at the time MYCIN is able to apply the rule.

The third component of the student model, called USED?, is relevant whenever the student states a partial solution. It records the program's belief that the student would mention a rule if asked to support his partial solution. This component combines indirect evidence by comparing conclusions made by rules with the student's conclusions, the record of what rules the student is believed to be able to use (STUDENT–APPLIED?), and evidence that the student may have remembered to apply the rule in this case (e.g., the rule mentioned earlier in the dialogue). This combined evidence affects how the program responds to the partial solution and feeds back into the USE–HISTORY component of the student model.

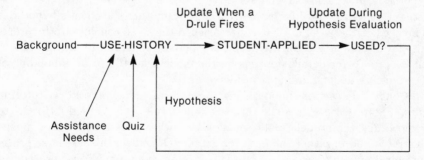

Figure C6–1.   Maintenance relations for student-model components (Clancy, 1979b).

Discourse Procedures and Alternative Dialogues

The student is allowed to explore MYCIN's reasoning by using options like FACTORS, shown earlier in the protocol excerpt. However, the tutor is not a simple, passive, information-retrieval system. In addition to clearly laying out data and inferences, the tutor has to reason about what constitutes reasonable, expected elaboration on the basis of what has been previously discussed. For example, in the excerpt, GUIDON provided details for an inference (rule 148) by offering to support achieved preconditions that were not mentioned in the tutorial dialogue up to that point.

Similarly, when the student takes the initiative by saying he has determined some subgoal, the tutor needs to determine what response makes sense, based on what it knows about the student's knowledge and shared goals for the tutorial session (topics or rules to discuss). The tutor may want to hold a detailed response in abeyance, simply acknowledge the student's remark, or probe him for evidence that he does indeed know the fact in question. Selection among these *alternative dialogues* might require determining what the student could have inferred from previous interactions and the current situation. In the dialogue excerpt shown above, GUIDON decides that there is sufficient evidence that the student knows the solution to a relevant subproblem, so detailed discussion and probing are not necessary.

Decoupling domain expertise from the dialogue program, an approach used by all ICAI systems, is a powerful way to provide flexible dialogue interaction. In GUIDON, *discourse procedures* formalize how the program should behave in general terms, not in terms of the data or outcome of a particular case. A discourse procedure is a sequence of actions to be followed under conditions determined by the complexity of the material, the student's understanding of the material, and tutoring goals for the session. Each option available to the student generally has a discourse procedure associated with it.

For example, if the student indicates, via the IKNOW option, that he has a hypothesis about some subgoal but MYCIN has not been able to make a decision yet, the procedure for requesting and evaluating a student's hypothesis is invoked. Otherwise, if MYCIN has reached the same conclusion, the procedure for discussing a completed topic is followed. Whether or not the student will be probed for details depends on the model that the tutor is building of the student's understanding (considered below).

Conditional actions in discourse procedures are expressed as tutoring rules. Figure C6–2 shows the tutoring rule (t-rule) that caused GUIDON to acknowledge the student's statement about what he knew in the dialogue illustrated above, rather than ask for details. Of course, this discourse procedure for discussing a completed topic is invoked from many other procedures besides the one corresponding to the IKNOW option: It may be invoked in the course of giving details about how a subgoal is determined, in responding to a student's hypothesis for a subgoal, when the program detects that the current

---

T-RULE5.02 *Directly state single, known rule.*

IF   1) There are rules having a bearing on this goal
               that have succeeded and have not been
               discussed, and

            2) The number of rules having a bearing on this
               goal that have succeeded is 1, and

            3) There is strong evidence that the student has
               applied this rule

THEN   Simply state the rule and its conclusion

Figure C6–2.   T-rule for deciding how to complete discussion of a topic.

subgoal (topic) is substantially completed (enough data have been given to make a strong conclusion), and so on.

Responding to Partial Solutions

Shown below is an annotated excerpt demonstrating how the program responds to partial solutions stated by the student. Tutoring rules are used both to update the model and to select the appropriate discourse procedures for responding. In this excerpt, while the student's hypothesis for a subproblem is correct, nevertheless, after analyzing the previous history of interaction with the student, GUIDON is not sure that the student really knows why his hypothesis is correct. Therefore, instead of accepting this answer, GUIDON requests relevant factors to support the hypothesis and probes further to see if the student knows why an alternative hypothesis is discredited.

> *GUIDON asks the student to state a hypothesis for a subgoal. The student may have volunteered to do this, or the program may be testing the student's understanding.*

What is the type of the infection?

** Bacterial

> *The program asks the student to support this hypothesis either because it is incorrect or, as in this case, the student model indicates that the student may not know all of the relevant rules. (GUIDON changes the prompt for student input to ">>" to indicate that specific input is expected and student-initiated options are not.)*

What facts about this case tell you that the type of the infection is bacterial?
(Enter one factor per line.)

>> PMNs

The percent of PMNs in the CBC is not relevant for determining
the type of the infection.

>> PMNs in the CSF
>> Cerebral-fluid glucose value
>> Protein of the CSF

*These factors are related to the rules used by MYCIN to conclude that the
infection is bacterial, and the student model is updated accordingly.*

You're right about the CSF protein, the percent of PMNs in
the CSF, and the CSF glucose value; however, you should have
mentioned the fact that the meningitis is partially treated,
the WBC from the CSF, and the fact that the simultaneous
blood glucose value is not known.

Other hypotheses are then discussed.

MYCIN rejected some possibilities you did not mention:

What facts about this case tell you that the type of the
infection is not viral?

Referring to the rules that MYCIN uses to solve subproblems (such as
determining whether a meningitis infection is bacterial, fungal, viral, or tuber-
culous), GUIDON decides which of these rules, if any, might have been used
by the student. That is, what inference chains are consistent with the student's behavior? This analysis is complicated by the fact that a particular
hypothesis about the problem may be indicated by more than one rule, or
negative evidence may outweigh positive evidence.

A potential weakness of the GUIDON program is that it attempts to
explain the student's behavior solely in terms of MYCIN's rules. If the student
is basing his questions and hypotheses on incorrect rules, GUIDON is not able
to formulate these rules and address them directly. It is possible as well that
the student's concepts are different from MYCIN's, so his conclusions might be
correct, but he will want to support them with reasoning that is different from
MYCIN's. This could involve something as simple as wanting to refer to the
patient's age in general terms (infant, adolescent), while MYCIN recognizes
only precise, numerical ages.

Modeling medical reasoning in terms of an alternative rule set (not just a
subset of MYCIN's rules) is a theory-formation problem that goes beyond the
current capabilities of AI. It is possible that the approach followed by Stevens
and Collins (see Article IX.C2) of collecting data about student misconceptions
and then incorporating these variations into the modeling process will prove
tenable for the medical domain.

Opportunistic Tutoring

It is sometimes advantageous for the tutor to take the initiative to present new material to the student. This requires that the tutor have presentation methods that opportunistically *adapt material to the needs of the dialogue.* In particular, the tutor has to be sensitive to how a tutorial dialogue fits together, including what kinds of interruptions and probing are reasonable and expected in this kind of discourse. GUIDON demonstrates its sensitivity to these concerns when it corrects the student before quizzing him about "missing hypotheses," asks him questions about recently mentioned data to see if he understands how to use them, quizzes him about rules that are related (by premise and action) to one that has just been discussed, follows up on previous hints, and comments on the status of a subproblem after an inference has been discussed ("Other factors remain to be considered...").

Pedagogical Style

There are many subtle issues—when to interrupt the student, how much to say, and the like—that constitute a pedagogical style and are implicit in GUIDON's teaching rules. For example, several tutoring rules in different situations may present short orientation lectures, but nowhere does GUIDON reason that its interaction will be of the tutorial type, which provides orientation when appropriate, in contrast with the coaching type (see Article IX.C5), which only makes interruptions. For this reason, it is useful to summarize the set of tutoring principles that appear implicitly in the tutoring rules:

1. *Be perspicuous:* Have an economical presentation strategy, provide lucid transitions, and adhere to conventional discourse patterns.

2. *Provide orientation to new tasks by top-down refinement:* Provide the student with an organized framework of considerations he should be making, without giving away the solution to the problem (important factors, subgoals, size of the task), thus challenging the student to examine his understanding constructively.

3. *Strictly guide the dialogue:* Say when topics are finished and inferences are completed, as opposed to letting the student discover transitions for himself.

4. *Account for incorrect behavior in terms of missing expertise* (as opposed to assuming alternative methods and strategies): Explain clearly what is improper from the tutor's point of view (e.g., improper requests for case data). This is, of course, more a statement of how GUIDON models the student than a principle of good teaching.

5. *Probe the student's understanding when you are not sure what he knows*, when you are responding to partial student solutions: Otherwise, directly confirm or correct the solution.

6. *Provide assistance by methodically introducing small steps* that will contribute to the problem's solution:

   a. Assistance should at first be general, to remind the student of solution methods and strategies he already knows;

   b. Assistance should encourage the student to advance the solution by using case data he has already been given.

7. *Examine the student's understanding and introduce new information* whenever there is an opportunity to do so.

Case and Domain Independence

Patient cases are entered into the MYCIN system for receiving a consultation or for testing the program, so the case library is available to GUIDON at no cost. This provides over 100 patients that GUIDON can discuss, clearly demonstrating the advantage that ICAI has over the traditional computer-based-instruction approach in which each lesson must be designed individually.

Besides being able to use the teaching procedures to tutor different cases, GUIDON can provide tutorials in any problem area for which a MYCIN-like knowledge base of decision rules and fact tables has been formalized (see van Melle, 1980). This affords an important perspective on the generality of the discourse and pedagogical rules.

Experimental tutorials using other knowledge bases have revealed that the effectiveness of discourse strategies for carrying on a dialogue economically is determined in part by the depth and breadth of the reasoning tree for solving problems, a characteristic of the rule set for each domain. When a solution involves many rules at a given level, for example, when there are many rules to determine the organism causing the infection, the tutor and student will not have time to discuss each rule in the same degree of detail. Similarly, when inference chains are long, an effective discourse strategy will entail summarizing evidence on a high level, rather than considering each subgoal in the chain.

Results

GUIDON demonstrated that teaching knowledge could be treated analogously to the domain expertise of consultation systems: It can be codified in rules and built incrementally by testing it on different cases. The framework of tutoring rules organized into discourse procedures worked well, indicating that it is suitable to think of a tutorial dialogue as being separated into relatively independent sequences of interaction. Moreover, the judgmental knowledge for constructing a student model can also be captured in rules utilizing certainty factors, showing that the task of modeling a student bears some relation to MYCIN's task of diagnosing a disease.

In contrast to GUIDON's teaching knowledge, the evaluation of MYCIN's rule set for this application was not so positive. While MYCIN's representational meta-knowledge made possible a wide variety of tutorial activity, students find that the rules are difficult to understand, remember, and incorporate into a problem-solving approach. These difficulties prompted an extensive study of MYCIN's rules to determine why the teaching points were not as clear as had been expected. GUIDON researchers discovered that important structural knowledge (hierarchies of data and diagnostic hypotheses) and strategic knowledge (searching the problem space by top-down refinement) were implicit in the rules. That is, the choice and ordering of rule-premise clauses constitute procedural knowledge that brings about good problem-solving performance in a MYCIN consultation but is unavailable for teaching purposes. Rather than teaching a student problem-solving steps (rule clauses) by rote, it is advantageous to convey an approach or strategy for bringing those steps to mind—the plan that knowledge-base authors were following when they designed MYCIN's rule set. To make this implicit design knowledge explicit, a new system, NEOMYCIN (Clancey and Letsinger, 1981), is being developed that separates out diagnostic strategy from domain knowledge and makes good use of hierarchical organization of data and hypotheses.

Moreover, besides reconfiguring MYCIN's rules so that knowledge is separated out and represented more declaratively, it is necessary to add knowledge about the justification of rules. Justifications are important as mnemonics for the heuristic associations, as well as for providing an understanding that allows the problem solver to violate the rules in unusual situations.

Finally, NEOMYCIN has additional knowledge about disease processes that allows it to use the strategy of "group and differentiate" for initial problem formulation, in which the problem solver must think about broad categories of disorders and consider competing hypotheses that explain the problem data. Thus, we want to teach the student the knowledge a human would need to focus on infectious-disease problems in the first place, essentially the knowledge (previously unformalized) that a human needs to use MYCIN appropriately.

In conclusion, GUIDON research sets out to demonstrate the advantages of separate, explicit representations of both teaching knowledge and subject material. The problems of recognizing student misconceptions aside, this research demonstrated that simply representing in an ideal way what to teach the student is not a trivial, solved problem. An unstructured set of production rules is inadequate. GUIDON's teaching rules are organized into procedures; NEOMYCIN's diagnostic rules are hierarchically grouped by both premise and action and are controlled by meta-rules. GUIDON research demonstrated that the needs of tutoring can serve as a "forcing function" to direct research toward more psychologically valid representations of domain knowledge, which potentially will benefit those aspects of expert-systems research that require human interaction, particularly explanation and knowledge acquisition.

References

GUIDON is described fully by Clancey (1979b); a shorter discussion is given in Clancey (1979a). Clancey and Letsinger (1981) describe the NEO-MYCIN research. The study of MYCIN's rule base leading up to this new system and some methodological considerations are provided by Clancey (in press-a, in press-b).

C7. BUGGY

BUGGY is a program that can determine accurately a student's misconceptions (bugs) about basic arithmetic skills. The system, developed by John Seely Brown, Richard Burton, and Kathy M. Larkin at Bolt Beranek and Newman, Inc., provides a mechanism for explaining why a student is making an arithmetic mistake, as opposed to simply identifying the mistake. Having a detailed model of a student's knowledge that indicates his (or her) misconceptions is important for successful tutoring.

A common assumption among teachers is that students do not follow procedures very well and that *erratic* behavior is the primary cause of students' inability to perform each step correctly. Brown and Burton (1978) argue that students are remarkably competent procedure followers, although they often follow the *wrong* procedures. By presenting examples of systematic incorrect behavior, BUGGY allows teachers to practice diagnosing the underlying causes of students' errors. Through BUGGY, teachers gain experience in forming hypotheses about the relation between the symptoms of bugs that students manifest and the underlying misconceptions. This experience helps teachers become more aware of methods or strategies available for diagnosing their students' problems properly.

Manifesting Bugs

Experience with BUGGY indicates that forming a model of what is wrong with a student's method of performing a task is often more difficult than performing the task itself. Consider, for example, the following addition problems and their (erroneous) solutions. They were provided by a student with a "bug" in his addition procedure:

$$
\begin{array}{ccccc}
41 & 328 & 989 & 66 & 216 \\
+9 & +917 & +52 & +887 & +13 \\
\hline
50 & 1345 & 1141 & 1053 & 229 \\
\end{array}
$$

Once you have discovered the bug, try testing your hypothesis by simulating the buggy student—predict his results on the following two test problems:

$$
\begin{array}{cc}
446 & 201 \\
+815 & +399 \\
\end{array}
$$

The bug is simple. In procedural terms, after determining the carry, the student forgets to reset the "carry register" to zero; he accumulates the amount carried across the columns. For example, in the student's second problem ($328+917 = 1345$), he proceeds as follows: $8+7 = 15$, so he writes 5 and carries 1; $2+1 = 3$ plus the 1 carried is 4; finally, $3+9 = 12$, but the 1

carried from the first column is still there—it has not been reset—so adding
it to the final column gives 13. If this is the correct bug, the answers to the
test problems will be 1361 and 700. (This bug is really not so unusual; a child
often uses his fingers to remember the carry and might forget to bend them
back after each column.)

The model built by BUGGY incorporates both correct and incorrect *subprocedures* that simulate the student's behavior on particular problems and
capture what parts of a student's skill are correct and what parts are incorrect.
BUGGY represents a skill, such as addition, as a collection of subskills, one
of which, for example, is knowing how to carry a digit into the next column.
The subprocedures in BUGGY that correspond to human subskills are linked
into a *procedural net* (Sacerdoti, 1974), which is BUGGY's representation of
the entire human skill. If all the subprocedures in BUGGY's procedural net
for addition work correctly, then BUGGY will do addition problems correctly.
On the other hand, replacing correct subprocedures with ones that are faulty
will result in systematic errors of the kind shown above. Brown and Burton
call a procedural network with one or more faulty subprocedures a *diagnostic
model*, because it is a way of representing systematic errors. The model has
been used in two ways. First, it can diagnose a student's errors and pinpoint
the bugs in the student's skill. Second, it can help train a teacher to diagnose student errors by playing the part of a student with one or more buggy
subskills.

When BUGGY is diagnosing a student's errors, its task is to modify the
correct procedural network of, say, subtraction until it accounts for all of
the student's answers, both right and wrong. This modification is done by
systematically replacing correct subprocedures with incorrect variants until
a consistent diagnostic model is found. There are currently 70 primitive
faulty subprocedures for subtraction. These are explored exhaustively while
attempting to determine a consistent diagnostic model. If a single variant or
bug is insufficient to explain a student's behavior, combinations of two bugs
are tried. (Because of the overwhelming number of combinations of three or
more bugs, they are not used to form diagnostic models.) In this manner,
330 bugs have been identified, each with a bug description. Interactions
among bugs and the ramifications of a buggy subprocedure's being called
by several high-order procedures constitute major challenges for designing
efficient simulations of multiple bugs. Note also that this technique requires
a large amount of compute time and is amenable only to domains where bugs
can be explicated in a more or less complete way.

The procedural network for subtraction (and its bugs) was evaluated in
an experiment based on the results of a test administered to 1,325 students in
the fourth, fifth, and sixth grades. The BUGGY model indicated that about
40% of the students exhibited consistently buggy behavior. That is, BUGGY
was able to construct a diagnostic model for students' errors demonstrating
that they were using nonrandom, though incorrect, procedures.

Using BUGGY to Train Teachers

BUGGY can also help train teachers to diagnose student errors. This facility is illustrated by the following protocol excerpted from Brown (1977), in which BUGGY presents a team of teachers with incorrectly solved mathematics problems and supervises their diagnosis of the bug.

```
Welcome to Bugland.  I have chosen a bug.
Here is an example of the bug.

17
+5
13
```

> *The system presents an example in which the student did not get the right answer.*

```
Now you can give me problems to determine the bug.

**  18      43
**  +6      +79
    15      23
```

> *The teachers suggest problems, and BUGGY solves them incorrectly, following a buggy procedure. The team is trying to diagnose the bug in BUGGY's addition procedures by presenting BUGGY with problems to solve. However, they are using problems similar to the original one, which is a poor strategy because it may leave other symptoms of the bug undiscovered.*

```
** Got the bug!
```

> *The team thinks that they know what the problem is. Omitted here for space (but illustrated later in the dialogue), BUGGY asks them to formulate the bug in English. This step has the effect of making the team verbalize the bug clearly. It is a difficult task, and the results are often ambiguous. BUGGY does not "read" the description of the bug, because it does not have the natural-language abilities to do so. Instead, it generates a series of problems for the team to solve. The team must solve them incorrectly, using the bug that they think they have identified, to convince BUGGY that they have, in fact, discovered the bug.*

```
Here are some problems to test your theories about the bug.
What is:

21
+39
** 51

That's not the bug I have.  Using my bug:
```

```
     21
    +39
     15
```

Try giving me some more examples...

> The team fails BUGGY's test by being unable to solve the given problem. That is, their bug is not the same one that BUGGY is using. If they had solved five problems "correctly" (i.e., incorrectly because of a bug), then BUGGY would credit them with a correct diagnosis. Now, however, they must set more problems for BUGGY to solve, in an attempt to deduce the bug.

```
**    51       99      68
**  +1707     +99      +9
      21       36      23
```

** Got the bug!

Please describe the bug you think I have:

** The student is adding all the digits together.

Here are some problems to test your theory about the bug. What are:

```
     33     1091      8      28     90
    +99      +60    +34     +70     +6
**   24       17     15      17     15
```

Very good. My description of the bug is:
The student always sums up all the digits,
with no regard to columns.

Summary

The central idea of this research is that *procedural networks* can be used to build diagnostic models. This representation scheme facilitates an appropriate decomposition of a skill into subskills, to make explicit the control structures underlying a collection of skills and to execute directly the resulting *diagnostic model*. Rather than being a subset or simplification of expert rules, as in *overlay modeling* (see Articles IX.B, IX.C4, and IX.C5), the procedural network is a model of a student's behavior that is structured in terms of semantically meaningful deviations from the correct procedure. Each subskill, whether correct or incorrect, is explicitly represented as a subprocedure in the network.

References

Brown and Burton (1978) is the most complete report on BUGGY. Recent extensions of this research are discussed by Van Lehn and Brown (1981). See also Brown, Burton, Hausmann, et al. (1977) and Brown, Burton, and Larkin (1977).

C8. EXCHECK

EXCHECK is an instructional system developed by Patrick Suppes and his colleagues at the Institute for Mathematical Studies in the Social Sciences (IMSSS) at Stanford University. It presents complete, university-level courses in logic, set theory, and proof theory. At a computer terminal, the student is presented lesson material followed by exercises consisting of theorems that he (or she) is to prove. The courses are taught on IMSSS's CAI system, which uses computer-generated speech and split-screen displays. Several hundred Stanford students take these courses each year.

From an AI point of view, the most interesting aspects of the EXCHECK system are the facilities that permit the interaction to take place in a natural style that closely approximates standard mathematical practice. The program's "expertise" consists of inference procedures that allow it to understand sketches of proofs, summarize proofs, and explain set-theoretical constructions. These inference procedures conform to the kinds of reasoning steps mathematicians make, called natural deduction (Suppes, 1957). EXCHECK has no student model, but its inference procedures allow it to make assumptions about a student's reasoning and track his solutions and thus it provides a "reactive environment" similar to that of SOPHIE (Article IX.C3).

Understanding Informal Mathematical Reasoning

The mathematical reasoning involved in the set theory and proof theory courses is complex and subtle. The fundamental AI problem of EXCHECK is making the program capable of understanding informal mathematical reasoning: It must be able to follow mathematical proofs presented in a "natural" manner. That is, just as the intent of natural-language processing is to handle languages in the manner in which they are actually written or spoken, the intent of natural proof processing is to handle proofs as they are actually done by practicing mathematicians. In general, such proofs are presented by giving a sketch of the main line of argument along with any other mathematically significant information that might be needed to reconstruct the proof completely. This style should be contrasted with the derivations familiar from elementary logic, where each detail is presented and the focus of attention is on syntactic manipulations rather than on the underlying semantics.

A major aspect of the problem of machine understanding of natural proofs is finding languages that permit users to express their proofs in the fashion described above. Such languages, in turn, must find their basis in an analysis or model of informal mathematical reasoning. Finding these natural proof languages should be compared to the problem of finding high-level "natural" or "English-like" programming languages. For more detailed discussions of these issues, see Blaine and Smith (1977), R. L. Smith (1976), and Smith et al. (1975). A simple example of understanding informal mathematical reasoning and a fuller discussion of the techniques involved follow.

A Student Proof

We present two proofs of the elementary theorem

$$\text{Thm: If } A \subset B, \text{ then } \neg(B \subseteq A);$$

where "$\subset$" indicates *proper subset* and "$\subseteq$" indicates *subset*.

First, the proof is given in the informal style of standard mathematical practice:

We want to show that if $A \subset B$, then $\neg(B \subseteq A)$.

Assume $A \subset B$. We show $\neg(B \subseteq A)$ by indirect proof. Assume that $B \subseteq A$. Since $A \subset B$, then, by definition, $A \subseteq B$ and $A \neq B$. Since $A \subseteq B$ and $B \subseteq A$, then $A = B$. But this is a contradiction and, hence, the assumption that $B \subseteq A$ is false. Therefore, $\neg(B \subseteq A)$.

The following typescript shows how one student did the proof in the EXCHECK system. Input from the student is underscored and comments are in italics; everything else is generated by the program. The program keeps track of the goal that the student is currently trying to establish; the initial goal is the theorem to be proved. EXCHECK indicates acceptance of an inference by returning the top-level prompt "**"; if a suggested inference is not acceptable, EXCHECK returns an error message.

```
Derive: If A ⊂ B then ¬(B ⊆ A)
** hyp (1) ** A ⊂ B
```

> *The hypothesis of the theorem is assumed. The goal is automatically reset to the consequent of the theorem.*

```
** raa
assume (2) **ᴳ B ⊆ A
```

> *The student begins an indirect proof (the command "raa" is a mnemonic for* reductio ad absurdum). *The program assumes the negation of current goal. The goal is now any contradiction.*

```
** 1definition Number or Name?  ** proper subset
1 Df. proper subset
        (3) A ⊆ B and A ≠ B
```

> *The definition of proper subset is applied to line 1.*

```
** 2,3establish ** B = A
2,3 Establish
       (4) B = A
```

The student asks the theorem prover to check the simple set-theoretic inference.

```
** 3,4contradiction
Using ** ok
3,4 Contradiction
       (5) B ¬ ⊆ A
```

The student indicates that lines 3 and 4 lead to a contradiction. EXCHECK returns the negation of assumption 2.

```
** qed
Correct
```

EXCHECK accepts the derivation.

The following informal *review* printout was generated by the program from the proof given in the above typescript.

```
Derive: If A ⊂ B then ¬(B ⊆ A)

Assume (1) A ⊂ B
By raa show: ¬(B ⊆ A)
Assume (2) B ⊆ A
From 1, by definition of proper subset,
       (3) A ⊆ B and A ≠ B
From 2,3 it follows that,
       (4) A = B
3,4 lead to a contradiction; hence, assumption 2 is false:
       (5) ¬(B ⊆ A)
```

Natural-inference Procedures

There are no significant structural differences between the detailed informal proof and the student's proof as presented to EXCHECK. The same steps occur in the same relations to each other. Such global or structural fidelity to natural proofs is a major research goal of the EXCHECK project and depends on the development of *natural-inference procedures*. Some of these, such as the HYPOTHESIS and INDIRECT PROOF procedures in the preceding proof, are familiar from standard logical systems. The procedure used in the application of the definition of proper subset to line 1 is called IMPLIES. It is used to derive results that, intuitively speaking, follow by applying a previous result or definition. It is considerably more complex than the inference procedures usually found in standard logical systems. An even more complex natural-inference procedure in the preceding proof is the ESTABLISH procedure. In general, ESTABLISH is used to derive results that are consequences of prior results in the theory under consideration, in this case, in the theory of sets, eliminating the need to cite specific results in the theory, which would disrupt the main line or argument. Both IMPLIES and ESTABLISH are discussed in more detail below.

The inference procedures in EXCHECK are intended not only to match natural inferences in strength but also to match them in degree and kind. However, there are differences. EXCHECK inference procedures must always be invoked explicitly—in standard practice, particular inference procedures or rules are usually not cited explicitly. For example, compare how the student expresses the inferences that result in lines 3 and 4 with their counterparts in the informal proof. The explicit invocation of inference procedures basically requires that two pieces of information be given: first, the inference procedure to be used and, second, the previous results to be used—in particular, explicit line numbers must be used.

Explicitness is not disruptive of mathematical reasoning. Neither is the reduction of complex inferences to smaller inferences nor is the use of explicit line numbers disruptive, in the sense of distracting the student from the main line of the mathematical argument. They are both simple elaborations of the main structure. However, having to think about what inference rule to apply can interrupt the main line of argument. The success of a system for interactively doing mathematics depends crucially on having a few powerful and natural inference procedures, with clear criteria for use, that are sufficient to handle all the inferences.

IMPLIES

IMPLIES is used to derive results by applying a previous result or definition as a rule of inference in a given context. This form of inference is probably the most frequent, naturally occurring inference. While the basic pattern is simple, the refinements that must be added to the basic form to handle most of the naturally occurring cases result in a computationally complex procedure. The following is a simple example of the basic pattern:

   (i) A is a subset of B

** i definition (Name or Number) ** subset

   (i) $(\forall x)(x \in A \rightarrow x \in B)$.

In this example, the student directed the program to apply the definition of subset to line i and IMPLIES generated the result: $(\forall x)(x \in A \rightarrow x \in B)$. It is important to note that, in an application of the IMPLIES procedure, the student indicates what axiom, definition, theorem, or line to apply to which lines, and the IMPLIES procedure generates the formula that is the result of the inference.

The IMPLIES procedure seems to correspond closely to naive notions of inference, in that logically unsophisticated but mathematically sophisticated users can use it very well after seeing the basic explanation and a few simple examples. However, the IMPLIES rule does have a fault. It is a purely logical inference procedure, and this can occasionally cause problems for users because mathematicians tend to think in terms of set-theoretic rather than logical consequence. The following discussion of the ESTABLISH rule carries this distinction further.

ESTABLISH

The following example of a simple use of ESTABLISH is taken from the earlier typescript, in which the student was trying to produce a contradiction:

```
    (2) B ⊆ A
    (3) A ⊆ B and A ≠ B
** 2,3establish ** B = A
2,3 Establish
    (4) B = A
```

The ESTABLISH rule allows users simply to assert that some formula is an elementary set-theoretic truth or is an elementary set-theoretic consequence of prior results. In the example above, ESTABLISH is used to infer from $B \subseteq A$ (line 2) and $A \subseteq B$ (line 3) that $A = B$, which in turn contradicts the other clause in line 3. $A = B$ is a set-theoretic consequence, but not a logical consequence, of $A \subseteq B$ and $B \subseteq A$.

If ESTABLISH handled only logical consequence, the student would have had to cite explicitly the relevant set-theoretic theorems or definitions needed to reduce the inference to a purely logical inference. This is not only disruptive of the line of argument but also difficult to do. Even the most experienced logicians and mathematicians have difficulty ferreting out all the axioms, definitions, and theorems needed to reduce even simple inferences to purely logical inferences.

All of the examples so far are extremely simple if considered in terms of the full capabilities of the ESTABLISH procedure. ESTABLISH incorporates a theorem prover that can prove about 85% of the first 200 theorems in the set theory course.

Proof Analysis and Summarization

EXCHECK contains procedures that generate informal summaries and sketches of proofs. Such analyses and summaries are useful not only as a semantic basis for the program, to understand and to present proofs better, but also to give guidance to the student, as illustrated in Figure C8–1. The summarization procedures analyze the proof by breaking it into parts (or subproofs) and isolating the mathematically important steps. They also permit a goal-oriented interpretation of the proof, in which the program keeps track of what is to be established at each point (i.e., the current goal); which lines, terms, and the like, are relevant; and how the current line or part fits into the whole structure. MYCIN's consultation explanation system (see Article VIII.B1) takes a similar approach. Goldstein (1977) also employs summarization techniques in the rhetorical modules of the WUMPUS coach (Article IX.C5).

The summaries presented in Figures C8–1 and C8–2 were generated by EXCHECK from a student proof of the Hausdorff maximal principle. The original line numbers have been retained (in parentheses) to give a sense of how much of the proof has been omitted in the summary. In Figure C8–1, only the top-level part of the proof is presented; the proofs of its subparts are omitted. All mathematically or logically insignificant information is omitted. In these proofs and summaries, "D contains E" is synonymous with "$E \subseteq D$." Also, C is a chain if and only if both C is a set of sets and, given any two elements of C, at least one is a subset of the other. Figure C8–1 is not the only summary that could be generated; it essentially presents only the main part of the proof. Subparts of the main part could have been included or even handled independently if so desired.

```
Derive:  If A is a family of sets then
                 every chain contained in A is contained in some
                 maximal chain in A
Proof:
                 Assume (1) A is a family of sets
                 Assume (2) C is a chain and C ⊆ A
                 Abbreviate: {B: B is a chain and C ⊆ B and B ⊆ A}
                         by: C!chains
         By Zorn's lemma,
                 (23) C!chains has a maximal element
         Let B be such that
                 (24) B is a maximal-element of C!chains
         Hence,
                 (25) B is a chain and C ⊆ B and B ⊆ A
         It follows that
                 (31) B is a maximal chain in A
         Therefore,
                 (32) C is contained in some maximal chain in A
```

Figure C8–1.   Informal summary of a proof of the Hausdorff maximal principle.

```
Derive: If A is a family of sets then
              every chain contained in A is contained in some
              maximal chain in A
Proof:
           Use Zorn's lemma to show that
           {B: B is a chain and C ⊆ B and B ⊆ A}
           contains a maximal element B. Then show that B is a
           maximal chain in A which contains C.
```

Figure C8–2.   An example of summarization.

The proof-analysis and proof-summarization procedures will also generate the summary presented in Figure C8–2, which is an attempt to sketch the basic idea of the proof.

The summarization presented in Figure C8–2 was obtained from the earlier one by tracing backward the history of the maximal chain in A that contains C. That is, the general form of the theorem to be proved is $(\exists x)FM(x)$, which is proved by showing $FM(t)$ for some term t. Usually, in proofs of this form, the most important piece of information is the term t. Tracing backward in this particular proof yields the information that there are two terms involved. The first is the set of all chains in A containing C, and the second is any maximal element of the set of all chains in A containing C.

Elementary Exercises and Dialogues

Another form of reasoning done by students is the solution of construction problems. A great many problems in elementary mathematics take the form of asking the student to give finite objects that satisfy certain conditions. For example, given the finite sets A and B, the student might be asked to give a function F that is a bijection (i.e., one-to-one and onto) from A to B.

For a large class of construction problems, there are procedures that will generate a tree of formulas and other information from the original statement of the problem. We call such trees *verification trees* for the problem. Essentially, the verification tree for a problem constitutes a reduction of the original (usually not directly verifiable) condition to a collection of directly verifiable conditions (the formulas at the leaves). These trees have the property that the failure of the formula at a node in the tree explains the failure of formulas at any of its ancestors. Similarly, the failure of a formula at a node is explained by the failure of formulas at any of its descendants.

For example, in the problem above of supplying a bijection F from A onto B, suppose that the student forgets to specify a value for some element of A, say, 3. The first response to the student might be: "The domain of F isn't A." The student might then ask, "Why?" The program would then answer (going toward the leaves), "Because there is an element of A that has not been assigned a value in B." The student might then ask, "Which one?" Since the routines that evaluate the formulas at the leaves provide counterexamples if those formulas fail, the program could then respond, "3." Or going back to the first response by the program ("The domain of F isn't A"), the student might say, "So?" The program could then move a step toward the root (the original statement of the conditions) and say, "Then F is not a map from A into B." The student might then again say, "So?" to which the program could respond, "F is not a bijection from A onto B."

The highly structured information in the verification tree provides the semantic base for a dialogue with the student in which the program can explain to the student what is wrong with the answer. It should be noted that more complex forms of explanation are available. In particular, the program could have said at the beginning, "Because 3 is not given a value by F, the domain of F is not A and hence F is not a bijection from A onto B."

Summary

A primary activity in mathematics is finding and presenting proofs. The EXCHECK instructional system attempts to handle natural proofs—proofs as they are actually done by practicing mathematicians—instead of requiring that these proofs be expressed as derivations in an elementary system of first-order logic. This objective requires the analysis of inferences actually made and the design and implementation of languages and procedures that permit such inferences to be easily stated and mechanically verified. Some progress has been made in handling natural proofs in elementary mathematics, but there is a considerable amount of work yet to be done.

References

See Blaine and Smith (1977), Smith et al. (1975), Smith and Blaine (1976), and Suppes (1981).

D.   OTHER APPLICATIONS OF AI TO EDUCATION

THE ICAI programs described in this chapter *teach* various subjects. Learning, however, does not always require teaching. Here, we discuss "learning by doing" and how, with this approach, Artificial Intelligence can help construct learning tools and provide a rich learning environment.

Learning by Doing

AI research has struggled repeatedly with the complexity of so-called commonsense knowledge and reasoning. Yet children can learn many complicated things without formal schooling. While some argue that much of this knowledge (e.g., the basic structures of language) is innate, the great diversity of human cultures and the observability of the learning process in children suggest that children actually do learn on their own.

Recent work in developmental psychology has underscored how very different this kind of learning seems to be from what takes place in schools. For example, Jean Piaget and his colleagues have amassed evidence that the child's *activity* is the key—learning must take place by "doing" (Piaget, 1970; Piaget and Inhelder, 1969). Accordingly, some educators have argued that this insight ought to be applied more in schools (see, e.g., Ashton-Warner, 1963; Holt, 1964), although others contend that it is fundamentally incompatible with formal schooling and that formal schooling should therefore be abolished:

> The totally destructive and constantly progressive nature of obligatory instruction will fulfill its ultimate logic unless we begin to liberate ourselves right now from our pedagogical hubris, our belief that man can do what God cannot, namely, manipulate others for their own salvation. (Illich, 1971, p. 73)

There is little room for the traditional "teacher" role in learning by doing, for the task provides its own feedback. Hence, the basic question in improving learning efficiency becomes: What are good things for students to "do"? Any activity is in some sense educational, but which activities pack the most value? And what are the right "powerful tools" to give them? A good example is "turtle geometry," which starts from the notion of *curvature* rather than points and straight lines (Euclidean geometry) or coordinate systems (analytic geometry) and results in a "discovery-rich" geometry from which one can gain an intuitive notion of the important underlying ideas (like number theory and topology) relatively quickly. (See Papert, 1980, Chap. 2; Abelson and diSessa, 1981.)

The Status Quo and Why AI Can Help

Educators occasionally experiment with learning-by-doing methods, but there are major hurdles to a more widespread use of such techniques:

1. A lot of careful thought goes into good "learning environments," especially into figuring out the real basics. A good example is arithmetic, as demonstrated by BUGGY (Article IX.C7): Arithmetic has a set of underlying issues, as reflected by "bugs," that should be addressed.

2. Such environments are expensive. "Doing" is only rarely compatible with the standard educational technology of paper and pencil.

3. Such instruction is highly individualized: Students cannot be rigidly controlled, the results are difficult to test, and the curricula are hard to standardize.

Computers and AI can help overcome these problems; for example,

1. AI can help build a theory of knowledge for a domain—a theory of what the "basics" are (see Papert, 1980, Chap. 6).

2. Computer and AI techniques are sufficiently general that the same resource (the computer system) can serve many learning needs, thus reducing the cost of innovative learning environments.

3. Because of its modeling flexibility and power, AI provides sophisticated approaches to accommodating different needs within a single (possibly mass-produced) program.

Thus, the computer and AI may help make previously "utopian" ideas like Illich's possible.

AI for Learning Resources

This brings us to the possibilities of AI for constructing "powerful tools" to help students learn by doing rather than by "being told." (It should be noted that useful computer-based learning tools, e.g., turtle geometry, do not necessarily require AI.)

Consider the effect of removing the tutoring components from SCHOLAR, SOPHIE, or EXCHECK. (WEST and WUMPUS would not be AI programs if their tutors were removed, but analogous, more interesting and complicated games conceivably would be.) There might actually be advantages to these truncated systems. Without tutoring, the students are freer to experiment, not having to worry constantly whether they are "right" or "wrong." No longer bound by what must inevitably be a narrow perspective of effective system usage, they can "browse," leave tasks unfinished, jump between unrelated tasks, and so on. (The GUIDON system, Article IX.C6, encourages this kind of browsing.) Suppose, for example, that students were allowed to go ahead and replace the wrong component in SOPHIE's "broken" circuit; the demonstration that the measurements from the supposedly corrected circuit are nearly unchanged may constitute more effective feedback than any verbal warning. And since students are allowed to "do" more in such modified systems, they may possibly learn more.

These examples fall short, however, in two respects. First, these ICAI systems were not designed for "nontutorial" use, and, second, they emphasize right-wrong distinctions inconsistent with teacherless learning. Better examples are operator-rich "learning environments" like LISP-based LOGO and its best-known application, turtle geometry (Solomon and Papert, 1976), message-passing SMALLTALK (Kay and Goldberg, 1977) and its constraint-resolving extension THINGLAB (Borning, 1979), and Kahn's actor-based DIRECTOR animation system (Kahn, 1976). In all of these, powerful programming-language features are tied to sophisticated graphics facilities that are not "frills" for motivational incentives but are central to the system—a means for presenting complicated ideas in the most efficient and accessible form. Except for the graphics, these systems look much like other cooperative, interactive AI systems, but with especially good tailoring to less sophisticated users—with informal formats, flexible user-specifications, and a carefully thought-out set of basic operators.

A tutor is a learning resource, and "hybrids" between ICAI ideas and learning-by-doing systems are possible. For instance, AI methods like parsing (see Chap. IV, in Vol. I) or inductive inference (Chap. XIV, in Vol. III) may be exploited to check, not whether the student is right or wrong, but whether his behavior is consistent with his explicitly defined goals (Miller and Goldstein, 1977a; Miller, 1979; Rowe, 1978). Thus, a very broad range of behavior may be allowed the student, yet tutorlike comments could be supplied as well.

AI Applied to Human Reasoning

One suspects that the more a student can "do" in a learning-by-doing situation—that is, the richer and more lifelike the environment is for him—the better he will learn; the role of the student in a computer-based learning environment should be mostly that of "programmer." The richer the environment becomes, the more the student can be seen as an integral part of the system, rather than as an appendage. Since we claim that AI ideas can be applied to modeling human reasoning (see Chap. XI, in Vol. III), we could make general reasoning and programming methods (e.g., modular problem decomposition, hierarchical organization, bugs, recursive problem solving) explicitly available to the student "programmer" to use as tools to manipulate complex systems (Papert, 1973, 1980, Chaps. 3 and 5; Howe and O'Shea, 1976). Students can learn these tools and carry them away from the computer-based learning environment. Furthermore, such tools can be applied naturally to many things having nothing to do with computers (see, e.g., Austin, 1974;

Bamberger, 1974). Thus, thanks to AI, we can teach problem solving as such more effectively, extending Polya's (1957) approach.

Applications of Education to AI

Finally, we can turn the tables and recognize that an approach to learning that proves to be particularly effective tells us something itself about the structure of what is being learned. For instance, if identifying the "bug types" of BUGGY makes it easier for students to learn arithmetic, this confirms that BUGGY's model of arithmetic as a set of procedures may be an important insight into arithmetic itself. Similarly, if students learn mathematical ideas better with turtle geometry than with Euclidean or Cartesian geometry, perhaps turtle geometry reflects better the "deep structure" of mathematics. Thus, we can think of educational applications as a laboratory for testing the epistemologies of various domains, including AI theories.

References

The books by Abelson and diSessa (1981) and Papert (1980) are highly recommended. See also Papert (1972a, 1972b).

Chapter X

Automatic Programming

CHAPTER X: AUTOMATIC PROGRAMMING

A. OVERVIEW

AUTOMATIC PROGRAMMING (AP) is the automation of some part of the programming process. As an application of Artificial Intelligence, AP research has achieved some success with experimental systems that help programmers manage large programs or that produce small programs from some *specification* of what they are to do (besides the code itself). Such specifications could be *examples* of the desired input/output behavior or a "higher level language" specification of the program, for example, in English. However, the importance of automatic-programming research in AI goes well beyond eventually relieving the plight of human programmers. In a sense, all of AI is a search for appropriate methods of automatic programming.

What Is Automatic Programming?

Programming can be defined as specifying the method for doing something the computer can do in terms the computer can interpret. In the simplest case, programmers code the steps of algorithms they want the machine to perform in terms of its hard-wired primitives for adding, subtracting, and moving numbers. But very few programmers really program that way any more. With the introduction of compilers—programs that translate a specification of an algorithm from a higher level language into the machine's primitive codes— programming became a much more reasonable task, since the activity took place at something closer to the human level than it did with the primitive machine code. For instance, in higher level languages, normal algebraic notation, such as $(N + 4)^2$, could be used to specify what is a substantially more involved procedure at the primitive level.

The first step toward automatic programming was, in fact, the development of compilers. The first FORTRAN compiler was even billed as an "automatic programming" system (Backus and Herrik, 1954; Backus, 1958). To reiterate, then, programming is the process of specifying what is to be done so that the computer can do it, and automatic programming uses another program, the AP system, to assist in this process, in particular, to raise the level at which instructions are specified. It is in this sense that AI itself can be viewed as automatic programming: There are some things that computers just cannot do, like flying. There are others, like becoming the world-champion chess player, that a computer might do if we could find a way of specifying the steps to winning chess games (see, however, Chap. II, in Vol. I).

There is a connection between AI and AP that is still deeper than this similarity of goals. At the core of AI is the ability of programs to reason about what they do—to reason about themselves as programs. This is why, for example, the ability to manipulate programs as data in LISP is so important (Chap. VI). And the ability to understand and reason about programs is the central research goal of automatic programming—an important open research problem in AI.

Returning to the more practical view of AP systems as programs that help people write programs, let us consider how the AP researchers themselves define the field. Since most of the research was begun in the 1970s, it is not surprising that there is some diversity of opinion as to the definition, scope, and direction of the endeavor. One definition says simply that AP is something that will spare people the chores of programming (Biermann, 1976a). Another states that an AP system carries out part of the programming activity currently performed by a human in constructing a program written in some machine-executable language, given the definition of the problem to be solved; here, the essence of an AP system is that it assumes some responsibilities otherwise borne by a human and thereby reduces the size of the person's task (Hammer and Ruth, 1979). Yet another definition states that AP means having the computer help write its own programs (Heidorn, 1977). AP is the application of a computing system to the problem of effectively utilizing that system or another computing system to perform a task specified by the user (Balzer, 1973b).

Other, more extensive definitions have been suggested. One definition (Balzer, 1973b) rates AP systems according to a measure of merit, which includes the following factors:

1. The time and effort required of the programmer to formulate and specify the desired program, which is determined in part by the system's *informality*, that is, the degree that the user's statements can be ambiguous or incomplete; its *language level*, that is, the degree to which the AP system can accept specifications in a terminology natural to the problem area under consideration; and its *executability*, that is, the degree to which the user need specify only what is wanted rather than how to obtain it;

2. The efficiency of the decisions made by the system in designing the program and, consequently, the overall efficiency of the program that is produced by the system;

3. The ease with which future modifications can be incorporated into the program;

4. The reliability and ruggedness of the program;

5. The computer resources, including time and memory, required by the system to produce that program;

6. The range, as well as the complexity, of the tasks that can be handled by the system.

Motivations for Automatic Programming

As mentioned above, the term *automatic programming* in the early days of computing meant writing a program in a high-level language (e.g., FORTRAN) and having a compiler transform the program into machine-language code. At that time, "real" programming referred to writing a program in machine or assembly language. Today, when most programming is done in high-level languages, AP implies programming in an even more advanced software environment.

In a general way, the forces responsible 20 years ago for FORTRAN are still the pragmatic reasons for developing AP systems today. Programmers were burdened with the need to specify many details, with the need to keep track of the many relations between these details, and with a programming environment that was not, perhaps, natural to the way in which they thought about the problem they were writing a program to solve. It was believed that new programming environments might be the answer and that the software technologies required for such environments might be feasible.

The situation with programming environments today seems even more critical. Software is costly and unreliable. Much time, money, and effort are currently being expended, with even greater expenditures forecast. Software is seldom produced within budget or on time. Quite often the supposedly finished product, when delivered, fails to meet specifications. As programming applications of increasingly greater complexity are addressed, not only does reliability become more difficult to achieve, but the costs of software, in terms of time, money, and effort, spiral upward.

To help alleviate these problems, AP aims at a general goal, namely, to restyle the way in which the programmer specifies the desired program. This restyling should allow the programmer to think of the problem at a higher and more natural level. AP would like to relieve the programmer of mundane portions of programming, that is, the need to keep track of inordinate amounts of detail. By improving the programming environment, AP could allow programmers to construct with greater ease and accuracy the programs of the present and to attempt with confidence the more complex programs of the future.

Characteristics of AP Systems

Automatic programming research in AI, then, refers to systems that assist humans in some aspect of programming. Each of these systems has four identifying characteristics: a *specification* method, a *target language*, a *problem area*, and an *approach* or method of operation.

Specification method. Programming involves some means or method for conveying to the computer the desired program. A variety of *specification methods* have been used in experimental AP systems.

Formal specification methods are those that might be considered to be *very high level* programming languages. In general, the syntax and semantics of such methods are precisely and unambiguously defined. Formal methods also tend to be *complete*; that is, the specification completely and precisely indicates what it is that the program is to accomplish, though, of course, the specification may not indicate the form of the program or how the program is to accomplish its task. On the one hand, many formal specification methods are not usually *interactive*, which is to say, the system does not interact with the user to obtain missing information, to verify hypotheses, or to point out inconsistencies in the specification. For example, it is comparable to the passive acceptance of a program's specification by a compiler of a high-level language (e.g., FORTRAN). On the other hand, there are some formal specification methods that are interactive (see McCune, 1979, which emphasizes interactive, formal specification techniques as a natural extension of *incremental compiling*).

Specification by examples is simply giving examples of what the desired program is to do—sufficient examples to allow the AP system then to construct it. The specification might consist of examples of the input/output behavior of the desired program, or it might consist of *traces* of how the program processed the input. There are many difficulties involved in specification by examples (or traces); for instance, this kind of specification is rarely *complete*, since a few examples will not fully describe the behavior of the desired program in all cases.

Natural language (e.g., English) is another method of specification. The user specifies "in so many words" what the desired program is to do. This method is often *interactive*—checking hypotheses, pointing out inconsistencies, and asking for further information (cf. Articles X.D1 on PSI and X.D7 on NLPQ).

A more detailed discussion of specification, including some advantages and disadvantages of the various methods, is presented in Article X.B.

Target language. The language in which the AP system writes the finished program is called the target language. The target languages of the AP systems described later in this chapter are high-level languages such as LISP, PL/1, and GPSS. In other words, the user of an AP system, possibly using examples of what he wanted the program to do, would expect the system to produce a program in, say, LISP that would do the right thing on the examples he used.

Problem area. Another characteristic of an AP system is its problem area, or area of intended application. For some AP systems, the scope of the problem area is relatively precise. For example, for the NLPQ system it is simple queuing problems, whereas for the Protosystem I project it is all input/output-intensive data-processing systems (including inventory control, payroll, and other record-keeping systems) and for the PSI system it is all symbolic computation (including list processing, searching and sorting, data storage and retrieval, and concept formation). The problem area of a system can have a bearing on the method of specification, introducing relevant terminology, influencing the method of operation or approach used by the AP system, and so forth.

Method of operation. Because AP is a young research area, the categorization of the methods used by existing systems is difficult. Article X.C discusses some of the more clear-cut approaches, including theorem proving, program formation, knowledge engineering, automatic data selection, traditional problem solving, and induction.

In the *theorem-proving approach*, the user specifies the conditions that must hold for the input data (to the desired program) and the conditions that the output data should satisfy: The conditions are specified in some *formal language*, often the predicate calculus (see Article III.C1, in Vol. I). A *theorem prover* is then asked to prove that, for all given inputs, there exists an output that satisfies the output conditions, and the proof yields as a side effect the desired program (Article XII.A, in Vol. III).

The *program-transformation approach* refers to transforming a specification or description of a program into an equivalent description of the program. The reason for the transformation might be to convert a specification that can be easily written and read into one that is more complicated but more efficient; alternately, the goal might be to convert a very high level description of the program into a description closer to a target-language implementation.

Knowledge engineering, applicable to many areas of AI besides AP, refers to identifying and codifying expert knowledge (see Article VII.A), and it often means encoding the knowledge as specific, rule-type data structures that can be added to or removed from the *knowledge base* of a system (Article III.C4, in Vol. I).

Traditional problem solving, also a general AI technique, refers to the use of goals to direct the choice and application of a set of operators.

These approaches overlap, and many systems utilize a method that may, in part, draw on elements from several. While it is hard to categorize the approaches of AP systems, there are now enough systems to be able to identify some common issues.

Basic Issues

Partial information pertains to systems whose methods of specification allow for partial or fragmentary descriptions of the desired program: Not all of the required information is present in the specification, or, where it is present, it may not be explicit. Systems that accept incomplete specifications, for example, natural-language specifications, are very much concerned with partial information. The NLPQ, PSI, and SAFE systems fall in this category. A classification of the different kinds of missing information that might occur in a natural-language specification is given in Article X.D2 on SAFE.

Usually going hand in hand with the problem of partial information is the problem of *consistency*. Incomplete methods of specification often permit inconsistency between different parts of the same specification. In such cases, the system must check for inconsistencies and, if they are found, resolve them.

In trying to fill in missing information in one part of the specification or checking for consistency between different parts and resolving any discovered inconsistencies, the system may use information that occurs either explicitly or implicitly in other parts of the specification. Also, it might utilize a knowledge base containing information about the problem area. Finally, the system may consult the user in an attempt to gain the sought-for information. One of the explicit devices for making use of such information is *constraints*. For examples of these, see Article X.D1 on PSI and especially Article X.D2 on SAFE.

Transformation is, simply, changing a program description, or part of a program description, into another form. All AP systems use transformation, if only to convert an internal description of the program into a target-language implementation (description). Even a compiler of high-level languages (e.g., FORTRAN, PL/1, ALGOL) will often transform a program description several times, taking it through several internal representations, the last of which is the machine-language description.

However, a compiler differs from an AP system in that it applies the transformations in a rigid, predetermined manner; in an automatic-programming system, the application of transformations may depend on an analysis and exploration of the results of applying various transformations. Systems that use extensive transformation on the program description, like DEDALUS and PECOS, have a knowledge base with many transformation rules that convert parts of a higher level description into a lower level description, closer to a target-language implementation. Such rules are repeatedly applied to parts of the program description with the goal of eventually producing descriptions within the target language. These systems develop a tree of possible descriptions of the program, with each descendant of a node being the result of a transformation. One of the goals, then, in developing the tree is to find a description that is a target-language implementation of the desired program. Another goal might be to find an efficient target-language implementation.

Other AP systems may use transformation rules in various ways. For instance, in the NLPQ system, transformation rules parse the natural-language input from the user, to generate natural-language output to the user and to generate the target-language program from an internal description.

Efficiency of the target-language implementation is another general concern of AP systems. The two systems described here that deal especially with this issue are Protosystem I and the PSI subsystem called LIBRA (Article X.D8). While the Protosystem I approach to creating efficient programs combines AI with the mathematical technique of dynamic programming, the LIBRA approach uses a more extensive range of AI techniques, employing a variety of heuristics, cost estimates, and other kinds of knowledge to guide its search for an efficient program.

When it is said that an AP system optimizes a program for efficiency, it does not mean that the system finds the absolutely most efficient implementation; *combinatorial explosion* makes such a task impossible, since there are usually many equivalent target-language implementations of any program. Rather, optimizing means making some reasonable choices in the implementation to achieve a relatively efficient program.

The basic concern of one of the systems described below, the Programmer's Apprentice, pertains more to *understanding* the program than it does to the issues discussed previously. In this situation, understanding a program might be defined as a system's being able to talk about, analyze, modify, or write parts of a program. It is the intention of the Programmer's Apprentice, though it should be kept in mind that this system is not yet operational, to bring about program understanding through the explicit use of *plans*. A plan represents one particular way of viewing a program, or part of a program (for a more detailed explanation, see Article X.D3). Understanding in the other systems is relatively implicit and does not reside in any one particular class of structure.

Overview of AP Research

The projects described in Section X.D cover much of the current research in AP and span the four basic issues discussed above, namely, transformation rules, search for efficiency, handling of partial information, and explicit understanding.

NLPQ is the first AP system to utilize natural-language dialogue as a specification method. The user specifies part of a simple queuing-simulation problem in English, and then the system, as necessary, answers questions posed by the user and queries the user to fill in missing information or to resolve inconsistencies. The partial knowledge that the system has obtained about the desired program is represented as a semantic net that is eventually used to generate the program in the target language, GPSS. Transformation rules analyze the user's natural-language specification, build and modify the semantic net, produce natural-language responses, and finally generate the target-language program.

The PSI system consists of many subsystems; it stresses the integration of a number of different processes and sources of knowledge. The problem-application area is symbolic (nonnumeric) programming, including information retrieval, simple sorting, and concept formation. The user can specify the desired program with a mixture of examples and mixed-initiative, natural-language dialogue; for an easier and more natural interaction with the user, the system maintains and utilizes a tree of the topics that occur during the specification dialogue. Through such a dialogue, PSI creates a complete, consistent description of the desired program. In the last phase, the system explores repeated application of transformation rules to convert the description into a target-language implementation. This last phase, the synthesis phase, is carried out by two subsystems: PECOS provides suitable transformation rules and LIBRA directs and explores the application of the rules, with the goal of obtaining an efficient target implementation. The PECOS and LIBRA subsystems are described separately in Articles X.D4 and X.D8.

Both PECOS and DEDALUS are examples of full-fledged, dynamic transformation systems. They each start out with a complete specification of the desired program. Each has a knowledge base of many transformation rules that are repeatedly applied to the specification. These repeated applications produce a sequence of specifications that eventually terminate with a specification that is a target-language implementation. Because more than one transformation rule can apply in some cases, each system actually develops a tree of specifications, with eventually one or more of the leaf nodes of the tree being a program implementation within the target language. Some of the differences between these two systems stem from the fact that DEDALUS is concerned with the logic of such programming concepts as recursion and subroutine. On the other hand, PECOS is more concerned with the multiplicity of implementations of very high level programming constructs and operations, because that is its task within the PSI system.

The SAFE system (Article X.D2) contains an extensive description of constraints and their use in handling partial information. SAFE processes a variety of constraints to fill in different kinds of information in the specification of the desired program and employs different methods of processing these constraints. There are constraints related to the type of object referenced in the specification, as well as some related to sequencing of steps. Constraints are processed by backtracking and by carrying out a form of symbolic execution.

One of the ideas of the SAFE project is that a completely specified program satisfies a very large number of constraints. Information in the user's partial, fragmentary specification (partial and fragmentary, since the specification does not mention all objects explicitly, or partially mentions other objects and may not specify explicit sequencing of actions) combined with the many constraints that a formal program satisfies (and possibly with information from a knowledge base of the application area or, in special cases, from information obtained from queries to the user) fully determine a complete and formal description of the program. No other system deals in so central a way with partial information and constraints.

The LIBRA and Protosystem-I projects are concerned with the efficiency of the target-language implementation. LIBRA uses an AI approach, while Protosystem I uses a combination of some AI with primarily the mathematical approach of dynamic programming. Dynamic programming, modified by approximations and heuristics, produces an optimized target-language implementation. On the other hand, LIBRA guides the application of the transformation rules furnished by the PECOS subsystem of PSI and directs the growth of the resulting tree (see the discussion of PECOS, above) with the goal of finding an efficient target implementation. LIBRA determines and utilizes estimates of what it is likely to achieve by exploring the development of a particular node. LIBRA has knowledge about how its own allocation of space and time should influence its strategy in searching for an efficient implementation. Though both Protosystem I and LIBRA are concerned with producing efficient implementations, they approach the problem in different contexts. The first explores configurations of a data-processing program and the second explores applications of transformation rules.

The Programmer's Apprentice is not necessarily intended to write programs automatically but, instead, to function as an apprentice to the user, assisting with such tasks as writing parts of the program, checking for consistency, explaining pieces of the program, and helping the user modify programs. The central concern of this project is *understanding*, through the explicit device of *plans*. A plan may be thought of as a template that expresses a viewpoint. Matching the plan to a part of a program description corresponds to understanding the part in that way. Several plans can match the same part of a program, corresponding to different ways of understanding that part. Plans can also be built up in a hierarchical fashion. The goal is that the Programmer's Apprentice, with the understanding gained through plans, can assist the programmer in correcting mistakes, writing parts of the program, and making modifications.

All of these are still research projects: Much work remains before most of these systems can be of use to programmers.

References

See Balzer (1973b), Biermann (1976a), Green (1975b, 1976b), Green and Barstow (1977a), Hammer and Ruth (1979), and Heidorn (1976, 1977).

B. METHODS OF PROGRAM SPECIFICATION

THE MEANS or method employed to convey to the AP system the kind of program the user wants is called *program specification.* The specification of the desired program might entail describing the program fully in some formal programming language or possibly just specifying certain properties of the program from which the AP system can deduce the rest. Alternately, it might involve providing examples of the input and the output of the desired program, giving formal constraints on the program in the predicate calculus, or interactively describing the program in English at increasing levels of detail.

Specification by Examples

Some simple programs are most easily described by giving examples of what the program is supposed to do.

Examples of input/output pairs. In this specification method, the user gives examples of typical inputs to the program he (or she) desires along with the corresponding outputs he expects. Consider describing, to someone who is unfamiliar with the concept of concatenation, a program that concatenates two lists. It might be most straightforward to use an example,

$$\text{CONCAT}[(ABC), (DE)] = (ABCDE),$$

which states that when the input of the function CONCAT consists of the two lists (ABC) and (DE), the corresponding output is $(ABCDE)$.

Given certain commonsense assumptions, this sample input/output pair should suffice to specify what it is that the desired program is to do. In slightly more complicated cases, where the commonsense assumptions are not sufficient, more examples must be given to specify the program uniquely. For instance, the example above could be misinterpreted as a "constant" program that always gives $(ABCDE)$ as output:

$$\text{CONCAT}[x, y] = (ABCDE).$$

In such a case, giving an additional example

$$\text{CONCAT}[(LM), (NOP)] = (LMNOP),$$

would probably clear up any confusion.

306

Another type of specification by examples is illustrated by the following specification of the function PRIME using a subset of its input/output pairs:

$$\mathrm{PRIME}(1) = 1$$
$$\mathrm{PRIME}(2) = 2$$
$$\mathrm{PRIME}(3) = 3$$
$$\mathrm{PRIME}(4) = 5$$
$$\mathrm{PRIME}(5) = 7$$
$$\mathrm{PRIME}(6) = 11 \ .$$

Generic examples of input/output pairs. In certain cases, generalizations of specific examples, or generic examples, are more useful in avoiding the problems inherent in partial specifications. For instance, the generic example

$$\mathrm{REVERSE}[(x_1 x_2 x_3 \ldots x_n)] = (x_n \ldots x_3 x_2 x_1)$$

describes a list-reversal function. Here, the $x_1, x_2, \ldots, x_n$ are variables and the list $(x_1 x_2 x_3 \ldots x_n)$ corresponds to any list of arbitrary length—a generic list. This specification is still partial but is more complete than any specification of this function given by nongeneric examples of input/output pairs.

Specification by program traces. Traces of the desired program's operation on sample data allow more imperative specifications than do sample input/output pairs alone. A sorting program, for example, may be specified with input/output pairs (e.g., Green et al., 1974), as in

$$\mathrm{SORT}[(3\,1\,4\,2)] = (1\,2\,3\,4),$$

but it would be hard to specify a program that specifically uses, say, an *insertion sort* algorithm in the same way. However, a program trace could express such a program as follows:

$$\mathrm{SORT}[(3\,1\,4\,2)] \to (\ )$$
$$(1\,4\,2) \to (3)$$
$$(4\,2) \to (1\,3)$$
$$(2) \to (1\,3\,4)$$
$$(\ ) \to (1\,2\,3\,4) \ .$$

Another example of specification by traces might be

$$\mathrm{GCD}(12, 18) \to$$
$$(6, 12) \to$$
$$(0, 6) \to$$
$$6$$

illustrating the operation of a program that uses the Euclidean algorithm to compute the greatest common divisor. An example of using a trace to specify part of a concept-formation program is presented in Article X.D1.

More formally, a trace may be defined as follows. A *programming domain* can be thought of as consisting of a set of abstract objects, a set of possible representations (called *data structures*) for these abstract objects, a basic set of operators to transform these representations, and a class of questions or predicates that can be evaluated on these data structures. A programming domain thus characterizes a class of programs that might be constructed to operate on representations of the set of abstract objects in the domain. For a given program operating on some data objects in the domain, a *trace* is a sequence of changes of these data structures and control-flow decisions that have caused these changes during execution of the program.

Traces are usually expressed in terms of domain operators and tests (or functional compositions of these). Traces are classified as *complete* if they carry all information about operators applied, data structures changed, control decisions taken, and so forth; otherwise, they are *incomplete*. An interesting subclass of the latter is the class of *protocols*, in which all data modifications are explicit but all control information (e.g., predicate evaluations that determine control flow) is omitted. A protocol is then a sequence of data-structure state snapshots and operation applications (for a more complete definition, see Article X.C).

Generic traces. Like generic examples of input/output pairs, generic traces of program operation can be used for specification. In general, there is a whole spectrum of trace specifications for a given program, depending on how much imperative information and descriptive information is presented. For instance, the traces above are completely descriptive, while traces that contain function applications or sequencing information tend to be more imperative.

Advantages and disadvantages of specification by examples. As stated above, generic examples are less ambiguous than are nongeneric examples. Traces are less ambiguous than input/output pairs and allow some imperative specification of the flow of control. On the other hand, to specify a trace, the user must have some idea of how the desired program is to function.

Specification by examples can be natural and easy for the user to formulate (Manna and Waldinger, 1977). Examples have the limitations inherent in informal program specifications: The user must choose examples so as to specify unambiguously the desired program. The AP system must be able to determine when the user's specification is consistent and complete and that the system's "model" of what the user wants is indeed the right program.

Formal Specifications

Formal methods of specifying programs are often used in conjunction with the theorem-proving-based approach to AP (Article X.C; see also Article III.C1, in Vol. I). Here one might specify a program as

$$\forall s_1.\,(P(s_1) \supset \exists s_2.\,Q(s_1, s_2)), \tag{1}$$

which states that for all values of *input variables* to the program, s_1, for which the predicate $P(s_1)$ is true, there are *output variables*, s_2, such that $Q(s_1, s_2)$ is true. The input predicate (or input specification) $P(s_1)$ gives the conditions that the inputs, s_1, can be expected to satisfy at the beginning of program execution. The output predicate $Q(s_2)$ gives the conditions that the outputs, s_2, of the desired program are expected to satisfy.

For example, a program that computes the greatest common divisor of two integers x and y might be specified by taking $P(x, y)$ as the condition that x and y are positive, and $Q(x, y, z)$ as the condition that z is the greatest common divisor. $P(x, y)$ could be written as

$$x > 0 \quad \text{and} \quad y > 0,$$

and $Q(x, y, z)$ could be written as

DIVIDE(z, x) and DIVIDE(z, y) and
$\qquad \forall r.\,((r > 0 \text{ and DIVIDE}(r, x) \text{ and DIVIDE}(r, y)) \supset z \geq r);$

that is, z divides both x and y and any r that also divides them is smaller than z.

Substituting these values for the predicates P and Q in expression (1) would produce a formula stating that for all positive integers x and y, there is a z such that z is their greatest common divisor. This expression would then be given to a theorem prover that produces a proof of the statement from which a program can be extracted as a side effect (see Chap. XII, in Vol. III). One is required to give to the theorem prover enough facts concerning any predicates and functions that occur in P and Q so that expression (1) is provable. Thus, in the above, one would have to specify a number of facts concerning the predicates DIVIDE, $<$, and $\geq$ over the integers.

A similar method of specification is used with the *program-transformation* and *very high level language* approaches to AP (see Article X.C). This specification method stresses the use of entities that are not immediately implementable on a computer, or at least not implementable with some desired degree of efficiency. There is considerable leeway in this classification. For instance, in some program-transformation systems the entities may be quite abstract, without any hint of the desired algorithm. In other systems, the algorithm most naturally suggested by the specification of the program could be inefficient, but the AP system will produce an efficient, if perhaps convoluted, program.

One example of a specification in program transformation is

GCD(x, y): **compute** MAX$\{z$: DIVIDE(z, x) and DIVIDE(z, y)$\}$
$\qquad$ **where** x and y are nonnegative integers greater than zero.

This expression states that the greatest common divisor of x and y is the maximum of all those z such that z divides x and y. Furthermore, it is assumed that x and y are nonnegative integers, one of which is nonzero. By successive transformations of this definition of GCD, the system would produce an efficient recursive program (see Article X.D5). Another example (Darlington and Burstall, 1973, p. 280) is

FACTORIAL(x): **if** $(x = 1)$ **then** 1 **else** TIMES$(x, $ FACTORIAL$(x - 1))$.

The system, then, by various transformations produces a more efficient non-recursive, though more tortuous, program.

Advantages and disadvantages of formal specifications. Specification by input and output predicates based on formal logic is completely general: Anything can be specified. On the other hand, the user must have a sufficient understanding of the desired behavior of the program to give a complete, formal description of the input and output. This understanding can sometimes be difficult to attain, even for simple programs. Also, the present state of theorem provers and problem-reduction methods makes synthesis of longer programs difficult.

The second type of formal specification, which is used with the program-transformation approach, does not have such arbitrary generality. However, the terminology in the specification often is closer to our way of thinking about a particular subject, and so it should be easier to create such specifications.

While some formal methods are arbitrarily general and others are not, they all are complete: The specification of the desired program fully and completely specifies what the program is to do. This is not true of some of the other methods, like specification by examples, where the specification does not uniquely determine what the program is to do. With such methods it becomes a concern whether the program produced by the system is actually what the user desires. Sometimes a system employing such a specification method may need to verify whether the program it produces is the program that the user wants (see Sibel, Furbach, and Schreiber, 1978).

Natural-language Specifications

Given an appropriate conceptual vocabulary, English descriptions of algorithms are often the most natural method of specification. Part of the reason is that natural language allows greater flexibility in dealing with basic concepts than do, say, very high level languages. This flexibility requires a fairly sophisticated representational structure for the model, with capabilities for representing the partial (incomplete) and often ambiguous descriptions that users provide. In addition, it may be necessary to maintain a database of domain-dependent knowledge for certain applications. Experience with implemented systems, such as SAFE (Article X.D2), suggests that the relevant issues are not in the area of natural-language processing but in how the specifications are modeled in the system and what "programming knowledge" the system must have.

Specification by Mixed-initiative Dialogue

A generalization of the entire concept of program specification involves an interaction between the user and the system as the system builds a model of what the user wants and tries to fill in the details of the algorithm. In addition to maintaining a model of the algorithm, interactive systems sometimes will even maintain a kind of model of the user to help the system tailor the dialogue to a particular user's idiosyncracies. Various techniques mentioned previously, such as examples or traces, could be incorporated into the dialogue as a description of some part of the algorithm. The system might be designed to allow users to be as vague or ambiguous as they please in the initial specification, since it ultimately takes the initiative and asks enough questions to fill in the model.

This method is probably the closest to the usual, natural method of program specification, allowing both the specifier and the programmer to make comments and suggestions. Users do not have to keep every detail in mind, nor need they present the specification in a certain order. The system will eventually question the user for missing details or ambiguous specifications. On the other hand, this method requires a system that deals with many problems of natural-language translation, generation, and representation. A versatile representation is also required for the system's model of the desired program.

The PSI system (Article X.D1) and the NLPQ system (Article X.D7) explore interactive program specification. Floyd (1972) and Green (1977) give hypothetical dialogues with such a system, illustrating the problems that researchers have encountered with this approach.

References

See Biermann (1976a) and Heidorn (1977).

C.   BASIC APPROACHES

THIS ARTICLE describes the basic approaches of automatic-programming systems to synthesizing desired programs from user specifications. There is not always a clear distinction between synthesis and specification paradigms. Furthermore, as will be seen in the articles in Section X.D describing important AP systems, some follow primarily one approach, while others have more elaborate paradigms that involve several approaches.

Theorem Proving

The theorem-proving approach is appropriate for the synthesis of programs whose input and output conditions can be specified in the formalism of the predicate calculus. As described in Article X.B, the user specifies the desired program as an assertion to be proved, which might take the following form (Green, 1969):

$$\forall s_1. (P(s_1) \supset \exists s_2. Q(s_1, s_2)),$$

where P is a condition that the input variables to the program, s_1, will satisfy and Q is the predicate that the output variables, s_2, are to satisfy after execution. The theorem prover must also have enough axioms about any other predicates appearing in this expression to be able to prove it.

The desired program is extracted as a by-product of the proof produced by the theorem prover. For instance, certain constructs in the proof will produce conditional statements, others will give sequential statements, and occurrences of induction axioms may produce loops or recursion. There are several variant methods of accomplishing these results (see Waldinger and Levitt, 1974; Kowalski, 1977; Clark and Sickel, 1977).

Although any interesting example would be far too long to work out in full detail here, it may be worthwhile to show how such a problem is set up. The interested reader is referred to Green (1969) for a more complete development of the following example. Consider the very simple problem of sorting in LISP the *dotted pair* of two distinct numbers (see Article VI.B on LISP). The axioms about LISP expressions that would prove useful for this synthesis would be:

1. $x = \text{CAR}(\text{CONS}(x, y))$
2. $y = \text{CDR}(\text{CONS}(x, y))$
3. $x = \text{NIL} \supset \text{COND}(x, y, z) = z$
4. $x \neq \text{NIL} \supset \text{COND}(x, y, z) = y$
5. $\forall x, y. (\text{LESSP}(x, y) \neq \text{NIL} \equiv x < y).$

The specification of the desired sorting program, that is, the theorem to be proved, would be:

$$\forall x. \exists y. [\text{CAR}(x) < \text{CDR}(x) \supset y = x] \land$$
$$[\text{CAR}(x) \geq \text{CDR}(x) \supset \text{CAR}(x) = \text{CDR}(y) \land \text{CDR}(x) = \text{CAR}(y)],$$

which says that for every *dotted-pair* input, x, there is a dotted-pair output, y, such that if x is already sorted, then y is the same as x, and if x is not sorted, then y is the interchange of the two elements of x. Using, for example, a *resolution theorem prover* (see Article XII.B, in Vol. III), we would obtain the following program:

$$y = \text{COND}(\text{LESSP}(\text{CAR}(x), \text{CDR}(x)), x, \text{CONS}(\text{CDR}(x), \text{CAR}(x))).$$

One of the major problems that synthesizing less trivial programs introduces is that some form of iteration or recursion is required. To form a recursive program, one needs the proper *induction axioms* for the problem. A general schema for the induction axiom sufficient for most programs is that of Green (1969):

$$[P(h(\text{NIL}), \text{NIL}) \land \forall x. [\text{ATOM}(x) \land P(h(\text{CDR}(x)), \text{CDR}(x)) \supset \dot{P}(h(x), x)]]$$
$$\supset \forall z. [P(h(z), z)],$$

where P is any predicate and h is any function. Somehow, this predicate and function must be determined. Requiring the user to supply the induction axioms for each program to be synthesized somewhat defeats the purpose of automating the synthesis, since it might be a lot easier to specify the entire program some other way. Because having the system randomly generate induction axioms until one of them works is out of the question, combinatorially, AP systems with this approach usually attempt to determine P and h by means of various *heuristics* that limit search (see Chap. II, in Vol. I).

There are several constraints inherent in the theorem-proving approach. First, for more complicated programs, it is often more difficult to specify correctly the input and output predicates of the program in the predicate calculus than it is to write the program itself. Second, the domain must be axiomatized completely; that is, one must give enough axioms to the theorem prover to make it possible for any statement that is true of the various functions and predicates in the specification of the program to actually be proved from the axioms—otherwise, the theorem prover may fail to produce a proof and thereby fail to produce the program. Third, present theorem provers lack the power to produce proofs for the specification of very complicated programs.

It should be noted that this approach does not lend itself to *partial specification:* Users cannot specify the program partially and have the system help them fill in details. On the other hand, when a theorem prover does succeed in producing a proof of the specification, the correctness of the extracted program is guaranteed. Thus, AP systems might incorporate theorem proving either where it is convenient or where correctness is an important requirement.

The Program-transformation Approach

The transformation approach is suitable for converting automatically an easily written, easily understood program into a more efficient, but perhaps convoluted program. One such system, described by Darlington and Burstall (1973), removes recursion, eliminates redundant computation, expands procedure calls, and takes discarded list cells into use.

Recursion removal transforms a recursive program into an iterative one, which is generally more efficient, avoiding the overhead of the stacking mechanism. Candidates for recursion removal are determined by performing pattern matching of the parts of the program against a recursive-schema input pattern. If the match is successful and if certain preconditions are met, the program is replaced by an iterative schema. A simple example of such a transformation rule is the following:

input pattern: $f(x)$: **if** a **then** b **else** $h(d, f(e))$;

precondition: h is associative, x does not occur free in h;

result pattern: $f(x)$: **if** a
               then result $\leftarrow b$
               else begin
                 result $\leftarrow d$;
                 $x \leftarrow e$;
                 while not a
                    do begin
                      result $\leftarrow h$ (result,d);
                      $x \leftarrow e$
                    end;
                 result $\leftarrow h$ (result,b)
               end

where a, b, d, e, f, and h in the input pattern are matched against arbitrary expressions in the candidate functions. For example, the function

FACTORIAL(x): **if** $(x = 1)$ **then** 1 **else** TIMES$(x, \text{FACTORIAL}(x - 1))$

would match the above input pattern with $f \leftarrow$ FACTORIAL, $a \leftarrow (x = 1)$, $b \leftarrow 1$, $h \leftarrow$ TIMES, $d \leftarrow x$, and $e \leftarrow (x - 1)$.

Eliminating redundant computations includes traditional subexpression elimination as well as combining loops that iterate over the same range.

Implicit iteration is part of the latter. Thus, if A, B, and C are represented as linked lists, the sequence

$$X \leftarrow \text{INTERSECTION}(A, B)$$
$$Y \leftarrow \text{INTERSECTION}(A, C),$$

is really two implicit iterations, each over the set A. A suitable transformation rule would convert these into a single iteration over the set A.

Expanding procedure calls generally involve substituting the body of a procedure for each of the calls to it. The potential benefit arises from simplifications made possible by use of the local context. This technique is the starting point for a general class of transformations explored by Burstall and Darlington (1975) and Wegbreit (1975a).

Program transformation also converts very high level specifications into target-language implementations (see Articles X.D4 and X.D5).

Knowledge Engineering

AP systems are said to be knowledge based when they are built by identifying the knowledge or *expertise* that is appropriate for program synthesis and understanding (i.e., the ability to manipulate and analyze programs) and by encoding this knowledge explicitly in some knowledge representation. Many of these systems use large amounts of many kinds of knowledge to analyze, modify, and debug large classes of programs. While the distinction is relative, it is possible to divide this knowledge into two types: programming knowledge and domain knowledge.

Programming knowledge includes both *programming-language knowledge* about the semantics of the target language in which the system will write the desired program and *general programming knowledge* about such general computation mechanisms as generators, tests, initialization, loops, sorting, searching, and hashing. Programming knowledge includes optimization techniques, high-level programming constructs (loops, recursion, branching), and strategy and planning techniques.

Domain knowledge is the information required for a system to infer how to go from the problem description or specification of a program in a certain program class (e.g., symbolic computation) to what needs to be done to solve the problem. This know-how includes how to structure the concepts in the domain or problem area and find their interrelationships. It must also include knowledge about how to achieve certain results in the problem domain (cf. HACKER's learning of procedures, Article XIV.D5c, in Vol. III). Moreover, it should be able to find alternative ways to define the problem and to solve the task—such knowledge represents an "understanding" of the domain.

Knowledge-based systems need a method of reasoning. Since they are not restricted to the traditional formalisms of logic, they often supply their own flexible reasoning techniques for guiding the synthesis. Some of these techniques are inference, program simplification, illustration and simplification for the user, decision trees, problem-solving techniques, and refinement.

The basic concern in representing the knowledge is that it be structured in such a way that the search for relevant facts not cause a combinatorial explosion. Various appropriate representations include—

1. PLANNER-like procedural experts (Article VI.C2);

2. Refinement rules (Article X.D4);

3. Modular, frame-like experts (OWL, Martin, 1974; BEINGS, Lenat, 1975);

4. Semantic nets (Article X.D7);

5. Amorphous systems that try several ad hoc techniques (Biggerstaff, 1976).

Methods of accessing knowledge bases include—

1. Pattern invocation (Article X.D4);

2. "When needed" (Sussman, 1975);

3. Frame relations and assertions, including filling in process models (Martin, 1974; Green, 1969; Lenat, 1975; see Articles X.D7, X.D1, and X.D2);

4. Subgoal or case analysis (Green, 1977; see Article X.D5).

Automatic Data-structure Selection

Automatic data-structure selection refers to the selection of efficient, low-level data-structure implementations for a program specified in terms of high-level, abstract information structures (e.g., sets, real numbers). Generally, programming languages with abstract data types employ default implementations that are a compromise between all likely uses of the data type; these choices may be far from efficient in any particular program. But a system with automatic data selection would choose, from a collection of possible implementations, one that is most efficient for the particular program under consideration.

For example, the abstract data-type *set* could be represented in low-level implementations as a linked list, a binary tree, a hash table, a bit string, or property-list markings. Some operations on sets are easier in one representation than in another—for example, the intersection of sets represented with bit strings is simply a logical AND operation, while iteration over a set is easier when it is represented as a linked list. Some implementations may not even be applicable in a given case (e.g., bit strings require that the domain of set elements be fixed and reasonably small, since one bit position is used for each possible element). Also, some representations may not permit all needed operations (e.g., the only way to enumerate the items in a set represented with property markings is to go through all the data in the system looking for ones with the appropriate property markings). By tailoring the representation to the particular programmer's intention, it is possible to produce much better code.

One such system that performs data-structure selection for the user is described by Low (1974, 1978). This system handles simple programs written in LEAP, a sublanguage of SAIL (Article VI.C4). It selects representations for sets, sequences, and relations from the fixed library of low-level data structures available in LEAP. The selection is guided by the goal of minimizing the product of the memory and time required to execute the resulting program.

Low's system begins with an information-gathering phase that searches out the relevant characteristics of the program's data structures, such as their expected size, their number, the operations performed on them, and their interactions. Some of this information is obtained by questioning the user and some by monitoring the actual execution of the program on typical data, with default representations for each structure. Then the system partitions into equivalence classes the variables whose values will be of the same type of data structure. The system employs a method similar to *hill climbing* to determine a (locally) optimal assignment of data structures to the equivalence classes (i.e., the representations assigned to the equivalence classes are repeatedly varied, one at a time, to see if an improvement will result).

Other AP systems are also concerned with the selection of an efficient set of data structures or file structures, but this concern is part of the general goal of writing an efficient program (see Articles X.D6 and X.D8).

Traditional Problem Solving

Traditional problem solving refers to using subgoals to direct the application of operations in a *problem-reduction space* (see Chap. II, in Vol. I). The Heuristic Compiler (Simon, 1972) regards the task of writing a program as a problem-solving process that applies heuristic techniques, like those of GPS (Article II.D2, in Vol. I). This pioneering work recognized the value of both a *state language*, to describe problem states and goals, and a *process language*, to represent the solver's actions.

In the Heuristic Compiler, the *State Description Compiler* is quite similar to later work on synthesis from examples. The program being synthesized is defined by specifying input/output conditions on the memory cells that it affects. The difference between the current state and the desired state is looked up in a table that specifies which operators to apply to transform the contents of the cells appropriately. The *Functional Description Compiler* is an important precursor to later work in automatic modification and debugging of programs. It uses a means-ends analysis to transform a known (compiled) routine into a new (desired) routine.

HACKER, a system built by Sussman (1975), adds to Simon's work, detecting and generalizing new differences (bugs) and defining appropriate operators to resolve them (patches). This system uses many significant AI techniques and language features: learning through practice how to write and debug programs; modular, pattern-invoked expert procedures (chunks of procedural knowledge); and hypothetical world models for subgoal analysis. Sussman's emphasis on generalizing from experience (trying old techniques in new situations), acceptance of the fact that users have an incomplete understanding of the desired program, and his goal-purpose annotation technique are all interesting directions in the development of automatic programming and *learning* systems (see Article XIV.D5c, in Vol. III).

However, HACKER's preference for ruthless generation of "buggy" code without detailed planning led to inadequate handling of subgoal conflicts. Training sequences had to be carefully ordered and, even so, the system exhaustively searched its base of world facts and programming knowledge. Such systems must constrain the problem of searching large knowledge bases. Other attempts to distribute knowledge among interacting specialists have encountered the same difficulty (Lenat, 1975).

Systems such as HACKER, which have been designed to operate like human programmers, promise a moderate degree of success compared to knowledge-impoverished formal methods. However, these systems are still often hampered by the rigid formalism that governs their application: In what order are operators to be applied? How can domain-specific information be specified as differences? The formalisms used to incorporate the various knowledge sources in these systems seem too methodical; the method is space and time bound because it is based on search.

Induction

Induction, or inductive inference, is the system's "educated guess" at what the user wants on the basis of program specifications that only partially describe the program's behavior. Such specifications are often the examples of input/output pairs and the program traces, in both regular and generic form (see Article X.B). For each of these kinds of specification, the corresponding AP system must determine the general rules on the basis of a specification that contains only a few examples (or in the generic specifications, a limited class of examples) of the program behavior.

The work in program synthesis from examples had its origin in research dealing with *grammatical inference*, in which the objective was to infer a grammar that described a language, given several examples of strings of the language (Feldman et al., 1969; Biermann and Feldman, 1970). In a natural way, this research was associated with the inference of finite-state machines from the sequence (string) of states that the machine passes through during execution. The association was natural in that finite-state machines are intimately related to the grammar that generates the strings of states representing legal behavior of the machine (Biermann and Krishnaswamy, 1974;

also Article IV.C1). This research opened up two new avenues of investigation in automatic programming: synthesis from examples and synthesis from traces.

The crucial issue for program synthesis from examples is the development of a generalized program, that is, one that can account for more than the examples given in the program specification. To do this, these programs break down the input, looking for recursively solvable subparts (Shaw, Swartout, and Green, 1975) or computation repetitions that can be fitted into a known program scheme (Hardy, 1975).

The work in program synthesis from trace specifications seeks to invert the transformations observed in a trace protocol to create abstractions that generalize into loops and variables (Bauer, 1975). Of all the induction-based synthesis paradigms, this is the one that is closest to grammatical inference. Biermann and Krishnaswamy (1974) have built a system that interprets traces as directions through a developing flowchart. Phillips (1977) has implemented a system for the inference of very high level program descriptions from a mixture of traces and example pairs in the context of a large automatic-programming system (see Article X.D1).

All inductive inference systems rely on a good *axiomatization of operations*. In other words, the system must know about all the possible primitive operations that can be applied to the data structures if it is to construct, by composition of these primitives, the desired program. Furthermore, a harmonious relation between the nature of the constructs in the specification and the most basic constructs in the target language is essential; for example, in Siklossy and Sykes (1975), the tasks of tree traversal and repetitive robot maneuvers are directly translatable into LISP recursion. Moreover, these programs are required to know quite a bit about generalization. After synthesizing the program, they test it on other examples, sometimes by generating test cases and sometimes by asking the user for approval.

The importance of induction from examples and from traces lies in the fact that, for certain classes of programs, examples and traces provide a natural way for the user to specify what the desired program is to do. These induction techniques are described in more detail below.

Program Induction from Examples of Input/Output Pairs

The synthesis of programs from a specification consisting of instances of input/output pairs strongly depends on the problem domain to which these programs belong (e.g., sorting, concept formation). A set of *program schemas* characterizes the entire class of programs for the domain. These schemas are like program skeletons and define the general structure of a program, omitting some details. The synthesis of a program thus amounts to (a) selecting a given schema that is representative of the program specified by the set of example pairs and then (b) using the information present in the examples to instantiate the unfilled *slots* of the schema. Thus, there are two steps:

a *classification* process, which selects the general structure (schema) of the target program, and an *instantiation* process, which completes the details of the target program.

What does the classification process require? Every schema defines a subclass of programs in the problem domain. Every set of example pairs defines a family of programs in the domain. Thus, the classification process must associate this set of example pairs with one of the subclasses of programs in the domain. To accomplish this task, a set of characteristics is associated with each schema (subclass) that, if present in the set of example pairs, guarantees that the set specifies a program of this type. Usually this task is accomplished by (a) providing a set of *difference measures* to be applied to the inputs and outputs of an example pair, as well as to different example pairs in the input collection (if it consists of more than one), and (b) providing a set of heuristics for each program schema that determine a *fit* measure of the example set that accompanies it. The task of classifying the example set is then reduced to choosing the schema with the highest value for fit.

During the instantiation process, in addition to the difference and fit metrics described above, every schema has an associated set of rules for filling its empty slots through the extraction of necessary features from the examples. For instance, in the domain of list-manipulation functions, cases in which the output list contains all elements in the input and cases where the output list contains only every other element, and so on, suggest different methods of constructing the output incrementally from the input. In the first case, the function maps down the input list; in the second case, it maps down the input with the LISP CDDR function. Slots are instantiated by these rules in terms of primitive operators of the domain and their functional compositions (in the above case, the basic LISP functions and their compositions).

Once a schema has been selected and instantiated, the synthesis algorithm must *validate* its hypothesis. This task is usually done either by generating some new examples for the program, evaluating the synthesized program on the example set, and checking the results with the user, or by presenting the program to the user and letting him (or her) verify its correctness.

In summary, the basic algorithm is as follows:

1. Apply the difference measures to the example set;

2. Based on this application, classify the set into a particular schema class;

3. Using heuristics associated with the particular schema, hypothesize a complete instantiation of the selected schema;

4. Validate this hypothesis.

In this basic algorithm, if there is a single input/output pair in the specification, the difference measures are just a set of feature-detecting heuristics. If there are more than one pair, the pairs may be ordered according to the complexity of the input. Difference measures will fall into two classes: those that associate the structure of a pair with a schema class and those that find differences between pairs. The latter are perhaps more crucial in the inference of a program. From these differences, a theory for the operation of the program is inductively inferred or, what is the same, a formation rule is derived. This operational theory might take the form of a certain schema class or of a recurrence equation that, in turn, specifies a schema class. In the classification phase it may be necessary to apply the classification rule to all pairs to infer the corresponding schema correctly. When several different schemas have been inferred, a decision rule is required to select the correct one.

An alternate approach is to reduce the whole problem to another paradigm for synthesizing programs. For example, if the problem domain has been formalized, so that there is a set of operators for the domain, it is possible to use a traditional problem solver to generate a solution to the input/output pair (considered as initial-state, goal-state) in the form of a sequence of operators that carry the input into the output. The solution so obtained can be considered a trace of the program to be synthesized and a trace-based paradigm may be employed (see below).

Specification by examples is suitable for synthesizing a program only in those cases where the task domain is small and easily axiomatized. It may also be a feasible approach in cases where the domain is repetitious enough that a small set of pairs is sufficient to specify the program, which is almost never the case in practical programming domains. Such a specification method tends to be quite limited and does not lend itself to useful generalization to large domains. Nevertheless, the power of examples for clarifying concepts is unquestionable. It seems that the main application that this specification formalism will have in future automatic-programming systems is restricted to the annotation and clarification of more formal program descriptions.

Program Induction from Traces

Inferring a program from a set of traces is, as mentioned earlier, very similar to inferring a description of a finite-state machine from a set of sequential states that the machine might pass through. The basic approach for synthesizing a program from a set of traces is to generate, in order of increasing complexity, the possible programs constructed from the programming-domain operators and tests and their functional compositions and then, after each new program is generated, to validate the given traces against the program. If the generated program accounts for the traces, it is the required solution. Notice that some kind of complexity measure is needed for the enumeration, such as program size (e.g., number of instructions in the program).

This basic approach suffers from the problems inherent to search in a large search space and thus admits improvement, in the form of reduction of the combinatorial explosion, by the use of heuristics to prune and guide the search process. It is thus not generally practical and suited only to the inference of small programs in very simple domains. Nevertheless, it has been applied with moderate success to the inference of programs from memory traces. Usually consisting of register assignments, tests, and memory-modification instructions, such programs and their traces are not very complex. Programs as complex as Hoare's FIND algorithm have been synthesized in this manner (Petry and Biermann, 1976). Though these systems tend to be knowledge impoverished, Phillips (1977) incorporates a methodology to compensate for this by utilizing problem-domain knowledge in the inference process. There are certain other special inference paradigms for particular classes of traces.

Program inference from protocols. Usually, traces mix information about operations applied to data objects, results of tests as to whether predicates hold at certain points during program execution, state snapshots of data values, and other information. Different classes of traces arise if restrictions are placed on the kind of information that may appear in them. *Protocols* are one such class, in which only operation applications and data-structure changes may appear and in which there is no information about control decisions that have been taken during the particular program execution reflected in the trace. An example of a typical protocol for a function that reverses a list would be:

```
input X
X = (A B C)
Y = (A)
X = (B C)
Y = (B A)
X = (C)
Y = (C B A)
output Y
```

Notice that the only information present in the protocol is operation applications and variable-state changes. All control information is omitted.

The inference of a program from a collection of protocols involves two phases: (a) constructing a program description that captures the nature of a program that could have generated a subset of the input protocols and then (b) modifying the program description as more protocols become available in order to validate them.

A natural algorithm would then be to hypothesize, by some feature-classification process or with the aid of a domain knowledge base, an initial description and debug it by forcing a unification of the protocol family with the description. The construction of the initial program description can be described as follows:

1. Match the protocols; that is, find common segments as well as differences by matching their structure.

2. Find substitutions that unify these protocols. Protocols may differ in variables that have different names, in the same data objects (at the same place in the protocols) having different values, and in differences in the operations that occur. The matching phase produces a set of such differences. The substitution phase finds substitutions that remove these differences. For example, if two protocols refer with different variable names to the same data object, this phase would propose a common name for the two variables. Such substitutions usually take the form: *constant* → *variable* or *variable-name* → *variable-name*.

3. Inductively form loops by detecting repeated equivalent subprotocols. Loop formation is the basic inductive step of this approach. For example,

```
protocol string: A B C D A B C D.
hypothesized loop:
                while <condition>
                do begin
                    A;
                    B;
                    C;
                    D;
                end;
```

Since there are infinitely many loop hypotheses for a given protocol, one of the tasks of the system designer is to provide a good set of heuristics to guide the search process during loop formation. For example, one such possible heuristic could be to consider first the loops with minimal nesting level.

4. Generalize remaining constants to variables.

At this stage, then, a description has been generated where all data-object snapshots have an associated variable name and where loop structures in the program have been inferred. The result of this matching, unification, and abstraction (generalization) process is a *semantic-net* representation of the program.

The next stage is to verify that the hypothesized program description agrees with any additional protocols and, if this is not the case, to modify it. This correction (debugging) phase can be described as follows:

1. Try to validate new protocols against the program representation—that is, to *symbolically execute* the program description to see if it can account for the given protocol.

2. Find any differences between predicted and actual protocol. The process of symbolic evaluation generates a set of differences that are due to the protocol's not matching the program description. This set of differences suggests the kinds of modifications that must be made to the description.

3. Form a theory for the difference; that is, hypothesize a suitable change to the program description that removes the particular difference. One way of accomplishing this is to use a classification process similar to the basic algorithm for inference from examples.

4. Modify the program representation accordingly.

This synthesis paradigm works only for complete protocols, that is, protocols in which all data-structure changes appear explicitly. Phillips (1977) has proposed a procedure for handling incomplete protocols in a unified framework for synthesis from examples and synthesis from traces or protocols. This procedure is basically as follows: For those segments of a protocol in which operations are missing, that is, in which two states of a data structure appear without intervening operations, the examples component of the system infers a piece of program description (i.e., a sequence of operations) that can take the data object from one state to the other. This program description is nothing but the sequence of missing operation applications. Merging all such sequences with the original incomplete protocol transforms it into a complete protocol, and the algorithm given above for dealing with complete protocols can be used.

Problem-solver-generated traces. If the domain is fully axiomatized, as may be the case for simple domains like those for robots, it may be possible to synthesize programs from example pairs by using a problem solver that produces a solution to the input pair in the form of a trace:

1. With the problem solver, synthesize a trace from an example pair.

2. Using the trace, a set of program schemas for the domain, and a set of schema-selection and schema-instantiation heuristics that operate on trace steps, produce a program in terms of domain operators and domain predicates that explain the example pair.

All these paradigms work only for complete traces and protocols. The problem of program inference from incomplete specifications is still under investigation. It is possible that the techniques outlined may be extended to cover the incomplete case by coupling the program synthesizer to a domain-based theory-formation module that could, so to speak, fill in the missing elements from the original specification. At this point, then, the methodology discussed above could be used.

Traces have the limitations inherent in informal program specifications, namely, the difficulty of specifying the required program uniquely with respect to the limited amount of information conveyed to the synthesizer. Thus, the problem of choosing a good description is left, as a burden, to the user. This problem might be alleviated by providing greater domain expertise—to produce the program that more nearly resembles the user's desired result.

Traces, and informal specification methods in general, promise to be useful for algorithm description and correction in future automatic-programming systems. The reason is clearly that these methods reflect closely the form in which humans understand and describe programs.

References

For theorem proving, see Green (1969), Waldinger and Levitt (1974), Kowalski (1977), and Clark and Sickel (1977); for program transformation, Darlington and Burstall (1973) and Wegbreit (1975a); for knowledge engineering, Martin (1974), Lenat (1975), Biggerstaff (1976), Sussman (1975), and Green (1977); for automatic data selection, Low (1978); for traditional problem solving, Simon (1972) and Sussman (1975); for induction from input/output pairs, Amarel (1972), Green (1975a), Hardy (1975), Shaw, Swartout, and Green (1975), Siklossy and Sykes (1975), and Summers (1977); for induction from traces, Bauer (1975), Biermann (1972a, 1976a), Petry and Biermann (1976), Phillips (1977), and Siklossy and Sykes (1975); and for induction from examples, Biermann and Feldman (1970) and Feldman, Gips, Horning, and Reder (1969).

D. AUTOMATIC PROGRAMMING SYSTEMS

D1. PSI and CHI

THE PSI system was developed by Cordell Green and his colleagues at Stanford University and at Systems Control, Inc. The design goal of PSI was the integration of the more specialized methods of automatic programming into a total system. This system, then, would incorporate knowledge engineering, model acquisition, program synthesis, efficiency analysis, and specification by examples, traces, or interactive natural-language dialogue. The research was directed toward determining the organization of such a system, the amount and type of knowledge such a system would require, and the representation of this knowledge. This research is continuing at the Kestrel Institute in Palo Alto where a successor system, CHI, has been developed by Green and his colleagues to extend the work in the direction of a supportive programming environment (see below).

PSI

In PSI, a program is specified by means of an interactive, *mixed-initiative dialogue*, which may include partial specifications by examples of input/output pairs or by traces (see Article X.B). It is planned also to allow program specification by means of a loose, very high level language. When the specification method is an interactive dialogue, the user furnishes both a description of what the desired program is to do and an indication of the overall control structure of the program.

The PSI system deals with programs in the general class of symbolic computation, including list processing, searching and sorting, data storage and retrieval, and concept formation programs. It is a knowledge-based system organized as a set of closely interacting modules, called *experts*. At present, these experts are the following:

1. PARSER/INTERPRETER
2. DIALOGUE MODERATOR
3. EXPLAINER
4. EXAMPLE/TRACE INFERENCE
5. TASK DOMAIN
6. PROGRAM–MODEL BUILDER
7. CODING
8. EFFICIENCY.

The overall operation of the system, illustrated in Figure D1–1, may be divided into two phases: (a) acquisition of a specification of the desired program and (b) synthesis of the program code. During the acquisition phase, several modules of the system—including the PARSER/INTERPRETER, EXPLAINER, DIALOGUE MODERATOR, and EXAMPLE/TRACE INFERENCE—will jointly interact with the user to construct a network data structure, called the *program net*, that describes the desired program. Then the PROGRAM–MODEL BUILDER module converts the net into a complete, consistent description of the program, called the *program model*. Afterwards, during the synthesis phase, the CODING and EFFICIENCY modules, interacting with each other, convert the program model, through repeated transformations, into an efficient implementation in the target language.

There were three reasons for separating the operation into acquisition and synthesis phases. First, the problems of designing such a system are more tractable with such a separation. Second, it was thought that code generators for different target languages and domain experts for different problem areas could be implemented to achieve a versatile, modular system. Third, acquisition requires interaction with the user, whereas, in PSI, synthesis does not.

In the overall operation, two of the primary interfaces within the PSI system are the *program net* and the *program model*. Both are very high level languages for describing programs and data structures. The program net forms a looser description of the program than does the program model. Fragments of the program net can be accessed in order of occurrence in the dialogue, rather than in order of eventual execution, which allows a less detailed, local, and partial specification of the program. Since these fragments correspond rather closely to what the user says, they ease the burden of the PARSER/INTERPRETER as well as of the EXAMPLE/TRACE INFERENCE module. The PROGRAM–MODEL BUILDER, on the other hand, includes complete, consistent, and interpretable, very high level algorithmic and information structures.

The remainder of this article describes briefly the PSI modules and then goes through several examples (Figs. D1–2 through D1–5) of the acquisition phase, including a specification by interactive natural-language dialogue, showing the resulting program net and program model, and a specification by trace.

The PARSER/INTERPRETER expert. In the acquisition phase, the PARSER/INTERPRETER expert (Ginsparg, 1978) first parses sentences and then interprets these parses into less linguistic and more program-oriented terms, which are then stored in the program net. This expert efficiently handles a very large English grammar and has knowledge about data structures (sets, records, etc.), control structures (loops, conditionals, procedures, etc.), and more complicated algorithm ideas (interchanges between the user and the desired program, set construction, quantification, etc.). It can sometimes

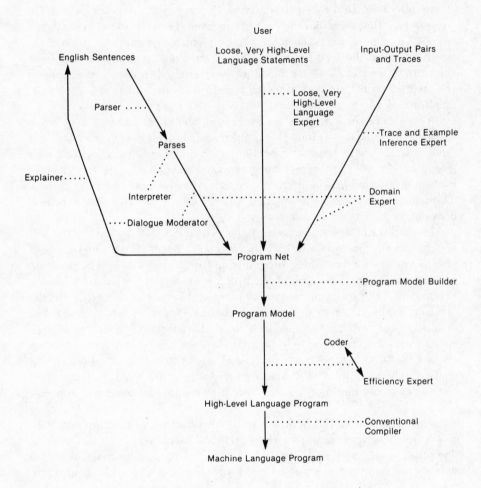

Figure D1–1.   Major paths of information flow in PSI.

assign a concept to an unknown word on the basis of the context in which the word appears.

The DIALOGUE MODERATOR expert. This expert (Steinberg, 1980) models the user, the dialogue, and the state of the system and selects appropriate questions and statements to present to the user. It also determines whether the user or the system has the initiative, and at what level on what subject, and attempts to keep PSI and the user in agreement on the current topic. It provides review and preview when the topic changes. The DIALOGUE MODERATOR decides which of the many questions being asked by the other experts should be passed on to the user. Since experts phrase questions in an internal form based on relations, the DIALOGUE MODERATOR expert gives questions to the EXPLAINER expert, which, in turn, converts them into English and presents them to the user.

The EXPLAINER expert. The EXPLAINER expert, developed by Richard Gabriel (1981), phrases questions in terms that the user finds meaningful, that is, in terms related to the problem domain and the previous sentences in the dialogue, rather than the more programming-oriented terms of the program net or the model builder. For example, rather than asking for the definition of "A0018," PSI asks what it means for "a trial set to fit a concept" (see Fig. D1-2). The EXPLAINER also generates English descriptions of the program net.

The EXAMPLE/TRACE expert. PSI also allows specification by traces and examples, since these are useful for inferring data structures and simple spatial transformations. This expert, developed by Jorge Phillips (1977), handles simple loop and data structure inference and incorporates several of the techniques discussed in Articles X.B and X.C (see also the example below).

The TASK DOMAIN expert. The TASK DOMAIN expert, also developed by Phillips, uses knowledge of the application area to help the PARSER/INTERPRETER and EXAMPLE/TRACE experts fill in missing information in the program net.

The PROGRAM–MODEL BUILDER expert. The PROGRAM–MODEL BUILDER (McCune, 1977) applies knowledge of what constitutes a correct program to the conversion of the program net into a complete and consistent program model, which then will be transformed during the synthesis phase into the target-language implementation. The PROGRAM–MODEL BUILDER completes the model by filling in the various pieces of required information and by analyzing the model for consistency; it checks to see that the model's parts are legal both with respect to each other and with respect to the semantics of the program-modeling language. Information is filled in by default, by inference mechanisms (which are in the form of rules and make use of consistency requirements), or by queries to other experts, which may eventually result in a query to the user.

For example, suppose that the program net contains "x part of y" and that the PROGRAM–MODEL BUILDER needs to fill in whether "part of" is to mean set membership, subset inclusion, component of y, or the image of x under some correspondence relation with y, or whether there might be an unspecified intervening subpart. Such information may be deducible from the structures of x and y, if and when these structures become known.

The PROGRAM–MODEL BUILDER also corrects minor inconsistencies, adds cross-references, and generalizes parts of the program description so that the synthesis phase has more freedom in looking for a good implementation. Thus, if the program net specifies that a certain object is to be a set of ordered pairs, the program model may, if appropriate, indicate that the object is to be a correspondence (i.e., a functional mapping).

The CODING and EFFICIENCY experts. These two experts are responsible for the synthesis phase (Barstow and Kant, 1977). The CODING expert's knowledge base contains rules that transform parts of a program description to forms closer to the target language. It is the goal of the EFFICIENCY expert to guide the choice of the different rules, so that an efficient target-language implementation eventually results. These two experts, also known as the systems PECOS and LIBRA, are discussed in detail separately in Articles X.D4 and X.D8, respectively.

Example of Specification by Interactive Dialogue

Figure D1–2 illustrates an interactive, natural-language dialogue held with the PSI system in which the user specifies a simple program, to be called CLASS. It includes many programming constructs necessary for more complex programs.

The user intends that the CLASS program input a sample set of items (e.g., a list of job qualifications) and then repeatedly input a trial set (e.g., the qualifications of an applicant), each time testing whether the sample set is a subset of the trial set and printing "FIT" or "DIDN'T FIT," accordingly. The user further intends that a person will be able to terminate CLASS simply by typing the word "QUIT," instead of a new trial set.

Based on its understanding of the dialogue, the PARSER/INTERPRETER expert produces the program net, which is summarized in Figure D1–3 (the algorithmic part of the net is shown in an ALGOL-like notation). Then the PROGRAM–MODEL BUILDER expert creates the very high level, complete, and consistent model of Figure D1–4. After repeated application of transformation rules during the synthesis phase, the CODING and EFFICIENCY experts will convert this model into an efficient target-language implementation.

An Example of Program Specification by Trace

Traces are another method of specification allowed by the PSI system. Figure D1–5 shows the use of a trace to specify part of the behavior of

What is the name of the program you want to write?
** CLASS.

Does CLASS have a special program type?
** Classification.

Please describe CLASS.
** CLASS first inputs a concept. Then it repeatedly accepts an
   input trial set from the user, classifies it based on whether
   or not it fits the concept, and outputs this classification to
   the user.

What is the structure of the concept?
** A concept is a collection of relations. Each relation is just
   a string.

What is the exit test of the loop?
** Stop when the user types "QUIT" instead of a trial set.

What is the structure of the trial set?
** The same as the concept.

Please define what it means for a trial set to fit a concept.
** A trial set fits a concept if all the relations in the concept
   are in the trial set.

What is the format of the classification output?
** Output "FIT" if the trial set fit, "DIDN'T FIT" if it didn't.

Are we finished?
** Yes.

Figure D1–2.   Specification by interactive natural-language dialogue: CLASS.

a program called TF ("Theory Formation"—a simplified version of Patrick
Winston's concept-formation program; see Winston, 1975). TF builds and
updates an internal model of a concept. A concept is a collection of "may" and
"must" conditions. TF builds and updates the model by repeatedly reading
in a trial set, guessing whether the trial set is an instance of the concept,

```
A2 is either a set whose generic element is a string
   or a string whose value is "QUIT."
A1 is a set whose generic element is a string.
A4 is the generic element of A1.
A3 is either TRUE or FALSE.


B1 is a variable bound to A2.
B2 is a variable bound to A1.
B3 is a variable bound to A4.



CLASS
  PRINT("Ready for the CONCEPT")
  A1 ← READ()
LOOP1:
  PRINT("Ready for the TRIAL SET")
  A2 ← READ()
  IF EQUAL(A2,"QUIT") THEN GOTO EXIT1
  A3 ← FIT(A2,A1)
  CASES: IF A3 THEN PRINT("FIT")
    ELSE IF NOT(A3) THEN PRINT("DIDN'T FIT")
  GOTO LOOP1

EXIT1:

FIT(B1,B2)
  FORALL B3 IMPLIES(MEMBER(B3,B2),MEMBER(B3,B1))
```

Figure D1–3.   Summary of the program net.

verifying with the person using TF whether the guess was correct or incorrect, and updating the model of the concept accordingly. The trace in Figure D1–5 shows the specification for only a part of the behavior of TF, the part that describes how TF is to update the model, given that a trial set does or does not fit a concept. The other parts of TF can be specified by trace or by natural-language dialogue. From this specification, the EXAMPLE/TRACE INFERENCE expert generates the following information about the desired program: If the trial set fits the concept, add to the concept all relations in the trial set but not present in the concept and mark them with "may." Otherwise, if the trial set does not fit the concept, change the marking of all relations marked "may" in the concept and not appearing in the trial set from "may" to "must."

```
program CLASS ;
   type
      a0032 : set of string ,
      a0053 : alternative of [string = "QUIT" , a0032] ;
   vars
      a0011 , a0014 , a0035 , a0036 : a0032 ,
      a0055 , m0080 : a0053 ,
      m0095 : string = "DIDN'T FIT" ,
      m0092 : string = "FIT" ,
      m0091 : Boolean ,
      m0081 : string = "QUIT" ;
   procedure a0067(a0036 , a0035 : a0032) : Boolean ;
      a0035 ⊂ a0036 ;
   procedure a0065(a0055 : a0053) : Boolean ;
      a0055 = "QUIT" ;
   begin
      a0011 ← input(a0032 , user , "READY FOR CONCEPT" ,
      "Illegal input. Input again: ") ;
      until A0051
      repeat
         begin
         m0080 ← input(a0053 , user , "READY" , "Illegal input. Input again: ");
         if a0065(m0080) then assert-exit-condition(A0051) ;
            a0014 ← m0080 ;
            m0091 ← a0067(a0014 , a0011) ;
            case
               ¬ m0091 : inform-user("DIDN'T FIT") ;
                 m0091 : inform-user("FIT") ;
            endcase
         end
      finally
      A0051 :
      endloop
   end ;
```

Figure D1-4.   The program model.

Work on the PSI system, which included developing a fully operational
system that could produce LISP code from some English specifications, has led
to the design and implementation of the CHI knowledge-based programming
system at the Kestrel Institute. Automatic-programming research in general,

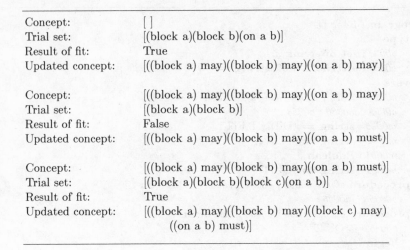

Concept:	[ ]
Trial set:	[(block a)(block b)(on a b)]
Result of fit:	True
Updated concept:	[((block a) may)((block b) may)((on a b) may)]
Concept:	[((block a) may)((block b) may)((on a b) may)]
Trial set:	[(block a)(block b)]
Result of fit:	False
Updated concept:	[((block a) may)((block b) may)((on a b) must)]
Concept:	[((block a) may)((block b) may)((on a b) must)]
Trial set:	[(block a)(block b)(block c)(on a b)]
Result of fit:	True
Updated concept:	[((block a) may)((block b) may)((block c) may) ((on a b) must)]

Figure D1–5.   A specification by trace.

including the PSI project, has concentrated on methods for compiling programs expressed in a very high level language. The goal in CHI is to provide not only a knowledge-based synthesis system, but also a supportive, high-level programming environment that includes knowledge-based specification acquisition, consistency checking, debugging, editing, and maintenance. In fact, the idea of a programming environment has been extended to include tools for aiding the human interactions necessary for the management of programming projects. The CHI system uses a common knowledge base about the programming process to support all of these activities.

The CHI knowledge-based programming environment emphasizes the use of a very high level, wide-spectrum language called "V" for specifying both programs and programming knowledge and for interacting with the programming environment. The V language includes constructs for sets, mappings, relations, predicates, enumerations, state-transformation sequences, program-synthesis rules, and control meta-rules. Rules are expressed more cleanly in CHI than in PSI.

One design goal is that CHI be a very adaptable and extensible environment. To this end, a self-description of the CHI environment itself is being produced in its own high-level language V. This high-level self-description is useful not only for self-compilation but also for modifying and extending the environment itself. In particular, the rule-compiler portion of CHI has been described in V, and CHI has compiled this description into efficient code. The compact, high-level description of the rule compiler is more easily comprehended, and is manipulable by the environment itself and so is more easily reasoned about, extended, or modified.

Research has progressed in developing program-refinement rules for handling data-structure selection and enumeration constructs and in producing concurrent programs from very high level program descriptions. A new research emphasis is on building tools for the more complex and creative part of the programming process, namely, algorithm design. An example of a powerful and frequently useful principle for structuring algorithm derivations is the incorporation of constraints or other operators into generators. Methods for incorporating constraints have been codified and applied to produce hand derivations of several prime-finding and shortest-path algorithms. Some of the methods were formalized and introduced into the CHI knowledge base and used in derivations of an efficient program for finding even, perfect-square numbers.

Key contributors to CHI, besides the project leader, Cordell Green, have been Jorge Phillips, who developed the philosophy of adaptable, self-described environments and shaped the V language and the knowledge base; Stephen Westfold, who implemented a structure-based editor for V and described the rule compiler in high-level V; Beverly Kedzierski, who is developing the project-management and communication aspect of the environment; Steve Tappel, who developed principles of algorithm design and applied them to diverse algorithms; and Tom Pressburger, who implemented some of those principles in CHI and developed a self-description of the knowledge base.

References

A short summary of the PSI work is given in Green et al. (1979). More detailed discussions of PSI are Green (1976b, 1977) and Green and Barstow (1977a); see also Barstow (1977a), Barstow and Kant (1977), Gabriel (1981), Green and Barstow (1978), Kant (1977), McCune (1977), and Phillips (1977).

A very short overview of the CHI research is found in Green et al. (1981a). A collection of reports that describe the research in more detail is found in Green et al. (1981b). The self-description of the rule compiler is found in Green and Westfold (1982). The project-management and communication-support aspect is presented in Kedzierski (1982).

D2. SAFE

THE SAFE system, developed at the Information Sciences Institute (ISI) of the University of Southern California by Robert Balzer, Neil Goldman, David Wile, and Charles Williams, accepts a program specification consisting of preparsed English, with limited syntax and vocabulary, including terms from the problem domain. The phrases and sentences of this specification, however, may be ambiguous and may fail to provide explicitly all the information required in a formal program specification. Therefore, using a large number of built-in constraints (which must be satisfied by any well-formed program), any specified constraints from the problem domain, and an occasional interaction with the user, SAFE resolves ambiguities, fills in missing pieces of information, and produces a high-level, complete program specification. To decide on missing pieces of information, SAFE employs a variety of techniques, including *backtracking* and a form of *symbolic execution.*

The SAFE system views the task of automatic programming as the production of a program from a description of the desired *behavior* of that program. There are four major differences between a conventionally specified program (a list of instructions for a "machine" to "execute") and a program described in terms of its desired behavior.

1. *Informality:* The behavioral description is informal. It has ambiguities (alternative interpretations yielding distinct behaviors) and "partial" constructs (constructs with missing pieces of information that must be supplied before any interpretation is possible). A conventionally specified program, on the other hand, is formal; its meaning is completely and unambiguously defined by the semantics of the programming language.

2. *Vocabulary:* The primitive terms in the behavioral description are those of the problem domain. General-purpose programming languages, on the other hand, provide a primitive vocabulary that is independent of particular problem areas.

3. *Executability:* Informality aside, it is possible, and sometimes desirable, to describe behavior in terms of relationships between the desired and the achieved states of a process, rather than by rules that specify how to obtain the desired state. Conventionally specified programs must give an algorithm for reaching the desired state.

4. *Efficiency:* Conventionally specified programs contain many details of operation beyond the desired input/output behavior. Among these are data representation, internal communication protocols, store-recompute decisions, and so forth, that affect a program's efficiency (utilization of time and computer resources). In general, these details do not appear in the description of the program's input/output behavior.

When one writes a program in the conventional manner, one must formalize the behavioral specification, translate the terms of the problem domain into those of a general programming language, guarantee that the specified algorithms actually achieve the desired results, and make a myriad of decisions for the sake of an efficient implementation.

The ISI group has attempted to split the task of creating a program into two separate parts by designing a formal, complete specification language (Balzer and Goldman, 1979) that allows behavioral specifications to be stated in terms specific to the problem domain while avoiding efficiency and representational concerns. This formal specification language acts as an interface between one project that deals with the first issue, translation from informal to formal specifications, and a second project that deals with the last issue, optimization of a formal specification. The former project is the subject of this article, while the latter is described elsewhere (Balzer, Goldman, and Wile, 1976). The issues of domain-specific vocabulary and executability are addressed within the formal specification language.

The SAFE project has concentrated on only the first of these specification issues: producing automatically a formal description from an informal description. It is not, therefore, a complete automatic-programming system. The user of the SAFE system provides a behavioral description in a preparsed, limited subset of English, including terms from the problem area. SAFE then seeks to determine a way of resolving all ambiguities and of filling in all missing information in a way that satisfies the system's knowledge of the constraints that all programs must satisfy. The result is a complete, unambiguous, very high level program specification in a language called AP2.

Partial Descriptions

After studying many examples of program specifications that had been written in English, the SAFE research group concluded that the main semantic difference between these specifications and their formal equivalents is that partial descriptions rather than complete descriptions were used. When such partial descriptions were used, it was because the missing information could be determined from the surrounding context. These partial descriptions have some of the useful properties of natural-language specifications that are lacking in formal languages. They focus both the writer's and the reader's attention on the relevant issues and condense the specification. Furthermore, the extensive use of context almost totally eliminates bookkeeping operations from the natural-language specification.

A partial description may have zero, one, or more valid interpretations in a given context. If a single valid interpretation is found for a description, it is unambiguous in that context. Multiple valid interpretations indicate that there is not sufficient information from the context to complete the description and that interaction with the user is required to resolve the ambiguity. If a partial description has no valid interpretation, it is inconsistent within the existing context.

The SAFE system allows the most prevalent forms of partial descriptions encountered in natural-language specifications:

1. *Partial sequencing:* Operations are not always described in the order of execution. While sequencing may sometimes be described explicitly, it is frequently implicit in the relationships between operations. Example: "Output generated while compiling is sent to a scratch file. This file must be opened in *write only* mode." (The file should, of course, be opened before compiling commences.)

2. *Missing operands:* The operands of operations are frequently omitted because they are recoverable from context. Recovering them may involve considering the operation's definition, other operands, and the procedural context. Example: "Do not mount a tape for a job unless the tape drive has been assigned" (to that job).

3. *Incomplete reference:* A description of an object may match several objects, whereas it was intended to refer to only one or possibly a subset of these objects. A complete description may be recovered by methods similar to the one for missing operands. Example: "When the mail program starts, it opens the file named MESSAGE" (in the directory of the job running the program).

4. *Type coercions:* Often, people using natural language do not precisely specify the object intended but instead specify an associated object or a subpart of an object. This situation can be recognized by a mismatch between the type of object actually specified and the type of object expected. Example: "Information messages are copied to each logged-in user" (i.e., to the terminal of the job of each logged-in user).

Operation of SAFE—Constraints on Programs

The goal of SAFE is to complete the various partial descriptions in the user's specification to produce a formal specification of the desired program. SAFE goes through several phases, but in all phases the system applies a variety of constraints to complete the partial descriptions. These include the built-in criteria that any formal program must meet (e.g., information must be produced before it is consumed) and the built-in heuristics that "sensible" programs will meet (e.g., the value of a conditional must depend on the program data), as well as any known or discovered constraints particular to a program's domain (e.g., each file in a directory has a distinct name). In fact, since programs are highly constrained objects, there are a large number of constraints that any "well-formed" program must satisfy, and this is one reason that programs are hard to write.

In general, each partial description has several different possible completions. Based on the partial description and the context in which it occurs, an ordered set of possible completions is created for it. But one decision cannot be made in isolation from the others; decisions must be consistent with each other and the resulting program must make sense as a whole, satisfying all the criteria for well-formed programs.

The problem of finding viable completions for a collection of partial descriptions provides a classical *backtracking* situation, since there are many related individual decisions that, in combination, can be either accepted or rejected on the basis of the constraints. SAFE utilizes the constraints so that early rejection possibilities can be realized.

The operation of SAFE consists of three sequential phases: linguistic, planning, and meta-evaluation. The cumulative effect of these phases is to produce a formal specification composed of declarative and procedural portions. The declarative part, or *domain model*, specifies the types of objects manipulated by the process, the different ways they may relate to each other, the actions that may be performed on various object types, and other global regularities of the problem domain. The procedural portion specifies the controlled application of actions to objects.

The *linguistic phase*, using production rules, transforms the parse trees of the English specification into fragments that retain the semantic content while discarding the syntactic detail. The production rules capture many context-sensitive aspects of natural language, such as the various uses of the verb *to be* and of quantifiers. The production rules may also add declarations to the domain model, with user approval, when this is required for interpretation of the input. This procedure is accomplished by distinguishing two sets of conditions on each rule: those relating to the linguistic form of the phrase being processed and those relating a form to the domain model. If the linguistic-form conditions are not satisfied (e.g., a clause with a transitive verb) but the domain-model conditions are (e.g., the verb names an action in the problem domain that has operands of types compatible with the verb arguments), the domain-model conditions are assumed.

The *planning phase* determines the overall sequencing of the operations in the program. It also determines which fragments belong together and how they are to interact. It does this by using explicit sequencing information in the description, such as *A is executed immediately after B* and *A is invoked whenever the condition C becomes true*, as well as static flow constraints on well-formed processes such as:

1. Before information is consumed (used by one fragment), it must be produced (created by the same or another fragment).

2. Expected outputs of the whole program or of a subprogram must be produced somewhere within that program.

3. The results of each described operation must be used or referenced somewhere.

The final phase, *meta-evaluation*, uses dynamic constraints to help determine the proper completion of partial descriptions. Dynamic constraints are those that apply, or at least relate, to the program during execution. Examples of such constraints are:

1. It must be possible (in general) to execute both branches of a conditional statement. (Otherwise, why would the user have specified a conditional?)

2. The constraints of a domain must not be violated.

Since no actual input data are available for testing the execution of the program and since the program must be well formed for all allowable inputs, inputs are represented symbolically. Instead of being actually executed, the program is symbolically executed on the inputs, which provides a much stronger test of the constraints than would execution on any particular set of inputs. The result is a database of relationships between the symbolic values and, implicitly, a database of relationships between program variables that are bound to these values.

All decisions concerning the proper interpretation of partial descriptions that affect the computation *to* some point in the execution (but not beyond) must be made before these dynamic criteria can be tested at that point in the execution. Thus, decisions are made as they are needed by the computation of the program, and the symbolic state of the program is examined at each stage of the computation. This arrangement allows the dynamic state-of-computation criteria to be used to obtain early rejection of infeasible alternatives.

There is a further point worth noting: Representing the complete state of a computation during symbolic execution is very difficult (e.g., it is quite hard to determine the state after execution of a loop or conditional statement) and more detailed than necessary for testing the constraints. Therefore, the SAFE system employs a weaker form of symbolic interpretation, meta-evaluation, which only partially determines the program's state as the computation proceeds (e.g., loops are executed only once for some "generic" element).

Notice that symbolic execution requires that the sequential relationships between the fragments be known; therefore, the meta-evaluation phase must follow the planning phase.

Finally, the global referencing constraints (e.g., the body of a procedure must make use of the procedure's parameters) test the overall use of names within the program and, thus, cannot be tested until all decisions have been made. These criteria can be tested only after the meta-evaluation is complete.

The prototype system has successfully handled the 75-to-200-word specifications of three quite distinct programs. In these cases, the SAFE output of a completed specification, including domain-structure definition, requires approximately two pages. One example concerned part of a system for scheduling transmissions in a communications network. Given a table containing entries for various network subscribers (SOL) and for various unassigned time slots (RATS), a schedule of absolute times when a particular subscriber could broadcast on the network was tabulated. The input specification to SAFE is shown in Figure D2–1.

```
((THE SOL)
 (IS SEARCHED)
 FOR
 (AN ENTRY FOR (THE SUBSCRIBER)))

(IF ((ONE)
     (IS FOUND))
    ((THE SUBSCRIBER'S (RELATIVE TRANSMISSION TIME))
     (IS COMPUTED) ACCORDING TO ("FORMULA-1")))

((THE SUBSCRIBER'S (CLOCK TRANSMISSION TIME))
 (IS COMPUTED) ACCORDING-TO ("FORMULA-2"))

(WHEN ((THE TRANSMISSION TIME)
       (HAS BEEN COMPUTED))
      ((IT)
       (IS INSERTED)
       AS (THE (PRIMARY ENTRY))
       IN (A (TRANSMISSION SCHEDULE))))

(FOR (EACH RATS ENTRY)
     (PERFORM)
     (: ((THE RATS'S (RELATIVE TRANSMISSION TIME))
         (IS COMPUTED) ACCORDING TO ("FORMULA-1"))
        ((THE RATS'S (CLOCK TRANSMISSION TIME))
         (IS COMPUTED) ACCORDING TO ("FORMULA-2"))))

((THE RATS (TRANSMISSION TIMES))
 (ARE ENTERED)
 INTO (THE SCHEDULE))
```

Figure D2–1.   Input (in preparsed English) for network
                         scheduler.

In formalizing this description, SAFE encountered and resolved the following characteristics of informal specifications:

Number of missing operands	= 7
Number of incomplete references	= 12
Number of implicit type-coercions	= 3
Number of implicit sequencing decisions	= 4

The robustness of the system has been increased by processing a number of perturbations of each of the major examples. These have involved specifying the same process but varying the syntax and vocabulary, the partial descriptions, and the formal knowledge about the problem domain.

Future Developments

The key technical restrictions of the prototype system appear to be (a) the sequential application of the three phases, which prohibits adequate interactions between the expertise embodied in each, and (b) the backtracking within the meta-evaluation phase, which corresponds to restarting the symbolic execution from an earlier point with much unnecessary search as a possible consequence. To correct these limitations, a reformulation of the SAFE system's architecture, along the lines of the HEARSAY–II speech-understanding system (see Article V.C1, in Vol. I), is currently in progress. This framework consists of a number of cooperating *knowledge sources* or experts interacting through a global *blackboard* database.

Simultaneously, the system is being scaled up to handle larger specifications (approximately 20 pages). Eventually, the project will consider the formalization of incremental informal specifications, so that it can also provide help during both specification formulation and maintenance activities.

References

See Balzer, Goldman, and Wile (1976, 1977, 1978) and Balzer and Goldman (1979).

D3.   The Programmer's Apprentice

THE PROGRAMMER'S APPRENTICE is an interactive system for helping
programmers with the task of programming. It is being designed and implemented at the Massachusetts Institute of Technology by Charles Rich, Howard
Shrobe, and Richard Waters. The intent of the Apprentice is that the programmer will do the difficult parts of design and implementation, while the
Apprentice will act as a junior partner and critic, keeping track of details
and assisting the programmer in the documentation, verification, debugging,
and modification of his (or her) program. To cooperate with the programmer
in this fashion, the Apprentice must be able to "understand" what is going
on. From the viewpoint of Artificial Intelligence, the central development of
the Programmer's Apprentice project has been the design of a representation,
called a *plan*, for programs and for knowledge about programming that serves
as the basis for this understanding. Developing plans and reasoning about
them are the central activity of the Programmer's Apprentice.

The plan for a program represents the program as a network of *operations*
connected by *links* explicitly representing data flow and control flow. The
advantage of this aspect of the plan formalism is that it is a level of abstraction
away from the specific syntactic constructs for control flow and data flow
used by various programming languages. The most novel aspect of the plan
formalism is that it goes beyond the specific level to create a vehicle for
expressing the *logical* relationships in a program, as follows.

First, a plan is not just a graph of primitive operations. Rather, it is
a hierarchy of segments within segments, where each segment corresponds
to a unit of behavior and has an input/output specification that describes
features of this behavior. The plan specifies how each nonterminal segment
is constructed from the segments contained within it. This segmentation is
important because it breaks the plan into localities that can be understood in
isolation from each other.

Second, the behavior of a segment is related to the behavior of its subsegments. This relationship is represented by explicit dependency links that
record the goal-subgoal and prerequisite relationships between the input/
output specification for a segment and those for its subsegments. Taken
together, the links summarize a proof of how these specifications for a segment follow from the specifications of its subsegments and from the way the
subsegments are connected by control flow and data flow.

A final aspect of the plan formalism is that there may be more than
one plan for a given segment of a program, with each plan representing a
different point of view on the segment. The data structures in a program are
represented by specifying their parts, their properties, and the relationships

between them in a method similar to *data abstraction* (Zilles, 1975; Liskov et al., 1977).

Knowledge about programming in general is also represented by plans and data-structure descriptions. This knowledge is stored in the Programmer's Apprentice in a database of common algorithms and data-structure implementations called the *plan library*. The Apprentice's understanding of a program is embodied in a hierarchical plan for it. In general, the subplan for each individual segment in terms of its subsegments will be an instance of some plan stored in the plan library. This structure gives the Apprentice access to all of the information stored in the plan library about the particular subplan as soon as it can make a guess as to what the subplan is.

A Scenario of Interaction with the Programmer's Apprentice

The following hypothetical conversation between a programmer and the Programmer's Apprentice is presented to illustrate the intended operation of the system. (Currently, most, but not all, of the modules that comprise the Apprentice system are running.) Commentary on the scenario is printed in *italics*. The scenario illustrates the following four basic areas in which the Apprentice can assist a programmer:

1. *Documentation.* One of the primary services the Apprentice provides is automatic, permanent, and in-depth documentation of the program. It remembers not only explicit commentary supplied by the programmer with the code, but also a substantial body of derived information describing the logical structure underlying the program, such as the dependency relationships between parts of the program.

2. *Verification.* The development of a program is accompanied by the construction of a sequence of plans at various levels of abstraction. At each step, the Apprentice attempts to verify that the current plan is both consistent and sufficient to accomplish the desired goal. As more information is specified, the Apprentice's reasoning about these plans approaches a complete verification of the program.

3. *Debugging.* Any discrepancy between the Apprentice's understanding of the programmer's intent and the actual operation of the program is reported to the programmer as a potential bug.

4. *Managing modification.* Perhaps the most useful aspect of the Apprentice is that it can help a programmer modify his program without introducing new bugs. Based on its knowledge of the logical relationships between parts of a program, the Apprentice is able to determine what parts of a program can be affected by a proposed change and how they can be affected. It can use this information to warn the programmer of impending difficulties.

The scenario presented below traces the design, coding, and subsequent modification of a program that deletes an entry from a hash table. The scenario picks up in the middle of a session, at a point where the programmer has already made many design choices and communicated them to the Apprentice. In particular, the user has stated the input/output specifications for the subroutine DELETE and chosen the basic data structures to be used. The hash table is implemented as an array of linked lists called *buckets*. Each of the entries in a bucket is a dotted pair whose CAR is the key for the entry (see Article VI.B on LISP).

Programmer: The plan for the routine DELETE has three main steps: The first one hashes the input key to get an index, the second one fetches the bucket corresponding to that index from the table, and the third splices out the entry in the bucket whose key part is equal to the input key.

> *The only feature of this scenario that is not a current research goal of the Programmer's Apprentice project is the use of English dialogue. Although the system should be able to support a sophisticated, natural-language "front end," no work has been done on this to date. As a result, the programmer would actually type in something like the following:*

```
(subsegments-of-DELETE step1-step2-step3)
(specifications-for-step1 (inputs-key1) (outputs-index)
        (assert-(=-index-(hash-key1)))) ...
```

> *From the programmer's outline of the design, the Apprentice builds a plan representing the program's intended structure. References to basic programming techniques such as splicing out (deleting elements from a linked list) trigger the retrieval of possibly appropriate plans from the plan library.*

Apprentice: I can't verify that this plan satisfies the specifications for DELETE. In particular, when the input key is equal to the key part of the first entry in a bucket, I can't prove that the entry is no longer in the table after DELETE is executed. Note that in this situation, the bucket after splicing out entries has a different initial cell from the bucket before splicing out entries and that therefore the table isn't changed.

> *After constructing a plan, the Apprentice uses its reasoning abilities to check for bugs. Above, it found one and reported it to the programmer. In general, it is the responsibility of the programmer to supply corrections. Below, the programmer corrects the plan by issuing semantically based editing commands to the Apprentice.*

Programmer: Modify the plan as follows. Add a final step that compares the bucket after splicing with the bucket before splicing and stores the new bucket in the table under the index if the two initial cells are not identical.

Apprentice: OK, the plan now seems correct.

The programmer then types in the code for DELETE. In cases where the programmer specifies the plan for a program as completely as he does here, he could ask the Apprentice to write the code. It is expected that the programmer will actually only write code in situations where it is easier to write the code than to fully explain the plan.

Programmer:

```
(DEFUN DELETE (KEY) ; hash table delete routine.
(PROG (BKT1 BKT2)
      (SETQ BKT1 (TBL (HASH KEY)) BKT2 (BKT-DELETE KEY BKT1))
      (COND ((NOT (EQ BKT1 BKT2))
                    ; check if first entry in bucket deleted.
             (STORE (TBL (HASH KEY)) BKT1)))))
```

To construct a plan, the Apprentice analyzes the code written by the programmer. Comparing this plan with the plan directly described by the programmer, the Apprentice discovers an implementation bug: In the last line of code, the user probably meant to store in the hash table not the first bucket, BKT1, but the second bucket, BKT2.

Apprentice: This code is not consistent with your plan. When the first entry is deleted, the code stores the bucket before splicing, rather than the bucket after splicing. Did you mean

```
(STORE-(TBL-(HASH-KEY))-BKT2) ?
```

Programmer: Yes, fix the code. Also, use the standard list-deletion algorithm to code BKT–DELETE, so that it splices out of the bucket all entries whose key equals the indicated value.

Apprentice:

```
(DEFUN BKT-DELETE (KEY BUCKET) ; list deletion routine coded by PA.
(PROG (CURRENT PREVIOUS)
      (SETQ CURRENT BUCKET  PREVIOUS NIL)
   LP (COND ((NULL CURRENT) (RETURN BUCKET))
            ((EQUAL (CAAR CURRENT) KEY)
                           ; if keypart equal, splice out entry.
             (COND (PREVIOUS (RPLACD PREVIOUS (CDR CURRENT)))
                   (T (SETQ BUCKET (CDR BUCKET)))))
                           ; special if first element deleted.
            (T (SETQ PREVIOUS CURRENT)))
      (SETQ CURRENT (CDR CURRENT))
      (GO LP)))
```

The Apprentice is able to code a program like this itself, even though the programmer did not specify a plan for it, because it is an implementation of a standard algorithm that corresponds to a plan in the plan library.

Code written by the Apprentice can be freely mixed with code written by the programmer, and each can edit the other's work.

Sometime later, it is necessary to modify the representation of the buckets. The Apprentice helps the programmer (perhaps a different person) maintain consistency.

Programmer: I want to make a change in the representation of buckets in the hashing programs. A bucket now has two parts: a count field and a list of entries as before. The count field will contain an integer equal to the length of the list of entries. Let a bucket be a dotted pair whose CAR is the count and whose CDR is the list of entries.

When the Apprentice inspects the logical dependencies in the plans, it discovers that a type requirement has been violated.

Apprentice: The proposed change will affect DELETE as follows: After the bucket is fetched, it is passed to BKT–DELETE, which does the actual deletion. However, BKT–DELETE requires a list of entries, while in this new implementation, a bucket is no longer just a list of entries.

Programmer: Explain the plan for BKT–DELETE, please.

Apprentice: BKT–DELETE is implemented following the standard list-deletion plan. The inputs are a key and a list of entries. The plan is a search loop with two pointers: a pointer to the current entry, which is initialized to the input list, and a trailing pointer, which is initialized to NIL. On each iteration, the loop tests the key of the current entry. If it is equal to the input key, the element is spliced out of the list by RPLACDing the trailing pointer.

Acting in its documentation role, the Apprentice describes the structure of BKT–DELETE by reporting the structure of its plan. The programmer then decides how to modify BKT–DELETE.

Programmer: Change the specifications of BKT–DELETE, so that it expects as input a bucket of the new type, rather than a list of entries. Also change the initialization of the pointers to read:

```
(SETQ-PREVIOUS-BUCKET-CURRENT-(CDR-BUCKET)) .
```

The Apprentice reanalyzes the program to verify that this change fixes the problem without causing any other problems. This analysis reveals the presence of inaccessible code, which the Apprentice reports to the programmer.

Apprentice: OK, this fixes the problem. However, now the special-case tests in BKT–DELETE and DELETE are not necessary, since PREVIOUS is never NIL and therefore elements are always deleted by side effect.

...and so the session continues with the Apprentice looking over the programmer's shoulder.

Operation of the System

The design of the Programmer's Apprentice is based on four modules—a surface analyzer, a recognizer, an interactive module, and a deductive module—and two databases—the plan library and a scratch pad called the design notebook. Only the first three modules have been implemented thus far. As described above, the plan library contains the Apprentice's knowledge of programming in general. The design notebook contains the Apprentice's evolving knowledge of the particular program being worked on and serves as the communication center for the system as a whole. The modules communicate with each other solely by making assertions in the design notebook. Each module has predefined trigger patterns that cause it to perform specific tasks (such as making a deduction or querying the user) whenever appropriate assertions appear in the notebook. Every assertion added to the notebook is also accompanied by a justification of its presence. These justifications make it possible for the Apprentice to account for its actions.

The *surface analyzer* is used to construct simple surface plans for sections of code written by the programmer. It is the only module whose implementation depends on the programming language. To date, surface analyzers have been implemented for both LISP and FORTRAN.

The *recognition module* takes over where the surface analyzer leaves off, to construct a detailed plan for a piece of code. It first breaks up the surface plan by identifying weakly interacting subsegments that can be further analyzed in isolation from each other. It then compares these subsegments with the plans in the library to determine more detailed plans for the program.

The *interactive module* is the communication link between the Apprentice and the programmer. It converts the programmer's input (which can consist of code, direct specification of a plan, or various requests) into assertions in the design notebook and decides what to say to the programmer based on the information currently in the notebook.

The *deductive module* operates in the background in cooperation with all of the other modules. It performs the deductions necessary to verify a proposed match between a program and a plan, to detect bugs in a plan, and to determine the ramifications of a proposed modification to a program or plan.

At a given moment, the *design notebook* holds the sum total of what the Apprentice knows about the program being worked on. This information triggers additional activity by the modules. If the recognizer and deductive modules are strong enough and the program is simple enough, this process will culminate in a complete understanding and verification of the program. However, this will typically not be the case, and some questions (such as the exact plan for a segment or the correctness of a specification) will remain unresolved in the notebook. The flexible architecture chosen for the Apprentice makes useful partial performance possible in this situation. The Apprentice can ignore what it does not understand and work constructively with what it does understand. The programmer can be called upon to fill in the gaps.

Current Status of the Programmer's Apprentice

Rich and Shrobe (1976) laid out the basic idea of a plan and the initial design of the Programmer's Apprentice. Since that time, Rich, Shrobe, and Waters have been working together on further aspects of the theory along with design and implementation of the Apprentice.

Rich's work (1979) centers on the plan library and the recognition process. Using the plan representation, he is codifying a large body of common programming strategies in the domain of nonnumerical programming. Rich is also designing a recognition module that will identify instances of plans in the library as they occur in combination in a programmer's program.

Shrobe (1978) has implemented a prototype deductive module that can reason about programs as represented by plans. An important aspect of its operation is that it maintains a record of the dependency relationships embodied in its deductions. In doing this, it builds up some of the logical structure that is a vital part of a plan for a program. Shrobe is currently designing an improved version of this deductive module.

Waters (1976, 1978) has implemented a system that can analyze the code for a program and produce the basic structure of a plan for the entire program. The system corresponds to the surface-analysis module and the initial phase of the recognition process. The basic idea in Waters' work is that plans for typical programs are built up in a small number of stereotyped ways and that features in the code for a program can be used to determine how the plan for the program should be built up.

The immediate goal is to construct a prototype system that can perform as shown in the scenario. To do this, an interactive module must be built, and the other modules must be connected together into an integrated system. Looking further ahead, additional modules (such as a simple program-synthesis module, and one dealing with efficiency issues) will be added to the Programmer's Apprentice, and the existing ones will be strengthened so that the Apprentice can assume an even larger role in the programming process.

References

See Rich and Shrobe (1978); also, Rich (1979), Shrobe (1978), and Waters (1978).

D4.   PECOS

DEVELOPED by David Barstow (1979) and based on ideas presented in Green and Barstow (1978), the automatic-programming system PECOS serves as the coding expert of the PSI project (see Article X.D1) at Stanford University. Though it can act in conjunction with the PSI system, PECOS can also stand on its own and interact directly with the user. The original problem area of PECOS was symbolic programming, which includes simple list-processing, sorting, database retrieval, and concept formation. This domain has been extended to graph theory and simple number theory. Programs are specified in terms of very high level constructs such as *data structures* (e.g., collections, mappings) and *operations* (e.g., testing for membership in a collection, computing the inverse image of an object under a mapping).

Knowledge about programming in the problem area has been codified (i.e., made explicit and put into machine-usable form) primarily as transformation rules, which make up PECOS's knowledge base. Most of the rules describe how constructs and operations can be represented or implemented in terms of other constructs and operations that are closer to, or actually in, the target language LISP. These rules can identify design decisions and can also serve as limited explanations.

The operation of the system proceeds by the repeated selection and application of the transformation rules in the knowledge base to parts of the program. Also referred to as *gradual refinement*, this transformation process reduces the high-level specification to an implementation fully within the target language. Each application of a rule is said to produce a partial implementation, or *refinement*, of the program, and the transformation rules are called *refinement* rules.

Conflict Resolution

At some points during the transformation process, a conflict may arise because several rules apply to the same part of the program. The handling of this *conflict-resolution* situation is important: The application of the several rules ultimately results in different target-language implementations that often vary significantly in terms of efficiency. There are three ways to handle this situation:

1. If PECOS is interacting directly with the user, the user may select which rule should be applied (and thus which implementation will be constructed).

2. For the convenience of the user, PECOS can choose one of the applicable rules, applying about a dozen heuristics to select the rule that leads to

350

the *most* efficient implementation. These heuristics handle about two-thirds of the choices that typically arise.

3. When no heuristic applies and the user is uncertain about which rule is "best" for his or her purposes, PECOS can apply each in parallel, constructing a separate implementation for each.

When the PECOS system functions as the CODING expert of the PSI system, choices between rules are made by an *efficiency expert* subsystem called LIBRA (Article X.D8), which incorporates more sophisticated analytic techniques than the simple heuristics of PECOS. The capability of developing different implementations in parallel is used extensively in the interactions between PECOS and LIBRA (Barstow and Kant, 1977).

The Knowledge Base of Refinement Rules

The system's knowledge base consists of about 400 rules dealing with a variety of symbolic-programming concepts. The most abstract concepts are those of the specification language (e.g., collection, inverse image, enumerating the objects in a collection). The implementation techniques covered by the rules include the representation of collections as linked lists, arrays (both ordered and unordered), and Boolean mappings, and the representation of mappings as tables, sets of pairs, property-list markings, and inverted mappings (indexed by range element). As a natural by-product, these rules also cover sorting within a transfer paradigm that includes simpler sorts such as insertion and selection. While some of the rules are specific to LISP, about three-fourths of the rules are independent of LISP or any other target language.

Internally, PECOS's rules are represented as condition-action pairs (production rules; see Article III.C4, in Vol. I). The conditions are particular configurations of abstract operations and data structures that are matched against parts of the developing program. Where the match is successful, the actions replace parts of the abstract concepts with refinements of those parts.

In the system of refinement rules, intermediate-level abstractions play a major role. One benefit of such intermediate-level concepts is a certain economy of knowledge. Consider, for example, the construct of a *sequential collection:* a linearly ordered group of locations in which the elements of a collection can be stored. Since there is no constraint on how the linear ordering is implemented, the construct can be seen as an abstraction (or generalization) of both linked lists and arrays. Much of what programmers know about linked lists is in common to what they know about arrays and hence can be represented as one rule set about sequential collections. A further benefit of these intermediate-level concepts is that they facilitate resolution of conflicts between alternative rules: Attention can be focused on the essential aspects of a choice while ignoring irrelevant details.

The Programming Knowledge Base

Most of the currently available sources of programming knowledge (e.g., books and articles) are too imprecise for effective use by a machine. The descriptions are often informal, with details omitted and assumptions unstated. Before this programming knowledge can be made available to machines, it must be made more precise—the assumptions must be made explicit and the details must be filled in.

PECOS's rules provide much of this precision for the domain of elementary symbolic programming. For example, consider the following rule (an English paraphrase of PECOS's internal representation):

> *A collection may be represented as a mapping of objects to Boolean values; the default range object is FALSE.*

Most programmers know this fact: that a collection may be represented by its *characteristic function*. Without knowing this rule, or something similar, it is almost impossible to understand why a bit string can represent a set (or, for that matter, why property-list markings work). Yet this rule is generally left unstated in discussions of bit-string representations. As another example, consider the following rule:

> *An association table whose keys are integers from a fixed range may be represented as an array subregion.*

The fact that an array is simply a way to represent a mapping of integers to arbitrary values is well known and usually stated explicitly. The detail that the integers must be from a fixed range is usually not stated. Note that if the integers are not from a fixed range, an array is the wrong representation and something like a hash table should be used.

PECOS's rules also identify particular design decisions that are part of programming. For example, one of the crucial decisions in building an enumerator of the objects in a sequential collection is selecting the order in which they should be enumerated. This decision is often made only implicitly. For example, the use of the LISP function MAPC to enumerate the objects in a list assumes implicitly that the stored (or "natural") order is the right order in which to enumerate them. While this is often correct, there are times when some other order is desired. For example, the selector of a *selection sort* involves enumerating the objects according to a particular ordering relation. A second major decision in building an enumerator involves selecting a way to save the state of the computation between calls to the enumerator. The use of a location (e.g., index or list cell) to specify the current state is based on knowing the following rule:

> *If the enumeration order is the same as the stored order, the state of an enumeration may be represented as a location in the sequential collection.*

Were the enumeration order different from the stored order (as in a selection sort), some other state-saving scheme would be needed, such as deleting the objects or marking them in some fashion.

Another interesting aspect of PECOS's rules is that they have a certain kind of explanatory power. Consider, for example, a well-known trick for computing the intersection of two linked lists of atoms in linear time: Map down the first list and put a special mark on the property list of each atom; then map down the second list, collecting only those atoms whose property lists contain the special mark. This technique can be understood on the basis of the following four PECOS rules (in addition to the rules about representing collections as linked lists):

> A collection may be represented as a mapping of objects to Boolean values; the default range object is FALSE.

> A mapping whose domain consists of atoms may be represented with property-list markings.

> The intersection of two collections may be implemented by enumerating the objects in one and, while enumerating them, collecting those that are members of the other.

> If a collection is input, its representation may be converted into any other representation before further processing.

Given these rules, the trick works by first converting the representation of one collection from a linked list to property-list markings with Boolean values and then computing the intersection in the standard way, except that a membership test for property-list markings involves a call to GETPROP rather than a scan down a linked list.

Status

PECOS is able to implement abstract algorithms (i.e., a very high level specification) in a variety of domains, including elementary symbolic programming (simple classification and concept-formation algorithms), sorting (several versions of selection and insertion sort), graph theory (a reachability algorithm), and even simple number theory (a prime-number algorithm). In each case, PECOS's knowledge about different implementation techniques permitted the construction of a variety of alternative implementations, often with significantly different efficiency characteristics.

The success of PECOS demonstrates the viability of the knowledge-based approach to automatic programming. In developing this approach further, two research directions seem particularly promising.

First, programming knowledge for other domains must be codified. In the process, rules developed for one domain may be found to be useful in other domains. With the hope of verifying the wider utility of PECOS's rules about collections and mappings, Yale University's Knowledge-based Automatic Programming Project codified the programming knowledge needed for some elementary graph algorithms (Barstow, 1978).

As an example, consider the common technique of representing a graph as an adjacency matrix. To construct such a representation, only one rule about graphs need be known:

A graph may be represented as a pair of sets: a set of vertices (whose elements are primitive objects) and a set of edges (whose elements are pairs of vertices).

The rest of the necessary knowledge is concerned with sets and mappings and is independent of its application to graphs. For example, to derive the bounds on the matrix, one need know only that primitive objects may be represented as integers, that a set of otherwise unconstrained integers may be represented as a sequence of consecutive integers, and that a sequence of consecutive integers may be represented as lower and upper bounds. To derive the representation of the matrix itself, one need only know PECOS's rules about Boolean mappings and association tables, plus the fact that a table whose keys are pairs of integers in fixed ranges may be represented as a two-dimensional matrix.

The second direction indicated by the PECOS research is that different kinds of programming knowledge need to be codified. Two types seem particularly important: efficiency knowledge and strategic knowledge. LIBRA (Article X.D8), which acts together with PECOS in PSI's synthesis phase, embodies a large amount of efficiency knowledge; but much remains to be done. Very little work on the use of general strategies (e.g., divide and conquer) in program synthesis has been done. The latter seems an especially important direction, since such strategies appear to play a major role in programming by humans.

References

See Barstow (1979); also, Barstow and Kant (1977) and Barstow (1978).

D5. DEDALUS

DEDALUS, the DEDuctive ALgorithm Ur-Synthesizer, developed by Richard Waldinger and Zohar Manna at SRI International, accepts an unambiguous, logically complete, very high level specification of a desired program and, through repeated application of transformation rules, seeks to reduce it to an implementation within a simple LISP-like target language. This target-language implementation is guaranteed to be correct (i.e., logically equivalent to the high-level specification) and to terminate. The knowledge that ultimately relates the constructs of the specification language to those in the target language is expressed in the transformation rules. But of special importance are certain rules that express general programming principles that are independent of the particular specification language and target language. These rules, which have constituted a major component of the DEDALUS effort, form conditional statements and recursive and nonrecursive procedures; they also generalize procedures, construct well-founded orderings to guarantee the termination of recursive calls, and write code that simultaneously achieves two or more goals. These general programming principles are described below in detail, with examples illustrating their application. As pointed out below in the section on the status of the project, some of the principles are fairly well understood, while others require further study. Not all the principles are implemented in the current DEDALUS system.

The DEDALUS specification language can contain constructs that are close to how the user actually thinks about the problem. Thus, the DEDALUS specification of the program LESSALL$(x\ l)$, which tests whether a number x is less than every element of a list l of numbers, and the program GCD$(x\ y)$, which computes the greatest common divisor of two nonnegative integers x and y, are specified as follows:

$$\text{LESSALL}(x\ l)\ \Leftarrow\ \textbf{compute}\ x < \text{ALL}(l)$$
$$\textbf{where}\ x\ \text{is a number and}\ l\ \text{is a list of numbers,}$$

$$\text{GCD}(x\ y)\ \Leftarrow\ \textbf{compute}\ \text{MAX}\{z\colon\ z\,|\,x\ \text{and}\ z\,|\,y\}$$
$$\textbf{where}\ x\ \text{and}\ y\ \text{are nonnegative, nonzero integers.}$$

Elements of DEDALUS's specification language, like the ALL construct in $P(\text{ALL}(l))$, indicating that the condition P holds for all elements of the list l, and the set constructor $\{u\colon P(u)\}$, indicating the set of elements for which P is true, will eventually be converted into target-language code through the repeated application of transformation rules. The specification language is not fixed: New constructs can be introduced by modifying or adding transformation rules.

The operation of DEDALUS consists of the repeated application of transformations to expressions to produce expressions that are closer to, or within,
the target language. In DEDALUS, the expressions that occur during the
transformation process specify not only programs, but also conditions to be
proved, as well as conditions to be made true. All these expressions are treated
as goals to be achieved: For an expression that specifies a program, the goal
is to convert that program into a target-language implementation; for an
expression that is a condition to be proved, the goal is to convert it to the
logical constant TRUE; for an expression that is a condition to be made true,
the goal is to construct a program that will make that condition true.

Transforming a subexpression into another subexpression requires rules
of the form

$$t \Rightarrow t' \text{ if } P,$$

the condition P being optional, indicating that the subexpression t can be
replaced by t'. If P is present, the rule can only be applied provided that
the system first proves that P is true; which is to say, before the rule can be
applied, the system must succeed in achieving the subgoal

Goal: **prove** P.

For example, consider

$$P(\text{ALL}(l)) \Rightarrow P(\text{HEAD}(l)) \text{ and } P(\text{ALL}(\text{TAIL}(l))) \text{ if not empty } (l),$$

which expresses the fact that a property P holds for every element of a
nonempty list l if it holds for the first element $\text{HEAD}(l)$ and for every element
of the list $\text{TAIL}(l)$ of the other elements. Before the system can apply this rule
to some part of an expression, it would have to succeed in proving that l is
not empty.

The application of transformation rules results in a tree of goals and
subgoals. Initially, the top-level goals of this tree are established by program
specifications. Thus, the common form of program specification

$$f(x) \Leftarrow \textbf{compute } P(x)$$
$$\textbf{where } Q(x)$$

establishes its output description as the top-level goal

Goal: **compute** $P(x)$,

and in trying to achieve this goal, the system assumes the truth of $Q(x)$. If
the top-level goals of trees are established by program specifications, most

subgoals are established as the result of transformations. Thus, by applying the transformation rule

$$u \,|\, v \text{ and } u \,|\, w \;\Rightarrow\; u \,|\, v \text{ and } u \,|\, w - v$$

to the top-level goal of the GCD program,

$$\text{Goal 1:}\quad \textbf{compute } \text{MAX}\{z\colon\; z \,|\, x \text{ and } z \,|\, y\}\,,$$

the system establishes

$$\text{Goal 2:}\quad \textbf{compute } \text{MAX}\{z\colon\; z \,|\, x \text{ and } z \,|\, y - x\}$$

as a subgoal. Such transformations express knowledge about specific constructs. In the DEDALUS system there is also knowledge of a more general sort.

General Programming Principles

This section describes five general programming principles and presents several examples to illustrate their application. The principles express knowledge about how to form conditionals and procedures (recursive and nonrecursive), how to replace two or more procedures by a generalized procedure, and how to achieve simultaneous goals. (As explained later in the article, the current implementation of DEDALUS does not incorporate the generalization of procedures or the achievement of simultaneous goals.)

Conditional formation. Many of the transformation rules impose some condition P (e.g., l is nonempty, x is nonnegative) that must be satisfied for the rule to be applied. Suppose that, in attempting to apply a particular rule, the system failed to prove or disprove the condition P, where P is expressed entirely in terms of the primitive constructs of the target language; in such a situation, the conditional-formation rule is invoked. This rule allows the introduction of case analysis to consider separately the cases in which P is true and in which P is false. Suppose the result is both a program segment S_1 that achieves the goal under the assumption that P is true and another program segment S_2 that achieves the goal under the assumption that P is false. The conditional-formation principle puts these two program segments together into a conditional expression

$$\textbf{if } P \textbf{ then } S_1 \textbf{ else } S_2\,,$$

which achieves the goal regardless of whether P is true or false. During the generation of S_2, the system could discover that a conditional expression was unnecessary: The generation of S_2 may not have required the assumption that P was false. In such a case, the program constructed would be simply S_2.

Recursion formation. Suppose, in constructing a program with specifications

$$f(x) \; \Leftarrow \; \textbf{compute } P(x)$$
$$\textbf{where } Q(x),$$

the system encounters a subgoal

Goal: **compute** $P(t)$,

which is an instance of the output specification, **compute** $P(x)$. Because the program $f(x)$ is intended to compute $P(x)$ for any x satisfying its input specification $Q(x)$, the recursion-formation rule proposes achieving the subgoal above by computing $P(t)$ with a recursive call $f(t)$. For this step to be valid, it must ensure that the input condition $Q(t)$ holds when the proposed recursive call is executed. To ensure that the new recursive call will not cause the program to loop indefinitely, the rule must also establish a *termination condition*, showing that the argument t is strictly less than the input x in some well-founded ordering. (A *well-founded ordering* is an ordering in which no infinite, strictly decreasing sequences can exist.) This condition precludes the possibility that an infinite sequence of recursive calls would occur during the execution of the program.

One example of recursion formation in the DEDALUS system is the program LESSALL($x \; l$), which tests whether a given number x is less than every element of a given list l of numbers. The specifications for this program are

LESSALL($x \; l$) $\; \Leftarrow \;$ **compute** $x <$ ALL(l)

where x is a number and l is a list of numbers.

In deriving this program, the system develops a subgoal

Goal: **compute** $x <$ ALL(TAIL(l)),

in the case that l is nonempty. This subgoal is an instance of the output specification of the original specification, with the input l replaced by TAIL(l); therefore, the recursion-formation principle proposes that the subgoal be achieved by introducing a recursive call LESSALL(x TAIL(l)). To ensure that this step is valid, the rule establishes an input condition that

x is a number and TAIL(l) is a list of numbers

and a termination condition that the argument pair (x TAIL(l)) is less than the input pair ($x \; l$) in some well-founded ordering. This termination condition holds because TAIL(l) is a proper sublist of l. As the final program, the system obtains

LESSALL($x \; l$) $\; \Leftarrow \;$ **if** EMPTY(l) **then** TRUE
else $x <$ HEAD(l) **and** LESSALL(x TAIL(l)).

Procedure formation. Suppose that, while developing a tree for a specification of the form

$$f(x) \;\Leftarrow\; \textbf{compute } P(x)$$
$$\textbf{where } Q(x),$$

the system encounters a subgoal

Goal B: **compute** $R(t)$,

which is an instance not of the output specification **compute** $P(x)$ but of some previously generated subgoal

Goal A: **compute** $R(x)$.

Then the procedure-formation principle introduces a new procedure, $g(x)$, whose output specification is

$$g(x) \;\Leftarrow\; \textbf{compute } R(x).$$

In this way, both goals A and B can be achieved by calls $g(x)$ and $g(t)$ to a single procedure. In the case where goal B has been derived from goal A, the call to $g(t)$ will be a recursive call; otherwise, both calls will be simple procedure calls.

An example of procedure formation occurs in the specification of the program CART$(s\ t)$ to compute the Cartesian product of two sets, s and t:

$$\text{CART}(s\ t) \;\Leftarrow\; \textbf{compute } \{(x\ y)\colon\ x \in s \text{ and } y \in t\}$$
$$\textbf{where } s \text{ and } t \text{ are finite sets.}$$

While deriving the tree for the program, the system obtains a subgoal

Goal A: **compute** $\{(x\ y)\colon\ x = \text{HEAD}(s) \text{ and } y \in t\}$,

given that s is nonempty. Developing goal A further, the system derives

Goal B: **compute** $\{(x\ y)\colon\ x = \text{HEAD}(s) \text{ and } y \in \text{TAIL}(t)\}$,

given that t is nonempty. Goal B is an instance of goal A; therefore, the procedure-formation rule proposes introducing a new procedure CART-HEAD$(s\ t)$ whose output specification is

$$\text{CARTHEAD}(s\ t) \;\Leftarrow\; \textbf{compute } \{(x\ y)\colon\ x = \text{HEAD}(s) \text{ and } y \in t\},$$

so that goal A can be achieved with a procedure call CARTHEAD$(s\ t)$, and goal B, with a (recursive) call CARTHEAD$(s\ \text{TAIL}(t))$.

When the CARTHEAD procedure is constructed by the techniques already described, the final system of programs becomes

$$\text{CART}(s\ t)\ \Leftarrow\ \textbf{if}\ \text{EMPTY}(s)\ \textbf{then}\ \{\ \}$$
$$\textbf{else}\ \text{UNION}(\text{CARTHEAD}(s\ t)\ \text{CART}(\text{TAIL}(s)\ t)),$$

$$\text{CARTHEAD}(s\ t)\ \Leftarrow\ \textbf{if}\ \text{EMPTY}(t)\ \textbf{then}\ \{\ \}$$
$$\textbf{else}\ \text{UNION}(\{\text{HEAD}(s)\ \text{HEAD}(t)\}$$
$$\text{CARTHEAD}(s\ \text{TAIL}(t)).$$

Generalization. Suppose, in deriving a program, that we obtain two subgoals

Goal A: **compute** $R(a(x))$

Goal B: **compute** $R(b(x))$,

neither of which is an instance of the other, but both of which are instances of the more general expression

compute $R(y)$.

In such a case, the extended procedure-formation rule proposes the introduction of the new procedure, whose output specification is

$$g(y)\ \Leftarrow\ \textbf{compute}\ R(y).$$

Thus, goal A and goal B can be achieved by procedure calls to $g(a(x))$ and $g(b(x))$, respectively.

Generalization is used in the synthesis of the program REVERSE(l), which reverses a list l. We first derive two subgoals:

Goal A: **compute** APPEND(REVERSE(TAIL(l))
                    CONS(HEAD(l)NIL))

Goal B: **compute** APPEND(REVERSE(TAIL(TAIL(l)))
                    CONS(HEAD(TAIL(l))
                    CONS(HEAD(l)NIL))).

Each is an instance of the more general expression

compute APPEND(REVERSE(TAIL(l))
                CONS(HEAD(l) m));

therefore, the extended procedure-formation rule proposes introducing a new procedure REVERSEGEN(l m), whose output specification is the more general expression:

$$\text{REVERSEGEN}(l\ m)\ \Leftarrow\ \textbf{compute}\ \text{APPEND}(\text{REVERSE}(\text{TAIL}(l))$$
$$\text{CONS}(\text{HEAD}(l)m))\,.$$

Although this procedure, which reverses a nonempty list l and appends the result to m, is a more general problem than the original REVERSE program, it turns out that REVERSEGEN is actually easier to construct. The final system of programs obtained is

$$\text{REVERSE}(l)\ \Leftarrow\ \textbf{if}\ \text{EMPTY}(l)\ \textbf{then}\ \text{NIL}$$
$$\textbf{else}\ \text{REVERSEGEN}(l\ \text{NIL})$$

$$\text{REVERSEGEN}(l\ m)\ \Leftarrow\ \textbf{if}\ \text{EMPTY}(\text{TAIL}(l))\ \textbf{then}\ \text{CONS}(\text{HEAD}(l)m)$$
$$\textbf{else}\ \text{REVERSEGEN}(\text{TAIL}(l)\ \text{CONS}(\text{HEAD}(l)m))\,.$$

Simultaneous goals. To deal with operations that produce side effects such as modifying the structure of data objects (e.g., assignment statements), DEDALUS introduces constructs such as ACHIEVE P, to denote a program intended to make the condition P true.

In constructing a program to achieve two conditions, P_1 and P_2, it is not sufficient to decompose the problem by constructing two independent programs to achieve P_1 and P_2. The concatenation of the two programs might not achieve both conditions because the program that achieves P_2 may in the process make P_1 false, and vice versa.

For example, suppose a program is desired to sort the values of three variables x, y, and z—in other words, to permute the values of the variables to achieve the two conditions $x \leq y$ and $y \leq z$ simultaneously. Assume the given primitive instruction SORT2 $(u\ v)$, which sorts the values of its input variables u and v. The concatenation

$$\text{SORT2}\,(x\ y)$$
$$\text{SORT2}\,(y\ z)$$

of these two segments will not necessarily achieve both conditions simultaneously; the second segment SORT2 $(y\ z)$ may, by sorting y and z, make the first condition $x \leq y$ false.

The simultaneous-goal principle, which was introduced to circumvent such difficulties, states that to satisfy a goal of form

$$\text{ACHIEVE}\ P_1\ \text{and}\ P_2\,,$$

a program F is first constructed to achieve P_1, and then F is modified to achieve P_2 while protecting P_1 at the end of F. A special *protection mechanism* (cf. Sussman, 1975) ensures that no modification is permitted that destroys the truth of the protected condition P_1 at the end of the program.

To apply this principle to the goal

$$\text{ACHIEVE } x \leq y \text{ and } y \leq z$$

in the sorting problem, for example, a system would first ACHIEVE $x \leq y$, by using the segment SORT2 $(x\ y)$. This program would then be modified to achieve the second condition $y \leq z$. But adding SORT2 $(y\ z)$ at the end of the program will not work because it destroys the truth of the protected condition $x \leq y$.

However, in general, a goal may be achieved by inserting modifications at any point in the program, not merely at the end. Introducing the two instructions

> **if** $y < x$ **then** SORT2 $(x\ z)$
>
> **if** $x \leq y$ **then** SORT2 $(y\ z)$

at the beginning of the program segment would simultaneously achieve both conditions $x \leq y$ and $y \leq z$. The resulting program would be

> **if** $y < x$ **then** SORT2 $(x\ z)$
>
> **if** $x \leq y$ **then** SORT2 $(y\ z)$
>
> SORT2 $(x\ y)$.

Status

Currently, the DEDALUS implementation incorporates the principles of conditional formation, recursion formation (including the termination proofs), and procedure formation, but it does not include generalization or the formation of structure-changing programs. The techniques for deriving straight-line, structure-changing programs were implemented in a separate system (see Waldinger, 1977).

Conditional formation and recursion formation are well understood. The method for proving termination of ordinary recursive calls does not always extend to the multiple-procedure case. The generalization mechanism and the extended procedure-formation principle are just beginning to be formulated.

The derivation of straight-line programs with simple side effects is fairly well understood, but much work remains to be done on the derivation of structure-changing programs with conditional expressions and loops, as well as on the derivation of programs that alter list structures and other complex data objects.

The DEDALUS system is implemented in QLISP, an extension of INTER-LISP that includes pattern-matching and backtracking facilities. The full power of the QLISP language is available in expressing each rule, since the rules are represented as QLISP programs in a fairly direct manner (see Chap. VI).

The following are some representative programs constructed by the current DEDALUS system:

Numerical programs:

—the subtractive GCD algorithm,
—the Euclidean GCD algorithm,
—the binary GCD algorithm,
—the remainder of dividing two integers.

List programs:

—finding the maximum element of a list,
—testing whether a list is sorted,
—testing whether a number is less than every element of a list of numbers (LESSALL),
—testing whether every element of one list of numbers is less than every element of another.

Set programs:

—computing the union or intersection of two sets,
—testing whether an element belongs to a set,
—testing whether one set is a subset of another,
—computing the Cartesian product of two sets (CART).

References

See Manna and Waldinger (1975, 1978) and Waldinger (1977).

D6.   Protosystem I

PROTOSYSTEM I, an automatic-programming system designed by William Martin, Gregory Ruth, Robert Baron, Matthew Morgenstern, and others of the M.I.T. Laboratory for Computer Science, is part of a larger research project aimed at modeling, understanding, and automating the writing of a data-processing system. (Hereafter, the data-processing system is referred to as a *data-processing program*, in accord with this chapter's terminology, which refers to the output of an automatic-programming system as a program.)

A model of the larger research project was developed that has five phases. The successive phases can be viewed as a series of transformations of the descriptions of the target program, beginning with a global conceptual description of the problem at hand and progressing, through increasing specificity, toward a detailed machine-level solution. The aim of the project is to develop stages of an AP system where each corresponds to one of the five phases of the model and each embodies the particular knowledge and expertise for that phase.

Phase 1: *Problem definition.* The specification of the data-processing program is expressed in domain-dependent terms in English.

Phase 2: *Specification analysis and system formulation.* The specification in phase 1 is viewed as a data-processing problem. This problem is solved, yielding a data-processing formulation of the desired program.

Phase 3: *Implementation.* The procedural steps, data representation, and organization of the target are determined by intelligent selection from, and adaptation of, a set of standard implementation possibilities.

Phase 4: *Code generation.* The implementation of phase 3 is transformed into code in some high-level language (e.g., PL/1).

Phase 5: *Compilation and loading.* The high-level code is transformed into a form that can be "understood" and executed by the target computer.

The first two phases involve such AI areas as natural-language comprehension, program-model formation, and problem solving. Since these areas of AI research are still in the early stages of evolution, the development of the first two phases has been deferred. At present, Protosystem I is limited to the automation of phases 3 and 4, since these phases were considered to be much more amenable to solution. Thus, the current system accepts a specification in terms of abstract relations (in a very high level language called SSL), and then it designs an optimized data-processing program and generates code for an efficient implementation. In automatic programming, it is usually impossible for a system to carry out a search for the absolutely optimal implementation; instead, a system works at optimizing a program only to a degree.

The particular problem area of Protosystem I is that of data-processing programs that are input/output intensive (file manipulation and updating) and batch oriented. Included in this area are programs for inventory control, payroll, and other record-keeping systems.

The specification method uses a description of the desired data-processing program in the SSL language. An SSL specification consists of a data division and a computation division. The data division gives the names of the data sets (conceptual aggregations or groupings of data), their keys, and their period of updating. The computation division specifies for each computed file the calculations to be performed when it is computed.

Figure D6-1 illustrates an SSL specification of a data-processing program for a warehouse inventory. In the proposed problem, the warehouse stocks a number of different items that are sent out daily to various stores. The data-processing program's task is to keep track of inventory levels, which items and how many of each item should be reordered from the producer (an item is reordered when less than 100 remain in stock), and how many items are received from the producer. In the data division are data sets (e.g., SHIPMENTS–RECEIVED, BEGINNING–INVENTORY, TOTAL–ITEMS), and in the computation division are the computation steps that involve these data sets (e.g., for each item, the beginning inventory is computed by adding the shipments received to the final inventory from the previous day).

When it has received the SSL specification of the desired program, Protosystem I transforms it into an efficient target-language implementation consisting of a collection of PL/1 programs and its JCL ("Job Control Language") for the IBM–360. To accomplish this transformation, the following specific design decisions are made with the goal of achieving an efficient implementation:

1. Design each keyed file, deciding what are to be its data items, organization (consecutive, index sequential, regional), storage device, associated sort ordering, and number of records per block;

2. Design each job step, determining which computations the step is to include, its accessing method (sequential, random, core table), its driving data set(s), and the order (by key values) in which the records of its input data sets are to be processed;

3. Determine whether sorts are necessary and where they should be performed; and

4. Determine the sequence of job steps.

DATA DIVISION

FILE SHIPMENTS-RECEIVED
    KEY IS ITEM
    GENERATED EVERY DAY

FILE QUANTITY-ORDERED-BY-STORE
    KEY IS ITEM, STORE
    GENERATED EVERY DAY

FILE BEGINNING-INVENTORY
    KEY IS ITEM
    GENERATED EVERY DAY

FILE TOTAL-SHIPPED
    KEY IS ITEM
    GENERATED EVERY DAY

FILE TOTAL-ITEM-ORDERS
    KEY IS ITEM
    GENERATED EVERY DAY

FILE FINAL-INVENTORY
    KEY IS ITEM
    GENERATED EVERY DAY

FILE QUANTITY-SHIPPED-TO-STORE
    KEY IS ITEM, STORE
    GENERATED EVERY DAY

FILE REORDER-AMOUNT
    KEY IS ITEM
    GENERATED EVERY DAY

COMPUTATION DIVISION

BEGINNING-INVENTORY IS
    FINAL-INVENTORY (*from the previous day*) + SHIPMENTS-RECEIVED

TOTAL-ITEM-ORDERS IS
    SUM OF QUANTITY-ORDERED-BY-STORE FOR EACH ITEM

QUANTITY-SHIPPED-TO-STORE IS

    QUANTITY-ORDERED-BY-STORE   IF BEGINNING-INVENTORY IS
                                         GREATER THAN TOTAL-ITEM-ORDERS

    ELSE

    QUANTITY-ORDERED-BY-STORE
    * (BEGINNING-INVENTORY / TOTAL-ITEM-ORDERS)
                         IF BEGINNING-INVENTORY IS NOT
                         GREATER THAN TOTAL-ITEM-ORDERS

TOTAL-SHIPPED IS
    SUM OF QUANTITY-SHIPPED-TO-STORE FOR EACH ITEM

FINAL-INVENTORY IS BEGINNING-INVENTORY − TOTAL-SHIPPED

REORDER-AMOUNT IS 1000 IF FINAL-INVENTORY IS LESS THAN 100.

Figure D6–1.   SSL relational description for a data-processing program.

These design decisions, especially the central ones of determining the final target data sets, computation steps, and sequencing of computation steps, are made by exploring the different ways of combining data sets and computation steps. The system carries out these explorations with the goal of minimizing the number of file accesses made during the run time of the target implementation. Sometimes, as explained below, the system also will seek to minimize a more detailed cost estimate of the target implementation.

Described in greater detail in the next section, the method employed by Protosystem I for achieving an efficient implementation does not rely solely on heuristics but uses instead what is essentially a dynamic-programming algorithm with heuristics added to the algorithm so that it can finish in a reasonable amount of time. An advantage of dynamic programming is that it can provide a good handle on global optimization when the results of individual decisions have far-reaching and compounding effects throughout the design of the data-processing program.

Operation of the System

Although the actual optimization process is performed by the optimizer module, several other modules provide preparatory and support services. First, the *structural-analyzer module* generates predicates for the operations in the SSL computation division. These predicates indicate the conditions under which data items in a data set will be either accessed or generated during an operation. For example, the condition

$$(\text{DEFINED } A(k_1)) = (\text{OR } (\text{DEFINED } B(k_1))(\text{DEFINED } C(k_1)))$$

would indicate that there is a record in data set A for a value of the key, k_1, only when at least one of the data sets B or C has a record for that value of the key. The structural analyzer also produces candidate driving-data-sets for each operation in the computation division. A driving data set of an operation is a data set whose records are "walked through" once in the order of their occurrence and the operation is executed once at each step (record).

The predicates produced by the structural analyzer are then used by the *question-answering module* to provide information to the optimizer about the average number of input/output accesses implied by tentative configurations (i.e., tentative choices for the data sets and computation steps) of the target implementation. The question-answering module maintains a knowledge base consisting of the predicates, characteristics of the data, and information obtained from interaction with the user, such as average data-set size or the probability of a predicate fragment's being true. This knowledge, along with knowledge about the probability calculus, is used to answer questions about the size of a data set and about the average number of items in the data set that are likely to satisfy a certain predicate (e.g., an access predicate).

When the knowledge is insufficient to answer an optimizer question, the question answerer initiates a dialogue with the user to elicit enough additional information to proceed.

The optimization process itself is performed by the *optimizer module*. This module intermittently obtains information from the question answerer about input/output accesses of tentative configurations of parts of the data-processing program, to explore the effects of such design parameters as the number of records per block, the file organization, the data items that are collected into a single data set, and the computations that are performed during a single reading of a file or files. Since the problem area of Protosystem I is that of input/output-intensive programs, the optimizer explores the various design parameters with the goal of minimizing the number of file accesses in their target-language implementation. Sometimes, however, after a number of more important design decisions have been made, the optimizer will further explore design alternatives by computing a more detailed cost estimate that attempts to approximate the charging structure of the particular installation on which the target system is to run (e.g., disk space, core-residency charges, explicit input/output).

The central part of the optimization process is concerned with the exploration of various ways of setting up data sets and computation steps. Basically, the optimization module starts with the data sets and computation steps in the data division and computation division of the SSL specification. Then, to minimize the number of file accesses, the module looks at data-processing programs that use various aggregations of these initial data sets and computation steps (an aggregation of two or more data sets is a data set that has all the data items of the original data sets, while an aggregation of several computation steps is a computation step that performs the functions of the original steps). The optimizer explores the aggregating data sets and the aggregating computation steps and develops and utilizes constraints on the sort order of both data sets and computation steps (an example of a sort-order constraint on a data set would be having the data-set records sorted first on a particular key).

To avoid the problem of combinatorial explosion, the module uses a form of dynamic programming with heuristics. Loosely speaking, *dynamic programming* is a set of parameterized recursive equations, which, in this case, express the cost of optimized longer segments of the program in terms of optimized shorter segments. A pure dynamic-programming algorithm, though it would find the absolute optimum target implementation, would require an excessive amount of time to do so. Therefore, for the algorithm to finish in a reasonable time, a number of heuristics are employed in the algorithm, including decoupling decisions where possible (and sometimes even where it is not completely possible) and carrying out local optimizations before making adjustments for global concerns. A full explanation of the algorithm is found in Morgenstern (1976).

Status

The SSL specification language has been completely defined, and there is an operational implementation of Protosystem I in MACLISP on a PDP–10 computer at M.I.T. The system is capable of producing acceptable target-language implementations. From a larger perspective, the Protosystem I project has developed a five-phase model of the process of writing a data-processing program (system), from its conception to its implementation as executable code. Twenty years ago, the fifth phase, compilation and loading, was automated. At present, a preliminary theory for and automation of the third and fourth phases, the generation of the system and translation into high-level code, are embodied in Protosystem I. Within the next decade, the theory and automation of the remaining two phases, including problem definition, specification analysis, and system formulation, should easily fall within the realm of presently developing AI technologies.

References

See Baron (1977), Morgenstern (1976), Ruth (1976a, 1978), and Hammer and Ruth (1979).

D7. NLPQ

THE NLPQ project (Natural Language Programming for Queuing Simulations) was begun by George Heidorn at Yale University in 1967 for a doctoral dissertation and completed at the Naval Postgraduate School during the years 1968–1972. The research area is that of simulation programs for simple queuing problems. The queuing problem's specification takes place during an interactive dialogue in English in which the user and the NLPQ system each can furnish information to, and request information from, the other. From this dialogue, the NLPQ system creates and maintains a partial internal description of the queuing problem. This partial description provides the basis for answering any questions that the user may ask, for generating questions that are to be asked of the user, and eventually, when completed by the dialogue activity, for generating the implementation of the simulation program in the target language GPSS. The system's processing—including creating the problem description and generating the GPSS program, as well as translating and generating sentences—is specified by *production rules* (see Article III.C4, in Vol. I).

Program Specification

In the English dialogue that constitutes NLPQ's method of specification, the user can make statements, give commands, ask questions, and answer questions. During this process, the system can ask and answer questions and respond to commands. In the brief dialogue of Figure D7–1, most of the features of the specification method are illustrated in a simple way (other, more complex dialogues are presented in Heidorn, 1972, 1974, 1975b, and 1976). In the dialogue, line numbers have been added for reference, and the lowercase typing was done by the user, while the uppercase typing was done by the computer.

This example concerns a queuing problem about cars that arrive at a station, get serviced, and leave. The user initially volunteered some information about how often the cars arrive and about the sequencing of actions, in lines 1 and 2, and then asked the system what other information was needed to complete the queuing model, in line 3. In lines 4 through 9, the system asked questions about times and actions, which the user answered, until the problem statement was complete, in line 10. Then, in line 11, the user asked a specific question about the queuing model concerning the mean time needed to service a car, a question that the system answered in line 12. In line 13, the user told the system to produce a description of the entire problem in English for verification purposes, which it did, in line 14. Finally, in response to the

1	every 6 minutes a car arrives at a station.
2	after arriving, it is serviced at a pump.
3	is the problem statement complete?
4	HOW LONG ARE THE CARS SERVICED AT THE PUMP?
5	from 3 to 7 minutes.
6	AFTER BEING SERVICED AT THE PUMP, WHAT DO THE CARS DO?
7	they leave the station.
8	HOW LONG SHALL THE SIMULATION BE RUN?
9	10 hours; use 1 minute as the basic time unit.
10	THE PROBLEM STATEMENT IS COMPLETE.
11	what is the mean of the time to service cars?
12	THE MEAN OF THE UNIFORM DISTRIBUTION IS 5 MINUTES.
13	describe the problem in english.
14	THE CARS ARRIVE AT THE STATION EVERY 6 MINUTES.

```
             AFTER ARRIVING AT THE STATION, THE CARS ARE SERVICED AT THE
             PUMP. THE TIME FOR THE CARS TO BE SERVICED AT THE PUMP IS
             UNIFORMLY DISTRIBUTED, WITH A MEAN OF 5 MINUTES AND A
             HALF-RANGE OF 2 MINUTES. AFTER BEING SERVICED AT THE PUMP,
             THE CARS LEAVE THE STATION. THE SIMULATION IS TO BE RUN
             FOR 10 HOURS, USING A BASIC TIME UNIT OF 1 MINUTE.
```

| 15 | write the gpss program. |
| 16 | |

```
             SIMULATE
STAT1    EQU             1,F,Q
PUMP2    EQU             2,F,Q
CAR1     EQU             1,T
1        TABLE           M1,1,1,2
*
*        THE CARS ARRIVE AT THE STATION.
         GENERATE        6
         ASSIGN          1,CAR1
*
*        THE CARS ARE SERVICED AT THE PUMP.
ACT1     QUEUE           PUMP2
         SEIZE           PUMP2
         DEPART          PUMP2
         ADVANCE         5,2
         RELEASE         PUMP2
*
*        THE CARS LEAVE THE STATION.
ACT3     TABULATE        P1
         TERMINATE
*
*        TIMING LOOP
         GENERATE        600
         TERMINATE       1
         START           1
         END
```

Figure D7–1.   A brief NLPQ dialogue.

user command in line 15, the system produced the GPSS program, in line 16, complete with English comments (preceded by *) and meaningful symbolic names.

Operation of the System

The processing to be done by NLPQ is specified by sets of production rules written in a language designed especially for the system. *Decoding rules* specify how strings of English text are to be converted into records in a semantic net, and *encoding rules* specify how records are to be converted into text. These are basically phrase-structure grammar rules (see Article IV.C1, in Vol. I), but they are augmented by arbitrary conditions and structure-building actions (Heidorn, 1975a).

The representation of the internal description of the simulation problem, as well as the representation of the syntactic and semantic structures, is in the form of a *semantic network* (Article III.C3, in Vol. I). A network consists of records that represent such things as concepts, words, physical entities, and probability distributions. Each record is a list of attribute-value pairs, where the value of an attribute is usually a pointer to another record but may sometimes be simply a number or character string.

Prior to a queuing dialogue, the system is given a network of about 300 "named" records containing information about words and concepts relevant to simple queuing problems. Also, it is furnished with a set of about 300 English-decoding rules and 500 English and GPSS encoding rules. As the dialogue progresses, the system uses the information it obtains from the English dialogue to build and complete a partial description of the desired simulation, a description that is in the form of a network called the Internal Problem Description (IPD).

Basically, an IPD network describes the flow of mobile entities, such as vehicles, through a queuing system consisting of stationary entities, such as pumps, by specifying the actions that take place in the system and their interrelationships. Each action is represented by a record whose attributes furnish such information as the type of action, the entity doing the action (i.e., the agent), the entity that is the object of the action, the location where it happens, its duration, its frequency of occurrence, and what happens next. For example, the action *The men unload the truck at a dock for two hours* could be represented by the record:

R1:	Type	unload
	Agent	men
	Object	truck
	Location	dock
	Duration	2 hours

The NLPQ system must obtain from the English dialogue all the information needed to build the IPD. Thus, the user must describe the flow of mobile entities through the queuing model by making statements about the actions that take place and about the relations between these actions. Each mobile entity must "arrive" at or "enter" the model. Then it may go through one or more other actions, such as "service," "load," "unload," and "wait." Then, typically, it "leaves" the model. The order in which these actions take place must eventually be made explicit by the use of subordinate clauses beginning with such conjunctions as *after*, *when*, and *before*, or by using the adverb *then*. If the order of the actions depends on the state of the queuing model, an "if" clause may be used to specify the condition for performing an action; a sentence with an "otherwise" in it is used to give an alternative action to be performed when this condition is not met.

The information needed to simulate the problem, including the various times involved, must also be furnished by the specification dialogue. It is necessary to specify the time between arrivals, the time required to perform each activity, the length of the simulation run, and the basic time unit to be used in the GPSS program. Activity times and times between events may be given as constants or as probability distributions, such as uniform, exponential, normal, or empirical. The quantity of each stationary entity should also be specified, unless 1 is to be assumed.

The user may either furnish this information in the form of a complete problem statement or he may state some part of it and then let the system ask questions to obtain the rest of the information, as was done above in lines 1 through 10 of Figure D7–1. The latter method results in a scan of the partially built IPD for missing or conflicting information and the generation of appropriate questions. Each time the system asks a question, it is trying to obtain the value of some specific attribute that will be needed to generate a GPSS program. To furnish a value for the attribute, the question may be answered by a complete sentence or simply by a phrase.

The user may ask the system specific questions about the queuing model, and the system will respond by generating the answers from the information in the appropriate parts of the IPD. To check the entire IPD as it exists at any time, the user may request that an English problem-description be produced. Such a description consists of all the information in the IPD as it is converted into English by the encoding rules (see line 14 of Fig. D7–1). Specifically, for each action in the IPD, the system generates one or more statements describing the type of action; its agent, object, and location; what action, if any, follows (if none, a new paragraph is started); and, if applicable, an inter-event time or duration. Conditional successor actions may result in two sentences, with the first one having an "if" clause in it and the second one beginning with "otherwise." After all of the actions have been described, a separate one-sentence paragraph is produced with the values of the run time and the basic time unit.

After the dialogue is finished and all the required information is obtained, NLPQ uses the IPD and the GPSS encoding rules to produce the desired program in the GPSS target language. Such a program was listed in line 16 of Figure D7–1. At the beginning of the program, the definitions for the stationary entities, mobile entities, and distributions are given. Then, for each action, a comment consisting of a simple English action-sentence is produced, followed by the GPSS statements appropriate to this action. For example, an "arrive" usually produces a GENERATE and an ASSIGN, a "leave" produces a TABULATE and a TERMINATE, and most activities produce a sequence like QUEUE, SEIZE, DEPART, ADVANCE, and RELEASE. These are usually followed by some sort of TRANSFER, depending upon the type of value that the action's successor attribute has. Finally, the GPSS program closes with a "timing loop" to govern the length of the simulation run.

Status

An NLPQ prototype system was demonstrated several times on a variety of problems. Although the capabilities of the prototype system are limited, the research did establish an overall framework for such a system and useful techniques were developed. Sufficient details were worked out to allow the system to carry out interesting interactions, as evidenced by the longer, more complicated dialogues shown in the first four references below. More details of the processing done by this system can be found in any of the references, especially Heidorn (1972).

References

See Heidorn (1972, 1974, 1975a, 1975b, 1976).

D8. LIBRA

LIBRA, the EFFICIENCY-ANALYSIS expert of the PSI system (Article X.D1), was developed by Elaine Kant in conjunction with the PSI project at Stanford University. The PSI system, through interaction with the user, constructs a very high level program specification called the program model. LIBRA, working together with the PECOS CODING expert (Article X.D4), converts the program model into a target-language implementation. The PECOS system supplies the transformation or *refinement rules* that can convert the program model into alternative target-language implementations. Using global efficiency analysis (with access to the entire program, as opposed to only a local segment), LIBRA directs and explores the application of the transformation rules to produce an efficient implementation.

The transformation process consists of repeated applications of transformation rules to parts of the program, in which every application results in a specification closer to a target-language implementation. Each such application of a rule is said to produce a partial implementation, or *refinement*, of the program. Thus, refinement rules applied to refinements produce further refinements. Because more than one refinement rule may be applicable to the same part of a refinement, the transformation process produces a tree of possible refinements (the actual situation is slightly more complicated, since the order in which the rules are applied can affect the tree that is produced). To avoid the problem of combinatorial explosion, LIBRA develops only part of the tree.

Operation of the System

It is LIBRA's function to analyze and guide the development of the refinement tree to achieve an efficient implementation. LIBRA determines which parts of the program to expand next and which parts not to expand at all. In particular, when more than one refinement rule is applicable, LIBRA may decide to apply them all, so that the resulting refinements can be considered in greater detail, or it may decide to apply only one of the rules. In the latter case, the refinement is implemented directly in the current node of the tree, and the other possibilities are permanently forgone.

One of the most important ways in which LIBRA attacks the problem of combinatorial explosion is by *estimating* the efficiency of possible target-language implementations. For each refinement in the tree, LIBRA maintains two cost estimates in the form of symbolic algebraic expressions that give the time and space requirements for executing a certain kind of target-language implementation. The first estimate is the default cost that might result if all the constructs and operators in the refinement were assigned default implementations. The second is the optimistic cost estimate that might result assuming (a) that certain efficient implementation techniques that have worked in similar situations will prove successful in the present situation and (b) that LIBRA expends enough of its own resources of time and space to carry out these implementation techniques.

Treating these two costs as upper and lower bounds on the costs of possible target-language implementations of the refinement, LIBRA obtains important guidance in directing the growth of the refinement tree. These upper and lower bounds can be used to prune a branch of the refinement tree (without further consideration of the branch) or to calculate the effect of a partial implementation decision on the global program cost. As discussed below in the section on rules, the upper and lower bounds help direct attention to high-impact areas, those areas in which effort is likely to yield the greatest increases in overall efficiency.

Another feature of the LIBRA system, a feature implicit in the above discussion, is the knowledge LIBRA has about the use and limits of its own resources of time and space. This feature is important because no system can devote unlimited effort to finding an efficient implementation—effort must be allocated. The way in which LIBRA performs this allocation is to assign available resources to high-impact areas, where the resources will do the most good.

When new high-level constructs (such as new types of sorts, or trees) are added to a program, new efficiency knowledge is needed to analyze these concepts (their subparts, running times, data-structure accesses, etc.). LIBRA has a model of programming concepts that is consulted when new concepts are added. Some of the necessary information can be deduced automatically, and the user is asked specific questions to obtain the rest. To help construct these estimation functions, LIBRA provides a semiautomatic procedure for deriving cost-estimation functions from the set of cost functions for the target-language constructs.

The knowledge for managing resources, computing upper and lower cost estimates, directing attention to different parts of the tree, making implementation decisions, and, in general, analyzing and directing the growth of the tree is in the form of rules. Each rule consists of a condition and an action to be performed if the condition is met. The knowledge that a rule expresses can easily be modified since the rules are replaceable and can be added, deleted, or altered without requiring that the system itself be modified (see Article III.C4, in Vol. I, on production systems).

Rules—LIBRA's Knowledge Base

The rules in LIBRA's knowledge base generally can be divided into three groups:

1. attention and resource-management rules,

2. plausible-implementation rules, and

3. cost-analysis rules.

Attention and resource-management rules describe when to shift attention to other nodes in the tree and also how to set priorities for refining the different constructs and operations within a refinement node. Some of the more important of these rules determine how LIBRA's own resources of time and space are to be allocated, on the basis of where they will have the greatest impact. One of the ways of determining impact is to consider the difference between the upper bound cost estimate (assuming default implementations) and the optimistic lower bound cost estimate (assuming both the successful application of efficiency techniques that have worked in similar situations and the sufficient expenditure of resources to carry the techniques to completion).

Other rules in this group state how to shift attention among nodes. These rules (a) cause complex programs to be expanded early to see what decisions are involved, (b) postpone trivial decisions until important ones are made, (c) look at all refinements in the tree and select for development the one whose optimistic cost estimate is lowest (when resources for developing a particular refinement are exhausted), and (d) apply a form of branch and bound stating that (when resources allocated for considering a particular decision are exhausted) attention should be directed to the whole tree and that all nodes whose optimistic cost estimate is worse than the default estimate of some other node should be eliminated. As described later, when cost-analysis rules compare estimates, they take into account the degree of uncertainty in the estimate.

Plausible-implementation rules express heuristics about when to limit expansion of nodes, by making a decision about some part of an implementation. For example, when the question of how to represent a set first arises, LIBRA performs a global examination of the program to determine all uses of the set. If there are many places where the program checks for membership in the set, a hash-table representation may be suggested. In general, plausible implementation rules express knowledge derived by human or machine analysis of commonly occurring situations, such as which sorting techniques are best for different-sized inputs. These rules also contain heuristics to make quick decisions. Thus, if LIBRA is running out of resources, heuristics that are not as dependable as the one just described are used to make decisions on the spot, without creating any new nodes. These heuristics generally express defaults, such as *Use lists rather than arrays if the target language is LISP;* they are used to make the less important decisions or to make all decisions if the total resources for writing a program are nearly exhausted.

Cost-analysis rules express how to compute, update, and compare upper and lower bound estimates of the cost of the final implementation. The cost estimates are in the form of symbolic algebraic expressions that may involve variables representing set sizes. The cost estimates are not computed once and for all: Whenever a partial implementation in the refinement tree is further refined, the cost estimates associated with that partial implementation are *incrementally updated* to produce estimates that are more accurate in view of the new information.

Cost estimates are constructed from a knowledge base that includes information on upper and lower bounds on costs for use of time and space by individual constructs and operations and on how to combine such cost estimates for composite programs. The knowledge needed to incrementally update the cost estimates is contained in rules corresponding to the particular construct or operation. The method of comparing the cost estimates of different refinements involves the addition of a bonus to the refinement that has a greater degree of completion and that consequently has a greater certainty in its cost estimates (default and optimistic). This feature favors a nearly complete refinement with a slightly worse lower bound over a less complete (more abstract) refinement with a slightly better lower bound. Such a preference is desirable, since the cost estimate of the more abstract refinement is less certain and therefore may not be achievable. By giving a bonus for the degree of completion, the cost-analysis rules take into account the likelihood of being able to achieve the low cost.

An Example—A Simple Sort Program

Suppose that a SORT is specified as a transfer of elements from a SOURCE sequential collection to a TARGET sequential collection that is ordered by some relation such as LESS-THAN. After the application of some preliminary refinement rules that do not require any decisions as to alternative choices, three choice points remain: choosing a transfer order, and choosing representations for SOURCE as well as for TARGET.

Since the transfer order is selected as the most important decision, LIBRA directs attention first to that choice point. A heuristic rule is applied that suggests the use of either an insertion sort from list to list or array to array, or a selection sort from list to array. The different refinement possibilities are added to the tree accordingly. Each of the branches is given a limited amount of resources and told to focus attention only on the parts of the program directly relevant to the transfer-order decision.

After these branches are refined within the limits of the assigned resources, the nodes of the tree are compared. The branch and bound method does not eliminate any of the alternatives here, but the insertion branch is selected as it has the best lower bound (taking into account factors related to uncertainty of estimates).

Refinement then proceeds in that node. The choice of a list or array representation for the TARGET is made by a heuristic that says that lists are easier to manipulate than arrays in LISP. This heuristic was applied because much of the time and space resources allocated for finding an implementation had been consumed in the above tasks and a quick decision was required. The choice of a list representation for TARGET forces a list representation for SOURCE because of a suggestion made under the transfer-order heuristic. Thereafter, the refinement process is basically straightforward, though several choices of whether to store or recompute local variables are made.

Status

LIBRA has guided the application of the PECOS refinement rules to produce efficient implementation of several variants of simple database-retrieval, sorting, and concept-formation programs (see Article X.D1 for an example of a concept-formation program). Current plans include extending the problem area to include simple algorithms for finding prime numbers and for reaching nodes in a graph. For an efficiency expert to be of use in a complete automatic-programming system, a good deal more research is needed. Higher level optimizations, extended symbolic analysis and comparison capabilities, and more domain expertise are some obvious extensions. Automatic bookkeeping of heuristics and perhaps even automatic generation of heuristics from an analysis of symbolic cost estimates of target-language concepts are some long-range goals.

To write more complex programs such as compilers or operating systems, additional efficiency rules would have to be provided, rules about concepts such as bit packing, machine interrupts, and multiprocessing. However, even with such additions, the efficiency techniques employed by the LIBRA system should be significant in controlling the problem of combinatorial explosion that arises during the search for efficient implementations.

References

See Kant (1979); also, Barstow and Kant (1977) and Kant (1977, 1978).

Bibliography

List of Abbreviations

ACM	Association for Computing Machinery
AFIPS	American Federation of Information Processing Societies
AMS	American Mathematical Society
CACM	Communications of the Association for Computing Machinery
IEEE	Institute for Electrical and Electronic Engineers
IFIPS	International Federation of Information Processing Societies
IJCAI	International Joint Conferences on AI
SIGART	ACM Special Interest Group on AI
SIGCSE	ACM Special Interest Group on Computer Science Education
SIGCUE	ACM Special Interest Group on Computer Uses in Education
SIGGRAPH	ACM Special Interest Group on Graphics
SIGPLAN	ACM Special Interest Group on Programming Languages
TINLAP	Workshops on Theoretical Issues in Natural Language Processing

BIBLIOGRAPHY

Abelson, H., and diSessa, A. 1981. *Turtle geometry: The computer as a medium for exploring mathematics.* Cambridge, Mass.: MIT Press.

Aikins, J. 1980. Prototypes and production rules: A knowledge representation for computer consultations. Rep. No. STAN–CSD–80–814, Computer Science Dept., Stanford University. (Doctoral dissertation.)

AIM Workshop Proceedings. Proceedings of the Annual AIM Workshops. 1975–1981. Computer Science Dept., Rutgers University.

Allen, J. 1978. *Anatomy of LISP.* New York: McGraw-Hill.

Amarel, S. 1972. Representation and modeling in problems of program formation. In B. Meltzer and D. Michie (Eds.), *Machine Intelligence 6.* New York: American Elsevier, 411–466.

Ashton-Warner, S. 1963. *Teacher.* New York: Simon and Schuster.

Atkinson, R. C. 1972. Ingredients for a theory of instruction. *American Psychologist* 27:921–931.

Atkinson, R. C., and Wilson, H. A. (Eds.). 1969. *Computer-assisted instruction.* New York: Academic Press.

Austin, H. 1974. A computational model of the skill of juggling. AI Memo 330, AI Laboratory, Massachusetts Institute of Technology.

Backus, J. W. 1958. Automatic programming-properties and performance of FORTRAN systems I and II. *Proceedings of the Symposium on the Mechanisation of Thought Processes.* Teddington, Middlesex, England: National Physical Laboratory.

Backus, J. 1978. Can programming be liberated from the von Neumann style? A functional style and its algebra of programs. *CACM* 21:613–641.

Backus, J. W., and Herrick, H. 1954. IBM 701 Speedcoding and other automatic programming systems. *Proceedings of the Symposium on Automatic Programming for Digital Computers, Office of Naval Research, Washington, D.C.*

Balzer, R. M. 1973. A global view of automatic programming. *IJCAI 3,* 494–499.

Balzer, R. M., and Goldman, N. 1979. Principles of good software specification and their implications for specification languages. *Proceedings of the IEEE Specification of Reliable Software Conference, Cambridge, Mass.*

Balzer, R. M., Goldman, N., and Wile, D. 1976. On the transformational implementation approach to programming. *Second International Conference on Software Engineering,* 337–344.

Balzer, R. M., Goldman, N., and Wile, D. 1977. Informality in program specification. *IJCAI 5,* 389–397.

Balzer, R. M., Goldman, N., and Wile, D. 1978. Informality in program specifications. *IEEE Transactions on Software Engineering* SE–4 2:94–103.

Bamberger, J. 1974. The luxury of necessity. AI Memo 312, AI Laboratory, Massachusetts Institute of Technology.

Baron, R. V. 1977. *Structural analysis in a very high level language.* Master's thesis, Massachusetts Institute of Technology.

Barr, A. 1979. Meta-knowledge and cognition. *IJCAI 6,* 31–33.

Barr, A., and Atkinson, R. C. 1977. Adaptive instructional strategies. In H. Spada and W. F. Kempf (Eds.), *Structural models of thinking and learning.* Bern: Hans Huber.

Barr, A., Beard, M., and Atkinson, R. C. 1975. A rationale and description of a CAI program to teach the BASIC programming language. *Instructional Science* 4:1–31.

Barr, A., Beard, M., and Atkinson, R. C. 1976. The computer as a tutorial laboratory: The Stanford BIP project. *International Journal of Man-Machine Studies* 8:567–596.

Barstow, D. 1977. A knowledge based system for automatic program construction. *IJCAI 5,* 382–388.

Barstow, D. 1978. Codification of programming knowledge: Graph algorithms. Rep. No. TR–149, Computer Science Dept., Yale University.

Barstow, D. 1979. *Knowledge-based program construction.* Amsterdam: Elsevier.

Barstow, D. R., and Kant, E. 1977. Observations on the interaction between coding and efficiency knowledge in the PSI system. In *Proceedings of the Second International Conference on Software Engineering.* Long Beach, Calif.: Computer Society, Institute of Electrical and Electronics Engineers, Inc., 19–31.

Bauer, M. 1975. A basis for the acquisition of procedures from protocols. *IJCAI 4,* 226–231.

Bennett, J. S., Creary, L. A., Engelmore, R. M., and Melosh, R. E. 1978. SACON: A knowledge-based consultant in structural analysis. Heuristic Programming Project Rep. No. HPP–78–23, Computer Science Dept., Stanford University.

Biermann, A. W. 1972a. Computer program synthesis from computation traces. *Symposium on Fundamental Theory of Programming, Kyoto University, Kyoto, Japan.*

Biermann, A. W. 1972b. On the inference of Turing machines from sample computations. *Artificial Intelligence* 3:181–198.

Biermann, A. W. 1976. Approaches to automatic programming. In M. Rubinoff and M. C. Yovits (Eds.), *Advances in computers* (Vol. 15). New York: Academic Press, 1–63.

Biermann, A. W., and Feldman, J. A. 1970. On the synthesis of finite-state acceptors. AI Memo 114, AI Laboratory, Stanford University.

Biermann, A. W., and Krishnaswamy, R. 1974. Constructing programs from example computations. Rep. No. OSU–CISRC–TR–74–5, Computer and Information Science Research Center, Ohio State University.

Biggerstaff, T. J. 1976. C2: A super-compiler approach to automatic programming. Tech. Rep. 76–01–01, Computer Science Dept., University of Washington. (Doctoral dissertation.)

Blaine, L. H., and Smith, R. L. 1977. Intelligent CAI: The role of curriculum in suggesting computational models of reasoning. *Proceedings: 1977 Annual Conference, ACM, Seattle.*

Blum, R. L., and Wiederhold, G. 1978. Inferring knowledge from clinical data banks: Utilizing techniques from artificial intelligence. In *Proceedings of the Second*

Annual Symposium on Computer Application in Medical Care, IEEE, Washington, D.C., 303–307.

Bobrow, D. G. 1972. Requirements for advanced programming systems for list processing. *CACM* 7:618–627.

Bobrow, D. G., and Wegbreit, B. 1973. A model and stack implementation of multiple environments. *CACM* 10:591–602.

Bobrow, D. G., and Winograd, T. 1977. An overview of KRL, a knowledge representation language. *Cognitive Science* 1:3–46.

Borning, A. 1979. THINGLAB: A constraint simulation laboratory. Rep. No. CS–79–746, Computer Science Dept., Stanford University. (Doctoral dissertation.)

Brown, G. P. 1977. A Framework for processing dialogue. Rep. No. TR–182, Laboratory for Computer Science, Massachusetts Institute of Technology.

Brown, H., and Masinter, L. 1974. An algorithm for the construction of the graphs of organic molecules. *Discrete Mathematics* 8:227.

Brown, H., Masinter, L., and Hjelmeland, L. 1974. Constructive graph labeling using double cosets. *Discrete Mathematics* 7:1.

Brown, J. S. 1977. Uses of artificial intelligence and advanced computer technology in education. In R. J. Seidel and M. Rubin (Eds.), *Computers and communications: Implications for education.* New York: Academic Press, 253–270.

Brown, J. S., and Burton, R. R. 1978a. Diagnostic models for procedural bugs in basic mathematical skills. *Cognitive Science* 2:155–192.

Brown, J. S., and Burton, R. R. 1978b. Multiple representations of knowledge for tutorial reasoning. In D. G. Bobrow and A. Collins (Eds.), *Representation and understanding: Studies in cognitive science.* New York: Academic Press, 311–349.

Brown, J. S., Burton, R. R., and Bell, A. G. 1974. SOPHIE: A sophisticated instructional environment for teaching electronic troubleshooting (an example of AI in CAI). BBN Rep. No. 2790, Bolt Beranek and Newman, Inc., Cambridge, Mass.

Brown, J. S., Burton, R. R., and de Kleer, J. In press. Knowledge engineering and pedagogical techniques in SOPHIE I, II, and III. In D. Sleeman and J. S. Brown (Eds.), *Intelligent tutoring systems.* London: Academic Press.

Brown, J. S., Burton, R. R., Hausmann, C., Goldstein, I., Huggins, B., and Miller, M. 1977. Aspects of a theory for automated student modelling. BBN Rep. No. 3549, Bolt Beranek and Newman, Inc., Cambridge, Mass.

Brown, J. S., Burton, R. R., and Larkin, K. M. 1977. Representing and using procedural bugs for educational purposes. *Proceedings: 1977 Annual Conference, ACM, Seattle,* 247–255.

Brown, J. S., Collins, A., and Harris, G. 1978. Artificial intelligence and learning strategies. In H. O'Neil (Ed.), *Learning strategies.* New York: Academic Press, 107–140.

Brown, J. S., and Goldstein, I. P. 1977. Computers in a learning society. *Testimony for the House Science and Technology Subcommittee on Domestic and International Planning, Analysis, and Cooperation.*

Brown, J. S., Rubinstein, R., and Burton, R. 1976. Reactive learning environment for computer assisted electronics instruction. BBN Rep. No. 3314, Bolt Beranek and Newman, Inc., Cambridge, Mass.

Brown, J. S., and Traub, J. F. 1971. On Euclid's algorithm and the computation of polynomial greatest common divisors. *J. ACM* 18:505–514.

Brown, J. S., and VanLehn, K. 1980. Repair theory: A generative theory of bugs in procedural skills. *Cognitive Science* 4:379–426.

Buchanan, B. G. 1976. Scientific theory formation by computer. *Proceedings of NATO Advanced Study Institute on Computer Oriented Learning Processes, Noordhoff, Leydon,* 515–530.

Buchanan, B. G., and Feigenbaum, E. A. 1978. DENDRAL and Meta-DENDRAL: Their applications dimension. *Journal of Artificial Intelligence* 11:5–24.

Buchanan, B. G., Smith, D. H., White, W. C., Gritter, R. J., Feigenbaum, E. A., Lederberg, J., and Djerassi, C. 1976. Applications of artificial intelligence for chemical inference XXII. Automatic rule formation in mass spectrometry by means of the Meta-DENDRAL program. *Journal of the American Chemical Society* 98:6168–6178.

Buchanan, B. G., Sutherland, G. L., and Feigenbaum, E. A. 1969. Heuristic DENDRAL: A program for generating explanatory hypotheses in organic chemistry. In B. Meltzer and D. Michie (Eds.), *Machine Intelligence 4.* Edinburgh: Edinburgh University Press, 209–254.

Buchanan, B. G., Sutherland, G. L., and Feigenbaum, E. A. 1970. Rediscovering some problems of artificial intelligence in the context of organic chemistry. In B. Meltzer and D. Mitchie (Eds.), *Machine Intelligence 5.* Edinburgh: Edinburgh University Press, 253–280.

Buchs, A., Delfino, A. B., Duffield, A. M., Djerassi, C., Buchanan, B., Feigenbaum, E. A., and Lederberg, J. 1970. Applications of artificial intelligence for chemical inference VI. Approach to a general method of interpreting low resolution mass spectra with a computer. *Helvetica Chemica Acta* 53:1394.

Burstall, R. M., Collins, J. S., and Popplestone, R. J. 1968. *The POP-2 papers.* Edinburgh: Edinburgh University Press.

Burstall, R. M., Collins, A., and Popplestone, R. J. 1971. *Programming in POP-2.* Edinburgh: Edinburgh University Press.

Burstall, R. M., and Darlington, J. 1977. A transformation system for developing recursive programs. *J. ACM* 24:44–67.

Burton, R. R. 1976. *Semantic grammar: A technique for efficient language understanding in limited domains.* Doctoral dissertation, Computer Science Dept., University of California, Irvine.

Burton, R. R., and Brown, J. S. 1976. A tutoring and student modelling paradigm for gaming environments. *SIGCSE Bulletin* 8:236–246.

Burton, R. R., and Brown, J. S. 1979a. An investigation of computer coaching for informal learning activities. *International Journal of Man-Machine Studies* 11:5–24.

Burton, R. R., and Brown, J. S. 1979b. Toward a natural-language capability for computer-assisted instruction. In H. O'Neil (Ed.), *Procedures for instructional systems development.* New York: Academic Press, 273–313.

Carbonell, J. R. 1970a. AI in CAI: An artificial intelligence approach to computer-aided instruction. *IEEE Transactions on Man-Machine Systems* MMS-11(4):190–202.

Carbonell, J. R. 1970b. Mixed-initiative man-computer instructional dialogues. BBN Rep. No. 1971, Bolt Beranek and Newman, Inc., Cambridge, Mass.

Carbonell, J. R., and Collins, A. 1973. Natural semantics in artificial intelligence. *IJCAI 3*, 344–351.

Carhart, R. E, and Smith, D. H. 1976. Applications of artificial intelligence for chemical inference XX. Intelligent use of constraints in computer-assisted structure elucidation. *Computers and Chemistry* 1:79.

Carhart, R. E., Smith, D. H., Brown, H., and Djerassi, C. 1975. Applications of artificial intelligence for chemical inference XVII. An approach to computer-assisted elucidation of molecular structure. *Journal of the American Chemical Society* 97:5755–5762.

Carr, B., and Goldstein, I. 1977. Overlays: A theory of modeling for computer aided instruction. AI Memo 406, AI Laboratory, Massachusetts Institute of Technology.

Chang, C. L. 1978. DEDUCE 2: Further investigations of deduction in relational databases. In H. Gallaire and J. Minker (Eds.), *Logic and databases*. New York: Plenum, 201–236.

Charniak, E., Riesbeck, C., and McDermott, D. 1979. *Artificial intelligence programming*. Hillsdale, N.J.: Lawrence Erlbaum.

Church, A. 1941. *Calculi of lambda conversion*. Princeton, N.J.: Princeton University Press.

Clancey, W. J. 1978. An antibiotic therapy selector which provides for explanations. Heuristic Programming Project Memo HPP–78–26, Computer Science Dept., Stanford University.

Clancey, W. J. 1979a. Dialogue management for rule-based tutorials. *IJCAI 6*, 155–161.

Clancey, W. J. 1979b. Transfer of rule-based expertise through a tutorial dialogue. Rep. No. STAN–CS–769, Computer Science Dept., Stanford University. (Doctoral dissertation.)

Clancey, W. J. 1979c. Tutoring rules for guiding a case method dialogue. *International Journal of Man-Machine Studies* 11:25–49.

Clancey, W. J. In press-a. The epistemology of a rule-based expert system: A framework for explanation. Submitted to *Artificial Intelligence*.

Clancey, W. J. In press-b. Methodology for building an intelligent tutoring system. To appear in W. Kintsch (Ed.), *Methods and tactics in cognitive science*.

Clancey, W. J., and Letsinger, R. 1981. NEOMYCIN: Reconfiguring a rule-based expert system for application to teaching. *IJCAI 7*, 829–836.

Clark, K., and Sickel, S. 1977. Predicate logic: A calculus for deriving programs. *IJCAI 5*, 419–420.

Clocksin, W. F., and Mellish, C. S. 1981. *Programming in PROLOG*. New York: Springer-Verlag.

Codd, E. F., Arnold, R. S., Cadiou, J. M., Chang, C. L., and Roussopoulos, N. 1978. RENDEZVOUS version 1: An experimental English-language query formulation system for casual users of relational databases. Rep. No. RJ–2144(29407), Computer Sciences Dept., Thomas J. Watson Research Center, IBM, Yorktown Heights, N.Y.

Collins, A. 1976. Processes in acquiring knowledge. In R. C. Anderson, R. J. Spiro, and W. E. Montague (Eds.), *Schooling and the acquisition of knowledge*. Hillsdale, N.J.: Lawrence Erlbaum, 339–363.

Collins, A. 1978a. Fragments of a theory of human plausible reasoning. *TINLAP-2,* 194–201.

Collins, A. 1978b. Reasoning from incomplete knowledge. In D. G. Bobrow and A. Collins (Eds.), *Representation and understanding: Studies in cognitive science.* New York: Academic Press, 383–415.

Collins, A., Warnock, E. H., and Passafiume, J. J. 1974. Analysis and synthesis of tutorial dialogues. BBN Rep. No. 2789, Bolt Beranek and Newman, Inc., Cambridge, Mass.

Corey, E. J., and Wipke, W. T. 1969. Computer assisted design of complex organic synthesis. *Science* 166:178–192.

Croft, J. 1972. Is computerized diagnosis possible? *Computers and Biomedical Research* 5:351–367.

Crowder, N. A. 1962. Intrinsic and extrinsic programming. In J. E. Coulson (Ed.), *Proceedings of the Conference on Application of Digital Computers to Automated Instruction.* New York: Wiley, 58–65.

Damerau, F. J. 1979. The transformational question answering (TQA) system: Operational statistics—1978. Rep. No. RC–7739 (No. 33522), Computer Sciences Dept., Thomas J. Watson Research Center, IBM, Yorktown Heights, N.Y.

Darlington, J., and Burstall, R. M. 1973. A system which automatically improves programs. *IJCAI 3,* 479–485.

Davies, D., et al. 1973. *POPLER 1.5 reference manual.* Edinburgh: University of Edinburgh.

Davis, R. 1976. Applications of meta-level knowledge to the construction, maintenance, and use of large knowledge bases. Memo AIM–283, AI Laboratory, and Rep. No. STAN–CS–76–552, Computer Science Dept., Stanford University. (Doctoral dissertation.) Reprinted in R. Davis and D. Lenat (Eds.), *Knowledge-based systems in artificial intelligence.* New York: McGraw-Hill, 1982, 229–490.

Davis, R. 1977. Interactive transfer of expertise: Acquisition of new inference rules. *IJCAI 5,* 321–328.

Davis, R. 1978. Knowledge acquisition in rule-based systems: Knowledge about representations as a basis for system construction and maintenance. In D. Waterman and F. Hayes-Roth (Eds.), *Pattern-directed inference systems.* New York: Academic Press, 99–134.

Davis, R. 1980. Meta-rules: Reasoning about control. *AI Journal* 15:179–222.

Davis, R., and Buchanan, B. 1977. Meta-level knowledge: Overview and applications. *IJCAI 5,* 920–928.

de Kleer, J., Doyle, J., Steele, G. L., Jr., and Sussman, G. J. 1979. Explicit control of reasoning. In P. J. Winston and R. H. Brown (Eds.), *Artificial intelligence: An MIT perspective.* Cambridge, Mass.: MIT Press, 93–116.

Doyle, J. 1979. A truth maintenance system. *Artificial Intelligence* 12:231–272.

Doyle, J. 1980. A model for deliberation, action, and introspection. Rep. No. TR–581, AI Laboratory, Massachusetts Institute of Technology. (Doctoral dissertation.)

Doyle, J., and London, P. E. 1980. Selected descriptor index bibliography to the literature on belief revision. *SIGART Newsletter* 71:7–23.

Duda, R. O., and Gaschnig, J. G. 1981. Knowledge-based expert systems come of age. *BYTE* 6:238–281.

Duda, R., Gaschnig, J., and Hart, P. E. 1979. Model design in the PROSPECTOR consultant system for mineral exploration. In D. Michie (Ed.), *Expert systems in the micro-electronic age.* Edinburgh: Edinburgh University Press, 153–167.

Duda, R. O., Gaschnig, J., Hart, P. E., Konolige, K., Reboh, R., Barrett, P., and Slocum, J. 1978. Development of the PROSPECTOR consultation system for mineral exploration. Final Report, SRI Projects 5821 and 6415, SRI International, Inc., Menlo Park, Calif.

Duda, R. O., Hart, P. E., Nilsson, N. J., Reboh, R., Slocum, J., and Sutherland, G. L. 1977. Development of a computer-based consultant for mineral exploration. Annual Report, SRI Projects 5821 and 6415, SRI International, Inc., Menlo Park, Calif.

Duffield, A. M., Robertson, A. V., Djerassi, C., Buchanan, B. G., Sutherland, G. L., Feigenbaum, E. A., and Lederberg, J. 1969. Applications of artificial intelligence for chemical inference II. Interpretation of low resolution mass spectra of ketones. *Journal of the American Chemical Society* 91(11):2977–2981.

Dugdale, S., and Kibbey, D. 1977. Elementary mathematics with PLATO. Computer-based Education Research Laboratory, University of Illinois, Urbana.

Engelmore, R. S., and Nii, H. P. 1977. A knowledge-based system for the interpretation of protein x-ray crystallographic data. Heuristic Programming Project Rep. No. HPP–77–2, Computer Science Dept., Stanford University.

Engelmore, R. E., and Terry, A. 1979. Structure and function of the CRYSALIS system. *IJCAI 6*, 250–256.

Fagan, L. 1979. *Knowledge engineering for dynamic clinical settings: Giving advice in the intensive care unit.* Doctoral dissertation, Computer Science Dept., Stanford University.

Fahlman, S. E. 1977. *A system for representing and using real world knowledge.* Doctoral dissertation, AI Laboratory, Massachusetts Institute of Technology.

Fain, J., Gorlin, D., Hayes-Roth, F., Rosenschein, S., Sowizral, H., and Waterman, D. 1981. The ROSIE language reference manual. Tech. Note N–1647–ARPA, Rand Corp., Santa Monica, Calif.

Fateman, R. J. 1976. An approach to automatic asymptotic expansions. *Symposium on Symbolic and Algebraic Computation, ACM.*

Feigenbaum, E. A. 1977. The art of artificial intelligence: Themes and case studies in knowledge engineering. *IJCAI 5*, 1014–1029.

Feigenbaum, E. A., Buchanan, B., and Lederberg, J. 1971. On generality and problem solving: A case study using the DENDRAL program. In B. Meltzer and D. Michie (Eds.), *Machine Intelligence 6.* New York: American Elsevier, 165–190.

Feigenbaum, E. A., Engelmore, R. S., and Johnson, C. K. 1977. A correlation between crystallographic computing and artificial intelligence research. *Acta Crystallographica* A33:13.

Feigenbaum, E. A., and Feldman, J. (Eds.). 1963. *Computers and thought.* New York: McGraw-Hill.

Feinstein, A. 1967. *Clinical judgment.* Baltimore: William and Wilkins.

Feldman, J. A., and Rovner, P. D. 1969. An ALGOL-based associative language. *CACM* 8:439–449.

Feldman, J. A., Gips, J., Horning, J. J., and Reder, S. 1969. Grammatical complexity and inference. AI Memo 89, AI Laboratory, Stanford University.

Feldman, J. A., Low, J. R., Swinehart, D. C., and Taylor, R. H. 1972. Recent developments in SAIL. Rep. No. STAN–CS–308, Computer Science Dept., and Rep. No. AIM–176, AI Laboratory, Stanford University.

Fikes, R. E. 1970. REF–ARF: A system for solving problems stated as procedures. *Artificial Intelligence* 1:27–120.

Fikes, R. E. 1975. Deductive retrieval mechanisms for state description models. *IJCAI 4,* 99–106.

Fischer, G., Brown, J. S., and Burton, R. R. 1978. Aspects of a theory of simplification, debugging, and coaching. *Proceedings of the Second Annual Conference of the Canadian Society for Computational Studies of Intelligence.*

Fletcher, J. D. 1975. Modeling the learner in computer-assisted instruction. *Journal of Computer-Based Instruction* 1:118–126.

Floyd, R. W. 1972. Toward interactive design of correct programs. In C. V. Freiman (Ed.), *Foundations and systems, information processing 71: Proceedings of IFIPS Congress 71* (Vol. 1). Amsterdam: North-Holland, 7–10.

Forgy, C., and McDermott, J. 1977. OPS, a domain-independent production system language. *IJCAI 5,* 933–939.

Friedman, D. P. 1974. *The little LISPer.* Chicago: Science Research Associates.

Furakawa, K. 1977. A deductive question answering system on relational databases. *IJCAI 5,* 59–66.

Gabriel, R. P. 1981. An organization for programs in fluid dynamics. Rep. No. STAN–CS–81–856, Computer Science Dept., Stanford University. (Doctoral dissertation.)

Gelernter, H. L., Sanders, A. F., Larsen, D. L., Agarival, K. K., Boivie, R. H., Spritzer, G. A., and Searleman, J. E. 1977. Empirical explorations of SYNCHEM. *Science* 197:1041–1049.

Genesereth, M. R. 1976. DB: A high level data base system with inference. Memo 4, MACSYMA Group, Massachusetts Institute of Technology.

Genesereth, M. R. 1977. The difficulties of using MACSYMA and the function of user aids. *Proceedings of the First MACSYMA Users' Conference.* Rep. No. CP–2012, NASA.

Genesereth, M. R. 1978. *Automated consultation for complex computer systems.* Doctoral dissertation, Division of Applied Sciences, Harvard University.

Genesereth, M. R. 1979. The role of plans in automated consultation systems. *IJCAI 6,* 311–319.

Ginsparg, J. M. 1978. Natural language processing in an automatic programming domain. Rep. No. STAN–CS–78–671, Computer Science Dept., Stanford University. (Doctoral dissertation.)

Goldberg, A. 1973. Computer-assisted instruction: The application of theorem-proving to adaptive response analysis. Tech. Rep. 203, Institute for Mathematical Studies in the Social Sciences, Stanford University.

Goldstein, I. 1977. The computer as coach: An athletic paradigm for intellectual education. AI Memo 389, AI Laboratory, Massachusetts Institute of Technology.

Goldstein, I. 1979. The genetic epistemology of rule systems. *International Journal of Man-Machine Studies* 11:51–77.

Gorry, G. A., Silverman, H., and Pauker, S. G. 1978. Capturing clinical expertise: A computer program that considers clinical response to digitalis. *American J. of Medicine* 64:452–460.

Gosper, R. W. 1977. Indefinite hypergeometric sums in MACSYMA. *Proceedings of the First MACSYMA Users' Conference*. Rep. No. CP–2012, NASA.

Green, C. 1969. The application of theorem proving to question-answering systems. Memo AIM–96, Electrical Engineering Dept., and Rep. No. STAN–CS–69–138, Computer Science Dept., Stanford University. (Doctoral dissertation.)

Green, C. 1975a. Unpublished lecture surveying automatic proramming. Computer Science Dept., Stanford University.

Green, C. 1975b. Whither automatic programming? (Invited tutorial lecture.) *IJCAI 4*.

Green, C. 1976. The design of the PSI program synthesis system. *Proceedings of the Second International Conference on Software Engineering*, 4–18.

Green, C. 1977. A summary of the PSI program synthesis system. *IJCAI 5*, 380–381.

Green, C., et al. 1979. Results in knowledge based program synthesis. *IJCAI 6*, 342–344.

Green, C., and Barstow, D. 1977. A hypothetical dialogue exhibiting a knowledge base for a program understanding system. In E. W. Elcock and D. Michie (Eds.), *Machine Intelligence 8*. New York: Wiley, 335–359.

Green, C., and Barstow, D. 1978. On program synthesis knowledge. *Artificial Intelligence* 3:241–279.

Green, C., Phillips, J., Westfold, S., Pressburger, T., Kedzierski, B., Angebranndt, S., Mont-Reynaud, B., and Tappel, S. 1981a. Progress on knowledge-based programming and algorithm design. Memo KES.U.81.1, Kestrel Institute, Palo Alto, Calif.

Green, C., Phillips, J., Westfold, S., Pressburger, T., Kedzierski, B., Angebranndt, S., Mont-Reynaud, B., and Tappel, S. 1981b. Research on knowledge-based programming and algorithm design—1981. Memo KES.U.81.2, Kestrel Institute, Palo Alto, Calif.

Green, C., Waldinger, R., Barstow, D., Elschlager, R., Lenat, D., McCune, B., Shaw, D., and Steinberg, L. 1974. Progress report on program understanding systems. Memo AIM–240, AI Laboratory, Stanford University.

Green, C., and Westfold, S. 1982. Knowledge-based programming self applied. *Machine Intelligence 10*. New York: Wiley.

Grignetti, M. C., Hausmann, C., and Gould, L. 1975. An intelligent on-line assistant and tutor—NLS–SCHOLAR. *Proceedings of the National Computer Conference, San Diego, Calif.*, 775–781.

Grossman, R. 1976. Some data base applications of constraint expressions. Rep. No. TR–158, Computer Science Laboratory, Massachusetts Institute of Technology.

Gund, P., Andose, J. D., and Rhodes, J. B. 1977. Computer assisted analysis in drug research. In W. T. Wipke and W. J. Howe (Eds.), *Computer-assisted organic synthesis*. Washington, D.C.: American Chemical Society, 179–187.

Gupta, M. M., Saridis, G. N., and Gaines, B. R. 1977. *FUZZY automata and decision processes.* New York: North-Holland.

Haas, N., and Hendrix, G. G. 1980. An approach to acquiring and applying knowledge. *Proceedings of the First Annual National Conference on AI, Stanford University,* 235–239.

Hammer, M., and McLeod, D. 1978. The semantic data model: A modelling mechanism for data base applications. *ACM,* 26–36.

Hammer, M., and Ruth, G. 1979. Automating the software development process. In P. Wegner (Ed.), *Research directions in software technology.* Cambridge, Mass.: MIT Press, 767–792.

Hardy, S. 1975. Synthesis of LISP functions from examples. *IJCAI 4,* 240–245.

Harris, L. R. 1977. ROBOT: A high performance natural language processor for data base query. *SIGART Newsletter* 61:39–40.

Hart, P. E. 1975. Progress on a computer based consultant. *IJCAI 4,* 831–841.

Hayes, P. J. 1975. A representation for robot plans. *IJCAI 4,* 181–188.

Hayes-Roth, F., Gorlin, D., Rosenschein, S., Sowizral, H., and Waterman, D. 1981. Rationale and motivation for ROSIE. Tech. Note N–1648–ARPA, Rand Corp., Santa Monica, Calif.

Hayes-Roth, F., Waterman, D. A., and Lenat, D. B. (Eds.). In preparation. *Building expert systems.*

Hearn, A. C. 1973. REDUCE–2 users' manual. Rep. No. UCP–19, Computational Physics Group, University of Utah.

Heathcock, C. H., and Clark, R. D. 1976. *Journal of Organic Chemistry* 41:636–643.

Heidorn, G. E. 1972. Natural language inputs to a simulation programming system. Rep. No. 55hd72101A, Naval Postgraduate School, Monterey, Calif.

Heidorn, G. E. 1974. English as a very high level language for simulation programming. *Proceedings of Symposium on Very High Level Language, SIGPLAN Notices* 9:91–100.

Heidorn, G. E. 1975a. Augmented phrase structure grammars. In B. L. Nash-Webber and R. C. Schank (Eds.), *Theoretical issues in natural language processing.* Association for Computational Linguistics, 1–5.

Heidorn, G. E. 1975b. *Simulation programming through natural language dialogue.* Amsterdam: North-Holland.

Heidorn, G. E. 1976. Automatic programming through natural language dialogue: A survey. *IBM J. Research and Development* 4:302–313.

Heidorn, G. E. 1977. The end of the user programmer? *The Software Revolution, Infotech State of the Art Conference, Copenhagen, Denmark.*

Heiser, J. F., Brooks, R. E., and Ballard, J. P. 1978. Progress report: A computerized psychopharmacology advisor. *Proceedings of the Eleventh Collegium Internationale Neuro-Psychopharmacologicum, Vienna, Austria.*

Hendrix, G. G., and Lewis, W. H. 1981. Transportable natural language interfaces to databases. *Proceedings of the Nineteenth Annual Meeting of the Association for Computational Linguistics, Stanford, University.*

Hendrix, G. G., and Sacerdoti, E. D. 1981. Natural-language processing: The field in perspective. *BYTE* 6:304–352.

Hewitt, C. 1971. *Description and theoretical analysis (using schemas) of PLANNER: A language for proving theorems and manipulating models in a robot.* Doctoral dissertation, AI Laboratory, Massachusetts Institute of Technology.

Hewitt, C. 1977. Viewing control structures as patterns of passing messages. *Artificial Intelligence* 8:323–364.

Holt, J. 1964. *How children fail.* New York: Delta.

Howe, J. A. M. 1973. Individualizing computer-assisted instruction. In A. Elithorn and D. Jones (Eds.), *Artificial and human thinking.* Amsterdam: Elsevier, 94–101.

Howe, J. A. M., and O'Shea, T. 1976. Computational metaphors for children. Rep. No. 24, Dept. of Artificial Intelligence, Edinburgh University.

Hunt, E. B. 1975. *Artificial Intelligence.* New York: Academic Press.

Illich, I. 1971. *Deschooling society.* New York: Harper and Row.

Jacquez, J. A. (Ed.). 1964. The diagnostic process. *Proceedings of a conference sponsored by the Biomedical Data Processing Training Program, University of Michigan Medical School, Ann Arbor.*

Jelliffe, R. W. 1967. A mathematical analysis of digitalis kinetics in patients with normal and reduced renal function. *Mathematical Biosciences* 1:305.

Jurs, P. C. 1974. Chemical data interpretation using pattern recognition techniques. In W. T. Wipke, S. R. Heller, R. J. Feldman, and E. Hyde, (Eds.), *Computer representation and manipulation of chemical information.* New York: Wiley, 265–285.

Kahn, K. 1976. An actor-based computer animation language. *Proceedings of the SIGGRAPH/ACM Workshop on User-Oriented Design of Interactive Graphics Systems,* 37–43.

Kant, E. 1977. The selection of efficient implementations for a high level language. *Proceedings of Symposium on Artificial Intelligence and Programming Languages. SIGART Newsletter* 64:140–146.

Kant, E. 1978. Efficiency estimation: Controlling search in program synthesis. In S. P. Ghosh and L. Y. Leonard (Eds.), *AFIPS Conference Proceedings: National Computer Conference,* 47:703.

Kant, E. 1979. *Efficiency considerations in program synthesis: A knowledge-based approach.* Doctoral dissertation, Computer Science Dept., Stanford University.

Kaplan, S. J. 1979. *Cooperative responses from a portable natural language data base query system.* Doctoral dissertation, Dept. of Computer and Information Sciences, University of Pennsylvania.

Kay, A., and Goldberg, A. 1977. Personal dynamic media. *Computer* 10:31–41.

Kedzierski, B. 1982. Communication and management support in system development environments. *Proceedings of the Human Factors in Computer Systems Conference, Gaithersburg, Md.*

Kellogg, C., Klahr, P., and Travis L. 1978. Deductive planning and pathfinding for relational databases. In H. Gallaire and J. Minker (Eds.), *Logic and databases.* New York: Plenum, 179–200.

Kimball, R. B. 1973. Self-optimizing computer-assisted tutoring: Theory and practice. Rep. No. 206, Institute for Mathematical Studies in the Social Sciences, Stanford University.

King, J. J. 1981a. Modelling concepts for reasoning about access to knowledge. *Proceedings of the Workshop on Data Abstraction, Databases, and Conceptual Modelling, Pingree Park, Colorado, 1980.*

King, J. J. 1981b. Query optimization by semantic reasoning. Rep. No. CS–81–857, Computer Science Dept., Stanford University. (Doctoral dissertation.)

Koffman, E. B., and Blount, S. E. 1973. Artificial intelligence and automatic programming in CAI. *IJCAI 3,* 86–94.

Koffman, E. B., and Blount, S. E. 1975. Artificial intelligence and automatic programming in CAI. *Artificial Intelligence* 6:215–234.

Kornfeld, W. A. 1979. ETHER—A parallel problem solving system. *IJCAI 6,* 490–492.

Kornfeld, W. A., and Hewitt, C. 1981. The scientific community metaphor. *IEEE Transactions on Systems, Man, and Cybernetics* SMC–11:24–33.

Kowalski, R. 1977. *Predicate logic as a programming language.* Amsterdam: North-Holland.

Kunz, J., et al. 1978. A physiological rule-based system for interpreting pulmonary function test results. Heuristic Programming Project Rep. No. HPP–78–19, Computer Science Dept., Stanford University.

Laubsch, J. H. 1975. Some thoughts about representing knowledge in instructional systems. *IJCAI 4,* 122–125.

Le Faivre, R. A. 1977. FUZZY reference manual. Computer Science Dept., Rutgers University.

Lederberg, J. 1964a. *Computation of molecular formulas for mass spectrometry.* San Francisco: Holden-Day.

Lederberg, J. 1964b. DENDRAL–64: A system for computer construction, enumeration and notation of organic molecules as tree structures and cyclic graphs. Part I. Notational algorithm for tree structures. Rep. No. CR–57029, NASA.

Ledley, R., and Lusted, L. 1959. Reasoning foundations of medical diagnosis. *Science* 130:9–21.

Lenat, D. B. 1975. Synthesis of large programs from specific dialogues. In G. Huet and G. Kahn (Eds.), *Proving and improving programs.* Rocquencourt, France: Institut de Recherche d'Informatique et d'Automatique, 225–241.

Lewis, V. E. 1977. User aids for MACSYMA. *Proceedings of the First MACSYMA Users' Conference.* Rep. No. CP–2012, NASA.

Lindberg, D. A. B., Sharp, G. C., Kingsland, L. C., Weiss, S. M., Hayes, S. P., Ueno, H., and Hazelwood, S. E. 1980. Computer based rheumatology consultant. In the syllabus for the *Tutorial on computers in medicine: Applications of artificial intelligence techniques,* Stanford University School of Medicine.

Lindsay, R., Buchanan, B. G., Feigenbaum, E. A., and Lederberg, J. 1980. *DENDRAL.* New York: McGraw-Hill.

Liskov, B. H., Snyder, A., Atkinson, R., and Schaffert, C. 1977. Abstraction mechanisms in CLU. *CACM* 8:564–576.

London, P. E. 1978. Dependency networks as a representation for modelling in general problem solvers. Rep. No. TR–698, Computer Science Dept., University of Maryland.

Long, W. 1980. Criteria for computer generated therapy advice in a clinical domain. *Conference on Computers in Cardiology, Williamsburg, Va.*

Low, J. R. 1974. Automatic coding: Choice of data structures. Memo AIM–242, AI Laboratory, Stanford University.

Low, J. R. 1978. Automatic data structure selection: An example and overview. *CACM* 5:21–25.

Manna, Z., and Waldinger, R. 1975. Knowledge and reasoning in program synthesis. *Artificial Intelligence* 6:175–208.

Manna, Z., and Waldinger, R. 1977. Synthesis: Dreams ⇒ programs. Rep. No. STAN–CS–77–630, Computer Science Dept., Stanford University.

Manna, Z., and Waldinger, R. 1978. DEDALUS—The DEDuctive ALgorithm Ur-Synthesizer. *National Computer Conference, Anaheim, Calif.,* 683–690.

Martin, W. A. 1974. OWL notes: A system for building expert problem solving systems involving verbal reasoning. Project MAC, Massachusetts Institute of Technology.

Masinter, L., Sridharan, N. S., Carhart, R., and Smith, D. H. 1974. Application of artificial intelligence for chemical inference XII: Exhaustive generation of cyclic and acyclic isomers. *Journal of the American Chemical Society* 96:7702.

Mathlab Group. 1977. MACSYMA reference manual. Computer Science Laboratory, Massachusetts Institute of Technology.

McCarthy, J. 1960. Recursive functions of symbolic expressions and their computation by machine. *CACM* 4:184–195.

McCarthy, J. 1978. History of LISP. *SIGPLAN Notices* 13:217–223.

McCarthy, J., Abrahams, P. W., Edwards, D. J., Hart, T. P., and Levin, M. I. 1962. *LISP 1.5 programmer's manual.* Cambridge, Mass.: MIT Press.

McCune, B. P. 1977. The PSI program model builder: Synthesis of very high-level programs. *Proceedings of the Symposium on Artificial Intelligence and Programming Languages, SIGART Newsletter* 64:130–139.

McCune, B. 1979. *Building program models incrementally from informal descriptions.* Doctoral dissertation, Computer Science Dept., Stanford University.

McDermott, D. V. 1975. Very large PLANNER-type data bases. Memo AIM–339, AI Laboratory, Massachusetts Institute of Technology.

McDermott, D. V. 1981. R1: The formative years. *AI Magazine* 2:21–29.

Miller, M. L. 1979. A structured planning and debugging environment for elementary programming. *International Journal of Man-Machine Studies* 1:79–95.

Miller, M. L., and Goldstein, I. 1977a. Problem solving grammars as formal tools for intelligent CAI. *Proceedings: 1977 Annual Conference, ACM, Seattle.*

Miller, M. L., and Goldstein, I. 1977b. Structured planning and debugging. *IJCAI 5.*

Minker, J. 1978. An experimental relational data base system based on logic. In H. Gallaire and J. Minker, (Eds.), *Logic and databases.* New York: Plenum.

Mitchell, T. M. 1977. Version spaces: An approach to rule revision during rule induction. *IJCAI 5,* 305–310.

Mitchell, T. M. 1978. Version spaces: An approach to concept learning. Rep. No. CS–78–711, Computer Science Dept., Stanford University. (Doctoral dissertation.)

Mitchell, T. M., and Schwenzer, G. M. 1978. Applications of artificial intelligence for chemical inference XXV: A computer program for automated empirical 13C NMR rule formation. *Organic Magnetic Resonance* 8:378.

Morgenstern, M. 1976. *Automated design and optimization of information processing systems.* Doctoral dissertation, Massachusetts Institute of Technology.

Moses, J. 1971. Symbolic integration: The stormy decade. *ACM* 14:548–560.

Moses, J. 1975. A MACSYMA primer. Mathlab Memo No. 2, Computer Science Laboratory, Massachusetts Institute of Technology.

Moses, J., and Yun, D. Y. 1973. The EZGCD algorithm. *Proceedings of the ACM National Convention.*

Musser, D. R. 1975. Multivariate polynomial factoring. *J. ACM* 2:291–307.

Mylopolous, J., Bernstein, P. A., and Wong, H. K. T. 1980. A language facility for designing database-intensive applications. *ACM* 5:185–207.

Newell, A., Shaw, J. C., and Simon, H. A. 1957. Programming the logic theory machine. *Proceedings of the Western Joint Computer Conference,* 230–240.

Nii, H. P., and Aiello, N. 1978. AGE (Attempt to Generalize): Profile of the AGE–0 system. Heuristic Programming Project Working Paper HPP–78–5, Computer Science Dept., Stanford University.

Nii, H. P., and Aiello, N. 1979. AGE (Attempt to Generalize): A knowledge-based program for building knowledge-based programs. *IJCAI 6,* 645–655.

Nilsson, N. (Ed.). 1975. Artificial intelligence—research and applications. SRI International, Inc., Menlo Park, Calif.

Nordyke, R., Kulikowski, C. A., and Kulikowski, C. W. 1971. A comparison of methods for the automated diagnosis of thyroid dysfunction. *Computers and Biomedical Research* 4:374–389.

Norman, A. C. 1975. On computing with formal power series. *ACM Transactions on Mathematical Software* 1:346–356.

Norman, D. A., Gentner, D. R., and Stevens, A. L. 1976. Comments on learning schemata and memory representation. In D. Klahr (Ed.), *Cognition and instruction.* Hillsdale, N.J.: Lawrence Erlbaum, 177–196.

Papert, S. 1972a. Teaching children to be mathematicians vs. teaching about mathematics. *International Journal of Mathematics, Education, Science, and Technology* 3:249–262.

Papert, S. 1972b. Teaching children thinking. *Programmed Learning and Educational Technology* 9(5):245–255.

Papert, S. 1973. Uses of technology to enhance education. AI Memo 298, AI Laboratory, Massachusetts Institute of Technology.

Papert, S. 1980. *Mindstorms: Children, computers, and powerful ideas.* New York: Basic Books.

Pauker, S., Gorry, G. A., Kassirer, J., and Schwartz, W. 1976. Towards the simulation of clinical cognition—Taking a present illness by computer. *American Journal of Medicine* 60:981–996.

Petry, F. E., and Biermann, A. W. 1976. Reconstruction of algorithms from memory snapshots of their execution. *Proceedings: 1976 Annual Conference, ACM, New York,* 530–534.

Phillips, J. V. 1977. Program inference from traces using multiple knowledge sources. *IJCAI 5*, 812.

Piaget, J. (D. Coltman, Trans.). 1970. *Science of education and the psychology of the child.* New York: Viking.

Piaget, J., and Inhelder, B. (H. Weaver, Trans.). 1969. *The psychology of the child.* New York: Basic Books.

Polya, G. 1954. *Mathematics and plausible reasoning* (2 vols.). New York: Wiley.

Polya, G. 1957. *How to solve it* (2nd ed.). New York: Doubleday Anchor.

Pople, H. 1977. The formation of composite hypotheses in diagnostic problem solving—An exercise in synthetic reasoning. *IJCAI 5*, 1030–1037.

Popplestone, R. J. 1967. The design philosophy of POP–2. In D. Michie (Ed.), *Machine Intelligence 3.* Edinburgh: Edinburgh University Press, 393–402.

Pratt, V. 1979. LISP. In J. Belzer, A. G. Holzman, and A. Kent (Eds.), *Encyclopedia of computer science and technology* (Vol. 10). New York: Marcel Dekker, 78–116.

Preston, K. 1976. Computer processing of biomedical images. *Computer* 9:54–68.

Reiser, J. F. 1975. BAIL: A debugger for SAIL. Rep. No. STAN–CS–75–270, Computer Science Dept., and AIM–270, AI Laboratory, Stanford University.

Reiser, J. F. (Ed.). 1976. SAIL. Rep. No. STAN–CS–76–574, Computer Science Dept., and Memo AIM–289, AI Laboratory, Stanford University.

Reiter, R. 1978. On reasoning by default. *TINLAP–2*, 210–218.

Rich, C. 1979. *A library of programming plans with applications to automated analysis, synthesis and verification of programs.* Doctoral dissertation, Massachusetts Institute of Technology.

Rich, C., and Shrobe, H. E. 1976. Initial report on a LISP programmer's apprentice. Rep. No. TR–354, AI Laboratory, Massachusetts Institute of Technology.

Rich, C., and Shrobe, H. E. 1978. Initial report on a LISP programmer's apprentice. *IEEE Transactions on Software Engineering* SE–4(6):456–467.

Rieger, C., Rosenberg, J., and Samet, H. 1979. Artificial intelligence programming languages for computer-aided manufacturing. *IEEE Transactions on Systems, Man, and Cybernetics* SMC–9(4):205–226.

Risch, R. 1969. The problem of integration in finite terms. *Transactions of the AMS* 139:167–189.

Rothstein, M. 1977. A new algorithm for the integration of exponential and logarithmic functions. *Proceedings of the First MACSYMA Users' Conference.* Rep. No. CP–2012, NASA.

Roussopoulos, N. D. 1977. A semantic network model of databases. Rep. No. 104, Computer Science Dept., University of Toronto.

Rowe, N. 1978. *An inductive tutor for context-free grammar construction.* Master's thesis, Massachusetts Institute of Technology.

Rulifson, J. F., Waldinger, J. A., and Derkson, J. A. 1971. A language for writing problem-solving programs. *Proceedings of IFIPS Congress '71, Ljubljana, Yugoslavia.*

Ruth, G. 1976. Automatic design of data processing systems. *Proceedings of the Third ACM Symposium on Principles of Programming Languages, Atlanta.*

Ruth, G. 1978. Protosystem I: An automatic programming system prototype. *Proceedings of the National Computer Conference, Anaheim, Calif., AFIPS* 47:675–681.

Sacerdoti, E. D. 1974. Planning in a hierarchy of abstraction spaces. *Artificial Intelligence* 5:115–135.

Sacerdoti, E. D. 1977. *A structure for plans and behavior.* New York: American Elsevier.

Sacerdoti, E. D., Fikes, R. E., Reboh, R., Sagalowicz, D., Waldinger, R. J., and Wilber, B. M. 1976. QLISP: A language for the interactive development of complex systems. SRI Tech. Note 120, AI Center, SRI International, Inc., Menlo Park, Calif.

Safrans, C., Desforges, J., and Tsichlis, P. 1976. Diagnostic planning and cancer management. Rep. No. TR–169, Laboratory for Computer Science, Massachusetts Institute of Technology.

Sandewall, E. 1978. Programming in the interactive environment: The LISP experience. *ACM Computing Surveys* 10:35–71.

Schank, R. C., and Riesbeck, C. K. 1981. *Inside computer understanding.* Hillsdale, N.J.: Lawrence Erlbaum.

Schmidt, C. F., and Sridharan, N. S. N. 1977. Plan recognition using a hypothesize and revise paradigm: An example. *IJCAI 5,* 480–486.

Schroll, G., Duffield, A. M., Djerassi, C., Buchanan, B. G., Sutherland, G. L., Feigenbaum, E. A., and Lederberg, J. 1969. Applications of artificial intelligence for chemical inference III. Aliphatic ethers diagnosed by their low resolution mass spectra and NMR data. *Journal of the American Chemical Society* 91:7440.

Self, J. A. 1974. Student models in computer-aided instruction. *International Journal of Man-Machine Studies* 6:261–276.

Shaw, D. E. 1980. Knowledge-based retrieval on a relational database machine. Rep. No. TR–823, Computer Science Dept., Stanford University.

Shaw, D., Swartout, W., and Green, C. 1975. Inferring LISP programs from examples. *IJCAI 4,* 260–267.

Sheikh, Y. M., Buchs, A., Delfino, A. B., Schroll, G., Duffield, A. M., Djerassi, C., Buchanan, B., Sutherland, G. L., Feigenbaum, E. A., and Lederberg, J. 1970. Applications of artificial intelligence for chemical inference V. An approach to the computer generation of cyclic structures. Differentiation between all the possible isomeric ketones of composition, C6H10O. *Organic Mass Spectrometry* 4:493.

Shortliffe, E. H. 1976. *Computer-based medical consultations: MYCIN.* New York: American Elsevier.

Shortliffe, E. H., Buchanan, B. G., and Feigenbaum, E. A. 1979. Knowledge engineering for medical decision making: A review of computer-based clinical decision aids. *Proceedings of the IEEE* 67:1207–1224.

Shortliffe, E. H., Scott, A. C., Bischoff, M. B., Campbell, A. B., van Melle, W., and Jacobs, C. D. 1981. ONCOCIN: An expert system for oncology protocol management. *IJCAI 7.*

Shrobe, H. E. 1978. *Reasoning and logic for complex program understanding.* Doctoral dissertation, Massachusetts Institute of Technology.

Sibel, W., Furbach, U., and Schreiber, J. F. 1978. Strategies for the synthesis of algorithms. *Informatik-Fadbendik* 5:97–109.

Siklossy, L. 1976. *Let's talk LISP.* Englewood Cliffs, N.J.: Prentice-Hall.

Siklossy, L., and Sykes, D. 1975. Automatic program synthesis from example problems. *IJCAI 4*, 268–273.

Silverman, H. 1975. A digitalis therapy advisor. Rep. No. TR–143, MAC Project, Computer Science Dept., Massachusetts Institute of Technology.

Simon, H. A. 1972. The heuristic compiler. In H. A. Simon and L. Siklossy (Eds.), *Representation and meaning*. Englewood Cliffs, N. J.: Prentice-Hall, 9–43.

Sleeman, D., and Brown, J. S. (Eds.). In press. *Intelligent tutoring systems*. London: Academic Press.

Smith, D. H. 1975. Applications of artificial intelligence for chemical inference XV. Constructive graph labelling applied to chemical problems. Chlorinated hydrocarbons. *Analytical Chemistry* 47:1176.

Smith, D. H., Buchanan, B. G., Engelmore, R. S., Adlercreutz, H., and Djerassi, C. 1973. Applications of artificial intelligence for chemical inference IX. Analysis of mixtures without prior separation as illustrated for estrogens. *Journal of the American Chemical Society* 95:6078.

Smith, D. H., Buchanan, B. G., Engelmore, R. S., Duffield, A. M., Yeo, A., Feigenbaum, E. A., Lederberg, J., and Djerassi, C. 1972. Applications of artificial intelligence for chemical inference VIII. An approach to the computer interpretation of the high resolution mass spectra of complex molecules. Structure elucidation of estrogenic steroids. *Journal of the American Chemical Society* 94:5962.

Smith, D. H., and Carhart, R. E. 1976. Applications of artificial intelligence for chemical inference XXIV. Structural isomerism of mono- and sesquiterpenoid skeleton 1,2-. *Tetrahedron* 32:2513.

Smith, D. H., and Carhart, R. E. 1978. Structure elucidation based on computer analysis of high and low resolution mass spectral data. In M. L. Gross (Ed.), *High performance mass spectrometry: Chemical applications*. Washington, D.C.: American Chemical Society, 325.

Smith, R. G., and Davis, R. 1981. Frameworks for cooperation in distributed problem solving. *IEEE Transactions on Systems, Man, and Cybernetics* SMC–11(1).

Smith, R. L. 1976. Artificial intelligence in CAI. Unpublished working paper, Institute for Mathematical Studies in the Social Sciences, Stanford University.

Smith, R. L., and Blaine, L. H. 1976. A generalized system for university mathematics instruction. *SIGCUE Bulletin* 1:280–288.

Smith, R. L., Graves W. H., Blaine, L. H., and Marinov, V. G. 1975. Computer-assisted axiomatic mathematics: Informal rigor. In O. Lacarme and R. Lewis (Eds.), *Computers in education, IFIPS* (Part 2). Amsterdam: North-Holland, 803–809.

Snape, K. 1974. Doctoral dissertation, University of Oxford.

Solomon, C., and Papert, S. 1976. A case study of a young child doing turtle graphics in LOGO. *Proceedings of the AFIPS National Computer Conference*, 1049–1056.

Sowa, J. F. 1976. Conceptual graphs for a data base interface. *IBM J. Research and Development* 20:336–357.

Sridharan, N. S. 1978. Special issue on applications in the sciences and medicine. *AI Journal* 1(1,2):195.

Stallman, R. M., and Sussman, G. J. 1977. Forward reasoning and dependency-directed backtracking in a system for computer-aided circuit analysis. *Artificial Intelligence* 9:135–196.

Stansfield, J. L., Carr, B. P., and Goldstein, I. P. 1976. WUMPUS Advisor I: A first implementation of a program that tutors logical and probabilistic reasoning skills. Memo 381, AI Laboratory, Massachusetts Institute of Technology.

Stefik, M. 1980. Planning with constraints. Rep. No. STAN–CS–80–784, Computer Science Dept., Stanford University. (Doctoral dissertation.)

Steinberg, L. 1980. *A dialogue moderator for program specification dialogues in the PSI system*. Doctoral dissertation, Computer Science Dept., Stanford University.

Stevens, A. L., and Collins, A. 1977. The goal structure of a socratic tutor. BBN Rep. No. 3518, Bolt Beranek and Newman, Inc., Cambridge, Mass.

Stevens, A. L., and Collins, A. 1978. Multiple conceptual models of a complex system. BBN Rep. No. 3923, Bolt Beranek and Newman, Inc., Cambridge, Mass.

Stevens, A. L., Collins, A., and Goldin, S. 1978. Diagnosing student's misconceptions in causal models. BBN Rep. No. 3786, Bolt Beranek and Newman, Inc., Cambridge, Mass.

Summers, P. D. 1977. A methodology for LISP program construction from examples. *J. ACM* 24:161–175.

Suppes, P. 1957. *Introduction to logic*. New York: Van Nostrand Reinhold.

Suppes, P. (Ed.). 1981. *University-level computer assisted instruction at Stanford: 1968–1980*. Stanford, Calif.: Institute for Mathematical Studies in the Social Sciences.

Sussman, G. J. 1975. *A computer model of skill acquisition*. New York: American Elsevier.

Sussman, G. J., and McDermott, D. V. 1972a. Why conniving is better than planning. AI Memo 255A, AI Laboratory, Massachusetts Institute of Technology.

Sussman, G. J., and McDermott, D. V. 1972b. From PLANNER to CONNIVER: A genetic approach. *AFIPS* 1171–1180.

Sussman, G. J., Winograd, T., and Charniak, E. 1971. MICRO–PLANNER reference manual. AI Memo 203A, AI Laboratory, Massachusetts Institute of Technology.

Swartout, W. 1977a. A digitalis therapy advisor with explanations. Rep. No. TR–176, MAC Project, Computer Science Dept., Massachusetts Institute of Technology.

Swartout, W. 1977b. A digitalis therapy advisor with explanations. *IJCAI 5*, 819–825.

Swartout, W. 1981. Explaining and justifying expert consulting programs. *IJCAI 7*, 815–822.

Szolovits, P., and Pauker, S. 1976. Research on a medical consultation program for taking the present illness. *Proceedings of the Third Illinois Conference on Medical Information Systems*.

Szolovits, P., and Pauker, S. 1978. Categorical and probabilistic reasoning in medical diagnosis. *AI Journal* 11(1,2):115–154.

Teitelman, W., et al. 1978. *INTERLISP reference manual*. Xerox PARC, Palo Alto, Calif.

Teitelman, W., and Masinter, L. 1981. The INTERLISP programming environment. *IEEE Transactions on Computers* C–14(4):25–35.

Terry, A. In preparation. *The hierarchical control of productions systems.* Doctoral dissertation, Computer Science Dept., Stanford University.

Trager, B. M. 1978. In preparation. *Integration of algebraic functions.* Doctoral dissertation, Computer Science Laboratory, Massachusetts Institute of Technology.

Trigoboff, M. 1978. *IRIS: A Framework for the construction of clinical consultation systems.* Doctoral dissertation, Computer Science Dept., Rutgers University.

Trigoboff, M., and Kulikowski, C. 1977. IRIS: A system for the propagation of inferences in a semantic net. *IJCAI 5,* 274–280.

van Melle, W. 1980. A domain independent system that aids in constructing consultation programs. Rep. No. STAN-CS–80–820, Computer Science Dept., Stanford University. (Doctoral dissertation.)

Varkony, T. H., Carhart, R. E., and Smith, D. H. 1977. Computer assisted structure elucidation, ranking of candidate structures, based on comparison between predicted and observed mass spectra. Paper presented at the ASMS meeting, Washington, D.C.

Varkony, T. H., Smith, D. H., and Djerassi, C. 1978. Computer-assisted structure manipulation: Studies in the biosynthesis of natural products. *Tetrahedron* 34:841–852.

Wahlster, W. 1977. HAM–RPM: A knowledge based conversationalist. *SIGART Newsletter* 61:36–37.

Waldinger, R. 1977. Achieving several goals simultaneously. In E. W. Elcock and D. Michie (Eds.), *Machine Intelligence 8.* New York: Wiley, 94–136.

Waldinger, R., and Levitt, K. N. 1974. Reasoning about programs. *Artificial Intelligence* 5:235–316.

Waltz, D. L. 1978. An English language question answering system for a large relational database. *CACM* 21:526–539.

Wang, P., and Rothschild, L. 1975. Factoring multivariate polynomials over the integers. *Mathematics of Computation* 29:935–950.

Warren, D., Pereira, L. M., and Pereira, F. 1977. PROLOG—The language and its implementation compared with LISP. *Proceedings of the ACM SIGART-SIGPLAN Symposium on AI and Programing Languages, Rochester, N.Y.*

Waterman, D. A., and Hayes-Roth, F. (Eds.). 1978. *Pattern-directed inference systems.* New York: Academic Press.

Waters, R. C. 1976. A system for understanding mathematical FORTRAN programs. Memo AIM–168, AI Laboratory, Massachusetts Institute of Technology.

Waters, R. C. 1978. Automatic analysis of the logical structure of programs. Rep. No. AI–TR–492, Massachusetts Institute of Technology. (Based on doctoral dissertation, *A Method for automatically analyzing the logical structure of programs,* 1978.)

Wegbreit, B. 1975a. Goal-directed program transformation. Rep. No. CSL–75–8, Xerox PARC, Palo Alto, Calif.

Wegbreit, B. 1975b. Mechanical program analysis. *CACM* 18:528–539.

Weiss, S. M., and Kulikowski, C. A. 1979. EXPERT: A system for developing consultation nodes. *IJCAI 6,* 942–947.

Weiss, S. M., Kulikowski, C. A., Amarel, S., and Safir, A. 1978. A model-based method for computer-aided medical decision-making. *Artificial Intelligence* 11:145–172.

Weiss, S. M., Kulikowski, C. A., and Galen, R. S. 1981. Developing microprocessor based expert models for instrument interpretation. *IJCAI 7*, 853–855.

Weiss, S., Kulikowski, C., and Safir, A. 1977. A model-based consultation system for the long-term management of glaucoma. *IJCAI 5*, 826–832.

Weissman, C. 1967. *LISP 1.5 Primer*. Belmont, Calif.: Dickenson.

Wescourt, K. T., and Hemphill, L. 1978. Representing and teaching knowledge for troubleshooting/debugging. Tech. Rep. 292, Institute for Mathematical Studies in the Social Sciences, Stanford University.

Wexler, J. D. 1970. Information networks in generative computer-assisted instruction. *IEEE Transactions on Man-Machine Systems* MMS–11:181–190.

Weyhrauch, R. 1979. Prolegomena to a theory of mechanized formal reasoning. Rep. No. STAN–CS–78–687, Computer Science Dept., Stanford University.

Wilber, B. M. 1976. A QLISP reference manual. Tech. Note 118, AI Center, SRI International, Inc., Menlo Park, Calif.

Winograd, T. 1975. Breaking the complexity barrier again. *SIGPLAN Notices* 1:13–30.

Winston, P. H. 1977. *Artificial intelligence*. Reading, Mass: Addison-Wesley.

Winston, P. H., and Horn, B. K. P. 1981. *LISP*. Reading, Mass.: Addison-Wesley.

Wipke, W. T., Braun, H., Smith, G., Choplin, F., and Sieber, W. 1977. SECS— Simulation and Evaluation of Chemical Synthesis: Strategy and planning. In W. T. Wipke and W. J. House (Eds.), *Computer-assisted organic synthesis*. Washington, D.C.: American Chemical Society, 97–127.

Yob, G. 1975. Hunt the Wumpus. *Creative Computing* 51–54.

Yu, V. L., Buchanan, B. B., Shortliffe, E. H., Wriath, S. M., Davis, R., Scott, A. C., and Cohen, S. N. 1979. Evaluating the performance of a computer-based consultant. *Computer Programs in Biomedicine* 9:95–102.

Yu, V. L., Fagan, L. M., Wraith, S. M., Clancey, W. J., Scott, A. C., Hannigan, J. F., Blum, R. L., Buchanan, B. G., and Cohen, S. N. 1979. Antimicrobial selection by a computer—A blinded evaluation by infectious disease experts. *J. American Medical Association* 242:1279–1282.

Zadeh, L. A. 1965. Fuzzy sets. *Information and Control* 8:338–353.

Zilles, S. 1975. Abstract specification for data types. IBM Research Laboratory, San Jose, Calif.

Zippel, R. 1976. Univariate power series expansions in algebraic manipulation. *Proceedings of an ACM Symposium on Symbolic and Algebraic Computation*.

Indexes

NAME INDEX

Pages on which an author's work is discussed are italicized.

SUBJECT INDEX

ABOUT THIS BOOK

The Handbook of Artificial Intelligence was designed and edited by Dianne Kanerva, who also established the production procedures and managed the production team that typeset the volumes.

The *Handbook* is unusual in that, from the soliciting and writing of manuscripts through the production of camera-ready copy, it was prepared entirely through the facilities of the three computer systems (SUMEX, SCORE, and SAIL) available to the Heuristic Programming Project at Stanford University. Volumes II and III were typeset at the Department of Computer Science using Donald Knuth's Tau Epsilon Chi (TEX), a computer-based typesetting system designed for mathematical text. The text of the volumes is set in the Computer Modern family of fonts designed by Knuth with his META-FONT system. Intermediate copy was produced with a Xerox Dover laser printer; final camera-ready copy was produced with an Alphatype CRS phototypesetter.

José González was responsible for tailoring and implementing a TEX macro package designed by Max Díaz to the requirements of the *Handbook*. González prepared the camera-ready copy of Volumes II and III of the *Handbook* and participated in editing. Dikran Karagueuzian prepared and typeset the bibliographies and name indexes of these last two volumes. The other individuals who participated in typesetting the *Handbook* were David Eppstein (especially the design of macros for the figures in Chap. XV and for the indexes), Jonni Kanerva (especially the layout and typesetting of Chap. XIII), and Janet Feigenbaum and Barbara Laddaga (especially the initial application of TEX to the task). Christopher Tucci operated the Alphatype CRS phototypesetter.

Printing, binding, jacket design, and artwork are by the publisher, William Kaufmann, Inc.